# INTO THE PAST

## Mycenaean Civilization

# WILLIAM A. McDONALD

PROFESSOR OF CLASSICS AND DIRECTOR OF THE HONORS
DIVISION, COLLEGE OF LIBERAL ARTS,
University of Minnesota

*Indiana University Press*
*Bloomington and London*

TO

# Elizabeth, Sue and Betsy

*for faith, hope and charity*

*in the busy months when these chapters*

*were being written*

# CONTENTS

# ILLUSTRATIONS

## MAPS

## PART TITLE ILLUSTRATIONS

Preface   Boar, fresco from Tiryns
   I      Sphinx, fresco from Pylos
   II     Warrior, metal inlay of a cup from Pylos
   III    Flying fish, fresco from Phylakopi, Melos
   IV     Bluebird, fresco from Knossos, House of Frescoes
   V      Nautilus, amphora from Kakovatos
   VI     Dolphin, floor painting from Pylos
   VII    Lion, metal inlay in a dagger blade from Mycenae,
             Grave Circle A
   VIII   Griffin, gold seal from Pylos
   IX     Octopus, pilgrim flask from Palaikastro

# PREFACE

IN A VERY REAL SENSE all scholarship is motivated by curiosity and an urge to investigate mysteries. So this is going to be a kind of detective story, a historical whodunit. Yet the analogy is not exact or complete. For example, you will not find "the answer" by peeking at the last chapter. Ironically enough, if a scientist is fortunate in "solving" a minor puzzle, the solution usually involves new and deeper mysteries.

In a standard mystery novel we finally learn that the culprit was the imperturbable butler or the harmless old gardener. In our story, on the contrary, such neat and satisfying solutions are conspicuously lacking. If we may be pardoned for comparing the Dorians with the butler and the "gray Minyan people" with the gardener, both are suspected of certain crimes of violence; but they as well as their victims are no longer available for questioning. Some intriguing clues have been left at the scene, however, and it may eventually be possible to construct an airtight case against them or to exonerate them completely. Meanwhile, it is entertaining to follow what the experts have so far made of the developing evidence and even to have a try ourselves.

The chief source of information in our search will be the clues unearthed by three detectives—or excavators, as they are known in archaeological circles. Each of them has made crucial contributions toward the solution of a complicated series of historical puzzles that can be summed up under the term "Mycenaean civilization." We shall also be interested in learning what these three and other scholarly sleuths have been able to discover about the relationship between this Mycenaean civilization and Homer's famous epic poems, the *Iliad* and the *Odyssey*.

Our three guides are giants and pioneers in their profession. This book is intended as a tribute to them, but it is not (we hope) an uncritical eulogy. Heinrich Schliemann laid the foundations of Greek prehistoric archaeology between 1870 and 1890; Arthur Evans in the next generation established its reputation as an exact field of research; Carl Blegen, still vigorous in the waning years of the third generation, guided the develop-ing science into responsible and flexible maturity.

The usual way to organize an account of any early civilization is to com-pose a synthesis of solid knowledge and responsible inference as it exists *at the moment of writing*. Scholars who made major contributions at vari-ous earlier stages of the reconstruction will of course be mentioned; but the approach will be *contemporary* and *encyclopedic*. The author will sum up as fairly as he can the verdict of his own day on the available informa-tion. Fortunately, several dependable handbooks of this sort have recently been produced by competent scholars in our field.

In contrast, however, we intend to use the *biographical* and *historical* approach to our subject. That is, we shall review the evidence on Myce-naean civilization as it has been gradually accumulating over the past ninety-five years. The successive discoveries and reactions to discoveries will be seen, as far as possible, through the eyes of the protagonists them-selves. Our method has unavoidable drawbacks and may at times tax the reader's patience and powers of recall and concentration. This approach is bound to take up more space, which means that we must be drastically selective to keep the account within reasonable bounds. Crucial conclu-sions and hypotheses have to be fully presented, even though some of them were subsequently disproved or modified. The discussion of a particular problem must be interrupted and then resumed when later evidence pro-duced new light on its solution. Yet, if followed faithfully and judiciously, the historical approach ought to result in a sounder appreciation of the *process* by which present-day evaluations have been reached. The reader can be drawn into a kind of active re-creation and partnership as the suc-cessive stages of discovery and interpretation are reviewed, rather than simply being informed about the end product.

On the biographical side, personal anecdotes about Schliemann, Evans and Blegen will be kept to a minimum. No connected account of extra-professional aspects of their careers will be attempted. We shall come to know these unusually able and fortunate men almost entirely in terms of their archaeological work—or, perhaps better, to see their professional accomplishments through their own developing experience. A valuable means to this end is to quote often and at length from their publications. Sometimes the way in which an idea is expressed reveals more about the speaker or writer than does the idea itself. Style and diction offer fascinating insights into the personality of eras as well as individuals.

We may as well attempt at this point to face a perfectly natural ques-tion: "Why single out only three protagonists? Aren't you slighting other pioneers of equal or nearly equal stature?" Very possibly we are, although we have tried not to. A separate chapter on Michael Ventris was at one time projected. His brilliant achievement, announced in 1952, would so far have to be ranked first among the claims of several contenders for primacy in the present (fourth) generation. As for contemporaries of the three we have chosen, other historians of the science might feel compelled to assign an equally prominent place to such great figures as Christos Tsountas, Wilhelm Dörpfeld and Alan Wace. And in a real sense, apart from such distinctions as chapter headings, these men do occupy a comparable position in our narrative.

The names and contributions of dozens of other talented scholars will of course be found on nearly every page. In a sense, every innovator who makes an independent discovery or sees a new and meaningful relationship in previous discoveries is a pioneer; and it may be unrealistic as well as risky to attempt to single out *the* outstanding figure in each generation of a science. Yet no one who has studied the record would deny that Schliemann, Evans and Blegen were authentic pacesetters. There is something mysterious about such individuals. They seem to possess a special blend of brilliance, self-assurance, intuition and luck. Scholars of this caliber do not appear very often in any field of study.

A colleague who generously consented to read these chapters in manuscript suggested that a fair number of important excavations and excavators find no place in the narrative. He appended a list of such items, which incidentally could easily be quadrupled. The only rejoinder is that this was intended from the start to be a selective, not a complete historical account. As such, it is sure to incur the criticism of some specialists, particularly those who may rightly feel that their own work has been slighted.

Perhaps a valid objection may also be made to the concentration on excavations and research published in English. Again, to attempt to justify the basis for selection may only make matters worse. It may or may not be a fair judgment that our German, French and Italian colleagues have been more interested in earlier or later horizons, or in Crete rather than the Greek mainland. Nevertheless, omissions of vital contributions by scholars of any nationality to the subject *as we have defined it* are to be attributed solely to ignorance; and sincere apologies are hereby offered.

Our story has two dimensions in time. One is the comparatively short span of slightly less than 100 years before the present. In it our pioneers and their colleagues lived their lives and made their contributions to Greek prehistory. The second is a much longer epoch, extending from about 1600 to 1100 years before the birth of Christ. In the Aegean area this period is technically known as the Late Bronze Age. Those far-off days when Mycenaean civilization grew and flourished and died became almost

as real to Schliemann, Evans and Blegen as the time into which they themselves were actually born. Indeed, every dedicated archaeologist and historian, as he gains familiarity with his chosen period of time, does begin to
lead a double life. If the following pages should succeed in producing something of the same effect on a few impressionable readers even for a matter
of hours, they will have more than fulfilled the author's hopes.

There are, of course, a great many interesting prehistoric cultures that
archaeologists all over the world are bringing to light. But our particular
chapter of man's kaleidoscopic past can perhaps claim a special place for
at least three reasons. The Mycenaean age is in a material sense better
documented than most of its fellows; it has the immense advantage of
contact (however complex and controversial) with the earliest known
European mythology and literature; and it left a rather impressive cultural
legacy to the classical Greek civilization that flourished roughly a thousand
years later.

Our geographical focus is the Greek mainland; but contemporary phases
at Troy and in Crete and some of the smaller islands form such an integral
part of the story that they have to be included. The contemporary situation
in the Near East is taken into account only so far as is necessary to understand Mycenaean contacts there or vice versa. For the same reason, the
whole of Europe is involved to some degree.

The criteria for material to be included in the following chapters were
originally based on relevance either to the work of our three pioneers or
to the illumination of the Homeric poems. Yet in practice such distinctions are extremely slippery. The story is really indivisible and cumulative.
An obviously relevant problem has a frustrating tendency to require the
inclusion of a less vital item, and so on. This eventually seemed to require
what might be called "synopses of syntheses" to link the three main chapters. That is, at three junctures (about 1900, 1920 and 1939) highlights
are excerpted from one or two publications that best sum up the state of
knowledge in their respective epochs. This method has the advantage of
ensuring the historical continuity; and it does not seem to obscure seriously the biographical context. It also became clear during the writing that
a somewhat comparable account was needed for the years since World
War II. And, finally, some kind of overview had to be attempted. These
subjects constitute the bases for the last two chapters.

A word now about Homeric parallels and comparisons. To Schliemann,
the connection was simple enough. Archaeology was the means of au-
thenticating and illustrating the poems, much as biblical archaeology is
still regarded in some quarters nowadays. Later excavators in our field
have usually been more cautious; but parallels in Homeric epic and tradi-

tional mythology are almost inevitably in the back of their minds as they handle new material and review former discoveries. We shall therefore pay particular attention to the way in which successive generations have assessed the connections and realized the discrepancies. Selected references (arabic numerals in the text, correlated with Homeric References, p. 439– 40) are supplied in particular contexts; but they should be regarded as samples only. A thorough correlation would have been tedious for the general reader; and a detailed account of the technical problems in each case would have been intolerably complicated. The reader whose interest is sufficiently piqued may browse among the specialized studies that are recommended in the list of Suggested Reading.

Those already familiar with the *Iliad* and the *Odyssey* will no doubt be at a considerable advantage as they follow our story. Homer-less readers might be well advised to spend a few hours with a good translation of the poems before plunging into this narrative. They will certainly not regret the experience. But the process can be reversed. A quick mind innocent of Homer should have little trouble in following the narrative; and this book will have truly accomplished its purpose if a few of its "graduates" decide that the next items on their reading list will be the Homeric epics themselves.

A few words may be required to draw attention to additional features of the book that are meant to be of assistance to the reader. The Glossary contains definitions and explanations of certain technical terms. They have been purposely kept to the minimum but a fair number are needed for clarity and brevity. Also included are identifications of ancient proper names that occur in the narrative. An asterisk (*) is printed with the first occurrence of each item to remind the reader of the existence of the *Glossary*. Also, throughout the book dimensions and distances, which are regularly indicated by the metric system in scientific publications, have been converted (even within quotes) to fairly close equivalents in English feet and miles.

The spelling of proper names and the use and formulation of technical terms may cause some unavoidable confusion because of the individual preferences of the various authorities whose direct words are quoted. Apart from quotations, however, it is hoped that the terminology is simple and consistent and that the spelling system is also as consistent and accurate as the complicated problems of transcription and usage allow. In the Index the stressed syllable in all unusual Greek proper names has been indicated, as in Zygouriés.

Geographical locations are essential to follow the narrative; and handy maps are of prime importance. Most locations are indicated in the general map (I) of the Aegean area (p. 454). The graph system has been adopted to save space and facilitate rapid reference. Thus, if the reader is unsure about the location of Kythera, he will check it in its proper location in the alphabetical list printed with the map. There a number (58) has been assigned to it along with the grid reference (J-4), so that a moment should suffice to identify the item on the map. Maps of the eastern (II) and western (III) Mediterranean areas are also provided (pp. 457, 458) to assist in locating the relatively few references to geographical points beyond our major focus. The text will normally make clear which map needs to be consulted. There are also detailed maps of the immediate area of the major sites of Troy, Mycenae, Knossos and Pylos.

The list of Suggested Reading is provided for those who become interested in following up the general subject or specific topics in more detail. The arrangement is alphabetical by author. The list is rather rigorously selective and is meant particularly for the reader whose only language is English. For the occasional reader who may want to check the source of specific quotations, detailed Chapter Bibliographies have been provided. Here again, however, there has been no attempt to supply a comprehensive bibliography on the whole subject.

Finally, some well-earned acknowledgments are due various persons. The original idea for the book evolved in 1962 during a canoe trip with two of my friends, Professors Walter Pattison and Reginald Allen. In the following year a College Honors Seminar provided the opportunity to develop it with a group of talented undergraduates majoring in a variety of departments. More of the content of Chapters II, IV and VI than I can now identify is owed to the stimulation and rapport of those pleasant weekly meetings.

As the book began to take shape, I discussed its progress (or lack of same) with a neighbor, Stanley Aschenbrenner, manager of Product Design and Coordination, Control Data Corporation. He most generously offered to read and criticize preliminary drafts of each chapter and to provide in advance the typical reactions of the kind of reader for whom the book is primarily intended. My wife, Elizabeth McDonald, skillfully typed and retyped the manuscript, showing no other reaction than an eye occasionally raised heavenward when presented with still another draft.

My colleagues Professor Erle Leichty and James Muhly of the Department of History at Minnesota gave me generous help—particularly on problems where the Aegean and Near Eastern evidence overlaps. Probably the deepest debt of all is owed to my friends John Chadwick, Lecturer in Greek in Downing College, Cambridge University, and Vincent Desborough, Lecturer in History, University of Manchester. They took time from busy schedules of teaching and research to read the next-to-final draft of the whole text and to send me detailed comments. Their control of the material in general as well as in their specialties has prevented many infelicities, inaccuracies and outright errors. If, as is very likely, others remain, they must not share the blame. The explanation would probably be either that they were too polite to pile Ossa on Pelion or else that the errors occur in passages added after the stage of the work that they saw.

A word must be said, too, about the relationship of the book to one of its "heroes." Professor Blegen has been my mentor and senior colleague and friend for twenty-seven years. At various times in that lengthy span we have talked over most of the problems here outlined, and a good many of the ideas that do not appear within quotes may stem from those discussions. But, again, he should not be charged with the shortcomings, and there are undoubtedly positions taken or theories suggested in the final chapter with which he will not agree. He was invited to read the manuscript, but since he had a general idea of his own prominent position in the text, he declined with characteristic modesty. His brother, Theodore Blegen, dean emeritus of the graduate school, University of Minnesota, who has always followed Carl's career with the closest interest, kindly consented to act as family arbiter on the Blegen chapter.

The illustrations were drawn by John Harris and William Williams. In general, Mr. Williams undertook the work connected with architecture and the vignettes, while Mr. Harris was responsible for the rest. The illustrations in books on Mycenaean civilization seem to me to have become largely standardized, with the chief variety consisting in the quality of the photographs. Since we could not hope to rival such photographs as Alison Frantz's, we have concentrated entirely on line drawings. It was my original intention to try to avoid the kind of illustration that is thoroughly familiar—and indeed hackneyed—to the veteran of many such books. But Mr. Aschenbrenner and others convinced me that some readers may never have seen the standard reproductions. Hence, our selection represents an attempt to combine these with some new material. It will be obvious to the experts that Mr. Harris and Mr. Williams have not attempted an absolutely faithful and literal reproduction but have instead sought to portray the "atmosphere" that they as artists feel in this material. I believe their results are both attractive and instructive; and the association with these gifted young artists has been an education to me at least.

The portrait of Schliemann is reproduced from Carl Schuchhardt's *Schliemann's Excavations;* that of Evans is a print of the painting done by Sir William Richmond and now in the Ashmolean Museum at Oxford. Miss Joan Evans very kindly arranged for the museum authorities to allow us to reproduce it. The photograph of Blegen was loaned by his brother.

The photographs of Tsountas, Dörpfeld, Wace and Ventris are reproduced respectively from *Epitoumbion Christou Tsounta* (published by the Society for Thracian Folklore and Linguistics); Peter Goessler's *Wilhelm Dörpfeld. Ein Leben im Dienst der Antike; Annual of the British School of Archaeology at Athens*, Vol. 46 (1951); and John Chadwick's *The Decipherment of Linear B*.

I am indebted to various publishers for permission to quote extensively from books and journal articles written by our major authorities in Chapters IV through VII. The following specific arrangements are hereby acknowledged: Society of Antiquaries of London for *Archaeologia*, Vol. 59; Methuen and Co., Ltd., for Pendlebury, *Archaeology of Crete* and Nilsson, *Homer and Mycenae*; Biblo and Tannen, Inc., and Agathon Press, Inc., for Evans, *Palace of Minos*; Williams and James, Gray's Inn, London, for *Scripta Minoa* and *Shaft Graves and Bee-hive Tombs*; Society for the Promotion of Hellenic Studies for *Journal of Hellenic Studies*, Vol. 32; Routledge and Kegan Paul, Ltd., for Glotz, *Aegean Civilization*; B. G. Teubner, Stuttgart, for Fimmen, *Die Kretisch-Mykenische Kultur*.

Finally, I wish to express my gratitude for three rather special acts of generosity: to the Managing Committee of the British School of Archaeology at Athens for the reproduction of numerous passages from the *Annual*; to Miss Joan Evans for full leave to quote from *Time and Chance*; and to Carl W. Blegen for permission to reproduce excerpts from a considerable number of his own publications.

La Pointe, Wisconsin
August 1966

# I

## Before Schliemann:
## Homer and the Philologists

BEFORE SCHLIEMANN'S EXCAVATIONS BEGAN IN 1870, what were the prevailing attitudes of professional scholars on the historical background of the earliest masterpieces of European literature? A brief review of the status of certain aspects of the so-called Homeric Question in the late nineteenth century may provide us with a useful starting point.

When Schliemann turned the first sod at Troy, debate concerning the composition, date and authorship of the *Iliad* and the *Odyssey* had been going on practically continuously for at least 2,500 years. Even now, almost a century later, most of the basic problems are unsolved; and some of them are probably insoluble in absolute terms. That is, we may never know exactly when (or even if) "Homer" lived, whether he was responsible for both of the great epics attributed to him, in what form the chronicles and legends and folk tales circulated before genius transformed and embedded them in monumental works of art, or what happened to the unified epics between Homer's time and the establishment of our text. With us, as with the ancient Greeks, belief in a historical Homer must to some extent constitute an "act of faith."

Yet in the past century much real progress has been made. In addition to the illumination of archaeological discoveries (which will be our major concern), the scholarly disciplines of philology, linguistics and comparative literature have made important contributions. The list of Suggested Reading contains readable descriptions of the fascinating discoveries being made about epic language and form, about the techniques still in use in out-of-the-way places for composing and perpetuating oral heroic poetry, and about comparable themes and thought patterns in the literature of the ancient Near East and elsewhere. Although satisfactory answers to many of the complex problems grouped under the Homeric Question still elude us, we now have far more evidence that bears on them than was available in any generation since the poems were composed.

In 1870 very little archaeological evidence from preclassical times was

available or recognized. A considerable amount of Greek sculpture, architecture, coins and other material remains of the fifth century B.C. and later
had, of course, long been known. Many classical art objects reflect Homeric
reminiscences, since the education of the artist—like that of all his contemporaries—was in a real sense based on Homer. But the archaeological
artefacts told no clearer story about the background and origin of the
epics than did classical literature. The later Greek artists and writers and
scholars did not, in fact, have dependable information about Homer and
the composition of the poems. Or, to put it more formally, they did not
receive from their distant ancestors, and so could not pass on to the modern world, solid and incontestable *external* evidence. The critics of Schliemann's day, therefore, had to base judgments on these unsatisfactory
ancient sources, plus their own analysis of the *internal* evidence preserved
in the poems themselves.

Some scholars of the nineteenth century were thorough skeptics. They
believed that the *Iliad* and the *Odyssey* contain no historical truth, that
Agamemnon and Pylos and the Trojan War had had no more real existence than Polyphemos or Lotus Land or the Council of the Gods on
Mount Olympus. Homer's poetic imagination, they said, soars far above
dull facts and has created a fiction truer than history. This attitude is
typified by the reaction of a famous scholar after reading Schliemann's
first account of his excavations at Troy. "I know as yet," he wrote, "of
one Ilion [Troy] only, that is, the Ilion as sung by Homer, which is not
likely to be found in the trenches of Hissarlik, but rather among the Muses
who dwell on Olympus."

At the other end of the spectrum were the readers who might be described as literalists or fundamentalists. Like the ancient Greeks, they
assumed that all of Homer's people had really lived and that every action
had taken place exactly as narrated. Even the geographical descriptions,
they thought, were accurately recalled from the poet's own memory, or
at the very least were passed on to him by a fully dependable and unbroken
tradition. Schliemann, for instance, refers to his boyhood trust in the
*Iliad,* "the exactness of which I used to believe in as in the Gospel itself."

Between the two extremes there was—and still is to some extent—a
bewildering variety of views. The major point at issue can perhaps be
phrased as follows: If we assume a long evolution in epic technique with
the present text of the poems as the end product, how can the history of
their composition be reconstructed? The critical methods applied to the
Homeric Question in the nineteenth century were very largely identical
with those brought to bear on the biblical narrative. In the broadest terms
there were two basically different and mutually exclusive theories. Both

depended on *internal* evidence, that is on analysis of the content of the poems themselves. One theory held that an original genius fashioned the poems out of already traditional and widely disparate materials, but that in the long process of transmission thereafter many major and minor changes were made by poets of varying merit, all of them far inferior to the master poet. The second reconstruction in effect eliminated Homer completely. Its adherents sought to prove that our *Iliad* and *Odyssey* are the result of a rather late, haphazard and awkward job of stitching together a large number of separate songs or "lays" of varying quality and age.

One can immediately see that to prove or disprove either viewpoint dependable criteria are needed for assigning an approximate date to the various units or episodes or lays (assuming their existence and correct identification). The evidence on which the critics formed their judgments was based mainly on details of style and language. But one serious drawback was that the specialists' opinions varied widely, not only on what constituted significant differences but on the implications of such differences for the history of the poems. The fields of linguistics and form analysis had not reached a point where reliable objective standards existed.

If form and language could not provide conclusive evidence, some scholars saw another possibility. The date of a given unit or story might be inferred from detailed descriptions of material objects or of political, social or religious institutions or customs that it embodied. If the time was even approximately known when a given type of political organization or a specially distinctive weapon or implement or item of jewelry was in use, then one might conclude that the section of the poems containing the relevant description was composed within those limits. At the very least, it could not have been composed *before* the institution or object was created.

But this method also had serious limitations. Very few such "dating brackets" were known with sufficient precision. And the late-nineteenth-century scholars saw no way to improve the situation. They did not believe that much progress could be made in chronological accuracy for such early periods by restudying the ancient texts. And most of them were unconvinced that excavation might uncover the towns where the stories were alleged to have originated or might find in the heroes' palaces and tombs material objects closely similar to those described by Homer. This was, of course, a shortsighted attitude in view of the archaeological discoveries already being made in western Europe, Egypt and other parts of the Near East. But they can hardly be blamed for failing to foresee the day when some of the places and objects described by Homer not only would be

found but could be quite closely dated by rigorous techniques that are
based only indirectly on written records.

The chapters to follow trace this progress into the past. But before we
leave the prearchaeological era, we might at least try to reconstruct the
viewpoint of the general reader of the poems in the nineteenth century
and before. What was his attitude, whether or not he had ever heard of
the Homeric Question? He probably looked on Priam and Odysseus and
their heroic companions very much as on King Arthur or Alexander the
Great. The "tale of Troy divine" had a tremendous romantic appeal to
a wide circle of readers and listeners; and this vogue had in turn stimu-
lated a long tradition of purely fictional elaboration and expansion. The
unsophisticated reader of Schliemann's time, as before and since, would
have been serenely unaware of any argument over fact versus fancy. Probably he would not have been much interested even if he had heard something of scholarly analyses and dissections. Fiction, legend, myth or history
—does it matter if all these elements and more are combined in a good
story? And, if they are, who could ever disentangle them after all these
centuries?

To such natural questions the Homeric scholar must have a reasonable
answer if he is concerned to justify his existence. He will certainly agree
that Homer's poems may be enjoyed simply as absorbing stories and
superb literary achievements. But he cannot stop there. The very fact of
their literary and technical perfection, standing as they do in the early
mists of European civilization, forces him to ask questions. Could this
perfection have been achieved suddenly and intuitively by one man? Could
the author have imagined his heroic civilization in all the splendid and
vital detail revealed in his elaborate word pictures? Is it possible that in
the poems precious evidence is embalmed about a real historical stage of
Greek civilization far earlier than classical times? How can we go about
definitely proving or disproving such conflicting hypotheses?

As a matter of fact, these questions need not be confined to scholars.
They could occur quite naturally to any intelligent lover of Homer and of
history. Western man has for so long located most of his intellectual and
cultural roots in classical Greece that simple curiosity about what preceded
*that* epoch is almost inevitable. It is only in the last century that some
fairly reliable answers are beginning to emerge and to win the adherence
of most serious students of Homer.

# II

## Schliemann, Priam and Agamemnon: 1870-1890

*"And now the treasure-digger has become a scholar"*

H EINRICH SCHLIEMANN, in his younger years, might be called an unsophisticated reader of Homer; and in his maturity he aspired to the status of professional scholar. But he was never really either the one or the other. He was a unique genius, and such a man can never be neatly labeled and confined to a single category.

This account is meant neither as another study of Schliemann's life nor as a detailed description of his excavations. Instead, as explained in the Preface, we want to review some of the highlights of his discoveries and to examine his theories of their relation to the civilization mirrored in the Homeric poems. Schliemann was the pioneer who made the decisive breakthrough into Greek prehistory. Knowledge about this tiny but important segment of human experience took a tremendous leap forward in his lifetime.

A few observations about the man and his methods are perhaps called for at the start. Psychologists and biographers have seen in his personality a strong element of psychotic compulsion. One can cite his devotion to his father and the shock following the breakup of his home in early boyhood, the long lonely search for the comfort of a wife and family of his own and the compensatory absorption in learning languages and making a fortune in business. Certainly he was egotistical, sensitive, volatile and hypochondriacal. His life was one continuous demonic drive to prove himself and his ideas to the world. But, again, he does not easily conform to a type. Some have maligned him as an avaricious megalomaniac, and others have flattered him as the more or less self-conscious founder of the science of archaeology. The variety of judgments during his lifetime and the continued interest of writers and readers are in themselves proof of the complexity of the man and the mystery of such prodigies.

Schliemann has for so long been associated in the public imagination with buried gold that nonspecialists are often unaware of the solid and lasting aspects of his work. The image of the "gold-seeker" was set early in his archaeological career, and clearly with his own encouragement. This was the line taken—as nearly always since in journalistic accounts of archaeology—in newspaper stories about his discoveries; and it is a very important element in the fascination that books by and about him have always had for their many readers. Archaeologists today profess impatience with the association of their profession and treasure trove. But the discovery of intrinsically valuable objects *was* clearly a major motivation for excavation all through the nineteenth century and earlier. It can probably be regarded as a more powerful stimulus to dig than is simple curiosity about one's predecessors. The search for buried treasure preceded scientific motivation by thousands of years. No present-day archaeologist has gotten completely beyond its lure, no matter how firmly he insists that he regards the commonest potsherd on the same terms as a golden diadem. Schliemann was quite frank about wanting to find treasure and supremely fortunate in fulfilling that wish.

But the truly significant result of his excavations was to show that there had been a brilliant and very distinctive civilization around the Aegean Sea *before the classical*. This fact, when eventually accepted by the experts, went a long way to "prove Homer right." And that was the hope, as Schliemann insists in his autobiography, that inspired the "great projects I formed when I was a poor little boy." The discovery of a prehistoric culture with firm Homeric connections was difficult for many contemporary scholars to accept, and the controversy provoked a "new War of Troy." They might with some justice criticize the rough-and-ready methods of his earlier excavations and his passion for making rash identifications of his finds with heroic people and places and things; but what upset them even more was the prospect of having to revise comfortable theories. Above all, Schliemann's work doomed the dogma that the Golden Age of classical Greek civilization had been created "out of nothing" by a few generations of supermen. Yet, for a doomed belief, it died hard; and its vestiges are with us even yet.

Schliemann was not usually overawed by learned authority and sometimes reacted to criticism in a not very tactful way. He apparently relished lengthy debates in newspapers and journals, enumerating for page after page the errors of fact committed by this or that "learned friend." In such situations, many authorities of our own day are inclined to sympathize with the experts. They feel that laymen do a disservice to science when they point out how "the scholars" were corrected by a courageous and gifted amateur. They fear that these irreverent disclosures may encourage the public to develop a skeptical attitude toward scholarly accomplishments. But a healthy skepticism is one of the qualities that education is supposed to plant and nourish. We all know that unquestioning public acceptance of the judgment of "the expert" can be dangerous. A "closed" science is on the way to becoming a mystery. The criticisms of crackpots will usually sputter out before long, as happened in the case of several of Schliemann's most malicious detractors. And the open-minded scholar will usually listen, as Schliemann did, when his mistakes are tactfully pointed out. The way should always be open for the gifted amateur to make himself heard. And Heinrich Schliemann is a prime example of the amateur of genius who became a scholar.

He not only had the originality to conceive the idea of testing an unpopular belief by excavation, but was persistent enough not to be discouraged by criticism and suspicion and lethargy. His successful earlier career in business was a useful background in this sense, for it was built on taking risks, outwitting his opponents and playing the brilliant hunch. The large fortune he had amassed gave him confidence and prestige in dealing with political authorities; and it freed him from the worry of finding funds to carry on his work. This brash amateur would probably have found it impossible to interest private donors or government agencies in financing his ambitious plans.

Schliemann's self-assertiveness irritated many, but without it he could never have forced himself to the attention of the learned world. And he was far from scornful of education and scholarly competence. His decision in 1866 to resume his own formal education at age forty-four, after a lapse of thirty years, shows clearly that he wanted to prepare himself to meet the experts on their own ground. And, when his own learning and fertile imagination failed to provide a satisfactory explanation for a problem, he did not hesitate to appeal for help. Reporting on his first campaign, he writes: "I find much in this stone period that is quite inexplicable to me, and I therefore consider it necessary to describe everything as minutely as possible, in the hope that one or other of my honoured colleagues will be able to give an explanation of the points which are obscure to me." In fact, there runs through his life a thread of insecurity that forms a striking complement to his more obvious egotism.

As the complexity of the job and the variety of the evidence gradually became clear to him, Schliemann tended more and more to associate various specialists in his work. In a very real sense, he anticipated by almost a century the "team approach" that is only recently gaining recognition in Greek archaeology. The only precedent then was the great French *Expédition Scientifique de Morée* (Peloponnese) more than a generation earlier; and it had the support of a government and the resources of a national treasury.

Of course, Schliemann hoped the opinion of the consultants would support his own and thereby strengthen his case against his critics; but the passionate desire to get at the truth from every possible angle shines out clearly. In the excavations at Troy in 1872 his staff included a professional surveyor and a professional photographer. The following year there was also a professional artist. Engineers and architects made elaborate and accurate plans of the structures uncovered and the sites examined. The "celebrated surgeon, Aretaeos of Athens" undertook a study of human skeletal material, the specialty we now call physical anthropology. Laboratory analyses and opinions by chemists, metallurgists, geologists and practicing goldsmiths are frequently quoted in the later publications.

Schliemann also realized the unique importance of the remains of the ancient highways that were still to be seen in the vicinity of Mycenae. He secured the services of Major Steffen, an army engineer, to measure and record this evidence in the course of his detailed survey of Mycenae and its environs. Steffen's report is still the only professional survey ever published on the evidence for land communications in the Aegean Bronze Age.

Emil Bournouf, director of the French School of Archaeology, provided assistance with the ceramic materials, and especially with the various decorative motifs on the pottery and other terra-cotta objects. At that time, however, no one knew much about the pottery of prehistoric periods. An indication of the fluidity of the situation is the varying opinion of eminent critics that the material Schliemann was unearthing should be dated as early as the Stone Age, as late as the third century A.D. or even the Middle Ages, or to assorted intermediate periods.

Schliemann gradually came to realize something of the crucial role that pottery must play in serious archaeological work. "Pottery . . . is the cornucopia of archaeological wisdom for those dark ages, which we, vaguely groping in the twilight of an unrecorded past, are wont to call pre-historic." He set out to learn all he could about it. On technical details such as clays, colors and glazes he consulted a professional chemist. He took increasing pains in recording the exact position, type and condition of the pottery uncovered. He compared his finds with other pottery from all over the world, sometimes suggesting reckless and misleading parallels. Yet before his death he had made himself a serious scholar of prehistoric ceramics.

The most valuable members of Schliemann's "team" were Rudolph Virchow and Wilhelm Dörpfeld. These two, especially Virchow, probably became the nearest equivalent of close friends that Schliemann ever had. His genuine respect for their ability seems to have acted as a brake on the violent outbursts of temper that made him a difficult colleague. Virchow was a fabulous polymath—a famous pathologist and member of a university faculty, as well as politician, social organizer, geologist, ethnographer and general scientist. Extremely generous with his time and learning both in correspondence and in the field, he carried out painstaking investigations of the geographical, botanical and meteorological features of the Trojan plain. We shall hear a great deal more about Dörpfeld, who became the acknowledged authority on Greek architecture in the following generation. His excavation technique and meticulous plans did much to inspire confidence in Schliemann's later campaigns at Troy and Tiryns.

As Schliemann's archaeological career unfolds over two decades, one can see the fiercely self-assertive egotist gradually becoming more mellow and cautious. Perhaps the change was due in part to the growing respect and recognition shown him by the public and by many scholars. Certainly, his happy second marriage in 1869 to the seventeen-year-old Sophia Engastromenou brightened his last twenty years. The tact and sympathy of the beautiful Sophia cushioned many a crisis. In a typical outburst of mingled love, pride and scholarly obsession, he speaks of "My dear wife, an Athenian lady, who is an enthusiastic admirer of Homer, and knows almost the whole of the 'Iliad' by heart . . ."

Before his death he had the satisfaction of knowing that he had won his main point. The scholarly world was reluctantly coming around to the admission that there *had* really been a Troy and a Mycenae before Homer, and that some features of their material culture *are* reflected in Homer's account so faithfully that coincidence is ruled out.

## ITHAKA

It is natural that Troy and Ithaka should have particularly attracted Schliemann since they are the chief locale of action in the *Iliad* and the *Odyssey*. In the first flush of leisure to take up his Greek studies, he briefly visited the island now called Ithaki or Thiaki and confidently identified various landmarks in the Ithakan countryside with Homer's topographical and geographical references. These observations are set forth in his first serious archaeological essay, *Ithâque, le Peloponnèse et Troie* (1869).

He returned to Ithaka ten years later for a more thorough survey. At that time he dug a few test trenches that showed that there had been a fair-sized town high up on Mount Aetos in the center of the island, at a spot that tradition called the Castle of Ulysses. But apart from emphasizing the "Cyclopean"\* nature of its fortifications and house walls, he is vague

---

\* Technical terms not explained in the text will be marked with an asterisk (\*) and defined in the Glossary (pp. 443–53).

about its date or claim to be really Odysseus' town. Soundings elsewhere on the island proved negative in the main, and his final verdict was that "systematic excavations for archaeological purposes are altogether out of the question here."

Yet Schliemann apparently never doubted that modern Ithaki had been Odysseus' home nor that Homer actually knew this particular island at first hand. It was left to Dörpfeld and others to carry on a lengthy and largely inconclusive controversy about which of the western (Ionian) islands was Odysseus' Ithaka. And, in spite of extensive search and excavation on both the island of Leukas and Ithaki, no recognizable trace of Odysseus' home has yet been discovered.

## TROY

Troy, on the other hand, occupied a major share of Schliemann's attention right up to his death. It was probably his favorite among all the sites he excavated or hoped to explore. After long and intricate negotiations with the Turkish authorities, he managed to carry out four major campaigns, in 1870–73, 1878–79, 1882 and 1890. Within an amazingly short time after all but the last season of digging he published a bulky book. Each report appeared in German, French and English, a gesture typical of the author's lavish scale of operations and of his well-founded expectation that the books would be widely read. The English edition of *Troy and Its Remains* appeared in 1875; of *Ilios: The City and Country of the Trojans,* in 1880; and of *Troja: Results of the Latest Researches,* in 1884. As in all his published reports, Schliemann combines in these absorbing volumes both day by day excavation notes and the results of at least a couple of years of over-all reflection and comparative study.

The Troy publications, along with his accounts of excavations at Mycenae and Tiryns, are the truest index to Schliemann's scientific accomplishments. They also provide at least as good a basis for understanding the man himself as all the books that have been written about him. The autobiography that forms the Introduction to *Ilios* is a fascinating example of the rags-to-riches story so dear to that epoch. For an outside evaluation of Schliemann's scientific accomplishments, Carl Schuchhardt's *Schliemann's Excavations* (1889; Eng. ed., 1891) is by far the most satisfactory. Written just at the end of Schliemann's life, it is a clear and sympathetic assessment that time has justified in the main.

Before Schliemann began his excavations some scholars would concede that a town called Troy (or Ilion) may have really existed before Homer in the northwest corner of Asia Minor (modern Turkey). But nearly all of them believed that its site was a high hill called Balli Dagh, near the village of Burnarbashi (see Map IV). They based their arguments almost entirely on its supposed correspondence with topographical descriptions in the *Iliad*. Now, there can be no objection to this "philological" or text-based kind of archaeological research if it is carried out with common sense. But the armchair archaeologists have too often tended to be so concerned with the traditions and opinions preserved by the ancient authorities that they neglect other types of evidence that may turn out to be more directly applicable. A case in point is that of the great English philologist R. C. Jebb. One of Schliemann's persistent critics, he tried to show that the majority of the finds from Troy were postclassical. Schliemann generally showed restraint in answering him, but on one occasion he was goaded into writing: "No courtesy on my part can save Professor Jebb from the fate on which an eminent classical scholar rushes when he mingles in an archaeological debate in ignorance of the first principles of archaeology."

Schliemann himself cannot wholly escape the criticism of putting too much trust in "book archaeology." He leaned on Homer and Pausanias* with a simple faith that few today would consider justified. And in his case, it must be admitted, the method proved its worth more than once. But he at least checked the ancient evidence on the ground. He used his own eyes and judgment in the modern countryside, which has not changed a great deal in its broader aspects since antiquity. Perhaps we should be charitable to the pre-twentieth-century scholars poring over the texts in their studies with the aid of bad maps. For them a trip to Greece or Turkey was usually out of the question or extremely difficult. But our contemporaries who shun field work and yet write learnedly on geographical and topographical problems can scarcely plead the same excuse.

The Burnarbashi theory shows how dangerous it is to place implicit and literal trust in Homer's geographical descriptions. One can point to a long series of attempts from antiquity to the present to prove geographical points by appealing solely to Homer's authority. It is not that these references are necessarily useless or misleading, or that the poet or his sources were demonstrably unfamiliar with the local topography; but most poetry is meant for readers or hearers who either already know the locale in question or do not care about precise geographical details. It is foolish to expect a singer in the court of a prehistoric king or an artist like Homer to supply, consciously or unconsciously, what would amount to an ancient traveler's handbook. In fact, not a single prehistoric site has ever been certainly identified solely by following descriptions in the poems, though learned treatises over the past 2,500 years are filled (not to say cluttered) with interminable attempts to do just that.

In any case, Schliemann looked carefully and with fresh eyes at the

Scamander plain, even though he kept a dog-eared copy of the *Iliad* in his pocket. He made brief and unproductive excavations at Burnarbashi in 1868 and 1871. His allusion to previous theorizing is rather amusing. "It [Burnarbashi] had been almost universally considered to be the site of the Homeric Ilium [Troy]; the springs at the bottom of that village having been regarded as the two springs mentioned by Homer,[1] one of which sent forth warm, the other cold water. But, instead of two springs, I found thirty-four . . . moreover, I found in all the springs a uniform temperature of . . . 62.6° Fahrenheit."

Schliemann, however, soon turned his full attention to a smaller hill called Hissarlik (see Map IV). The name means "fortress" or "acropolis" in Turkish, originally from the Arabic. Hissarlik lies about four miles south of the Dardanelles (ancient Hellespont) and rises some 100 feet above the plain. Its top surface is only about 225 by 175 yards, which had been a factor in causing searchers to look elsewhere for a bigger and more imposing site conforming better to the heroic account.

Schliemann describes the panorama from Hissarlik in rather picturesque language.

> The view from the hill . . . is extremely magnificent. Before me lies the glorious Plain of Troy, which, since the recent rain, is again covered with grass and yellow buttercups; on the north-north-west, at about an hour's distance, it is bounded by the Hellespont. The peninsula of Gallipoli here runs out to a point, upon which stands a lighthouse. To the left of it is the island of Imbros, above which rises Mount Ida of the island of Samothrace, at present covered with snow; a little more to the west, on the Macedonian peninsula, lies the celebrated Mount Athos, or Monte Santo, with its monasteries. . . . Between the . . . mounds [in the plain to the west—traditionally associated with the burial places of Homeric heroes] we see projecting above the high shores of the Aegean Sea the island of Tenedos. To the south, we see the Plain of Troy, extending again to a distance of two hours, as far as the heights of Burnarbashi, above which rises majestically the snow-capped Gargarus of Mount Ida, from which Jupiter witnessed the battles between the Trojans and the Greeks.

Hissarlik had been the focus of a large Greek and Roman town called Ilion and was almost universally believed in classical antiquity to be the site of Priam's Troy. The major voice raised against it in those days was that of the geographer Strabo*, who lived about the time of Christ. The adoption of his skeptical view by the majority of scholars in Schliemann's day has a curious parallel, as we shall see, in the case of Nestor's Pylos. But Hissarlik had at least a few modern champions. Several earlier scholars had declared in its favor; and Frank Calvert, the American vice-consul at the Dardanelles, had dug a small trial trench on the part of the hill that he owned. Calvert took Schliemann to see the site and helped him in many ways during his early negotiations and excavations. But it was his own reading of the ancient evidence (especially the *Iliad*) and an uncanny intuition that made Schliemann decide to excavate at Hissarlik. "Ever since my first visit," he wrote later, "I never doubted that I should find the Pergamus [citadel] of Priam in the depths of this hill."

## The Campaign of 1870–1873

The first seasons at Troy were admittedly more of a rape than a scientific examination. But nearly all archaeological excavations were rough-and-ready affairs in those days; and Schliemann was inexperienced and without expert assistance. A horde of untrained workmen averaging 150 in number hacked great rents through the hill. Schliemann was determined to get to the bottom of the mound, since he had no doubt that Homer's Troy was the first settlement on the site and so the deepest. His great north-south trench bisected the mound, and nothing was allowed to stand in its path. With good reason the workmen named it "the grandmother of the trenches." Schliemann and Sophia were utterly unable to supervise the work properly and to decide what foundations should be preserved and where the digging could proceed deeper without too much damage. Remains of relatively well-preserved buildings were lost for all time when the foundations were wrenched out with no thought of exact measurement or detailed photography before their removal. Schliemann candidly admits that, "Unfortunately, owing to the great extent of my excavations, the hurry in which they were carried on, and the hardness of the *débris,* by far the greater portion of the terra-cotta vessels . . . were brought out more or less broken." Of course, much of the pottery recovered in the most careful excavation is found in crushed condition; but Schliemann's material would surely have shown too many fresh breaks. And there are ominous references to the use of battering rams and great iron levers to remove house walls and fortifications that impeded the impetuous downward thrust.

But in all fairness, if Schliemann's own naïve reports on his early methods are used to discredit him, as they were so often by his critics, other remarks such as the following should not be forgotten. "As every object belonging to the dark night of the pre-Hellenic times, and bearing traces of human skill in art, is to me a page of history, I am, above all things, obliged to take care that nothing escapes me." Elsewhere he says: "Archaeology shall on no account lose any one of my discoveries; every article which can have any interest for the learned world shall be photographed, or copied by a skilful draughtsman, and published in the Appendix to this work; and by the side of every article I shall state the depth in which I discovered it." And in still another place, "I have therefore thought it in the interest of science to fill the excavation up again, in order to preserve the house for future times." These are remarkable statements of principle in the 1870s, even if they were not always observed in practice. If all of his successors in hundreds of excavations had imposed on themselves as conscientious a code in excavation and publication, much valuable evidence would not have been lost forever.

In the reports of those first seasons one can sense that difficulties and perplexities were the chief reward. He had envisioned the rapid uncovering of the "city of Priam"; and his rationalizations for the lack of immediate and striking results are not entirely convincing.

> My expectations are extremely modest; I have no hope of finding plastic works of art [*i.e.,* monumental sculpture, the main motivation of excavations at that time]. The single object of my excavations from the beginning was only to find Troy, whose site has been discussed by a hundred scholars in a hundred books, but which as yet no one has ever sought to bring to light by excavations. If I should not succeed in this, still I shall be perfectly contented, if by my labours I succeed only in penetrating to the deepest darkness of pre-historic times, and enriching archaeology by the discovery of a few interesting features from the most ancient history of the great Hellenic race.

For Schliemann as for anyone else in his day, the proof that he had found Homeric Troy would have to be the remains of great fortification walls, monumental buildings and above all portable wealth in the form of precious metals. So the workmen were urged, in imminent peril of their own and their directors' lives, to burrow ever deeper. They penetrated in places more than 50 feet before reaching what he calls "primary soil."

Schliemann gradually came to believe that he could recognize four major levels of ruins below those of the Greek town of Ilion, which he thought had been founded about 700 B.C. He felt sure that these four prehistoric "nations" had all belonged to a related culture, because he could see a continuity in the artefacts. And he thought that the lower strata contained the artefacts of finer quality; that is, the level of culture had deteriorated as time went on. Furthermore, these people were all "Aryan" in race (a mania with nineteenth-century European students of early cultures), because designs such as the swastika inscribed on various small objects,

Figure 1

particularly on whorls*, reminded him and others he consulted of religious motifs found in India (Fig. 1).

Perhaps the most striking find extending through all four levels of the ruins was a series of large globular "owl vases," with handles like upraised arms or wings rising from the shoulder (Fig. 2). Eyes and nose (and later ears, too) were modeled on the neck or sometimes on a separate lid; and female breasts, navel and vulva were often shown on the body of the vessel. Schliemann regarded these interesting objects as representations of Athena, the protecting goddess of Homer's Troy. He was sure the scholars were wrong in translating *glaukōpis* (Homer's favorite epithet for Athena) as "gray-eyed" or "bright-eyed"; it must rather mean "owl-eyed," since *glaux* is the classical Greek word for "owl" and the owl was Athena's bird.

Figure 2

For some time Schliemann continued to believe that the lowest of his four prehistoric levels must be Homer's Troy. This conviction was shaken toward the end of the campaign by the appearance in the second level from the bottom of well-preserved foundations of a "Great Tower" (Fig. 13). Beside it there had been a "double gateway" with a paved ramp leading out through the fortification wall and dipping steeply toward the southwest edge of the hill. The gateway soon became the Scaean Gate, where Homer locates the famous recognition scene. "Here . . . sat Priam, the seven elders of the city, and Helen; and this is the scene of the most splendid passage in the Iliad. From this spot the company surveyed the whole Plain, and saw at the foot of the Pergamus the Trojan and the

Achaean armies face to face about to settle their agreement to let the war be decided by a single combat between Paris and Menelaus."[2]

It followed in Schliemann's reconstruction that the ruins of a large structure built on an artificial elevation immediately inside the Scaean Gate ought to mark the "palace of Priam." He could only partially uncover its ground plan since it extended under the temporary buildings where the staff lived. But prospects were getting brighter. The terra-cotta vases found within the "palace" were especially fine, and in or near it a silver vase and a cup made of electrum* were discovered.

So the stage was set for the high point of the first series of excavations. In the spring of 1873, while work was proceeding at the base of the fortification wall slightly west of the Scaean Gate, Schliemann reports that he detected through the dust and rubble "a large copper article of the most remarkable form, which attracted my attention all the more as I thought I saw gold behind it." He immediately told Sophia to announce a recess for the workmen.

> While the men were eating and resting, I cut out the Treasure with a large knife, which it was impossible to do without the very greatest exertion and the most fearful risk of my life, for the great fortification-

Figure 3

wall, beneath which I had to dig, threatened every moment to fall down
upon me. But the sight of so many objects, every one of which is of
inestimable value to archaeology, made me foolhardy, and I never
thought of any danger. It would, however, have been impossible for me
to have removed the Treasure without the help of my dear wife, who
stood by me ready to pack the things which I cut out in her shawl and
to carry them away.

One may observe parenthetically that his dear wife was apparently in equal
peril of her life and also that, as will be seen, she must have had an extremely capacious shawl.

Below a copper "shield" (really a very large basin) lay a copper cauldron
with horizontal handles, a silver jug (Fig. 3), a globular gold bottle and two
gold cups (Fig. 4). One of the cups has two handles and two unusual
spouts (Fig. 5). The form is very distinctive, and we now call it a sauceboat*. It regularly has but a single longer spout and is the most typical vase
shape on the Greek mainland in the mid-*third* millennium. Schliemann,
of course, could not know this and immediately saw in the cup an example of Homer's *depas amphikypellon**.[3] Since the double-sauceboat shape

Figure 4

Top View

0   in   2

Figure 5

turned out to be unique, Schliemann later extended the equation to include another very common and distinctive two-handled conical goblet
(Fig. 6).

In a transport of delight, Schliemann goes on and on with the inventory of "the Treasure"—more cups and vases of precious metals, lances,
daggers, axes, knives. Many of the objects were fused and deformed by
intense heat. Packed into the largest silver vase, he records "two splendid
gold diadems . . . a fillet*, and four beautiful gold ear-rings of most exquisite workmanship: upon these lay 56 gold ear-rings of exceedingly curious form and 8750 small gold rings, perforated prisms and dice, gold
buttons, and similar jewels, which obviously belonged to other ornaments;
then followed six gold bracelets, and on the top of all the two small gold
goblets."

Schliemann's reconstruction of the way the treasure reached this spot
is typical of his vivid imagination.

As I found all these articles together, forming a rectangular mass, or
packed into one another, it seems to be certain that they were placed
on the city wall in a wooden chest, . . . such as those mentioned by
Homer as being in the palace of king Priam.[4] This appears to be the

more certain, as close by the side of these articles I found a copper key [it later proved to be a chisel]. . . . It is probable that some member of the family of king Priam hurriedly packed the Treasure into the chest and carried it off without having time to pull out the key; that when he reached the wall, however, the hand of an enemy or the fire overtook him, and he was obliged to abandon the chest, which was immediately covered to a height of from 5 to 6 feet with the red ashes and the stones of the adjoining royal palace.

This fabulous discovery finally convinced Schliemann that he must change his view about which stratum represented Homer's Troy. "I formerly believed," he writes, "that the most ancient people who inhabited this site were the Trojans [of Homer] . . . but I now perceive that Priam's people were the succeeding nation. . . . In consequence of my former mistaken idea, that Troy was to be found on the primary soil or close above it, I unfortunately, in 1871 and 1872, destroyed a large portion of the

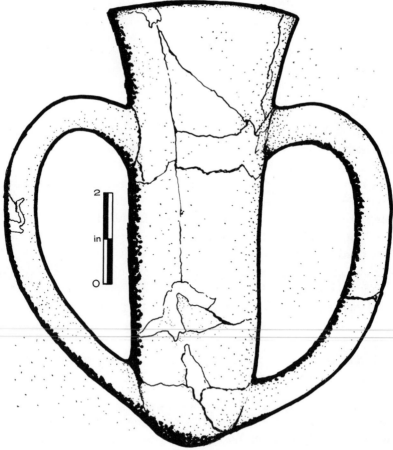

Figure 6

[second] city, for I at that time broke down all the house-walls in the higher strata which obstructed my way." One can hardly condone the impetuosity, but the frank admission of the mistake is courageous.

In another important respect, too, Schliemann had to change his thinking. All through the first three years he carefully datelined his field reports "Pergamus of Troy." Now Pergamus is the name Homer gives to the citadel as distinct from the lower town surrounding it. But Schliemann's soundings outside the fortified acropolis showed no signs of prehistoric habitation, and he finally came to the reluctant conclusion that the area within the walls must represent the total extent of the town. "I now most emphatically declare that the city of Priam cannot have extended on any one side beyond the primeval plateau of this fortress. . . . I am extremely disappointed at being obliged to give so small a plan of Troy; nay, I had wished to be able to make it a thousand times larger, but I value truth above everything, and I rejoice that my three years' excavations have laid open the Homeric Troy, even though on a diminished scale."

The higher stratum that we now believe to represent Homeric Troy was, as it later turned out, considerably larger than Schliemann's "second city" (Fig. 13); but it is still a characteristic failing of classical enthusiasts to form an inflated impression of the monumental size of ancient Greek "cities." Schliemann continues his apology:

> I venture to hope that the civilized world will not only not be disappointed that the city of Priam has shown itself to be scarcely a twentieth part as large as was to be expected from the statements of the Iliad, but that, on the contrary, it will accept with delight and enthusiasm the certainty that Ilium did really exist, that a large portion of it has now been brought to light, and that Homer, even although he exaggerates, nevertheless sings of events that actually happened. . . . But this little Troy was immensely rich for the circumstances of those times, since I find here a treasure of gold and silver articles, such as is now scarcely to be found in an emperor's palace; and as the town was wealthy, so was it also powerful, and ruled over a large territory.

As he finished the 1873 season, Schliemann had no idea of returning to "this little Troy" but was impatient to start work at Mycenae.

> I have excavated two-thirds of the entire city; and, as I have brought to light the Great Tower, the Scaean Gate, the city wall of Troy, the royal palace . . . I have also made an exceedingly copious collection of all the articles of the domestic life and the religion of the Trojans; and therefore it is not to be expected that science would gain anything more by further excavations. If, however, my excavations should at any time be continued, I urgently entreat those who do so to throw the *débris*

of their diggings from the declivity of the hill, and *not* to fill up the colossal cuttings which I have made with such infinite trouble and at such great expense, for they are of great value to archaeology, inasmuch as in these cuttings all the strata of *débris,* from the primary soil up to the surface of the hill, can be examined with little trouble.

We note here the first faint gropings toward scientific stratigraphy*, so vital to modern archaeology, already forming in his agile brain.

The stealthy removal of the treasure and nearly all of the other finds from Turkey to Athens is not a happy story. But, apart from charges and countercharges about broken agreements, one can point out that Schliemann was simply following accepted practice. In those days the fortunate discoverer of archaeological riches in the soil of "underdeveloped" countries took it for granted that he would carry home the loot. Sometimes he smuggled it out; but more often that was unnecessary, particularly if he had diplomatic immunity or powerful friends. And we are hardly entitled nowadays to pass moral judgment on such practices of the past when we know that rare antiquities illegally removed from the country of their origin (and probably discovered in illegal excavations) still appear in the museums and private collections of "overdeveloped" countries.

The publication of his first series of excavations did not have the positive effect that Schliemann had hoped. It was admitted that he had unearthed important evidence for early civilization in the Troad*, but most experts were critical of the methods by which he had gathered his material and of the conclusions he had drawn from it. One prominent scholar suggested that the funds might have been put to much better use by more experienced excavators. There were even slanderous insinuations that Schliemann had "planted" the more striking finds in advance of excavation. Few scholars saw any close connection between the antiquities he had unearthed and the Trojan buildings and artefacts described in the *Iliad.* In fact, Schliemann's confident association of various discoveries with Homer's people and places became something of a laughing stock in the public press as well as in scholarly circles, particularly in his native Germany. The Burnarbashi site still remained the favorite location for Homer's Troy, if it had ever actually existed.

## THE CAMPAIGN OF 1878–1879

We have gained enough insight into Schliemann's character to guess that he would not give up the struggle at this point. He quickly changed his earlier attitude that no further excavation at Hissarlik was necessary and began the extremely difficult negotiations with the Turkish Government for a new permit. A lengthy lawsuit over the ownership of the treasure resulted in an order for him to pay the Turks an indemnity of 10,000 francs. He promptly paid five times the amount assessed and brought the precious objects out of their hiding places in the homes and farms of Sophia's numerous Greek relatives. With the support of many powerful friends, including Sir Austen Henry Layard, British Ambassador to Turkey and himself a renowned excavator in the Near East, permission to continue the work was finally obtained. Although the exciting excavation of the Shaft Graves* at Mycenae intervened, we shall defer that episode until we have reviewed the remaining campaigns at Troy. But it should be noted that Schliemann returned to Troy in 1878 with considerably more excavation experience than when he had left.

Unfair though some of the criticisms had been, their total effect was beneficial. Schliemann now refers more cautiously to the "city chieftain's house" and the "great Treasure" rather than to Priam's Palace and Priam's Treasure. Bournouf and Virchow were now associated with him in the field. The latter says, in his Preface to the publication of this second series of excavations: "I recognize the duty of bearing my testimony against the host of doubters, who, with good or ill intentions, have never tired of carping alike at the trustworthiness and significance of his discoveries." Virchow does indeed stake his own impeccable scholarly reputation, insisting, "This excavation has opened for the studies of the archaeologist a completely new theatre—like a world by itself. Here begins an entirely new science." Virchow's verdict is indeed a responsible statement of fact. Mistakes and vacillations would still occur, but from now on one senses that Schliemann and his staff are in control of the situation and are investigating specific and manageable problems.

Schliemann even found the patience to submit to the presence of armed soldiers and a Turkish commissioner, who held the keys to the building where the finds were stored. "The ten gensdarmes . . . were of great use to me, for they not only served as a guard against the brigands by whom the Troad was infested, but they also carefully watched my labourers whilst they were excavating, and thus forced them to be honest." We shall soon see the special point of this last remark.

The second campaign had two principal purposes, both of them responses to the previous adverse criticism. The first was to clear the ruins of the fortifications and of the large building of the second level near which the treasure had been discovered. The expedition succeeded in uncovering almost the whole western half of the mound down to this "Homeric" level. The second project was a very thorough and wide-ranging study of the whole Trojan plain—its topography, geology, flora, fauna and economic basis, as well as the antiquities of all periods. This, of course, was a reaction to the charge that Homer had no firsthand acquaintance with the area, or at least that Hissarlik did not correspond with ancient literary references to Troy.

The very title of the second book, *Ilios: The City and Country of the Trojans,* suggests the wider scope. Schliemann discusses in detail all the ancient literary evidence, the history and mythology of Troy and the ethnology of the Trojans and their allies. He and Virchow outline their research on the mountains, rivers, climate, zoology and botany of the area. They stress its strategic location, with command of the easiest land and sea routes between Europe and Asia. Virchow insists on Homer's "surprising knowledge of the meteorology of the district, of the flora and fauna, and the social peculiarities of its population. Three thousand years have not sufficed to produce any noteworthy alteration in these things. . . . The truth of this warrants us in assuming that the poet did visit the country, though perhaps he may not have stayed there long, and it does not exclude the hypothesis that a body of legend, though disjointed and incongruous, already existed before his time."

We see here that the possibility of a long gap between the Trojan War and Homer's lifetime is coming into focus. Virchow, in fact, frankly admits, "It is very questionable whether he [Homer] ever saw with his eyes even the ruins of the fallen city." This must have been a bitter blow to Schliemann's naïve credulity. But, to his credit, he does not dispute it; and, of course, his major thesis is still untouched.

Schliemann continues his bulky book with a full review of the controversy over the exact site of Homer's "city" and argues as strong a case as has ever been made since for Hissarlik. Then he begins at the bottom and describes, layer by layer, the *seven* successive settlements that they had by then succeeded in distinguishing. The introductory diagram makes it all appear deceptively simple. Stratum I occupies 52½ feet to 45 feet below the modern surface; Stratum II, 45 to 33 feet; Stratum III, 33 feet to 23 feet; Stratum IV, 23 feet to 13 feet; Stratum V, 13 feet to 6½ feet; Stratum VI, 6½ feet to 6 feet; Stratum VII, 6 feet and up. But even this schematic representation indicates tremendous progress in precision compared to the "four nations" discussed so vaguely only a few years before. In fact, the later work of Dörpfeld and Blegen in large part authenticated Schliemann's seven occupation levels, although two major phases were added; and with modern stratigraphical techniques Blegen was able to demonstrate a far more complex pattern of subphases in the long story of Trojan prehistory.

Schliemann was trying hard to improve on his past methods, but we shall see that not every change from earlier conclusions was a correction of error. What had previously been called the lowest level is now divided into the First and the Second City. He notes that the house walls (and possibly the fortifications) at the lower level were made of much smaller stones; but it is particularly the pottery types that are now recognized as being "so vastly, so entirely different."

With a new caution he says of the so-called Aryan motifs on the spindle whorls, "I abstain from discussing whether this ornamentation may be symbolical or not . . ." Similarly, in describing some little bird-faced statuettes, he hedges slightly compared with his previous confident identification of the owl vases with Athena. "As all these rude figures represent the same form, there can be no doubt that they are idols of a female goddess, the patron deity of the place, whether she may have been called Até* or Athené, or have had any other name . . ." But he still cannot resist the urge to tie in his finds with mythology and adds: "There appears to be the highest probability that all of them are copies of the celebrated primeval Palladium* [image of Pallas Athene], to which was attached the fate of Troy, and which was fabled to have fallen from heaven."

Laboratory analyses of thirteen stone axes, or celts*, from the lowest level showed that they were of jade (nephrite)—one of them a rare white variety—which must have been imported in rough or finished form from very distant eastern sources. Pure copper, not bronze, was the basic metal, and the art of gilding was known. "We, therefore, find in use among these primitive inhabitants of the most ancient city on Hissarlik, together with very numerous stone implements and stone weapons, the following metals: gold, silver, lead, copper, but no iron; in fact, no trace of this latter metal was ever found by me either in any of the pre-historic cities of Troy, or at Mycenae. Nothing, I think, could better testify to the great antiquity of the pre-historic ruins at Hissarlik and at Mycenae, than the total absence of iron."

The *new* Level II represents the occupation of a "different people." Since there are no signs of fire between this and the first "city," there may have been an intervening period when the hill was unoccupied. The house walls were more solidly built of large white limestone blocks, which presumably reached right up to the roofs, and the fortifications were in the monumental Cyclopean style. The Scaean Gate and its street paved with white slabs was built then; so perhaps were some house walls found *below* the foundations of the "house of the town chieftain" (*now* assigned to Level III), which might point to the existence of a "palace" belonging to Level II on the same spot.

Figure 7

One of the ceramic innovations in Level II was the presence of many large clay storage jars, or pithoi*, some of them over 6 feet in height and as much as 5 feet in diameter (Fig. 7). In a characteristic example of his incorrigible habit of name-dropping, Schliemann records: "As his Highness Prince Otto Bismarck, the Chancellor of the German Empire, ingeniously remarked to me . . . the manufacture of these large jars proves already a high degree of civilization, for to make them is just as difficult as to bake them . . ." Also, the owl vases begin in Level II and continue in the following three strata; so do the equally distinctive conical goblets (Fig. 6). The connection of the one with "owl-eyed" Athena and of the other with Homer's double-handled drinking cup is reaffirmed. Carl Schuchhardt, the first scholar to review Schliemann's over-all achievement, remarks that this "Trojan cup would be exactly suited for guests sitting in a circle at their meal. It cannot stand, and it must therefore be emptied at one draught, or else be passed round, and this would be much facilitated by the two big handles . . ."

The settlement now called "the third, the burnt city" was built on the leveled ruins of its predecessor, probably after the hill had been abandoned for a long time. Schliemann continues to identify these ruins with the fabled Troy that the Greeks captured, but it has lost its earlier designation as the Second City because of the additional stratum recognized below it. The new people built the lower part of their walls of reddish stones laid in clay mortar; and "they, and they alone of all the prehistoric people who lived here, used bricks." Brick and timber superstructures crowned their fortifications and buildings, and the final conflagration left a layer of brick and ashes 6 to 10 feet deep.

Schliemann reasons that the Scaean Gate had been reused in this phase and that a new paving of reddish slabs was laid over the white ones of the earlier roadway. Several houses were excavated. "By far the most remarkable . . . is undoubtedly the mansion immediately to the north-west of the gate, which I attribute to the town-chief or king: first, because this is by far the largest house of all; and secondly, because . . . I found in or close to it nine out of the ten treasures which were discovered, as well as a very large quantity of pottery, which, though without painting and of the same forms as that found elsewhere, was distinguished, generally speaking, by its fabric." The exterior dimensions were approximately 24 by 49 feet. The surviving ground plan is peculiar, but Schliemann argued on the analogy of modern houses in the area that the surviving first level was simply a storage cellar. It would have been reached by wooden stairs from the floor above, and the deep layer of burned debris might indicate that there had been as many as five or six stories!

Now we can follow up the discovery of the *ten* treasures just mentioned. It will be remembered that Schliemann thought that someone had been trying to carry off the great treasure from this very building. "This was certainly my opinion at the time of the discovery; but since then I have found, in the presence of Professor Virchow and M. Bournouf [note the careful reference to reliable eyewitnesses], on the very same wall, and only a few yards to the north of the spot where the large treasure was discovered, another smaller treasure, and three more treasures on and near the walls of the adjoining royal house. I, therefore, now rather believe that all these treasures have fallen in the conflagration from the upper storeys of the royal house." The remaining hoards of precious objects came from spots in the same general area and level.

Although Schliemann never suspected it at the time, the great treasure was not the only precious find of the 1873 campaign. Again, we can best get the flavor by quoting his own version of what happened.

> I now come to the three smaller treasures, found . . . at a depth of 30 feet on the east side of the royal house and very close to it, by two of my workmen. . . . [They] had stolen and divided the three treasures between themselves, and probably I should never have had any knowledge of it, had it not been for the lucky circumstance that the wife of [one] . . . had the boldness to parade one Sunday with the ear-rings and pendants. . . . This excited the envy of her companions; she was denounced to the Turkish authorities . . . who put her and her husband in prison; and, having been threatened that her husband would be hanged if they did not give up the jewels, she betrayed the hiding-place, and thus this part of the treasure was at once recovered. . . . The pair also denounced their accomplice . . . but here the authorities came too late, because he had already had his part of the spoil melted down. . . . Thus this part of the treasure is for ever lost to science.

Schliemann then describes the gold earrings, bracelets, pendants and necklaces that were recovered, and he continues: "Both thieves concur in their statement that the other part of the treasures . . . contained, amongst other jewels . . . a very large round plate of gold with most curious signs engraved on it. The loss of this latter object grieves me more than anything else." Here we can detect the scientist winning out over the gold-seeker. Schliemann desperately wanted to find written records in the earlier levels but was doomed to disappointment—as are all prehistoric archaeologists *by definition.*

No wonder a determined effort was made to supervise the later work more closely! And fortunately this change came before the complete excavation of the "house of the chieftain," because the list of separate hoards of precious objects, usually enclosed in a terra-cotta vase, becomes almost monotonous. Hundreds of articles of gold, silver and electrum jewelry, as well as various bronze weapons, were recovered in and around the ruins of the building. This time most of them were turned over to the museum in Constantinople, but Schliemann retained the rights of publication. Among the most striking objects were heavy gold bracelets and brooches with applied decoration of spirals and rosettes, a fine gold eagle, an elegant silver spoon and a ceremonial dagger of silver (Fig. 8). Clearly the occupants of the "palace" had been exceedingly wealthy; and equally clearly the fire had left no time to rescue or pillage valuables, and their later recovery had for some reason been impracticable.

Schliemann was wise enough to consult an expert about the techniques of manufacturing shown by his unique collection of delicate jewelry. Carlo

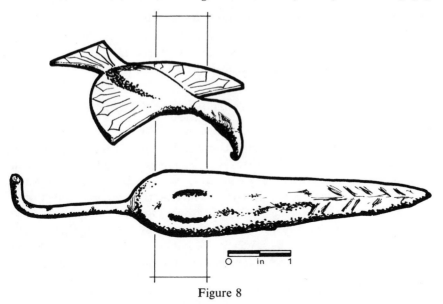

Figure 8

Giuliano, a famous London goldsmith and connoisseur of antiques, found that the gold was in general very pure (up to 23 carats fine) and that the craftsmen had been expert in making thin wire, punching complicated patterns from gold leaf and soldering microscopic beads (granulation). But "how the primitive goldsmith could do all this fine work . . . without the aid of a lens . . . is an enigma even to Mr. Giuliano." Schliemann draws a few vague parallels in details of design (especially the spirals and rosettes) with his recent finds from Mycenae, but he is not very optimistic about what the future might provide in the way of comparative material. "As nothing similar to any one of these various articles of gold has been ever found elsewhere, it will for ever remain a riddle to us whether they were home-made or imported; but if we compare them with the rude works of terra-cotta or the implements and weapons of stone or bronze found in the third city, we certainly feel inclined to think that they were imported."

Schliemann's "for ever" is somewhat of an overstatement. We now know that fortified settlements with comparable riches amassed in the chief's treasure rooms were fairly common in the same general period in the northern Aegean islands and in Anatolia. They testify to widespread trade and probably to piracy as well. But it is still difficult to define the sources of metals and other precious materials, as well as the precise centers of manufacture.

Implements and weapons of unalloyed or almost pure copper were common. But two different experts analyzed drillings from several axes and found that they were copper with between 5 per cent and 10 per cent tin; that is, the metal is proper bronze. Schliemann speculates on the source of the tin, which is not known to have occurred in any quantity in the east Mediterranean area and which he regards as a sure sign of long-distance commerce.

Among the terra-cotta vases, the big pithoi, or storage jars, interest him particularly.

> The number of large jars which I brought to light in the burnt stratum of the third city certainly exceeds 600. By far the larger number of them were empty, the mouth being covered by a large flag of schist or lime-stone. This leads me to the conclusion that the jars were filled with wine or water at the time of the catastrophe, for there appears to have been hardly any reason for covering them if they had been empty. Had they been used to contain anything else but liquids, I should have found traces of the fact; but only in a very few cases did I find some carbonized grain in the jars . . .

He is bothered by the continuing crudeness of the "monstrous representations of the tutelary deity" on the very numerous owl vases, when there is at least some evidence that the Trojans could model fair representations of normal human features. A possible explanation occurs in the well-known phenomenon of religious conservatism. A great many of the vases have tripod bases, but Schliemann is disappointed by the complete lack of proper tripods in metal, which are such a prominent article of exchange and value in the Homeric poems. Numerous globular jugs have a peculiar bent-back neck (Fig. 9), and there are a fair number of joined multiple vases. Both types show similarities to vases found in Cyprus. There are also some terra-cotta containers in the form of animals—hedge-hogs, pigs and even a hippopotamus.

We can follow here, too, the infancy of the science of physical anthropology. Although very few burials were found in any of the prehistoric strata, several human skeletons were recovered in this level. Two of them were apparently warriors; they were wearing helmets and a bronze lance was beside one. Virchow studied the skulls carefully and found that the warriors were young males, long-headed (dolichocephalic*), with cranial indexes (the proportion of width to length) of 68.6 and 73.8. Another well-preserved skull was that of a young female, round-headed (brachy-cephalic*), with an index of 82.5. The considerable disparity perplexes him. "Thus we are led naturally to the question, whether we have not here before us the remains of a mixed race. . . . The temptation is very great to make further suppositions regarding the extraction of the individual persons and their social position." His good sense gets the upper

Figure 9

hand, as he adds, "This temptation, I believe, I must resist, because our real knowledge of the craniology of ancient peoples is still on a very small scale." Yet the urge to see early evidence for the master race is, after all, too much and a few lines later he confides, "But if besides the skull index we take into consideration the entire formation of the head and the face of the dolichocephalic skulls, the idea that those men were members of the Aryan race is highly pleasing."

Schliemann naturally gives a particularly careful description of the material remains recovered in his Level III, since he is still as sure as ever that it must be Homer's Troy. Yet he practically admits that the correspondences with the *Iliad* are not nearly so close as he had once believed, and he now echoes Virchow in accounting for the discrepancy. "I wish I could have proved Homer to have been an eye-witness of the Trojan war! Alas, I cannot do it! At his time swords were in universal use and iron was known, whereas they were totally unknown at Troy. . . . Homer

gives us the legend of Ilium's tragic fate, as it was handed down to him
by preceding bards, clothing the traditional facts of the war and destruction
of Troy in the garb of his own day." Such a far-reaching hypothesis has a
strangely modern ring and no doubt was in part the result of reading (in
German) E. Buchholz's *The Homeric Artefacts*, which had appeared
since Schliemann's first campaign.

We can be quite brief about the upper strata. Schliemann finds hints
in legend that Troy was not permanently and completely destroyed by the
Greeks, and he insists that archaeology has proved this true. In fact, he
says, "We find among the successors of the burnt city the very same
singular idols; the very same primitive bronze battle-axes; the very same
terra-cotta vases, with or without tripod feet. . . . The only difference is
that, in general, the pottery . . . is coarser and of a ruder fabric; and that
we find . . . many new forms of vases and goblets." He complains particularly about the slovenliness of the housewives in Level IV. "The masses
of shells and cockles accumulated in the *débris* of the houses are so stu-
pendous, that they baffle all description. . . . A people which left all their
kitchen-refuse on the floors of their rooms must have lived in a very low
social condition." Present-day archaeologists, on the other hand, are more
likely to complain when ancient housewives have been so tidy that their
house floors are found swept clean.

No monumental fortification walls could be clearly associated with
Levels IV and V. In the latter there was considerably more wheel-made
pottery, and metal largely replaces stone for implements and weapons.
Schliemann, noting the elements of both innovation and continuity, theorizes
that the old stock continued to live alongside newcomers.

Between the fifth and "the seventh, the Greek Ilium," Schliemann
found a thin deposit that definitely puzzled him. He calls it "the Sixth
city, most probably a Lydian settlement." He could associate with it no
fortifications and scarcely any house walls. He correctly suggests that the
reason is a drastic leveling of the hilltop for the later Greek town. Some
pottery shapes like the pithos continue; and we are reminded of the
legendary Diogenes by the reference to one great jar, which "was lying
. . . before my house at Hissarlik, and was always used as a lodging by
one of my workmen; it even lodged two of them in rainy weather."

Most of the "Lydian" pottery in this sixth level is quite unparalleled in
the lower strata, and it will prove to have a mighty importance for prehistoric archaeology (Fig. 10). "I found a vast quantity of very curious
pottery, partly hand-made, partly wheel-made, which in shape and fabric,
in colour and in the clay, is so utterly different from all the pottery of the
preceding pre-historic cities, as well as from the pottery of the upper

Figure 10

Aeolic* Ilium, that I hesitate whether to refer it to pre-historic or to historic times." The color is black or gray, occasionally yellow or brown. Favorite shapes include cups and bowls with one or (more commonly) two high-swung handles. Many have sharp ridges, parallel grooves and abrupt sur-face transitions.

Schliemann, as usual, looked around the museums of Western Europe for parallels and concluded: "From the great resemblance this pottery has to . . . vases . . . found in Italy . . . held to be either archaic Etruscan or prae-Etruscan pottery, we think it likely that there may have been a Lydian settlement on Hissarlik contemporary with the colonization of Etruria by the Lydians, asserted by Herodotus, and that the Lydian dominion may have been established over the whole Troad at the same epoch." The fabulously wealthy Lydian kingdom, located in the coastal area of west central Turkey, was absorbed by the Persians in the sixth century B.C. Herodotus reports the story—still very controversial—that the mysterious Etruscan civilization in western Italy north of Rome owed its origin to a band of Lydians who were forced by famine to emigrate.[5]

When he feels that he has to suggest even an approximate date for Troy VI, Schliemann is naturally uncomfortable and vague. "Now, regarding the chronology of this Lydian city, I think every archaeologist will admit that all the articles which we have passed in review . . . denote an early state of civilization. . . . It is pretty certain that the immigration of the Etruscans into Italy took place before the Dorian invasion of the Peloponnesus [traditionally dated about 1104 B.C.] . . . ." Such remarks are a commentary on the dense fog in which the pioneer was groping his way toward some kind of firm link between his own discoveries and the chaotic and vague prehistoric time scale of his day. We now know that his "Lydian" pottery is far earlier, and the earliest evidence for Etruscan culture considerably later than 1100.

## THE CAMPAIGN OF 1882

The publication called *Troja,* which reports the results of the third campaign, is dedicated to "Her Imperial and Royal Highness Victoria . . . Princess Royal of Great Britain . . . illustrious patron of art and science." At the beginning Schliemann confesses that he had become increasingly unhappy about his identification of "the small town, the third in succession from the virgin soil" with the mighty Troy of legend. He finally felt compelled once more to recheck the evidence in the field. This time he was assisted by the architects Dörpfeld and Joseph Höfler. They were responsible for a completely new survey of the excavations. Time after time in the course of his last major Trojan publication Schliemann frankly and courageously admits that "my excellent architects have proved to me" that this or that previous theory was wrong.

One perceives throughout this book a more relaxed and mellow tone. The site and equipment were in good shape when they returned. The weather was good. Their quarters were larger and more comfortable. And, even more important, the commissary had improved. "My honoured friends, Messrs. J. Henry Schröder & Co., of London, had kindly sent me a large supply of tins of Chicago corned beef, peaches, the best English cheese, and ox-tongues, as well as 240 bottles of the best English pale ale." A footnote on this page probably represents the most personal remark ever made by the author of a serious archaeological publication. "I was the sole consumer," Schliemann confesses, "of these 240 bottles of pale ale, which lasted me for five months, and which I used as a medicine to cure constipation, from which I had been suffering for more than thirty years . . ." The only real irritant was that the Turkish authorities, still mindful of the disappearance of the treasure in 1873, had posted as overseer a certain suspicious and malicious Beder Eddin Effendi. "A wretch like him," comments Schliemann, "is an unmitigated plague in archaeological pursuits."

The results of the third campaign required no major revision in the previous conclusions about Level I. It was a small fortified citadel with relatively few buildings. But we are startled to see references to "the *second,* the burnt city." What, we wonder, has happened to "the *third,* the burnt city"? Schliemann apologizes quite candidly: "My architects have proved to me that, together with M. Bournouf, my collaborator in 1879, I had not rightly distinguished and separated the ruins of the two following settlements, namely, the Second and Third . . ." His explanation of this serious mistake is long and involved; but it amounts to the fact that the deep layer of burned debris (especially bricks) really marks the destruction of the buildings of the *second* level, and that the buildings of the next level were set immediately on this debris, sometimes sunk down into it and resting directly on earlier fortifications and house walls that had not been too much ruined. So, all references in the 1880 publication to the "*third,* the burnt city" must be erased from our minds, and we are back to the earlier equation of 1875: Level II=burned city=Homer's Troy.

To those who wonder why we bother to record such wavering, one may point out that it is often by means of a series of corrected hypotheses that archaeology or any other science reaches or approaches the truth. The usual statement that Schliemann believed that Level II was Homer's Troy is an oversimplification and in a sense a falsification of the record. The conclusion was not reached nearly as directly as that. In fact, as we have seen, his identification of Homeric Troy varied over those early years from Level I to Level II to Level III and back to II. And to anticipate for a moment, in his very last year of life he was apparently convinced that he would have to change his pronouncement once again—to Level VI. And even that equation did not stand the test of time, for we now believe that Homeric Troy was Level VIIa! Schliemann no doubt had an embarrassing habit of rushing into print; but no apology is needed in any scholarly field for a change of mind necessitated by new evidence. The unpardonable sin, indeed, is for a scholar to refuse to consider the possibility that a cherished theory may be mistaken. And archaeological annals, as we shall see, contain notable examples of such failings.

But to return to 1882, for the first time the foundations of buildings in the center of the fortified area of Level II were systematically cleared. Especially noteworthy were two large structures with heavy brick walls (Fig. 13). They "are most probably temples: we infer this in the first place from their ground plan, because they have only one hall in the breadth; secondly, from the proportionately considerable thickness of the walls; thirdly, from the circumstance, that they stand parallel and near each other, being only separated by a corridor about 20 inches broad; for if they had been dwelling-houses they would probably have had one common wall—a thing never found yet in ancient temples."

The larger structure (A) had an almost square porch at the front and a main room about 33 feet by 66 feet. The two rooms are called pronaos* (porch) and naos* (sanctuary) in the technical terms of classical temple architecture.

> Precisely in the middle of the naos is a circular elevation. . . . It consists, like the floor, of beaten clay, and seems to have served as the substruction to an altar or as a base for the idol; but we cannot say this with certainty, the greater part of the circle having been cut away by the great north trench. . . . Like all edifices in the prehistoric cities of Troy, this temple had a horizontal roofing, which was made of large wooden beams, smaller rafters, and clay. This is evident from the entire absence of any tiles, as well as from the existence in the interior of the edifice of a layer of clay 12 inches thick, mixed with calcined rafters and some large well-preserved pieces of wood. . . . This kind of roofing is still in general use in the Troad.

The smaller edifice (B) was built later than A, since there was no clay coating over the bricks of the exterior wall next to A. Its ground plan consisted of three rooms about 15 feet wide and one behind the other: pronaos; naos, about 24 feet long; and a rear room, about 30 feet long. "Although the division of the temple B into three rooms answers in a striking manner to the division of the house of Paris, according to Homer's description[6] . . . nevertheless the reasons given above seem to prove, with the greatest probability, that both the edifices, B as well as A, were temples." One can read between the lines that Schliemann would have very much preferred to call these buildings houses or even palaces; but he was overawed by Dörpfeld, who was fresh from the exciting German discovery of classical temples at Olympia.

Only one new cache of metal objects was discovered in Level II, and Schliemann's description of the fate of one item suggests the satisfaction he took in outwitting the obnoxious Beder Eddin Effendi. "By far the most interesting object of the little treasure was a copper or bronze idol of the most primitive form. . . . I think it probable that it is a copy or imitation of the famous Palladium. . . . Fortunately . . . it had broken into three fragments; I am indebted to this lucky circumstance for having obtained it in the division with the Turkish Government; for the three pieces were covered with carbonate of copper and dirt, and altogether undiscernible to an inexperienced eye" (Fig. 11).

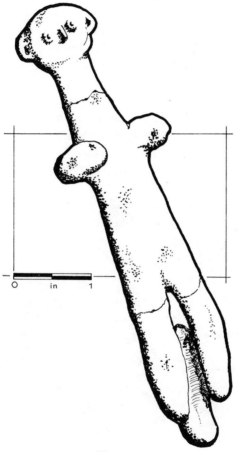

Figure 11

No significant changes are made in the brief discussion of Levels IV, V and VI. The latter is still called Lydian. He describes the results of his research in the uppermost level of Greek and Roman times and reviews the latest explorations in the plain of Troy. Then, with uncharacteristic detachment, which perhaps suggests that he was tiring, he sums up the whole series of campaigns: "My work at Troy is now ended for ever, after extending over more than the period of *ten years,* which has a fated connection with the legend of the city. How many tens of years a new controversy may rage around it, I leave to the critics: *that* is their work; *mine* is done."

## THE CAMPAIGN OF 1890

The controversy that Schliemann predicted has indeed continued to the present day, though perhaps not along the lines he foresaw; but his own work at Troy was not quite done. The fabulous discovery of the royal Shaft Graves just inside the Lion Gate at Mycenae had kindled the hope that their counterparts might still exist undetected at Troy. The belief seems to have taken increasing hold of Schliemann that excavation around the main gate in the southwest section of wealthy Troy II would "pay off." And so in 1890, the last year of his eventful life, the old man was once more back at Hissarlik with Dörpfeld; and a new field railroad system

Figure 12

with metal track and dump cars was installed to dispose more quickly of the earth.

They found no gold-filled tombs associated with Troy II, but they made a discovery of far greater importance for the true understanding of the site. For Schliemann it must have been a tragically unwelcome realization. Troy II was apparently not "Homer's Troy" and the wonderful treasures had no connection with Priam. For on the slope outside the circuit of its walls they discovered the ruins of two buildings of excellent construction that had belonged to Troy VI, the "Lydian city"; and on the floors, mixed with the gray pottery that Schliemann still called Lydian, were a fair number of vase fragments clearly identical with those they already knew well from the most prosperous phases of Mycenae and Tiryns on the Greek mainland (Fig. 12).

The conclusion was inevitable. It was Level VI and not Level II that

| 0 | ft | 200 |

| I | "House of Chieftain" |
| 2 | Great Treasure |
| 3 | Megaron A |
| 4 | Megaron B |
| 5 | "Scaean Gate" |
| 6 | Great Ramp |

Figure 13

was contemporary with the period of Mycenae's greatness; and it therefore would have been Troy VI that was attacked by the Greek armada. Between Levels II and VI lay the remains of three distinct phases of occupation, which showed that Troy II must be far older than the epoch of the Trojan War. With characteristic honesty and energy Schliemann saw that the shattering new evidence had to be followed up. His earlier excavations had largely missed or misinterpreted any monumental remains of the Lydian level. He had believed that segments of its marvelously constructed walls, encountered more than once in earlier campaigns, belonged to classical Greek times. They had enclosed a much larger area than had the walls of Troy II. Peripheral areas would probably yield a good deal of information about Troy VI, even though its higher central section had been destroyed when later Greeks and Romans leveled off the site (Fig. 13).

We can hardly pass over one discovery from Level II during this last excavation. Near the center of the citadel a "treasure" of stone objects was uncovered. The finest of the contents are four magnificent, highly polished artefacts that truly deserve the name "battle-axes" (Fig. 14). Three are of greenish stone said to be nephrite, and one bluish one resembles lapis

Figure 14

lazuli. Both the exotic materials and the elegant craftsmanship suggest that these, like the smaller objects of jade, probably come from much farther east—perhaps from Bessarabia.

Schliemann immediately began planning for a major campaign in the spring of 1891. But in December, when he was in Naples en route to be with his family for Christmas after an ear operation in Germany, death intervened. Perhaps it was just as well. Adjustment to the new evidence and explanations of all his earlier confident claims would have been a difficult ordeal. Now he could finally find a well-deserved resting place, as Dörpfeld writes, "in Athens, his second home, in sight of the acropolis."

## POSTHUMOUS REVISIONS

For Schliemann's last word on the Trojan excavations, however, it is proper to add the modifications published by Schuchhardt. He had repeatedly conferred with Schliemann during the preparation of his German edition, which appeared in 1889; and Schliemann had given permission for his own summary of the 1890 campaign to be printed in the English edition (1891).

One important change was the realization that buildings A and B in Level II were indeed the remains of a "palace," and not temples at all. This had been made clear by the discovery of much later buildings of similar plan on the acropolises of Tiryns and Mycenae in mainland Greece. The central unit of the mainland palaces had been given the name "megaron*," which is Homer's own word to denominate the palace—or at least the throne room—of a king. The fragmentary circular structure about 13 feet in diameter in the center of the main room of the Trojan megaron A is recognized as the hearth "which Homer tells us is situated in the innermost part of the house and marks its most sacred spot."[7]

Confusion between the ground plan of prehistoric megaron and classical temple was a natural error, since the royal palace of the Bronze Age was apparently in a real sense a shrine as well as a dwelling, and there seems to have been a straight line of development from it to the stately building that sheltered deity in later times. The later connection of still another architectural feature first discovered at Troy is also more fully recognized. Schuchhardt points out that the monumental plan of the city gates and propylaea* (entranceway) of Level II is "not only found again at Tiryns and Mycenae, but it became the model for all subsequent Greek gate construction."

The "owl vases" were finally recognized as nothing more than primitive attempts to model the main features of the female body. The similarity to an owl—and therefore the connection with an "owl-eyed" Athena—was purely accidental. On another issue, Schliemann, as well as several eminent philologists, had at first professed to see writing symbols in the complicated patterns inscribed on some of the clay spindle whorls, balls and seals. In particular, several equations had been proposed between certain of these signs and the early writing systems of Cyprus and Hittite Asia Minor. Schuchhardt, however, states flatly: "On none of them . . . can anything beyond mere decoration be made out."

In his summary of Schliemann's work at Troy, Schuchhardt apparently makes just one rather awkward and oblique reference to the chronological revelations of the last campaign. We can accept, he asserts, "one fact as incontestable: there existed on the site of Hissarlik, at a period far anterior to any we know of on Greek soil, a proud and royal city [presumably Level II], mistress of sea and land; and the singers of the Trojan War, just as they were familiar with Ida and Skamander, with the Hellespont and the Isle of Tenedos, knew also of this city, knew of its golden age and of its mighty downfall." He seems here to be aware of the contemporaneity of Mycenae with Troy VI and yet still to link Troy II with the epic.

So it remained for Dörpfeld and Blegen to try in their turn to set the Homeric story in its proper archaeological context at Troy. As we shall see, they worked in a later epoch with new knowledge and new techniques— and yet always in the shadow of the pioneer.

## MYCENAE

In his first archaeological book, Schliemann not only had insisted that modern Ithaki is Odysseus' island and that Hissarlik is Priam's Troy, but also had proposed a new theory about Agamemnon's Mycenae. In the case of Mycenae, there could be no question about the identification of the site. A strong and reverent tradition had apparently clung to the citadel, probably without a serious break, for fifteen centuries or more when its ruins were visited and described in the second century A.D. by the famous traveler Pausanias. And since then the Lion Gate (Fig. 15) itself was enough to keep the record clear. Indeed, the very massiveness of the remains continued to protect them, so that practically everything that Pausanias saw has been visible ever since. Naturally, a good many treasure hunters and archaeological dilettantes had probed among the monuments of "golden Mycenae" before Schliemann saw the site.

Figure 15

Pausanias was a conscientious antiquarian who took the grand tour of Greece in the heyday of the highly civilized *Pax Romana* when Hadrian and the later Antonine emperors had set the fashion of interest in "ancient" Greek history and archaeology. Local guides, who then as now mixed true traditions and solid fact with legend and personal imagination, gave him "the pitch." His notes on Mycenae, published in the monumental *Description of Greece,* are worth quoting at some length.

Among other remains of the wall is the gate, on which stand lions. They [the walls and the gate] are said to be the work of the Cyclopes, who built the wall for Proteus at Tiryns. In the ruins of Mycenae is the fountain called Perseia and the subterranean buildings of Atreus and his children, in which they stored their treasures. There is the sepulchre of Atreus, and the tombs of the companions of Agamemnon, who on their return from Ilium were killed at a banquet by Aegisthus. . . . There is the tomb of Agamemnon and that of his charioteer Eurymedon, and of Electra. Teledamus and Pelos were buried in the same sepulchre, for it is said that Cassandra bore these twins, and that, while as yet infants, they were slaughtered by Aegisthus together with their parents. . . . Clytemnestra and Aegisthus were buried at a little distance from the wall because they were thought unworthy to have their tombs inside of it, where Agamemnon reposed and those who were killed with him.[8]

To Schliemann, as he first stood on the acropolis with his copy of Pausanias in hand, almost everything seemed right (see Fig. 16). He had only to follow Pausanias' directions and to "get digging." He could see the massive Cyclopean fortification walls surrounding the acropolis, the famous Lion Gate at its northwest angle, and the Perseia fountain. To the west, outside the fortifications, the great domed underground structure, long recognized as Pausanias' "Treasury of Atreus," was accessible; and five other partially collapsed examples of the same type of monumental construction had been discovered in the vicinity.

On the other hand, the *tomb* of Atreus, those of Agamemnon and his companions, and of their murderers, Aegisthus and Clytemnestra, who "were buried at a little distance from the wall," were not so easy to identify. Modern scholars who had visited Mycenae before Schliemann understood Pausanias' "wall" to refer to the slight traces of a line of fortifications northwest of the citadel. This outer line (actually of Hellenistic* date) had presumably enclosed the lower town. So they expected the tombs of Agamemnon and the rest to lie *outside* the great fortified citadel and those of Clytemnestra and Aegisthus to be still farther on the periphery, beyond the city limits.

But Schliemann thought otherwise:

Pausanias could only speak of such walls as he *saw,* and not of those which he did *not see.* He saw the huge walls of the citadel, because they were at his time exactly as they are now; but he could not see the wall of the lower city, because it had been originally only very thin, and it had been demolished 638 years before his time [when Argos destroyed the little classical town of Mycenae in 468 B.C.]; nor was he an archaeologist, to search for its traces or still less to make excavations to find them. . . . For these decisive reasons, I have always interpreted the famous passage in Pausanias in the sense that the five tombs [Atreus; Agamemnon; Eurymedon; Cassandra and twins; Electra] were in the Acropolis.

Figure 16

And it was *inside* the monumental fortifications of the acropolis that
Schliemann had made up his mind to search for Agamemnon's mortal
remains.

Negotiations for a permit from the Greek authorities were complicated
by the controversy with the Turks over the ownership of the Trojan treasure
and by widespread criticism of Schliemann's lack of care in the first campaign at Hissarlik. He was allowed to sink some experimental shafts at

Mycenae in 1874, but it was only in late summer of 1876 that the Greek government authorized a full-scale excavation. Even then, he had to give assurances that digging would be concentrated at only one spot at a time, that no damage would be done to structures uncovered and that a manageable number of workmen would be hired. Most galling of all, "a government clerk by the name of Stamatakes" (in fact a trusted and senior member of the Archaeological Service) was sent to see that the stipulations were followed.

Schliemann's motivation for the excavations at Mycenae was exactly the same as at Troy. In the dedication of his book titled *Mycenae* (1878) he speaks of "this account of discoveries made at Mycenae and Tiryns, tending to illustrate the POEMS OF HOMER." Incidentally, the book was dedicated to "The Right Honourable William Ewart Gladstone, M.P.," who had been prevailed upon to write a Preface. The great Gladstone maintained throughout his busy political life continuing research and reading in classical literature. Only two years earlier he had published the third of his book-length studies of Greek epic, *Homeric Synchronisms: An Enquiry into the Time and Place of Homer*. Gladstone was one of Schliemann's earliest and staunchest supporters; and Schliemann was almost pathetically grateful.

Schliemann's description of the site (see Map V), while perhaps not as lyrical as what he wrote at Troy, is still worth quoting.

The situation of Mycenae is beautifully described by Homer, "in the depths of the horse-feeding Argos,"[9] because it lies in the north corner of the plain of Argos, . . . whence it commanded the upper part of the great plain and the important narrow pass, by which the roads lead to Phlius, Cleonae, and Corinth. The Acropolis occupied a strong rocky height, which projects from the foot of the mountain behind it [the lofty Prophitis Elias] in the form of an irregular triangle sloping to the west. This cliff overhangs a deep gorge, which protects the whole south flank of the citadel. . . . The cliff also falls off precipitously on the north side. . . . Between these two gorges extended the lower city. The cliff of the citadel is also more or less steep on the east and west side, where it forms six natural or artificial terraces.

Excavation was concentrated just inside the Lion Gate. "I began the great work," writes Schliemann, "on the 7th August, 1876, with sixty-three workmen, whom I divided into three parties. I put twelve men at the Lions' Gate, to open the passage into the Acropolis; I set forty-three to dig, at a distance of 40 feet from [inside] that gate, a trench 113 feet long and 113 feet broad; and the remaining eight men I ordered to dig a trench on the south side of the Treasury [later called the tomb of Clytemnestra] in the lower city, near the Lions' Gate, in search of the entrance." The third area was under his wife's supervision.

It soon became clear that the accepted belief that the final destruction of the little classical town occurred in 468 B.C. was in error. Schliemann showed definitely that the upper three feet or so of fill contained potsherds, terra-cotta statuettes and coins that belong to Hellenistic times. "I presume that the new colony may have been founded in the beginning of the fourth, and may have been abandoned in the beginning of the second century B.C." One is immediately struck by the comparative precision with which the chronology of the historic material could even then be fixed.

Everywhere below this level, however, he found "fragments of those splendidly-painted archaic vases" (Fig. 12) whose shapes and decorative motifs he illustrates in the publication. He knew, of course, that comparable pottery had been known for some time from Attica, Rhodes, Cyprus, and even Egypt. In an Egyptian tomb, along with fragments of this distinctive pottery, was a scarab* with a "cartouche* of Amunoph III, who is thought by Egyptologists to have reigned not later than B.C. 1400." Here already is a strong contrast to the groping for parallels and the lack of any hint at absolute* chronology for the Trojan material. Almost from the beginning this "Mycenaean" culture could be placed in at least an approximate historical context because of Egyptian synchronisms.*

He also notes the discovery of many terra-cotta "idols of Hera, more or less broken, in the form of a woman or in that of a cow" (Fig. 17). As with the Trojan "owl-eyed Athena," he immediately recognizes in these little figures a connection with a Homeric deity, in this case Hera *bo-ōpis* ("ox-eyed").

Figure 17

But more exciting finds soon began to appear in the big trench inside the Lion Gate. "I have brought to light two tombstones, which stand in a direct line from north to south, and are ornamented with bas-reliefs of the highest interest." Both showed chariot scenes. There is a single charioteer, and the horse (he uses the singular) is at full gallop. Underneath the horse portrayed on the slab, or stela*, that he identifies as #1, a dog and deer are running; while on stela #2 (Fig. 18) a man with a raised sword is shown just in front of the chariot group. Framing the figured scenes, particularly in the second example, is a careful border of parallel straight lines and elaborate spirals.

Schliemann immediately notices an odd feature in the sculpture. "I find such a marvellous accuracy and symmetry in all the spiral ornamentation, that I feel almost tempted to think such work can only have been produced by a school of sculptors which had worked for ages in a similar style. On the other hand, the men and the animals are made as rudely and in as puerile a manner as if they were the primitive artist's first essay to represent living beings." Above all, he is pleased with the new evidence on chariotry,

Figure 18

the first archaeological proof that the institution so typical in Homer was at home in prehistoric Greece. "The chariot gives us a unique and most precious specimen of the Homeric chariot, of which we had before but a confused idea."

Soon they uncovered two parallel rows of plain stone slabs, which "appear to form, with the part in the adjoining field, a full circle." The circular structure proved to be a low barrier formed by laying horizontal slabs on top of the two parallel lines of vertical ones (Fig. 19). The barrier was interrupted by an entrance, which faced the Lion Gate, and Schliemann long believed (with others) that he had found an example of the "sacred circle" of the Homeric agora, or assembly place.[10] Two more sculptured stelae were found within the circle. They were in the same line and farther south than the previous two. The third has in an upper register a chariot scene very similar to #2; and the lower part is adorned with running spirals within two circles linked in a horizontal figure-eight design. Stela #4 has no figured scene but simply three vertical panels, the middle plain, the others sculptured in a wave pattern. Several additional complete or fragmentary stelae were encountered at the same depth of 10 to 13 feet below the surface.

With serene confidence Schliemann states in the day-to-day diary his conviction that the "four sculptured and five unsculptured sepulchral slabs undoubtedly mark the sites of tombs cut deep in the rock. . . . I also found at the feet of most of the tombstones grey ashes of burnt animal matter, which I at first thought was from human bodies; but as I found together with them bones which on closer investigation turn out to be those of animals, I now think the ashes must be from sacrifices."

Furthermore, he has no doubts about the identity of the tombs he has not yet located. "Who have the great personages been, and what immense services did they render to Mycenae, to have received the signal honour of such a burial place? I do not for a moment hesitate to proclaim that I have found here the sepulchres which Pausanias, following the tradition, attributes to Atreus, to the 'king of men' Agamemnon. . . . But it is utterly impossible that Pausanias should have seen these tombstones. . . . He could only have known of the existence of these sepulchres by tradition."

Work was also proceeding beyond (south of) the circle of slabs in a "vast Cyclopean house." Later it was called the House of the Warrior Vase because it contained, among other finds, "fragments of a large vase, with two or three handles, the ends of which have been modelled into the shape of cowheads. . . . Some of the fragments . . . represent six full-armed warriors, painted with a dark red colour on a light yellow dead [dull monotone] ground; they are evidently setting out on a military expedition,

Figure 19

and all wear coats of mail which reach from the neck down to below the hips. . . . The shape of the lances is such as we were led to expect from the Homeric *'dolichoskion enchos'* [long-shadowing spear], for they are very long . . ."

He proceeds as follows with the description of the scene on the Warrior Vase, which is still the best-known and perhaps the most informative of all Mycenaean paintings (Fig. 20):

Figure 20

Now, with regard to the physiognomy of the six warriors, it is most decidedly not Assyrian or Egyptian. All have exactly the same type— very long noses, large eyes, small ears, and a long well-dressed beard. . . . Five of the warriors are followed by a woman, seemingly a priestess, who is dressed in a long gown fastened at the waist by a girdle. . . . Only her right arm remains, which is uplifted, and by the curve it forms it appears that the woman has lifted her joined hands and is praying to the gods to be propitious to the departing warriors, and to grant them a safe return. This custom of lifting both hands when praying is continually found in Homer.[11] On other fragments of the same vase are represented two warriors. . . . The armour . . . is perfectly identical . . . except for the head-dress, which, instead of bronze helmets, consists here seemingly of a low helmet of boarskin, with the bristles outside. In fact, these helmets vividly remind us of the low helm of oxskin which Ulysses put on his head when he and Diomede went in the night as spies to the Trojan camp.[12]

Back inside the circular agora the workmen were probing deeper, and the most spectacular find in the history of Greek archaeology was about to be made. Schliemann tells of the discovery of the first grave under dateline of December 6. His prose is curiously restrained when compared with the description of the great Trojan treasure found only three years before. "I excavated on the site of the three [tombstones] with the bas-reliefs representing the warriors and the hunting scene, and found a quadrangular tomb, 21 ft. 5 in. long and 10 ft. 4 in. broad, cut out in the slope of the rock." Before he could reach its bottom, however, a heavy rain occurred and he shifted operations about 20 feet away where the two unsculptured tombstones had been found.

> At a depth of 15 ft. below the level of the rock, or of 25 ft. below the former surface of the ground . . . I reached a layer of pebbles, below which I found, at a distance of three feet from each other, the remains of three human bodies, all with the head turned to the east and the feet to the west. . . . They had evidently been burned simultaneously. . . . There were the most unmistakable marks of three distinct funeral pyres. . . . These could not have been large, and had evidently been intended to consume merely the clothes and partly or entirely the flesh of the deceased; but *no more,* because the bones and even the skulls had been preserved . . .

He then records the offerings buried with the dead—gold diadems, small gold "crosses," badly decomposed objects of glass, terra-cotta figurines, obsidian* knives, a large silver vase, and "most remarkable wheel-made terracottas [vases]" (Fig. 21).

This grave he labeled II, and we shall retain the original numbering. It is worth remarking here that, although one would never guess the fact from his continual use of the first person singular, the hands that delicately cleared each of the precious objects in all of these graves were not Heinrich's, but Sophia Schliemann's. For those twenty-five days of continuous and incredibly painstaking work his excitable temperament simply would not have held up. We can imagine the scene—workmen dismissed, armed soldiers ringing the grave, Schliemann busily taking notes and counting the treasure, Stamatakes and officials watching and recounting, but Sophia down in the deep hole for hours on end in cramped and uncomfortable positions doing the real work.

The report resumes.

> Encouraged by the success obtained in the second tomb, I took out the two large unsculptured tombstones of the third line, which stood almost due south of the former. . . . In digging deeper I found . . . two sepulchres, of which I shall describe the smaller one. . . . I call [it] the Third Tomb. . . . [It measures] 16 ft. 8 in. long and 10 ft. 2 in. broad. . . . I found in this sepulchre the mortal remains of three persons who, to

Figure 21

judge by the smallness of the bones and particularly of the teeth, and by the masses of female ornaments found here, must have been women. . . . The bodies were literally laden with jewels, all of which bore evident signs of the fire and smoke. . . . The ornaments of which the greatest number was found were the large, thick, round plates of gold, with a very pretty decoration of *repoussé** work, of which I collected 701 [Fig. 22].

Grave III also contained masses of other gold objects in the form of seals, griffins*, lions, nude female figurines with doves perched on head and arms, octopus, butterflies, eagles. Many of them showed holes for attachment, and Schliemann concluded that they had been sewn on the dresses of the dead women. Near one cranium was a magnificent gold crown decorated in repoussé with intricate designs within circles, and a smaller gold diadem was still in place on another skull. There were seven simpler and smaller diadems, six crosses, a jewelbox with lid, a brooch, pendants, numerous earrings, pins, wheels, combs and various other gold objects for which he could not immediately determine the purpose. The grave also contained masses of amber beads of various sizes, objects of

Figure 22

rock crystal, ivory, engraved gems. In addition to jewelry he inventories
several vases of gold (Fig. 23), two of silver and a number of terra-cotta.

Less than 5 feet from III lay Grave IV. Exactly over its center they
found an "almost circular mass of Cyclopean masonry with a large opening in the form of a well," which Schliemann identified as a "funeral altar—
erected in honour of those whose mortal remains reposed" in the grave
below. Grave IV contained the skeletons of five men, three lying with
head to the east and the other two with head to the north. The type of
tomb and the method of burial were exactly similar to that in Graves II

and III; that is, the tomb had been hollowed in the rock of the hillside, the walls lined with rubble and the floor covered with pebbles "intended to procure ventilation for the pyres." Schliemann adds some details that later proved significant: "Here, as well as in the first and third tombs, I have noticed that, for a reason unknown to me, the burned bodies, with their golden ornaments, had been covered, after the cremation, with a layer . . . of . . . white clay. . . . On this layer of clay was put the second layer of pebbles."

He was apparently becoming somewhat uneasy about his diagnosis of cremation, and perhaps for this reason he insisted on it all the more. "The cremation . . . has been officially authenticated by the three government clerks, whom the Director-General of Antiquities at Athens . . . has sent here to assist me in guarding the treasures . . . and by the thousands of people who flock hither from all parts of the Argolid to see these wonders; and, therefore, anyone who doubts the exactness of my statements as to the cremation is requested to apply to the said Director-General or to the

Figure 23

Ministry of Public Instruction at Athens." Naturally, he wanted the burial rite in these Mycenae graves to correspond with the cremations described in the *Iliad*.

Apropos of the intense public interest, Schliemann adds one of his characteristic and imaginative historical gambits:

For the first time since its capture by the Argives in 468 B.C., and so for the first time during 2,344 years, the Acropolis of Mycenae has a garrison, whose watch-fires seen by night throughout the whole Plain of Argos carry back the mind to the watch kept for Agamemnon's return from Troy, and the signal which warned Clytemnestra and her paramour of his approach.[13] But this time the object of the occupation by soldiery is of a more peaceful character, for it is merely intended to inspire awe among the country-people, and to prevent them from making clandestine excavations in the tombs . . .

Figure 24

Figure 25

The five bodies in Grave IV had been literally smothered in costly burial offerings. In view of the previous warning, the following sentence will provoke a tolerant smile. "We have to do the work ourselves; the task is exceedingly difficult and painful to us, particularly in the present rainy weather, for we cannot dig otherwise than on our knees, and by cutting the earth and stones carefully away with our knives, so as not to injure or lose any of the gold ornaments." Among the finds were many objects that are still the finest examples known for their class and time. Schliemann's descriptions are really quite brief; yet they and the illustrations occupy more than twenty pages in the original publication. We can mention only a few of the most outstanding: a silver vase in the form of a bull's head (called a rhyton*) with golden horns (Fig. 24); three remarkable and awe-inspiring gold face masks (Fig. 25), apparently modeled on the actual features of the deceased; two large gold signet rings showing chariot scenes of battle and hunting; a massive gold bracelet; gold breastplates, diadems and a "shoulder-belt"; nine golden goblets and vases, including the famous "cup of Nestor" (Fig. 26); three "models of a temple" in gold; a number of fragments of silver vessels and one silver pitcher; more than 400 beads of amber; a large three-handled vase of alabaster; thirty-two copper cauldrons; a copper tripod; various adornments for armor and weapons; obsidian arrowheads; perforated boar's tusks; forty-six bronze

Figure 26

swords and daggers; four lances; three knives; numerous terra-cotta vases.

At least a few of Schliemann's observations on these discoveries must be recorded. Analysis of the bronze showed an alloy consisting of copper with 10 to 13 per cent tin. He notes that the Mycenaean goldsmiths, unlike those of Troy, did not practice soldering but made connections with "pins" (rivets). Also, they apparently could not plate gold over silver, except by using an intervening layer of copper. He also observes that the spiral decoration on some of the objects in the graves is "perfectly similar" to that on the grave stelae.

As for the representational art, he is sure that the long, rectangular shield portrayed in the battle scene on a gold ring (Fig. 27) is "one of the large Homeric shields, which were so enormous that the poet compares them to towers."[14] And after describing the scenes on the bezels of the two gold rings, he adds, "When I brought to light these wonderful signets, I involuntarily exclaimed: 'The author of the *Iliad* and the *Odyssey* cannot

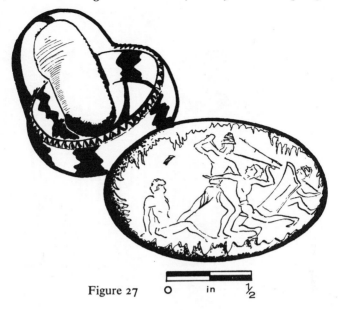

Figure 27    O    in    ½

but have been born and educated amidst a civilisation which was able to produce such works as these. Only a poet who had objects of art like these continually before his eyes could compose those divine poems.' "

In discussing the golden goblet that "vividly reminds us of Nestor's cup,"[15] Schliemann comes to the conclusion that "the shape of the Nestorian goblet may be imagined as perfectly similar to the goblet before us, because this really has four handles; namely, the two horizontal ones, on which the pigeons lie, and the two lower ones which are produced by the thick vertical straps, which join them at the foot. If so, the only difference would be that Nestor's goblet had one more pigeon on each of these double handles." The three so-called temple models of gold, "perhaps the most curious objects of all," show a tripartite building, open at the front, with a column like those in the sculpture of the Lion Gate in the center of each opening. Motifs such as pairs of horns are shown at the base of each column, as well as above the roof of the higher central part. And birds perch above each of the outer parts (Fig. 28).

He notes that the swords are very long and narrow and that there is evidence from particles still attached to them that many had had sheaths of linen. The human bones in Grave IV were better preserved and "all which are not too much decayed will be displayed in the National Museum at Athens together with the treasures."

A fifth grave was discovered immediately to the northwest of the fourth and directly under four tombstones. It is important to note that two of

Figure 28

the stelae were found about 12 feet below the surface and two more, "evidently much older" and unsculptured, were about 10 feet below the others and only 3 feet above the grave itself. Grave V contained only one skeleton. The skull had a golden diadem around it, and the offerings included a lance, two small bronze swords and two long bronze knives, a golden goblet, a broken vase of "light green Egyptian porcelain" and many terra-cotta vases. One of the latter was "light red . . . ornamented with black spiral lines, and with two female breasts surrounded by circles of black strokes." Schliemann refers in this connection to the Trojan owl vases but sees an even closer parallel in vases found in 1866 on the island of Thera (Santorin) "in the ruins of the prehistoric cities which . . . were covered by an eruption of that great central volcano which is believed by competent geologists to have sunk and disappeared about 1700 to 1800 B.C." Geological dating, although sporadically attempted from that time to the present in archaeological contexts, is necessarily less exact than synchronisms with literate cultures.

When the mud in Grave I had dried sufficiently, its excavation was continued. There were three skeletons here. One had no offerings around it nor clay coating over it, which made Schliemann suspect that there had been later tampering. The bones indicated that the three men had been unusually large, while their position suggested to Schliemann that the bodies had been "forcibly squeezed into the small space of only 5 feet 6 inches which was left for them between the inner walls."

But the climax of the whole series of discoveries was still to come. Here, at least, is what Schliemann writes:

> Of the third body, which lay at the north end of the tomb, the round face, with all its flesh, had been wonderfully preserved under its ponderous golden mask; there was no vestige of hair, but both eyes were perfectly visible, also the mouth, which, owing to the enormous weight that had pressed upon it, was wide open, and showed thirty-two beautiful teeth. From these, all the physicians who came to see the body were led to believe that the man must have died at the early age of thirty-five. The nose was entirely gone. . . . The colour of the body resembled very much that of an Egyptian mummy. . . . A druggist from Argos, Spiridon Nicolaou by name, rendered it hard and solid by pouring on it alcohol, in which he had dissolved gum-sandarac.

An artist was also called in to make an oil painting, which is reproduced in the publication. Then, after being carefully undercut and boxed, the mysterious semimummy was transported to Athens.

The richness of the offerings in Grave I was surpassed only by those in IV and the types are comparable. It is indeed completely understandable that Schliemann unhesitatingly associated these graves with the acme of power and prosperity of Homer's "golden Mycenae." There were a great many swords, usually in fragments. Among the unusual finds were considerable fragments of wood in recognizable shape—three lids of boxes, and two sides of a small box on each of which are carved in relief a lion and a dog. "Food seems also to have been deposited . . . for I gathered in it a large quantity of oyster-shells, and among them several unopened oysters."

In the interval between the clearing of the tombs and the publication, Schliemann obviously thought a great deal about the significance of his finds; and the first scholarly reactions to the discovery were already known to him. He writes:

> I now proceed to discuss the question, whether it is possible to identify these sepulchres with the tombs which Pausanias, following the tradition, attributes to Agamemnon, to Cassandra, to Eurymedon, and to their companions. . . . For my part, I have always firmly believed in the Trojan war; my full faith in Homer and in the tradition has never been shaken by modern criticism, and to this faith of mine I am indebted for the discovery of Troy and its Treasure. . . . I never doubted that a king of Mycenae, by name Agamemnon, . . . had been treacherously murdered . . . and I firmly believed in the statement of Pausanias, that the murdered persons had been interred in the Acropolis. . . . My firm faith in the traditions . . . led to the discovery of the five tombs, with their immense treasures . . .

He proceeds to insist that these really are the graves of Agamemnon and his friends, foully murdered, although he is silent as to why their bodies would have been loaded with rich funeral offerings.

The identity of the mode of burial, the perfect similarity of all the tombs, their very close proximity, the impossibility of admitting that three or even five royal personages of immeasurable wealth, who had died a natural death at long intervals of time, should have been huddled together in the same tomb, and, finally, the great resemblance of all the ornaments, which show exactly the same style of art and the same epoch—all these facts are so many proofs that all the twelve men, three women, and perhaps two or three children, had been murdered simultaneously and burned at the same time. . . . The site of each tomb was marked by tombstones, and when these had been covered by the dust of ages and had disappeared, fresh tombstones were erected on the new level, but precisely over the spot where the ancient memorials lay buried. . . . I think it therefore highly probable that the erection of the Agora coincides with the renewal of the tombstones . . .

On the chronological question he is on particularly slippery ground. "The period of the kings of Mycenae belongs to a very remote antiquity. Royalty ceased there at the Dorian invasion, the date of which has always been fixed at 1104 B.C. . . . But, in agreement with all archaeologists, I hold to the conclusion that, on the evidence of the monuments of Troy, the capture and the destruction of that city, and consequently also the Dorian invasion [which traditionally occurred eighty years later], must have occurred at a much earlier date." His early groping for a firm chronological link between Troy II and the monumental fortified sites on the Greek mainland was, of course, superseded by the results of the last Trojan campaign. But he already seems to have sensed correctly that the Egyptian evidence of a date around 1400 for the developed phases at Mycenae was too late for Troy II. Incidentally, he must have been in a particularly euphoric state when he refers to his "agreement with all archaeologists" about the chronological implications of the Trojan excavations.

Before we discuss the modified views on the graves in the agora that had developed by the time of Schliemann's death, we should very briefly summarize his opinions about the "treasuries" outside the acropolis walls. The largest and only uncollapsed structure was apparently the one attributed to Atreus by Pausanias (Fig. 38). Since it had been partially cleared in the early nineteenth century, Mrs. Schliemann was put in charge of excavating the most impressive of the others that lay just outside the Lion Gate. Describing the type, Schliemann says, "These conical buildings, 50 feet high, were constructed under the slope of a hill, and were destined to remain subterranean: for . . . the outside surface of the stones is quite irregular, and the whole building is covered all round with a thick layer of stones, the weight of which holds the masonry fast together. I feel certain that the tradition is correct which says that these mysterious buildings served as the store-houses of the wealth of the early kings. . . ." This, we remember, is how Pausanias explained their purpose.

The long horizontal entrance passage, or dromos*, of Mrs. Schliemann's "treasury" was nearly as monumental as that of the uncollapsed example attributed to King Atreus. Here too, at the inner end of the dromos, mighty doors had been flanked by half-columns, and above the great lintel was a triangular space, which Schliemann reasoned had once held a sculptured block comparable to that over the Lion Gate. He found no evidence of holes in the underside of the blocks of the great domed tomb chamber like those in the Atreus building, which were supposed to indicate that the curved surface had originally been decorated with bronze rosettes.

In commenting on the relative dating of the "treasuries" and the newly discovered graves within the citadel, Schliemann says, "I perfectly share Mr. Newton's opinion, that all the five immense and magnificent Treasuries in the lower city and in the suburb must necessarily be more ancient than the five royal tombs in the Acropolis; and if we reflect that princes, who used such magnificent underground palaces as storehouses of their wealth, should have been huddled away like impure animals into miserable holes, we find in this ignominious burial alone a powerful argument in favour of the veracity of the tradition which points to these sepulchres as those of the king of men, Agamemnon, and his companions . . ." Professor C. T. Newton, as we shall see, had a dominant voice in English classical circles and, to Arthur Evans at least, he typified the "old guard" who felt themselves threatened by the phenomenal growth of interest in Greek prehistory.

Schuchhardt in 1891 emphasizes three new sources of evidence on Mycenae. The first was the excavation we have been reviewing of "the pit graves filled with gold." The second, also carried out under Schliemann's auspices, was "Steffen's map of Mycenae in 1881." Lastly, Schuchhardt points to the importance of the "excavations of the Greek Archaeological Society in 1886 to 1888, when the palace was discovered on the summit of the citadel." We shall review this development in the next chapter.

In Schuchhardt's account we can readily see the major changes that had already been made in Schliemann's first impressions and theories. The so-called treasuries were shown to be real tombs, because at Menidi, near Athens, a similar structure had been found with six undisturbed skeletons lying on the floor and their funeral offerings around them. In any case, as Schuchhardt drily points out, "No prince would ever have kept his treasures outside the walls of his citadel." So before 1900 the great domed "tholos*," or "beehive" tombs are recognized as one of the most striking characteristics of Mycenaean civilization. At that time only five examples were known outside of Mycenae. But the older discredited theory of their use that goes back to Pausanias still persists to our own day in the common designation of the finest example, the magnificent intact tholos tomb at Mycenae, as the Treasury of Atreus.

The five graves within the circle of slabs were soon augmented by a sixth found by Stamatakes. It is typical of Schliemann's blind faith in the ancient authors that he stopped digging when he had found the five graves memorialized by Pausanias. In Schuchhardt's book the six graves within the circle are called "Shaft Graves*," by which designation they have been known ever since. Schuchhardt rejects the idea that the ring of slabs represents a Homeric agora. He insists that the construction was a later feature to mark the position of the Shaft Graves when the great existing fortification wall was built. At that time the sloping area inside the new walls was filled to such a height that the Shaft Graves were deeply buried. The stelae found near the modern surface would have been set up at the higher level within the circle, while the deeper stelae and the altar above Grave IV would mark an earlier stage of veneration of the buried royalty.

Most scholars had also hesitated to accept Schliemann's theory of the burial of all the bodies in the Shaft Graves on one single occasion. But, since the graves had apparently been immediately filled up and there seemed to be practically no sign of later disturbance, it was difficult to see how successive new burials could have been made. Dörpfeld, however, reviewed the chronicle of their excavation (he was not present himself) and realized that there was proof that the graves had been roofed. Schliemann had thought that slabs of schist that were found scattered just above the skeletons had lined the vertical walls; but Dörpfeld saw that they had really been laid horizontally over big wooden beams that in turn rested on the rubble walls that lined the graves. Four enigmatic copper "boxes" with long copper nails still holding rotted wood, found in Grave III, were now recognized as ornamental coverings over the ends of two great beams. And the layer of clay regularly found just above the skeletons and tomb furniture had clearly been spread over the stone slabs to make the grave coverings watertight. So, as long as the beams held firm, it would have been relatively simple to remove the overlying earth and reopen a grave for a new burial (Fig. 29).

Also, there was increasing doubt about Schliemann's insistence that

Figure 29

the bodies had been at least partially cremated. A great funeral pyre is of course the universal method of burial for Homer's heroes, and Schliemann was always overanxious to point parallels between his finds and the poems. But it appeared from his own account that both the bodies and the fabulous funeral offerings had been largely untouched by fire. The graves did contain ashes and traces of the effects of fire, but this could be explained as the remains of sacrifices or purificatory rites or simply fumigation.

On the crucial matter of the identification of the Shaft Graves with those of "Agamemnon and his friends" pointed out to Pausanias, there was almost universal skepticism. The burials had certainly extended over a considerable length of time, perhaps a century. Stamatakes' sixth grave showed simpler and poorer offerings. It seemed to suggest a grouping with Schliemann's II and V; while Graves I, III and IV were much richer and presumably later.

Schuchhardt reviews the contents of the Shaft Graves in the light of the first careful examination by numerous authorities. They confirm Schliemann's insight that there is a curious dichotomy between two distinct artistic traditions, the one specializing in conventional geometric motifs such as spirals and linear patterns, the other preferring naturalistic scenes with plant, animal and human representations. And even in the second tradition, there is an astonishing gap between the immaturity and crudity of workmanship exhibited in scenes such as those on the stelae and the mastery of naturalistic representations on many other objects. Of all the magnificent examples in the latter category, the inlaid scenes on several of the newly cleaned daggers were especially striking (Fig. 30). These decorative friezes had completely escaped Schliemann's eagle eye at the time of discovery. Schuchhardt is impressed both by the technical skill required for this complicated "metal painting" and by the apparent historical implications of the representation of fighting and hunting in the light of Homeric descriptions.

Figure 30

## TIRYNS

Schliemann's discovery of the Shaft Graves was the most spectacular, and in many ways the most far-reaching in its historical implications, of any archaeological find ever made in Greece. With eyes dazzled by the gold of Mycenae, one has to think again about Herodotus' famous assertion that "Poverty is always a companion to Greece."[16] Yet only some eight miles to the south, another great fortified citadel was soon to produce new evidence that, in its way, was equally novel and important.

Apparently the Homeric name "Tiryns" has clung to it with equal tenacity through later ages. Its mighty walls rise around the edges of an isolated outcropping of rock dominating the plain of Argos only a little over a mile inland from the Gulf of Nauplia. Both here and at Mycenae the relatively complete state of the fortifications is probably to be explained by the huge size of the individual blocks, which made it too dangerous and laborious for conquerors to dismantle them or peasants to reuse them.

Pausanias speaks only of the impressive fortifications, with scarcely a word at this point on Tiryns' important mythological connections: "Nothing is left of the ruins of Tiryns except the wall, which is a work of the Cyclopes, and is made of unwrought stones, each stone so large that a pair of mules could not even stir the smallest of them. In ancient times small stones have been fitted in so as to bind together the large stones."[17] This is a useful description of the typical wall construction at that time, except that large and small stones were further solidified with a strong clay mortar in the interstices.

Perhaps it was the great fortifications of these prehistoric sites, even more than the pottery and other artefacts associated with them, that puzzled so many scholars of the late nineteenth century. As we have seen, they found it difficult to believe that "the Greeks" could have succeeded many centuries before classical times in developing a civilization so technically and artistically advanced. So they searched the literature for mention of an intrusive people to whom the wonders could be attributed; and many were convinced that they had found the explanation in a persistent tradition—noticeable as early as the *Odyssey* and popular with the later Greeks —that "Phoinikes" ("Red Men," "Phoenicians") had once occupied parts of the peninsula and introduced the civilizing arts to Greece. Schliemann long and stoutly resisted their theories and never adopted them in his official publications. But it was a lonely struggle for a self-made scholar against prestigious and plausible experts. We should not, therefore, be too surprised or disappointed to learn that in his later years he wavered and perhaps actually capitulated. In a letter to Virchow, dated 1885, he even appears to play down his earlier courageous attitude. "I have been at pains," he writes, "to demonstrate that Tiryns and Mycenae must have been built and inhabited by the *Phoenicians,* who in a remote prehistoric age flooded Greece and the islands of the Ionian and Aegean seas with colonies, and who were only finally expelled, around 1100 B.C., by the so-called Dorian Invasion." Fortunately, as we shall see, this aberration was firmly rejected by the leading scholars actually working in Greece.

As he first stood on the Tiryns acropolis and looked up inland toward Mycenae, Schliemann must have wondered about the relationship of these two contemporary sites separated by so short a distance. In fact, he never suggests a theory to explain the existence of a second fortress almost along-side "golden Mycenae." Nor has any later scholar proposed a wholly satisfactory solution for this contiguous pair of citadels, to say nothing of others that have been discovered on the mainland at Orchomenos-Gla, on Crete at Phaistos-Haghia Triada and (most recently) at Knossos-Arkhanes. Tiryns seems to belong to an older cycle of heroic stories than those that figure prominently in Homer's poems. It was reputed to be the home of the mighty Herakles, and in the time of the Trojan War it may have been the capital of Diomedes.[18] But, apart from its less striking heroic connections, excavation at Tiryns must have seemed almost as attractive as at Mycenae or Troy, and Schliemann was not the kind of man to leave any beckoning stone unturned.

Eight years separated the first trial trenches on the acropolis of Tiryns from the two excavation seasons of 1884 and 1885. Dörpfeld, who had proved his worth at Troy, was with him the first year and assumed sole charge during the second, while Schliemann was being lionized in London. Dörpfeld also wrote over his own name the section on the architectural remains in the publication *Tiryns*. This major concession to his assistant shows clearly that the old egotist Schliemann was mellowing and tiring.

Like Troy and unlike Mycenae, Tiryns produced no spectacular tombs. Nor have "royal" tombs like the Shaft Graves or tholoi (except for one possible unexcavated example) been since discovered in the vicinity. But at Tiryns for the first time reasonably well-preserved ruins of a Mycenaean palace were uncovered. "The dwelling-house of a ruler in the Heroic age," says Dörpfeld, "was until now only known to us by the descriptions of Homer. Nothing remained of the palaces of Menelaus, of Odysseus, or the other heroes [a rather premature assertion]. . . . How clearly, on the other hand, rises before us from these discoveries at Tiryns the image of the home of the prehistoric king!" Dörpfeld then conducts the reader on a tour of the main features of the inner citadel. Keeping an eye on the plan (Fig. 31), we may profitably follow along.

Figure 31

1 Ramp
2 Gateway
3 Corbelled Galleries
4 Propylon
5 Outer Court
6 "Altar"
7 Vestibule
8 Megaron
9 Bath
10 "Women's Megaron"

We first ascend a great ramp leading to the main gate in the east wall. The approach was so arranged that the right side of attacking warriors, unprotected by their shield, would be exposed to arrows and spears from the wall. Turning left inside the gate, we follow a wide corridor, pass through a second massive gateway (#2) and on to the southeast corner of the citadel where the false-vaulted (or corbeled*) galleries (#3) within the thickness of the wall are best preserved. Turning to the right through a stately propylon* (#4) with columned porches on both sides, we enter a large outer court (#5) from which another turn to the right through a similar propylon brings us to the main inner courtyard. Columned porches lined the south, west and east sides, while the two columns between the end walls of the main megaron on the north side completed the effect of a shaded peristyle*. In the court just to the right of the propylon and on the main axis of the megaron we see a rectangular stone curb surrounding a shallow circular depression (#6). Dörpfeld identified this structure as an altar or sacrificial pit, and we immediately think of the circular structure found over the fourth Shaft Grave at Mycenae. But it has been since shown that the curb (if not the pit) dates from much later times when a large building, perhaps an early temple, was apparently built over part of the Tiryns megaron.

We enter between the columns of the megaron porch and notice along the base of the short wall on our left a low frieze made up of seven alabaster blocks, alternating in width from narrow to square. Although badly damaged, these blocks retained traces of an elaborate inset design in blue glass paste (Fig. 32). The scheme consists of elongated half-rosettes on the square blocks and on the narrow blocks two vertical rows of small rosettes separated by a vertical space. Virtually the same intricate design was already known from better-preserved carved stone blocks at Mycenae and from small pieces of glass paste (no doubt from inlays) found in the tholos at Menidi in Attica. Dörpfeld feels confident that this kind of architectural decoration is reflected in Homer's description of the blue (*kyanos*) frieze around the walls of the palace of Alkinoos.[19] The resemblance to the triglyph-metope frieze* over the columns in classical Doric architecture is striking and scarcely accidental.

Figure 32

From the porch we pass through the central of three doors into an antechamber or vestibule (#7). Beyond the vestibule lies the main throne room (#8), which perhaps alone deserves the Homeric name "megaron." The stucco floor of this main room was divided into a pattern of squares, each with painted decoration; and a slightly raised circular curb on the floor at the center of the room indicates the position of what Dörpfeld took to be a great ceremonial hearth. A rectangular interruption in the floor pattern toward the east wall opposite the hearth testified to the original location of a wooden construction, probably the king's throne (Fig. 36).

Placed symmetrically around the hearth were the stone bases of four columns. Dörpfeld reasoned that the columns must have supported a higher roof (clerestory*) over the central part of the building, thus providing for the escape of smoke and admission of light. After thoroughly reviewing the Homeric descriptions of royal palaces, particularly that of King Alkinoos,[20] Dörpfeld concludes: "This [Homeric] description agrees very well with the arrangement of the megaron of Tiryns. . . . Most probably the ground-plan . . . was a typical one, occurring in an identical manner in many heroic palaces." It now became clear that the so-called temple A in Level II at Troy, though it had no anteroom, was an essentially similar and much earlier megaron, with the hearth still partially preserved in the center of the main room. And we may add that Dörpfeld's inference of a standard plan for Mycenaean palaces proved remarkably accurate.

Retracing our steps to the anteroom, we pass through a door in its west wall and enter a winding passage leading to a small room paved with a single huge flat stone and with a drain carefully let into the east wall (#9). "I think it certain," says Dörpfeld, "that we have here found the bath-room, which must have existed in every Homeric palace. In the room there must have stood a *tub,* to be filled with water for the bather. . . . When washed and anointed, . . . [a visitor] went through the . . . corridor to the anteroom, and thence into the megaron."

We then circle around to the east behind the megaron and enter a smaller structure (#10) constructed parallel to the main building. It too has its own little court as well as the megaron plan, though it lacks the anteroom. In the center of the main room there is a rectangular gap in the floor, where again a hearth was presumably located. Dörpfeld confidently identified this as the "women's hall," which is said to have been a regular feature of important houses in classical times. Scholars have disputed whether the Homeric descriptions of palaces take for granted a separate hall for women. Dörpfeld feels that the Tiryns plan provides the needed confirmation. But the identification has never really been settled; and, as we shall see, the plan of the Pylos palace raises the question again.

Dörpfeld believed that all Mycenaean buildings, as well as those at Troy, had flat roofs and that remains of stairways pointed to access to the roof rather than to a second story. He emphasized that the evidence of heavy burning reinforces the theory that construction methods involved the use of a large amount of wood. The walls were built in the so-called half-timber construction—sun-dried brick in timber framework—and col-

umns and roofbeams were of wood. He points to the Lion Gate sculpture
at Mycenae as a likely model of the type of column, with slender proportions and diameter decreasing toward the base.

In addition to broken pottery similar to that found at Mycenae, the
ruins of the Tiryns palace yielded numerous fragments of wall plaster on
which were paintings in fresco* technique. These and some of the most
interesting vase fragments are reproduced in twenty-four excellent color
plates in the *Tiryns* publication. Most of the fresco fragments show elaborate nonrepresentational designs of spirals, rosettes and other conventionalized naturalistic and geometric patterns. But some pieces proved
that certain walls had been decorated with panels depicting figured scenes.
The best preserved composition shows a charging bull and a man perform-
ing some kind of acrobatic feat on or over its back (Fig. 33). This scene
aroused lively interest because of the references in classical literature to
prehistoric bull worship and Theseus' famous encounter with the Minotaur
("Minos Bull") at Knossos in Crete.

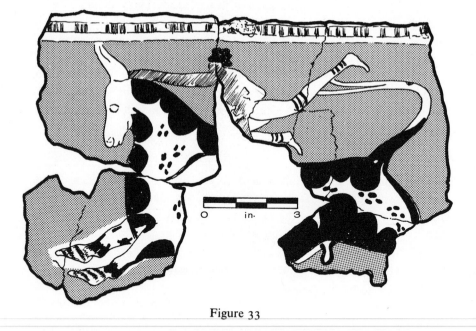

Figure 33

## ADDITIONAL SITES

Schliemann's boundless energy and driving ambition kept him always
on the lookout for new sites to explore. In northern Boeotia a great tholos
tomb, like the "treasuries" of Mycenae, had announced its location to the

nearby villagers many years before when the dome collapsed with a thunderous roar. The existence of such a monument was realized as a strong indication that the capital of a prehistoric kingdom must have been situated in the vicinity; and the site had been identified as the famous Orchomenos, where Pausanias had admired a "treasury of Minyas." He says of it: "There is no greater marvel either in Greece or elsewhere. It is made of stone: its form is circular, rising to a somewhat blunt top, and they say that the topmost stone is the keystone of the whole building."[21]

"Minyan Orchomenos," as it is called by Homer,[22] had a reputation in mythology for wealth second only to Mycenae. Lord Elgin, who saved (or raped, depending on your point of view) the Parthenon sculptures, had tried to clear the Orchomenos tholos but had been discouraged by the great accumulation of fallen stone. In three short campaigns between 1880 and 1886 Schliemann carried out this task and opened a few graves in the vicinity. The main chamber was badly ruined, but a side chamber like that of the Treasury of Atreus at Mycenae yielded some remarkable sculptured blocks that had lined the walls and ceiling. They were of green schist with exquisitely carved patterns of spirals, rosettes and palmettes. Clearly, this must once have been a royal tomb that rivaled the magnificence of those at Mycenae. But perhaps Schliemann's most lasting contribution at Orchomenos was the recognition of a class of smooth gray wheel-turned pottery, which he called Minyan* after Minyas, the legendary king of Orchomenos. This pottery was to play a crucial role in the reconstruction of an important phase of Greek prehistory; and although Schliemann apparently did not realize it, "Minyan ware" is practically indistinguishable from the pottery that he had found in the sixth ("Lydian") level at Troy.

There were other spots on the mainland—and on islands such as Kythera —where Schliemann made soundings. The two sites that probably interested him most were eventually to loom as large in Greek prehistoric archaeology as Troy, Mycenae and Tiryns. One was in the far southwest, where tradition located Pylos, the capital of Homer's garrulous old hero Nestor. Some very minor probing around the Frankish castle at the north end of the great bay of Navarino (see Map VII) produced nothing spectacular.

The second site was near the north coast of central Crete, which some minor excavation had already connected with the legendary Knossos, capital of King Minos and later the power center ruled by the Homeric hero Idomeneus. Schliemann was sure that the ruins of Minos' palace still lay under a great mound called Kephala (see Map VI) about three miles inland from the town of Candia (Iraklion). In a letter written only two years before his death, he said, "I would like to end my life's labours with

one great work—the prehistoric palace of the kings of Knossos in Crete."
He actually secured an excavation permit from the Turkish authorities
but had trouble in reaching a financial agreement with the owner of the
land. In his posthumously published report on the 1890 campaign at Troy
he confides, "I had thought . . . that I could turn my attention to Crete,
where I hoped to discover the original home of Mycenaean civilisation.
This plan was, however, frustrated by various difficulties, and finally by
the recent disturbances [revolt against Turkish control] in Crete, which
made excavation there impossible."

Fate may have decreed that this ambitious human had already won his
full share of fame and enjoyed his fair quota of excitement. At any rate,
the startling secrets hidden beneath the vineyards at Kephala and under
the olive trees crowning an obscure hill near Pylos were reserved for other
pioneers, in their own way as fascinating personalities as Heinrich Schliemann. Chapters IV and VI will record these later phases of the unfolding
story.


## SUMMATION

By 1885 imposing architectural remains and numerous and varied
movable finds from a number of Greek sites were beginning to provide a
basis for a credible reconstruction of a preclassical civilization that seemed
to have at least some valid points of contact with Homeric descriptions.
Schuchhardt recorded:

> There were plenty of discerning people who held that the Homeric
> shields decorated with marvellous art, the splendid cups, the palaces of
> magical beauty, had not all been evolved out of nothing, but must have
> been suggested by things that actually existed. On the other hand, there
> were the faint-hearted, who held all this for idle fantasy and fable, be-
> cause not supported by actual finds. Now we have the great civilisation
> of the Mycenaean period before our eyes, and can no longer doubt that
> this is the civilisation which underlay those Homeric descriptions, where
> every detail is so fondly dwelt upon.

We note that already the term "Mycenaean period" is assuming natural
use, although its wider implications and its chronological limits are not
yet clearly established.

Schuchhardt's summation was no doubt a healthy antidote to skepticism
at the time, but his implication that the question was already settled in
Schliemann's favor is rather misleading. A more perceptive comment on

Schliemann's contribution was written by the great Homeric scholar Walter Leaf. "Dr. Schliemann," says Leaf, "was essentially 'epoch-making' in his branch of study, and it is not for epoch-making men to see the rounding off and completion of their task. That must be the labour of a generation at least. A man who can state to the world a completely new problem may be content to let the final solution of it wait for those that come after him."

# III

## Before Evans:
## The Situation in 1900

W HAT WAS THE SUM of knowledge and theory about Mycenaean civilization when Evans began his first campaign at Knossos in 1900? The personality and achievements of a giant like Schliemann are so overpowering that we are in danger of forgetting that there were others who had also made vital contributions.

One scholar in particular deserves far more credit than he has generally received. Christos Tsountas was one of the very greatest archaeologists of native Greek descent who have excavated in their own country. He was the logical scholar to be designated by his government to continue Schliemann's work at Mycenae. This might have been considered an anticlimactic assignment because of Schliemann's legendary luck and flair for publicity. But Tsountas' efforts revealed important new features of that inexhaustible site; and he achieved notable results in various excavations elsewhere. In addition to his work in classical and Mycenaean contexts, he laid the foundation for the exploration of a brilliant phase of neolithic* civilization that had flourished in northeastern Greece, especially in Thessaly. And on several of the central Aegean islands he found evidence for an important development of "Cycladic*" culture that he recognized as being considerably earlier than the Mycenaean.

Tsountas' most valuable contribution, however, may well have been a brilliant synthesis, called *Mycenae and Mycenaean Civilization,* published in Greek in 1893. His book shows the startling volume of new information that had already accumulated in twenty-three years. But even more valuable than the collection of the data is Tsountas' attempt to systematize and digest the results of that first exciting generation of excavation. The importance of such an overview by an able practicing field archaeologist is obvious enough; but it is a curious fact that for seventy years thereafter, as new information has continued to pour in from many sources, no one of similar background and experience took up the challenge to bring Tsountas' seminal work up to date.

The desirability of making Tsountas' book known to a wider public was immediately realized by an American, Professor J. Irving Manatt of Brown University. Tsountas was willing to authorize a somewhat expanded edition in English; and the names of Tsountas and Manatt appear as coauthors of *The Mycenaean Age: A Study of the Monuments and Culture of Pre-Homeric Greece* (1897). In Manatt's Preface we detect a typical late-nineteenth-century note of confidence—perhaps of overconfidence.

> As I come to date this preface, I am reminded that there could not well be a more auspicious moment for bringing out a work like the present. It signalizes the end of the second decade of Mycenaeology [a term which, fortunately, did not become current]. Just twenty years ago to-day the wires flashed from Mycenae to King George's palace at Athens Schliemann's jubilant message that he had found the Royal Tombs, with their heroic tenants still masked in gold and their heroic equipage about them. That find was the crowning historical revelation of our time, and out of it has sprung a science whose progress is hardly less marvelous than its origin,—a science which has already in great measure restored the landmarks of pre-Homeric Greece, and with them the real background of the Homeric poems.

## NEW DEVELOPMENTS AT TROY

Before following Tsountas' account, however, we shall pause to review the new Trojan evidence. But it should be noted that Troy, while it retains a definite relevance to Homeric studies, is increasingly recognized as just one of many sites peripherally in touch with Mycenaean civilization. Dörpfeld was now director of the German Archaeological School in Athens and the leading foreign authority. It is natural that he should have been asked to write the Introduction to *The Mycenaean Age* and also an Appendix called "The Mycenaean Troy."

By this time the campaigns of 1893 (financed by Sophia Schliemann) and 1894 (financed by Kaiser Wilhelm II) were completed. Dörpfeld's "Table of Nine Layers" in his little book *Troja 1893* provides a convenient summary of the new conclusions. Level II is there described as follows: "Prehistoric citadel of Troy; with strong defensive fortifications and large dwelling houses of sundried brick. Three times destroyed and rebuilt. Monochrome pottery. Many objects of bronze, silver and gold. Estimated period 2500 to 2000 before Christ." His characterization of Troy VI, on the other hand, is a far cry from Schliemann's "Lydian" level: "Citadel of Mycenaean times. Mighty fortification walls with a great tower and handsome houses built of well cut stone blocks. The Pergamus of Troy sung about by Homer. Developed monochrome Trojan pottery. With it imported Mycenaean vases. About 1500 to 1000 before Christ." .

In so matter-of-fact a tone Dörpfeld announces the new stratigraphical equation foreshadowed in 1890 and proved by 1893. For the first time there was a dependable synchronism provided by Mycenaean pottery in a Trojan level, even though the chronology of Mycenaean civilization itself was still far from precise. The dating bracket now assigned to Troy II was even more uncertain—really little more than an educated guess. It was based on a gross calculation of 500 years for the interval occupied by the intervening of phases III, IV and V. There was still no means of even approximating absolute dates for Trojan material earlier than 1500.

On the northwestern and southwestern slopes of the Hissarlik mound Dörpfeld had now uncovered sizable sections of the fortifications of Troy VI (Fig. 34) with substantial buildings close inside them. Both walls and

Figure 34

houses had been constructed entirely of carefully worked stone. He estimated that the fortified acropolis was about 22,000 square yards, which compares with about the same size for Tiryns, 28,000 for Athens, and 33,000 for Mycenae. On the other hand, the fortified citadel of Troy II was less than 9,000 square yards.

Where their ground plans were preserved, the major buildings of Troy VI showed essentially the same type of freestanding megaron plan already noted in Troy II. Again Dörpfeld is tempted to see in at least one or two of them the Trojan temples mentioned by Homer.[23] In one building a row of wooden columns had stood on stone bases along the main axis, and this same plan had just been shown to have characterized a temple of the early classical period at Neandria, not far from Troy. But he finally inclines to the view that all of the Troy VI buildings are private houses, the "chambers of polished stone" that Homer describes on the Pergamus of Troy.[24] Their closeness in date and plan to the mainland palaces is obvious, though in the small area examined at Troy there were at least sixteen separate examples. In contrast, the main megaron at Tiryns and at Mycenae (which Tsountas had meanwhile discovered) were flanked by a complex of smaller and subsidiary units. Dörpfeld makes a comparison of the size of the main room of the various known megara and finds that at Tiryns it was about 130 square yards, at Mycenae about 166, at Troy between 117 and 194.

In spite of the chronological link, Level VI was in some ways a less attractive candidate for Homeric Troy than Level II. The latter had produced rich treasures, and their abandonment or the attempt to hide them seemed to indicate a sudden enemy attack. This impression was further strengthened by the clear evidence that Troy II met its doom in a furious conflagration. In contrast, there was little trace of fire in the destruction of Troy VI, and it had failed to produce much evidence of wealth, except for its size and the monumental style of its fortifications and buildings. Pottery analysis was still in its infancy, and Dörpfeld merely remarks that on the house floors, along with a fair number of imported Mycenaean sherds, vases of Schliemann's "Lydian" fabric were lying. This smooth gray pottery with metallic profile and appearance still held its secret. Alfred Brueckner, who wrote the chapter on pottery, sees in the gray ware the "old Trojan shapes" and believes there is "no ground for ascribing it to another people."

Dörpfeld was of course an architect and not a philologist, but in *Troja 1893* he dares to enter the age-old controversy. "In my opinion," he writes, "this part of the Trojan Question is solved. I pronounce with increasing confidence . . . that it is the Mycenaean, not a later culture, which lies at the base of the Homeric epics. Now we are concerned with another aspect of the Homeric Question; now it must be established how completely the poet's descriptions correspond with reality. Perhaps we will succeed in this way in gaining a new and sounder basis for research into the origin and development of epic poetry." Dörpfeld here foresees a basic direction that prehistoric archaeology and Homeric studies have taken. Yet the establishment of the correspondence he obviously expected has turned out to be a very complex and often a baffling pursuit.

## MYCENAEAN CIVILIZATION: A SYNTHESIS

To return now to the Greek mainland and Tsountas' *Mycenaean Age,* the excavations at Mycenae in the last decade of the century did not seriously upset Schliemann's major conclusions; but they supplemented the earlier work in several important respects. Tsountas cleared the summit of the acropolis and discovered the location of the palace (Fig. 35). Badly ruined foundations of a large building complex were found just southwest of the highest outcropping of rock. A ramp and monumental stairs had led up to it from the Lion Gate. The southern half of the megaron had collapsed into the deep ravine below, but almost all of the preserved features corresponded to those already known from Tiryns. There was the same court in front, the same tripartite ground plan of columned porch, anteroom and main room with column bases near the center. About one-third of the actual curb of a low circular hearth was still in place between the northern column bases, but the floor surface where the throne might have been set had disappeared. So, as Dörpfeld had predicted, a kind of canon of the "megaron type" was emerging from the approximately contemporary sites of Troy VI, Tiryns and Mycenae.

Figure 35

A main corridor and the bases of stairways to the north of the Mycenae megaron indicated that the rest of the palace had lain higher up, on or near the summit; but leveling for a later temple in that area had almost completely destroyed all traces. "If we now . . . reproduce in imagination a Mycenaean palace," writes Tsountas, "our impression of it must be in many respects a brilliant one. There is the Great Hall, with the pillars upholding the roof and inclosing the great round hearth with its rich polychrome designs; the smooth concrete floors, scratched in checkers of red and blue; the walls frescoed in bands, now of animals or linear designs, now of hunting or battle scenes, and crowned with richly carved friezes, while the doorways and the woodwork generally are agleam with noble bronze" (Fig. 36).

The most interesting result of Tsountas' study of the Mycenaean fortifications was that in the eastern part of the acropolis a secret passageway through the north wall led to a series of ninety-nine steps that descended to a deep underground reservoir (Fig. 37). The water was presumably

Figure 36

Figure 37

piped from the famous spring of Perseus about 100 yards outside the wall. This ingenious arrangement would have helped to ensure the all-important water supply in case of a siege.

Deliberate excavation is not by any means the only method by which archaeological evidence is recovered from the earth. An ambitious modern engineering project in the early 1890s drained the big shallow Copaic basin in north central Boeotia and made this rich area available for farming. But the French and English engineers found that they had had predecessors. Tremendous drainage channels or canals had been constructed along the northern and southeastern edges of the lake. Wherever possible, the steep natural slope of rock had been utilized for the outer retaining wall. The artificial banks were mighty earthen structures up to 200 feet in width and reinforced with stone walls. Excess water emptying into the western part of the basin, both from abundant springs and from seasonally swollen rivers, was thus caught and conducted to the northeastern corner of the basin. There the two main channels united and carried the water to one of the natural emissaries or sink-holes from which it found its way underground through the mountain barrier to the sea.

It would appear that the resulting desiccation was most complete in the northwestern part of the basin and archaeologists realized that the chief beneficiary must have been Orchomenos. This ambitious hydraulic system certainly provided a very large and fertile addition to her agricultural resources. And since both tradition and rather meager archaeological evidence pointed to her acme of prosperity in the Late Bronze Age, the Copaic drainage project was termed "the greatest public works of the Mycenaean age." It clearly required as expert supervision and as highly organized a social and political system as did the mighty fortifications of Tiryns and Mycenae or the great tholos tombs.

The southern drainage channel passed close to a rocky eminence, called Gla, which had apparently been an island in the northeastern part of the lake. A mile or so farther to the northeast the two main channels coalesced. Archaeologists for the first time carefully studied Gla's great Cyclopean fortifications and excavated within them. The circuit enclosing Gla is far longer than at Tiryns and Mycenae, measuring almost two miles in circumference, with four gates and protective towers. It appears to have been built at roughly the same time as the fortifications at Tiryns and Mycenae.

A French excavator named A. deRidder worked at Gla for one short season (1893) and showed that a monumental building had been constructed against the north wall and that a large rectangular area to the south of it and in the approximate center of the fortified area had contained other less impressive buildings. This whole area had been enclosed by a second, internal line of fortifications. The so-called palace at the north was quite different in plan from the type established at Tiryns and Mycenae. It was composed of two wings laid out in an L shape. No obvious megaron was identified. There was no evidence of stairways leading to roofs or second stories. Only one room and vestibule showed fragments of frescoed walls. The whole complex at Gla suggested a regional stronghold rather than a royal capital, with much more unoccupied space than in other citadels. The scarcity of small finds indicated that it had not been occupied very long. But, in spite of anomalies, Gla emerged as a third great fortified Mycenaean site, the first discovered north of the Isthmus of Corinth.

Tsountas' most important chapters are those entitled "The Dwellings of the Dead: Shaft Graves" and "The Dwellings of the Dead: Beehive and Chamber Tombs." In the first place we notice that the relative dating of the different grave types is now confidently stated. "The Mycenaean tombs are of two general types. The first is that of the oblong pit [*i.e.,* the shaft grave] sunk vertically in the ground, very much like the modern grave; the second includes the beehive or tholos-structure and the rockhewn chamber, approached alike by an avenue [dromos] cut horizontally into a hillside. It is the second which offers the great monuments of sepulchral architecture; but the shaft-graves are obviously earlier in origin . . ." Tsountas' relative chronology is not based on the pottery types contained in the different kinds of tomb. This is, of course, the most effective modern proof; but he has to rely, rather tenuously, on the generally richer contents of the Shaft Graves (an odd argument) and on the absence or scarcity in them of such objects as engraved gems, ornaments of ivory, mirrors and razors, all of which were common in the tholos tombs.

Tsountas believes that Schliemann's account of the wonderful state of preservation of at least one body in the Shaft Graves must be taken seriously and that some process of embalming was at least occasionally employed. "From the Homeric poems we know that the bodies of the chiefs lay in state for days, and even weeks, before being consigned to the tomb, and without embalming this would have been impossible." He refers to Thetis' inserting ambrosia and red nectar through the nostrils of Patrokles* "that his flesh might abide the same continually,"[25] and he reminds the reader that Aphrodite anoints the body of Hector* with "rose-sweet oil ambrosial."[26] He points to Homer's use of the verb *"tarchuein"* for "bury,"[27] though its primary meaning is "pickle" or "embalm." So he feels that the Mycenaeans may have taken measures to preserve the bodies of important men for lengthy preburial rituals, although the partial parallel with Egyptian customs should not be used to argue that the Mycenaeans held similar views about the future life.

It was now clear that the Shaft Graves within the grave circle were simply the most important of a whole series of similar burials that had once occupied the slope; but "after the change due to the enlargement of the acropolis, these humbler tombs were neglected and houses were built over them, while the royal tombs were preserved." Tsountas assumes that all six Shaft Graves within the circle of stone slabs belonged to a single dynasty and must form a closely related series. He calls renewed attention to the animal bones found scattered above the graves, which suggest that there was a final funeral feast after the earth was replaced. The sacrificial pit above Grave IV would suggest a continuing cult. Several human burials that were found above the Shaft Graves and were unaccompanied by rich objects are not necessarily from a later period, according to Tsountas, but probably represent "the bodies of slaves or captives immolated on the master's tomb."

After the days of the "shaft-grave dynasty" at Mycenae comes a time when the kings were buried in tholos or beehive tombs (Fig. 38) while the "mass of the people" constructed simpler chamber tombs* for their last

Figure 38

resting place (Fig. 39). Both types have in common the long horizontal entrance corridor, or dromos, cut into a sloping rock face. The chamber tombs are square or oblong rooms excavated in the soft rock at the inner end of the dromos; whereas the tholoi are constructed by sinking a circular shaft from the surface, lining it with a stone wall of gradually decreasing diameter until a single stone closed the dome. The tholos walls were packed with clay mortar and weighted on the outside with earth and stone. Since the dome usually protruded above normal ground level, the earth covering formed a mound, or tumulus*, over the grave. At the time Tsountas wrote, twenty-one tholos tombs were known on the Greek mainland, with by far the greatest concentration (eight) at Mycenae. Three had been discovered near the Argive Heraion (famous sanctuary of the goddess Hera in classical times), which was connected to Mycenae by a carefully built highway leading southward some five miles. Three tholoi had been located at Thorikos in eastern Attica, and single examples were scattered from Dimini in Thessaly to Kampos near the Gulf of Messenia and Vaphio near Sparta. So Homer's picture of a series of kingdoms throughout central and southern Greece was beginning to come into focus.

Tsountas emphasizes the monumental character of the tholos tombs and speculates on the wealth and manpower that must have been at the command of the rulers who ordered their construction. In a detailed description of the so-called Treasury of Atreus at Mycenae, he calls it "the type of the tholos tomb in its highest structural perfection, as well as the most

Figure 39

perfectly preserved monument of Mycenaean architecture." And he adds, "Every visitor must be awed by it, even apart from its august and immemorial story."

Due to their conspicuous mounds, nearly all of the tholoi had been plundered long ago. Tsountas conjectures that the Dorian conquerors were the first robbers, but he seems to feel that the offerings originally placed with the deceased royalty in the tholoi were far less rich than those in the Shaft Graves, which preceded them. This would certainly be the case if he was right that "the tombs of Vaphio, Menidi, Demini, Kampos, and one at the Heraion were found substantially intact." Of these the Vaphio tholos contained the richest grave furniture and, since Tsountas was himself the excavator, we may best follow the discovery in his own words.

"In the doorway . . . we found a pit. . . . This was empty, though a thin layer of ashes covered the bottom. . . . The reasonable supposition is that it was a sacrificial pit for the worship of the dead. Within the rotunda [main circular tomb chamber] . . . there was another pit 7½ feet long, 3½ feet wide, and 3 feet deep—paved, walled and covered with stone slabs. This pit, which we found intact, was a man's grave, and was furnished with a great number of precious offerings . . ."

He then goes on to enumerate the grave goods.

On the floor of the round chamber [*i.e.,* not in the "pit," or cist*] . . . were found thirteen engraved gems, two gold rings, silver and bronze needles, some smaller gold ornaments, and a few leaves of gold. But the most and finest of the offerings lay in the pit . . . and, as they had never been disturbed, it is worth while to describe their arrangement. . . . We found no bones, for they had long ago mouldered away, but everything went to show that the body had lain with the head to the west, just as the Greeks bury their dead at the present day. Doubtless this was only that the dead might face the door of his tomb, which happens to front the east; at least during the *prothesis* or lying in state, it was the custom from Homeric times for the dead to be laid upon the bier facing the vestibule.[28] Near where the head had lain were two bronze vessels (one of them a sort of skillet, possibly for sacrificial uses); a bronze sword, 3 feet long; two spear-heads; seven bronze knives; the bronze scepter-sheath; a large bronze spoon; a mirror disk; ten smaller disks of five different sizes, probably making up five pairs of balances; five leaden disks (possibly used as a sort of currency in trade); two stone basins; two alabaster vases, with a little silver spoon in one of them; two terra-cotta vessels; and three other terra-cottas which look like lamps. All these objects were disposed as if to form a pillow for the head.

As Tsountas continues to list the remainder of the contents of this single cist grave we ought to keep in mind (in connection with his impression that the offerings in tholoi were less rich than in the Shaft Graves) that there were often at least two cists, that burials were usually made on the floor of the circular tomb chamber itself and that Spartan kings were probably not the wealthiest of Mycenaean leaders.

> Where the neck and breast must have lain, we found some 80 amethyst beads, with two engraved gems, apparently forming a necklace of two chains. On the left lay a gold-plated dagger, and in the middle of the grave a silver cup with a gold-plated rim. At either hand lay two more cups, one of silver and one of gold: the latter are the now famous Vaphio cups [Fig. 40]. . . . At either hand lay a heap of twelve engraved gems, —the two heaps obviously once forming a pair of bracelets,—with three more silver objects, including an ear-pick, and three rings, one of gold, one of bronze, and one of iron. At the foot lay a bronze knife, two bronze axes . . . and four more lead disks.

It certainly does not appear that this one member of the royal generation using the tholos was any more poverty-stricken than some of the individuals buried in the Shaft Graves.

Turning to the simpler chamber tombs, Tsountas describes the characteristics of more than sixty examples that he had opened in the vicinity of the Mycenae acropolis, as well as others scattered throughout the whole

Figure 40

area of east central and southern Greece and some of the Aegean islands. An interesting feature of the Mycenae chamber tombs is that they cluster in clearly differentiated groups, which suggests that the people lived in small villages around the fortified acropolis. The divisions would presumably have been on the basis of clan (*i.e.,* blood relationship), as in later Sparta. The chamber tombs did not have elaborately decorated entrances and doors, as in the finer tholoi, but the doorway was carefully blocked with a wall of stone or sun-dried brick.

In the chamber tombs, as in the tholoi, it is clear that several burials had usually been made. The funeral customs in both types of tomb seem to have been similar. Normally the bodies were simply placed on the floor, usually in a reclining position with the head propped up and the offerings placed around them. They were not covered with earth or placed in a coffin. As additional burials were made, the earlier bones and offerings were likely to be swept aside rather unceremoniously to make room for the newest occupant. Sometimes a pit is cut into the floor, as at Vaphio, and this indicates to Tsountas a special status for the individual so buried. An even more favored position would be in a side chamber with which only a few tholoi and chamber tombs were provided.

Tsountas discusses at great length a puzzling problem implicit in the continuing use of the chamber tombs and tholoi. When a new burial was made and the immediate funeral rituals were completed, did the dromos of the tomb remain open or was it filled with earth? And, if the latter, was it completely cleared on the occasion of the next burial? He firmly argues for the repeated covering and reopening of the dromos in the case of "all the chamber-tombs and most of the tholoi." He concedes that the richly ornamented entrance façades of some tholoi make this hard to believe but finally concludes that even they were "in the strictest sense subterranean, and that their splendors were displayed only on recurring funeral occasions."

He also points to the evidence for subsequent funeral offerings and some sort of continuing cult or at least memorial rituals.

For the funeral sacrifices, we have evidence in the charred bones sometimes found in the vaulted and chamber tombs. These are the bones of burnt-offerings, for we know that the bodies of the dead were not burned. In the doorway of the Vaphio tomb . . . was a deep pit never occupied as a grave. . . . It was doubtless a sacrificial pit: over it the victim's throat was cut, that the blood-offering might stream through it to the dead beneath; and into it were doubtless poured other libations dear to the dead, such as Odysseus offers in that weird underworld scene which throws so strong a light on the whole subject.[29] . . . But the libations of wine, honey, and milk, and the slaughter of victims over the sacrificial pit—all indispensable to the well-being of the dead—did not cease with the solemn funeral. These rites were observed not only on special occasions, but also at fixed times, namely,—if we may carry back so far the known usages of historical Greece,—on the third, ninth, and thirtieth days after death, and annually thenceforward. That these rites were kept up at the Royal Sepulchre [the grave circle] of Mycenae is proven by the circular altar. . . . In Homer the funeral feast—either before or after the burial—is indispensable.[30] . . . That these feasts were customary in the Mycenaean Age is evident. . . . In case of the vaulted and chamber tombs, the bones of animals are found especially in the dromos before the doorway.

On much less dependable evidence Tsountas insists that prisoners, slaves, and even favorite wives may have been forced to accompany the king on his last journey.

Following up the Homeric parallels, we observe that Achilles, when he burns his comrade's body,—not content with holocausts of sheep and oxen, and horses and dogs, to garnish the great pyre a hundred feet square,—adds a yet sterner sacrifice. "And twelve valiant sons of great-hearted Trojans he slew with the sword,—for he devised mischief in his heart,—and he set to the merciless might of the fire to feed on them."[31] This awful immolation . . . [had] apparently now gone out of use and memory, so that the poet, borrowing here from an earlier lay, feels the need of accounting for the act. A like usage prevailed among other peoples related to the Hellenic stock, and must be assumed for the Mycenaeans as well. We have already spoken of the human skeletons found in the *débris* above the acropolis graves, and not infrequently bodies are found buried in the passages of the chamber-tombs. . . . The woman buried in the dromos of the Clytemnestra tomb must have been a slave, and one highly prized. For, while as a rule there are no offerings with the other bodies buried in these passages, this grave yielded two bronze mirrors with richly carved ivory handles . . . as well as several small ornaments of gold. . . . May we not go a step farther and venture the surmise that she was a favorite slain to follow her master to the underworld?

He should, at least, have considered the parallel in the Christian catacombs, where it was considered a coveted honor to be assigned a burial spot (when the natural time came) as close as possible to important personages.

Tsountas next tries to sum up the evidence for "Dress and Personal Adornment," mainly from both scanty and sketchy representations on gems, frescoes and vases. Men are often depicted wearing nothing but a very abbreviated pair of shorts, for which the nineteenth century used such decorous names as "breech-clout" and "loin apron"; but the record is confused by wide variations in the date of the representations and the occasion shown. For instance, the kings buried in the Shaft Graves were dressed very differently from the soldiers shown going off to battle on the Warrior Vase. These later soldiers could perhaps be said to have something in common with Homer's description of Odysseus' father, old Laertes, who was "clothed in a . . . chiton* [a close-fitting shirt], with . . . leggings of ox-hide bound about his knees . . . and on his head he wore a goat-skin cap."[32]

Some kind of sandals with exaggeratedly pointed toes are commonly shown. The hair was worn long and sometimes bound with a ribbon or fillet. Fairly long, carefully trimmed beards are the rule. The upper lip is usually shaved, and we note the bronze razors sometimes found in the graves. On the other hand, some of the gold masks of the Shaft Graves depict luxurious moustaches. Men seem to have been as fond as women of necklaces, bracelets, brooches and other jewelry. Elaborately decorated round metal objects may once have sheathed the handles of the wooden scepters that were the badge of royalty in Homeric descriptions.

The female costume was naturally more complicated. An outer garment fell in full horizontal flounces down to the ankles. The bodice, perhaps of a different material, was diaphanous and followed the lines of breasts and shoulders. Some experts were sure that the artist meant to show the breasts completely nude. Pointed sandals were worn, and the long hair was elaborately curled and braided. Like most of her sex at other times and places, the Mycenaean lady had a whole arsenal of ornaments and toilet accessories, best represented by the fantastic variety from the Shaft Graves.

Of course, it is hardly fair to suggest any generalization from the queens and princesses of the Shaft Graves or even from the priestesses (or goddesses?) depicted on the rings and gems; yet Tsountas' summation is appealing. "We may now picture to ourselves the Mycenaean lady in full dress . . . soft woollen of sea-purple stain, and glistering linen . . . The diadem of gold is on her brow, golden fillets and pins of exquisite technique shining out of her dark hair; golden bands about her throat and golden necklaces falling upon her bosom; gold bracelets upon her arms, gold rings chased with inimitable art upon her fingers, and finally her very robes agleam with gold. Thus she stands forth a golden lady, if we may borrow Homer's epithet for Aphrodite . . ."[33]

Perhaps the best index on the degree of correspondence between actual Mycenaean objects and Homer's word pictures is in the category of weapons and armor. In life, war was the ultimate test of manliness; and apparently a dead warrior needed to be fully armed to continue his prowess in a future existence. While the disintegration of wood and leather has taken its toll, art representations of fighting and hunting piece out the testimony of material objects from the graves. Again, unfortunately, Tsountas' generation was seriously impeded in utilizing the available evidence by their almost total inability to differentiate relative dates within the long Mycenaean time span.

A great man-covering shield, perhaps comparable to that wielded by Homer's Ajax,[34] is shown in two forms on objects such as the inlaid daggers from the Shaft Graves. One type is oblong, the other pinched at the center into a kind of figure eight. These mighty contraptions could not be held in front of one by a handle but were slung over the shoulder with a strap, or telamon. No wonder the warrior so equipped could not move easily and needed a chariot to convey him to and from the battle. The shield shown on the Warrior Vase, on the other hand, is a much smaller, lighter, oval-shaped object, the handle grasped in the left hand, and displaying such blazons as a crescent moon or stars set in a silver field.

A bronze corselet, or cuirass*, covering the upper part of the body is mentioned by Homer,[35] and something of the sort—probably not of metal— is apparently shown on the Warrior Vase; but corselet and greaves* may have been unnecessary with the bigger shields. Homer's favorite epithet for the Greeks is "well-greaved,"[36] and greaves, or shin-protectors, perhaps of leather rather than metal, are depicted on various monuments such as the Warrior Vase. The helmet was usually a conical cap made of the skin of an animal. Several varieties appear, but none seems to be of metal.

The most striking Homeric parallel in this category is between the description[37] of a helmet covered with gleaming tusks of wild boar and archaeological discoveries of boar's tusks and of art objects showing such a helmet (Fig. 41). Schliemann found sixty tusks in a single Shaft Grave. They were ground flat on one side and perforated for attachment. Also, a small ivory head from Mycenae shows a helmet apparently covered with overlapping rows of boar's tusks and with a wide chin strap or cheek piece similarly covered. "This was in all probability an early Mycenaean practice," says Tsountas. The flashing plumes so prominent on the helmets of Homer's heroes are depicted on the Warrior Vase, and some helmets have a kind of button at the apex into which plumes might have been set. On the Warrior Vase, too, some of the helmets are shown surmounted by two "horns," which would further enhance the threatening aspect of the wearer.

Offensive weapons are much better preserved. The basic implement for close-up fighting was the sword or dagger. There are about 150 of these in bronze from the Shaft Graves alone. They are obviously meant for thrusting rather than slashing. Some are more than 3 feet long, but those from later burials tend to be shorter. The most elaborate were magnifi-

Figure 41

cently decorated with inlaid scenes of battle and hunting. Scabbards were
no doubt of wood, leather or even linen, and the baldric, or sword belt,
of leather. Some of the gold appliqué in the Shaft Graves may have decorated the baldrics. Before engaging at close range, the Homeric hero used
his spear. The bronze spearhead had a socket to receive the long wooden
shaft, which was riveted to the metal.

Chisel-shaped or double-edged battle-axes are occasionally found.
Tsountas is particularly proud of a discovery at Vaphio of a very unusual
type of battle-ax (Fig. 42). "It is crescent-shaped, with two large holes
(possibly to lighten the blade), while the back is cut out in three teeth.
. . . With this unique specimen before us, we can at last understand the
feat of Odysseus in sending an arrow through the rings of twelve axes
set up in a row."[38] Much later, it was realized that this ax reflects Egyptian
influence on a basically Syrian form; but the fact that it was not native
to Greece does not necessarily exclude Tsountas' theory.

Figure 42

Arrowheads of obsidian and bronze abound in the tombs, and representations such as the siege scene on a badly damaged silver rhyton found in the fourth Shaft Grave show kneeling bowmen and standing slingers. This unique object was, like the inlaid daggers, so encrusted and fragmentary that it was not recognized and cleaned until years after Schliemann's excavations (Fig. 43). The vase had a gold rim and a series of gold figure-eight shields just below the rim. The body was of silver, with the figured scene in relief. "Fortunately, now," says Tsountas, "we have recovered at least one Mycenaean battle-picture. . . . Out of the rocky slope—very much as we see it at Mycenae—springs the fortress wall, and behind rise other squared structures which may stand for towers, or for houses in the citadel; before the wall grow trees which we take for wild olives. Upon the wall are five women . . . in attitudes of frenzy and supplication."

He continues with the description of what is preserved of the battle scene on the Siege Rhyton.

Figure 43

Before the walls we see the archers and slingers in the heat of conflict, —speeding their shafts and hurling their missiles at the beleaguering foe, whose figures must have filled the missing foreground . . . and in the rear, just under the wall, are two figures . . . [who may represent] aged non-combatants, watching the conflict; and we have a scene the very counterpart of one wrought by Hephaestus on the shield of Herakles.[39] . . . On other fragments, we make out fallen warriors stretched upon the rocky ground; others carrying off the dead or wounded. . . . How vividly it brings before us the savagery and horror of ancient war. . . . The offending town is beleaguered, and the defense is maintained with the savage fury of men who feel that all is at stake, cheered on by women who know too well the doom awaiting them if once the stronghold be mastered, their husbands and sons put to the sword, and their homes given to the flames. For war is but a higher order of hunting, and women the only game worth taking alive. It is this that nerves the arm of Hector, when Andromache would hold him back from battle.[40]

Tsountas' account of Mycenaean art and architecture is imprecise, naïve and occasionally marred by unlikely hypotheses. Yet in 1897 who could have predicted the startling discoveries so soon to be made on the island of Crete and their special bearing on this particular phase of Mycenaean civilization? One criticism at least seems to be called for, however, in connection with the early evaluation of Mycenaean art. The nineteenth-century scholars, including Schliemann, showed an extremely casual interest in the evolution of shape and decoration of the omnipresent clay vases. They concentrated almost entirely on objects in precious metals. Yet the latter, because of their very rarity and uniqueness (in terms of survival), offer far less opportunity for any systematic reconstruction of the development of art forms.

One chapter in *The Mycenaean Age* is devoted to a question that was considered more or less settled in the negative for a whole generation following 1900. Were the Mycenaeans literate? The lack of written material seemed to provide yet another parallel with the illiterate civilization depicted in the Homeric poems. At the time Tsountas was writing, only six inscribed vessels of stone or terra-cotta had been discovered. They bore, incised or painted on their shoulders or handles, one to five symbols that were apparently written characters. They seemed to be typical local Mycenaean vessels, and the inscription had preceded the firing. Tsountas himself had published two of them (Fig. 44) and had remarked on the similarity of some characters to those of the "pre-Greek" syllabary* with which some of the inhabitants of Cyprus had written Greek in classical times. Also, at two sites in the Egyptian Fayum the British excavator Flinders Petrie had discovered a good deal of pottery identical with Mycenaean types and "often inscribed with characters similar to, and in some cases identical with, those found in Greece."

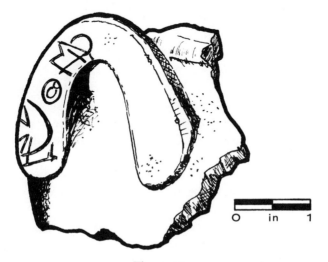

Figure 44

Most significant of all were the recently published results of Arthur Evans' explorations in Crete in the closing years of the century. In a long article in the *Journal of Hellenic Studies* (1894) and then in a book called *Cretan Pictographs and Pre-Phoenician Script* (1895), Evans reviewed the material available at that time. "The evidence which I am now able to bring forward," he wrote, "will, I venture to think, conclusively demonstrate that as a matter of fact an elaborate system of writing did exist within the limits of the Mycenaean world, and moreover that two distinct phases of this art are traceable among its population. The one is pictographic in character like Egyptian hieroglyphics, the other linear and quasi-alphabetic, much resembling the Cypriote and Asiatic syllabaries."

Tsountas accepts Evans' general conclusions; but he shows a prophetic instinct in distinguishing between the mainland and Crete, a distinction which was soon to be highly controversial.

Mycenaean culture in Greece belongs to the Greeks: this view is daily gaining ground. True, peoples of other stock were drawn within the sphere of its influence; but in Peloponnesus and on the adjoining Mainland, and for the most part in the Islands too, this civilization was Greek, and cultivated by Greeks. For all that, the system of writing to which the "Mycenaean" symbols belong seems not to have been a Greek invention, nor primarily intended for the Greek language. . . . It is of course now well known that the Cypriote alphabet as well was devised by a non-Hellenic stock, and subsequently adapted to the Greek language, whose sounds it could but imperfectly represent.

But when he is forced to take a stand on the meaning of the very minor existing evidence from the mainland, Tsountas decides that these are stray imports. "Three years ago, in publishing two inscribed vase-handles, we stated that facts seemed to show that writing was neither used nor known among the Mycenaean peoples. To-day we must reiterate the same judgment; . . . Perhaps the future may reveal fresh data; but in Greece at least the Mycenaean epoch has been pretty thoroughly explored, and this exploration has yielded us a great mass of monuments,—utensils, ornaments and other products of Mycenaean art; and these afford negative proof against the existence of writing." We smile now to think that anyone could have believed seventy years ago that "the Mycenaean epoch has been pretty well explored"; it would be a debatable statement even today.

So Tsountas took the wrong road, and others followed him for over forty years. It is clear throughout his chapter dealing with writing that Tsountas is unhappy with his reading of the evidence. At the end he says: "This [the absence of writing] is a surprising fact when we consider how splendidly nature had endowed them for other tasks, and how constantly they were in touch with nations that had long known and employed that art." When he tries finally to answer the question "Why did the Mycenaeans not adopt or invent a writing system?" he is scarcely convincing. "It may be that the primitive peoples of Greece felt no need of writing. They had other ways of learning and communicating what they would. Each state, even imperial Mycenae, lay within very narrow bounds; a patriarchal form of government prevailed; social relations were very simple; there were few temples and no sacerdotal class; . . . Finally, there were the winged songs of the troubadours who published the *klea andrōn* [famous deeds of heroes] to a much wider circle than could be reached by inscriptions set up in some one place."

Yet it would be unfair to Tsountas to ignore a remark he made in quite another context, for this pronouncement proved to be truly prophetic. "We may hope, at least," he says, "if this ancient culture ever recovers its voice, to find it not altogether unfamiliar; we need not be startled if we catch the first lisping accent of what has grown full and strong in the Achaean epic." Tsountas' instinct on this point was as near the truth as it was completely missed by the dogma of some of his successors a whole generation later.

In 1897, as to a large extent even now, the religious beliefs and practices of the Mycenaeans had to be deduced from material remains. Tsountas' inventory includes "the actual altars at Mycenae and Tiryns; the funeral offerings and the clear traces of continued ministration to the dead; the adoration scenes occurring in Mycenaean art [especially on rings and gems]; the rude images which are hardly less abundant in Mycenaean remains than the eikon in modern Greece or the crucifix in Catholic countries." He echoes Schliemann's surprise at the relative crudeness of the distinctive little terra-cotta figurines in comparison with the delicacy and perfection of other art forms. The predominantly female representations, with folded or upraised arms, occasionally holding a child, and with garments and ornaments summarily indicated in dark paint show "how religious conservatism had consecrated these divine simulacra as it continued to consecrate the wooden *xoana*\* in the very presence of the Phidian masterpieces." It is clear, he notes, that "female deities decidedly outnumber the male. With barely the two exceptions . . . [where] we have ventured to recognize Zeus, the monuments give us goddesses exclusively, Aphrodite, Artemis, Hera, Earth. . . . With the exception of Aphrodite, whose cult was brought in by the Phoenicians, all the female deities identified on our monuments are but slightly differing forms of that goddess whose worship is primeval—Mother Earth, the universal life-giver" (Fig. 17).

These deities—at least Aphrodite—apparently had dwelling places built by their worshipers' hands, to judge from such objects as the little golden tripartite buildings with hovering doves that had been found in the Shaft Graves. Yet in excavation no ruined building had yet been found whose plan or furnishing would suggest that it had been a temple or shrine.

As for Tsountas' chapter on "The Problem of the Mycenaean Race," perhaps the less said the better. Not that twentieth-century archaeologists and anthropologists have settled the problem; but they have learned to beware of the broad generalizations and reckless hypotheses so dear to former generations who speculated on this slippery topic. Tsountas is completely under the spell of the "northern mirage." The Mycenaeans must be "Aryans." He tries to connect them with the pile-dwelling peoples who inhabited the marshy areas of northern Italy and Switzerland. Homer's various names for the Greeks and other features of the mythological tradition are pressed into service, with the Danaans representing these earlier "marsh-men" (akin to the Minyans who drained Lake Copais in Boeotia) and the Achaeans* equated with the "lands-men," a later branch of the same race (he speaks also of "two races") who had learned to fortify high citadels. The Shaft Graves could then be conveniently ascribed to the marsh-men (the Perseid* dynasty of mythology) and the tholos tombs to the lands-men (the Pelopid* dynasty). The fusion of these two peoples made up the "Hellenic" race, and they were responsible for a "native growth" of Mycenaean art, "influenced though it was by the earlier civilizations of the Cyclades and the East."

On problems connected with the so-called Dorian invasion, Tsountas' position is the "orthodox" one that has generally prevailed from later antiquity almost to the present. "Can we determine the race or races among the Greeks known to history to whom the achievement of Mycenaean civilization is to be ascribed? In this inquiry we may set aside the Dorians, although many scholars (especially among the Germans) still claim for them the marvelous remains of the Argolid. . . . [This view] cannot stand the test of chronology. For tradition refers that migration to the end of the twelfth century B.C., whereas the Mycenaean people were established in the Argolid before the sixteenth, probably even before the twentieth century."

Against another theory—that the Dorian migration was a myth or belonged to the immemorial past—Tsountas urges that excavation has shown clearly that the Mycenaean civilization perished in a great catastrophe.

The palaces . . . were destroyed by fire after being so thoroughly pillaged that scarcely a single bit of metal was left in the ruins. Further, they were never rebuilt; . . . How are we to account for this sudden and final overthrow otherwise than by assuming a great historic crisis, which left these mighty cities with their magnificent palaces only heaps of smoking ruins? And what other crisis can this have been than the irruption of the Dorians? And their descent into the Peloponnese is traditionally dated at the very time which other considerations have led us to fix as the lower limit of the Mycenaean age. Had that migration never been recorded by the ancients nor attested by the state of the Peloponnese in historic times [generally an area of Doric dialect], we should still be led to infer it from the facts now put in evidence by the archaeologist's spade.

By Tsountas' time Greek prehistoric archaeology had already passed somewhat beyond the predicament that he describes as follows: "A dateless era and a nameless race . . . are facts to be accepted only in the last resort. The student of human culture cannot look upon the massive walls, the solemn domes [tholoi], the exquisite creations of what we call Mycenaean art, without asking—When? By whom? In default of direct and positive evidence, he will make the most of the indirect and probable." Schliemann had given prompt and confident, if rather imprecise, answers to these questions. The epoch, he thought, was during and just before the Trojan War, traditionally dated in the early twelfth century. The people were Homer's Greeks, called variously Danaoi, Achaioi, Argeoi. But by Tsountas' day it was realized that the problem was not so simple.

We have followed his rather abortive attempt to pin down the origin of these people. On the question of chronology, however, a firm over-all framework had now been laid. The method employed is still standard for dating as far back as 3000—that is, to establish synchronisms between the culture in question and another culture with an *absolute* chronology that can be calculated from written records. "Here we call in the aid of Egyptology," says Tsountas. "In Greece we find datable Egyptian products in Mycenaean deposits, and conversely in datable Egyptian deposits we find Mycenaean products." He then lists the chief known synchronisms: a late Mycenaean vase in an Egyptian tomb dating within fifty years of 1100; a large group of the "Mycenaean false-necked vase or Bügelkanne*" (we now usually call them stirrup jars* [Fig. 45]), which Flinders Petrie, the first exponent of sequence dating*, had found at various Egyptian sites and arranged in a stylistic series dated between 1400 and 1100; tomb frescoes of Thothmes III (about 1500) at Egyptian Thebes on which were shown "princes of the land of Keftu" (presumed to be Crete) with vases of distinct Mycenaean style in their hands; scarabs found both at Mycenae and Ialysos in Rhodes bearing cartouches of "Amenophis III and of his queen Tiy" (latter half of the fifteenth century).

There had also been some attempt, in addition to Petrie's work, to dis-

Figure 45

tinguish between an "earlier" and "later" phase. "The earlier period of Mycenaean art is thus shown to be anterior to the reign of Thothmes III; and, as that period cannot conceivably be limited to a few short generations, the sixteenth century is none too early for the upper limit of the Mycenaean age. . . . For the lower limit . . . we have taken the twelfth century, though certain archaeologists and historians are inclined to a much more recent date—some even bringing it three or four centuries farther down." Tsountas refutes the latter theory by pointing out that "if the beehive and chamber-tombs at Mycenae are to be assigned to a period as late as the ninth century, the rare occurrence of iron in them becomes quite inexplicable."

So the destruction of Mycenaean civilization is confidently placed in the twelfth century, and the agents are identified as the Dorians. But Tsountas is at pains to insist that the influence of Mycenaean civilization survived the Dorian destruction. In fact, certain architectural features such as the plan of the megaron and propylon as well as the column and lintel construction became "an enduring possession of Hellenic art, and so of the civilized world."

This theme leads naturally to the subject of his final chapter, "The Mycenaean World and Homer." We hear no more of Schliemann's early and impetuous conviction that the Mycenaean world *is* Homer's world;

but the connection is no less firmly argued. "That Mycenaean art outlasted the social *régime* under which it had attained its splendid bloom is sufficiently attested by the Homeric poems. Doubtless, the Achaean system, when it fell before the aggressive Dorian, must have left many an heirloom above ground. . . . And, again, the poems in their primitive strata undoubtedly reflect the older order . . ." Tsountas sounds an even more modern note in another passage: "Homer avowedly sings of heroes and peoples who had flourished in Greece long before his own day. Now it may be denied that these represent the civilization known to us as Mycenaean; but it is certainly a marvellous coincidence (as Schuchhardt observes) that 'excavations invariably confirm the former power and splendor of every city which is mentioned by Homer as conspicuous for its wealth or sovereignty.' "

In the historical reconstruction that ends *The Mycenaean Age* we detect a characteristic nineteenth-century attitude (possibly to be attributed mainly to Manatt). It was by manifest destiny that the inventive and forward-looking West clashed with and defeated the ancient and conservative East, which sat astride the land and sea routes between Europe and Asia. "The sea power in the Aegean [Mycenae] and the land power on the Hellespont [Troy] could no more avoid an Eastern Question then than can England and Russia to-day."

But the weakened victors of the long struggle celebrated by Homer returned home only to face and succumb to the Dorian threat. "The Dorian migration marks the beginning of long dark ages, the mediaeval epoch of Greece, out of which she emerges only in the Homeric Renaissance. . . . To the isles and shores of Asia Minor, the descendants of the conquerors [of Troy] return as refugees; and of all they carry with them the most precious possessions are the old songs." Tsountas and his contemporaries tended to think of the new colonial milieu in which Homer lived as a "ferment of races and conditions" that gradually produced the complex and more or less unified civilization mirrored in the poems as we have them. "On the establishment of the new order with a new accumulation of wealth, some of the old arts revive, while others have to be created afresh." Political, social and religious institutions described in the Homeric poems are largely the reflection of this post-Dark Ages renaissance rather than of Mycenaean times. Yet it was a far less splendid age than the one that saw the mighty heroic deeds and produced the original heroic songs inspired by them. "As compared with the Mycenaean, the Homeric civilization marks decadence. The arts especially are stationary or even retrograde; and the Phoenicians have resumed their old lead in art as well as in commerce."

Again in the very last sentences, the confident note of late-nineteenth-century optimism is struck. "We set the epic picture against the real background, and the harmony is too close and manifold to have happened [*i.e.,* to be accidental]. To bring out the full measure of that harmony, we have only to go on unearthing the relics of prehistoric Greece and at the same time to delve yet deeper in the inexhaustible mines of Homer." This seems a naïve faith in the light of the archaeological and philological results of the first two generations of the twentieth century. Yet when one reflects on the extraordinary forward leap in solid knowledge documented in Tsountas' book as compared with a generation before, when Schliemann began his excavations, it must be admitted that there *was* considerable reason for such a confident attitude.

# IV

## Evans, Crete and Minos:
## 1900-1914

*"Evans had come to the site in the hope of finding*

*a seal impression and a clay tablet, and Time and Chance*

*had led him to discover a civilization."*


WHEN SCHLIEMANN WAS NEGOTIATING for his first excavation at Troy, a young man of very different background but with many similar traits of personality was entering Oxford University. Particularly for his earlier years we shall depend heavily on recollections and documents published by his half sister, Joan, in her book, *Time and Chance*.

Throughout more than half of his life Arthur Evans was simply the "son of John Evans the great." The older Evans was a Fellow of the Royal Society, Honorary Secretary of the Geological and Numismatic Societies of London, a distinguished, wealthy, widely traveled and politically sophisticated businessman and scholar-gentleman. Such books as *The Ancient Stone Implements, Weapons and Ornaments of Great Britain* (1872) had established his reputation as one of the founders of the new science of prehistory. The son grew up "belonging of right to the world of learning and the lesser world of archaeology; in having an instinctive judgment of date and style and use, acquired by living among the collections at Nash Mills [the Evans manor house]; in possessing a knowledge of prehistory and numismatics learned so gradually and so easily that it had become unconscious. There were solid advantages . . . in being the son of a man who provided . . . an allowance of £250 a year without question or condition, and would always help in a financial emergency . . ."

While profiting all his life from his family's prominence, Arthur was determined to make his mark on his own terms. In school debates he criticized the classical curriculum and attacked the Conservative government. He refused to take any interest in the family papermills and after his college years spent much of his time abroad. Until close to middle age he lived and traveled mainly in the Balkans. There he combined archaeological and historical exploration with an ardent interest in the current political struggle. As correspondent for the *Manchester Guardian* and free-lance writer, he sent home impassioned dispatches supporting the native aspirations for self-government.

At the age of twenty-seven Evans married Margaret Freeman, whose father was a distinguished medieval historian. They made their home at Ragusa on the Dalmatian coast during the earlier portion of their fifteen years of life together. Actually, the bridegroom continued his constant travels, with or without his bride; and Margaret soon became resigned to frequent separations. Their parents, anxious to lure them back to England, urged Arthur to try to qualify for a new studentship in archaeology at Oxford. An excerpt from his reply tells a good deal about his own attitude and the archaeological climate of the day: "It is quite evident that Athens and no other earthly site is Newton's goal. . . . In that case the studentship ought not to be called a studentship of Archaeology in general. The great characteristic of modern Archaeological progress has been the revelations as to periods and races of men about which history is silent; and for pre-historic Archaeology, no European field is perhaps now more important than the unworked Illyrian one [the area where he was then living] . . . Oxford, however, seems to have set itself to ignore every branch of Archaeology out of its own classical beat."

Evans' resentment of what he felt was a current overemphasis on classical antiquity can again be sensed in his sister's account of a trip to Greece in 1882.

They rode . . . by Orchomenos, where Schliemann had excavated a prehistoric tomb two years before, to Thebes and Athens. . . . They saw the Schliemanns, heard all about the finds at Orchomenos, and laughed a little at the odd little man and his preoccupation with Homer; but Arthur found his gold work from Mycenae beautiful, exciting, and puzzling: it was art of a kind that appealed to him, because it was not classical: but how did its quasi-Assyrian and quasi-Egyptian elements come to be combined with the Aegean octopus? . . . By Aegina and Nauplia they made their way to Tiryns, where Evans was enormously impressed by the Cyclopean walls, and to Mycenae, where he could not get over the extraordinary contrast between its architecture and that of classical Greece.

In 1884 Evans became Keeper of the Ashmolean Museum in Oxford. It is probably fair to infer that the appointment depended more on family connections than on any wide professional reputation that Arthur had earned up to that time. As a matter of fact, the post had for generations been a sinecure, with a motley collection and no funds for its proper maintenance or improvement. But Evans always relished a challenge, and he was soon announcing his intention to collect and display in the Ashmolean a selection of artefacts representing archaeology in the broadest sense. Here was a vision that was far more sweeping than Schliemann's passion to authenticate Homer. It had first stirred a few brilliant and audacious minds in John Evans' generation and was still making slow and painful progress against the weight of orthodox and entrenched dogma.

In his inaugural address, "The Ashmolean Museum as a Home of Archaeology in Oxford," Arthur Evans eloquently sounded the keynote.

> Our theme is History, the history of the rise and succession of human Arts, Institutions, and Beliefs in our historic portion of the globe. . . . The unwritten History of Mankind precedes the written, the lore of monuments precedes the lore of books. . . . Consider for a moment the services rendered within quite recent years by what has been called Prae-historic Archaeology, but which in truth was never more Historic, in widening the horizon of our Past. It has drawn aside the curtain, and revealed the dawn. It has dispelled, like the unsubstantial phantoms of a dream, those preconceived notions as to the origin of human arts and institutions at which Epicurus and Lucretius already laughed, before the days of biblical chronology. . . . We have as yet too little in our Museum to illustrate these early chapters in the history of human arts . . .

The status and prestige of the Ashmolean did improve dramatically under Evans' forceful direction, but the endless negotiating over accessions and funds and building plans bored and exasperated him. Joan Evans writes:

> A new vision was beginning to haunt him: Crete. It is hard to say what chance had first drawn his attention to the unknown island; it seems as if a thousand tiny facts and things had drifted like dust and settled to weigh down the scales of his decision. His father's acquaintance, Henry Schliemann, had revealed a bright new world by his excavations at Troy, Mycenae, Tiryns and Orchomenos: excavations conducted Homer in hand, with no thought of relating them to anything but the epic story. For Evans, as for others, they were not Homeric illustrations but bronze age sites, and for that very reason offered problems more complex than any Schliemann found. There seemed, especially at Mycenae, to be things of many dates, drawn from various sources; and those sources were for the most part still unknown. Schliemann himself had planned to excavate "broad Knossos," but had never done so; and now the same unavowed intention was dawning on the mind of Arthur Evans. On February 3, 1892, he was in Rome, and made friends with Halbherr, an Italian archaeologist who had already explored many of the classical sites in Crete. What he told him of the earlier remains on the island, unexplored and unexplained, fired his imagination and confirmed his interest, though as yet his purpose was hardly formed.

After his wife's premature death in 1893, Evans began to concentrate more and more on Aegean prehistory, particularly on the evidence for a system of writing that he was discovering on engraved gems and seals. "Evans was extremely short-sighted, and a reluctant wearer of glasses. Without them, he could see small things held a few inches from his eyes in extraordinary detail, while everything else was a vague blur. Consequently the details he saw with microscopic exactitude, undistracted by the outside world, had a greater significance for him than for other men." After Schliemann's death, it was possible to work over the finds from his excavations with more freedom, and Evans detected written symbols on two of the objects. Also, in the antique shops in Athens he discovered engraved hieroglyphics on gems that the dealers said had originated in Crete. Similar objects in the Berlin Museum undoubtedly came from Crete, although Adolph Furtwängler, the foremost expert on Mycenaean art, believed that they were to be dated later than Mycenaean times.

Other scholars were also beginning to look toward Crete. The German authority Milchhöfer, in a book entitled *Beginnings of Art* (1883), had inferred that to explain the discoveries at Mycenae and Tiryns one would have to follow the trail back through the Aegean islands (especially Melos) and eventually to Crete. We have already mentioned Schliemann's frustrated plans at Knossos. In 1893 some sherds had been brought to the museum at Candia (now Iraklion, the largest town in Crete) from a cave called Kamares* high up on the southern face of Mount Ida. They were closely similar to pottery that Flinders Petrie had discovered in twelfth-dynasty tombs at Kahun in the Egyptian Fayum and had with marvelous intuition identified as "Aegean imports." So the stage was set to press an investigation in Crete itself as soon as political conditions would permit.

Arthur Evans visited Crete for the first time in 1894, the very year in which his first article on the Cretan inscriptions appeared. His sister draws an interesting contrast in his literary style during the Balkan and Cretan years. The earlier documents were "as much occupied with people and scenery as with objects of antiquity: the records of a desultory quest for interest and adventure"; but after 1894 the letters become "brief and businesslike, devoid of fine writing, and yet imbued with a curious steady purpose." She infers from this sudden change that "before he landed Evans had determined on the archaeological conquest of the island."

A few excerpts from his letters will suggest the exciting atmosphere of those first days on Cretan soil.

The site of Knossos is most extensive and occupies several hills [see Map VI]. The Mykenaean akropolis however seems not to be the highest but that to the south west, nearest to the gorge. . . . Here at a place called *ta pithária* ["the storage jars"] are the remains of Mykenaean walls and passages (where the great pots, Pithoi, were found) noted by W. J. Still-

man [a British diplomat and amateur archaeologist] and others. . . .
I copied the marks on the stones, some of which recall my "hieroglyphics." . . . I was brought a remarkable fragment of a black basalt
vessel. At first I thought it was a bit of some kind of Roman relief
ware, but to my astonishment I found it was Mykenaean, with part of
a relief representing men perhaps ploughing or sowing—an altar?—
and a walled enclosure with a fig tree: a supplement to the Vapheio
vases and contemporary in style!

On March 20 he continues:

Halbherr arrived with the President of the Syllogos [Archaeological
Council] Hadjidakis. . . . [March 22] Long conversation with [Joseph]
Hadjidakis about the excavations of Knossos. Schliemann proposed to
dig here. . . . I took the responsibility of saying he [Hadjidakis]
might buy it [a quarter-share of the site] for me and that I would raise
the money for the entire purchase in England when that was feasible.
The possession of a part can legally compel sale. I said that the "Cretan
Exploration Fund"—at present non-existent—would agree to the same
terms as the Germans at Olympia and that the Cretans should keep
these antiquities only reserving to us the right of publication and such
specimens as were *not needed or could be spared by the Museum of
the Syllogos.* . . . Halbherr would act for the Cretan Exploration Fund
as epigraphic* explorer; he knows of countless places where material
could be gathered and great discoveries made . . .

Having gotten negotiations started in this rather breezy manner, Evans
set out on a long journey of exploration—the first of many—through central and eastern Crete. Everywhere, he recognized the broken potsherds
marking the sites of towns that had existed long before the classical period.
He also bought or took impressions of many engraved seals and gems that
the Cretans called *galopetras* ("milkstones"). Mothers wore them as
charms to guarantee that their milk would prove adequate for their babies.
The antiquities acquired in those first explorations formed the beginning
of the great Cretan collection of the Ashmolean Museum.

One ancient site, at Goulas near Kritsa, particularly impressed Evans.
"What a mighty centre this must have been! There is no one object here
to fix the attention like the Lion Gate; the walls are not so massive as those
of Tiryns, but for vastness of extent, for the preservation of its inner
buildings, for sublimity of site, Goulas throws all competitors into the
shade. . . . There seems to be no trace of anything Hellenic here . . . there
is nothing that is not Mykenaean or prae-Mykenaean." We can already
catch the first glimmer of a theory that was to become Evans' abiding
conviction for the next forty-five years. "What one feels," he writes, "is that

here [in Crete] perhaps was really the great original focus of Mykenaean culture . . ." It is a minor irony that Goulas, the site on which he seems to have first based the hypothesis, was later proved not to be prehistoric at all.

The following year Evans was back in Crete, accompanied by John L. Myres, "a Ulysses of twenty-six, black-bearded and quick spoken, learned in many lores and a fit companion for Homeric adventure." As their explorations continue, Evans sees increasing evidence for close connections with the prehistoric phase already known on the mainland. "The golden age of Crete lies far beyond the limits of the historical period: its culture . . . is practically identical with that of the Peloponnese and a large part of the Aegean world. . . . The great days of Crete were those of which we still find a reflection in the Homeric poems—the period of Mycenaean culture, to which here at least we would fain attach the name 'Minoan.' " Minos was perhaps a generic name for the ruler of Knossos, like Pharaoh in Egypt and Caesar in Rome. The adjective "Minoan" soon came to connote for Evans a culture originating in Crete, particularly at Knossos, and completely dominating its "Mycenaean" counterpart on the mainland. One of our major themes from now on will be the developing evidence for Minoan-Mycenaean interrelations; and for this reason we must be familiar with at least certain aspects of Minoan civilization.

## THE SEASON OF 1900

The final Cretan phase of the Greek War of Independence prevented Evans' return until 1899. The next year the acquisition of the Knossos site and the excavation permits were finally in order, and Evans began to dig on March 23, 1900. Like Schliemann thirty years before, Evans was a middle-aged man with practically no experience in excavation when he undertook the uncovering of a crucial site. His half sister frankly admits that he "except at Aylesford [a Late Celtic urnfield in Kent excavated in 1891] had done none but occasional and surreptitious excavation." It is fortunate therefore that he acquired as his assistant a reticent and capable Scot named Duncan Mackenzie.

During the previous four years Mackenzie had been a member of the staff of the first major excavation conducted by the British School of Archaeology at Athens. This was at the deeply stratified and complex site of Phylakopi on the island of Melos. Mackenzie was site supervisor throughout that undertaking and assumed complete charge during the final campaign. We shall later review some of his conclusions and inferences on the Phylakopi discoveries.

At Knossos Mackenzie seems again to have performed the duties that we would now designate as those of the site supervisor. But the exact nature of his responsibilities, the limits of his authority and the personal relationship between him and Evans are something of an enigma. The problem has important scientific implications in view of the controversy that has developed since 1962 about the dependability of some aspects of Evans' publications. The conundrum, in short, concerns the exact roles that the two men played in the gradual evolution of theories from the moment of discovery of crucial evidence until the final arguments and conclusions appeared in definitive publications.

Differences of opinion and personality clashes may occur among the members of any excavation staff, just as in other small groups that are temporarily isolated from normal living and working habits. Whether these tensions were particularly aggravated in the case of Evans and Mackenzie is not clear. According to his half sister, Evans "endured his [Mackenzie's] suspicious temper and his valetudinarian ways with exemplary patience." This would suggest that in the bosom of the family Evans sometimes unburdened certain resentments and frustrations. Yet Evans too was undoubtedly a difficult man with whom to be closely associated. And the situation may well have been aggravated by the almost complete dependence of one scholar on the other for his economic livelihood. One gets the impression, rightly or wrongly, of an annually renewed contract at Knossos, rather than a full-fledged collaboration such as seems to have developed between Schliemann and Dörpfeld.

In any case, we must turn to the chronicle of some of the major discoveries in those fabulous early years. Although one is likely to think of the Knossos excavations as a long series of slow, methodical campaigns extending through the first two or three decades of the century, the fact is that almost all of the major excavation in the palace and much of the exploration of its environs were completed within five years. The season usually lasted from two to four months in the spring and early summer. The nature of the finds soon required the services of a trained architect and a skilled artist. The supervisory staff was always very small and the workmen extremely numerous, by modern standards. And one looks in vain for mention of additional supervisors to direct and control 100 to 200 eager laborers.

Mackenzie, for all his experience and instinct for complete and precise recording, must have been pressed very hard. Evans' own role is less clear; but it would appear that he was more concerned with the preliminary examination of the finds themselves than in methodically checking their exact position and association as they came out of the ground. In short, the early excavation of Knossos was conducted with no more refined technique than Schliemann's later campaigns. No sudden revolution in methodology took place between 1890 and 1900; and it is in fact unrealistic to assume that it should have.

We shall try as far as is practicable to follow the progress of the work by quoting from Evans' letters to his family and especially from his annual reports. The latter were regularly printed in the place of honor at the beginning of each number of the prestigious *Annual of the British School at Athens* for the years 1900 to 1905. First, for a rather more complete description of the geographical setting (see Map VI):

> The site of ancient Knossos . . . about four miles inland from Candia, is shut in by higher hills in three directions. Somewhat South however of the scanty remains of the Roman City, the ground gradually rises into a rounded hill generally known as Kephala. . . . This hill lies at the confluence of a tributary stream with the ancient Kairatos (now *Katsabás*), and descends somewhat steeply towards these channels on the South and East. To the West of the hill . . . runs a road, the antiquity of which is shown by the rock tombs that extend along its further course. This road must in all ages of Cretan history have formed the natural lines of access [to the interior of the island]. . . . Although overlooked by loftier heights beyond the streams and the road, the partial isolation of the hill of Kephala, and the fact that it immediately commanded this natural line of communication, must have made it in early times something of a key position.

Attention was concentrated that first year mainly on the western part of the mound. We cannot hope to provide a detailed and systematic reconstruction of the spectacular finds that came pouring out almost as soon as the surface was scratched. It was not only the quantity and variety that amazed Evans, but above all their quality and novelty. The discoveries on the mainland had hardly prepared anyone for this revelation of a lively, imaginative and exuberant people who had once populated the mythical Knossos. In his formal publications Evans strikes a rather ponderous and detached note, which contrasts strongly with Schliemann's naïve enthusiasm. But the letters show that his reactions were not so very different when he first saw the inscribed tablets, painted pottery, monumental architectural remains and particularly the frescoes.

For instance, in the southwestern section of the hill in what was soon to be called the Corridor of the Cupbearer (Fig. 52), he writes that "two large pieces of Mycenaean fresco" were recovered on which was preserved "far and away the most remarkable human figure of the Mycenaean Age that has yet come to light" (Fig. 46). Later known as the Cupbearer, *she* is described by Evans as follows: "One [fragment] represented the head

Figure 46

and forehead, the other the waist and part of the skirt of a female figure holding in her hand a long Mycenaean 'rhyton' or high funnel shaped cup. . . . The figure was life size, the flesh colour of a deep reddish hue. . . . The profile of the face was of a noble type: full lips. . . . The eye was dark and slightly almond shaped. In front of the ear is a kind of ornament and a necklace and bracelet are visible. The arms are beautifully modelled. The waist is of the smallest . . ." After cleaning and study prior to the first tentative published report, Evans describes the painting as follows: ". . . on the floor level . . . face uppermost, [lay] two large pieces of fresco. These pieces together formed the greater part of a life-sized figure of a youth clad in the same close-fitting and richly embroidered loin-cloth as those of the 'Corridor of the Procession' . . . The modelling of the face and limbs show an artistic advance which in historic Greece was not reached till the fifth century before our era, some eight or nine centuries later than the date of this Knossian fresco."

A few days later a letter describes the uncovering of a "bath chamber," which was soon recognized as the famous Throne Room.

> On the other side of the North wall was a short bench, like that of the outer chamber, and then separated from it by a small interval a separate seat of honour or throne. It had a high back . . . which was partly imbedded in the stucco of the wall. It was raised on a square base and had a curious moulding below with crockets. (Almost Gothic!) Probably painted originally so as to harmonize with the fresco at its side. This was imperfectly preserved, but showed the upper foliage of a palm tree (No! reeds). . . . On the N. E. wall was another study in foliage, reed like plants in front of a tree (No! hills) and curving lines below apparently indicating flowing water . . ."

Again, in the preliminary publication, a good many changes can already be noticed. The "bath chamber" has become the Throne Room, and the sunken area in front of the throne that suggested the original designation is possibly an aquarium or fish pond (this distinctive feature of Minoan palaces is now usually called a lustral area*). The stone throne itself had been stuccoed and painted, and great wingless griffins with elaborate crests are recognized as the major theme on the frescoed walls. In addition to the throne, "the specially rich character of the relics found in the chamber itself corroborates the conclusion that a royal personage once sat here for council. . . . The stone benches round may have afforded room for twenty counsellors." Furthermore, Evans feels that the room has "an appearance of freshness and homogeneity that makes it improbable that at the time of the great overthrow it had long existed in its present form" (Fig. 47).

Figure 47

The frescoes, whether in place on the lower walls or fallen in tumbled fragments, had to be promptly and carefully cleaned, conserved and copied by an expert. Evans summoned from Athens the Swiss artist Étienne Gilliéron, who had carried out similar work for the French School of Archaeology. For almost a generation the Gilliérons, father and son, were associated with the Knossos excavations. Most of the reconstructions of fresco panels and other art objects are their work. We must, of course, be grateful to the modern artist and the excavator for such striking re-creations of Minoan art. But, as in the case of the restoration of the palace architecture, reconstruction poses serious problems when certainty cannot be attained. How far should one man's imagination and judgment decide for others? Many a visitor to the museum in Iraklion (where most of the movable finds from Knossos are displayed) is startled to discover how little of the original fresco compositions Evans really recovered and how much is restored. And the restored areas are so artfully blended with the original fragments that the innocent student is likely to assume from reproductions in books that the total composition is certain.

As more fresco fragments came out, Evans realized that the Minoan artists had followed the Egyptian convention of using white for the flesh of women and red for men. He also began to suspect that the paintings were not all contemporary. For instance, this is part of his description of the famous "Blue Boy" composition (Fig. 48):

Figure 48

There are eight pieces of this design, which can be put together sufficiently to show the greater part [but missing the head] of a small figure
of a boy in a field of white crocuses, some of which he is placing in
an ornamental vase of "kantharos" shape. This fresco, remarkable in
many ways, apparently belongs to an earlier date than any yet discovered in the Palace. . . . The whole tone of the painting differs from
that of the mature Mycenaean style of the Knossos frescoes, and the
tint of the boy's body, here a pale blue, differs from the regular Mycenaean convention, in which male figures are painted a reddish-brown,
while the women are white.

His instinct about date proved to be right; but a blue *tail* was later detected on one fragment of this composition and the subsequent discovery
of a Knossian scene clearly depicting a blue *monkey* leaves little doubt
that the color convention had not been violated in this case.

Another group of fresco fragments in "miniature style" depicts crowds
of people watching spectacles such as bull baiting or dancing.

At a glance we recognize Court ladies in elaborate toilette. . . . In the
best executed pieces these *décolletées* ladies are seated in groups with
their legs half bent under them, engaged in animated conversation em-

phasised by expressive gesticulation. . . . The men, none of whom are bearded, are naked except for the usual loin-cloth and the foot-gear with banded gaiter-like continuations above the ankle, resembling the buskins worn by the warriors on the fresco-fragments from Mycenae. . . . These unique representations of great crowds of men and women within the walls of towns and palaces supply a new and striking commentary on the familiar passage of Homer describing the ancient populousness of the Cretan cities.[41]

It soon appeared that the Minoans had also used monumental relief sculpture to decorate some wall surfaces. Near the northwest corner of the mound, where Evans suspected that a major entrance to the palace had been located, sizable fragments were discovered of a painted plaster relief of a bull's head (Fig. 49). "It is life-sized, or somewhat over, and modelled in high relief. . . . [It] is the most magnificent monument of Mycenaean

Figure 49

plastic art that has come down to our time . . . full of life and spirit. It combines in a high degree naturalism with grandeur, and it is no exaggeration to say that no figure of a bull at once so powerful and so true was produced by later classical art." Here we can sense again a deep-seated urge to find material not only earlier but "better" than the widely praised original sculpture of the fifth century B.C. that was being recovered in Greece, and particularly at Olympia. And on occasion Evans' imagination is no less fertile than Schliemann's in suggesting historical or mythological associations for his finds. "What a part these creatures [bulls] play here! On the frescoes and reliefs, the chief design of the seals, on a steatite vase, above the gate it may be of the Palace itself. Was not some one or other of these creatures visible on the ruined site in the early Dorian days [after the destruction], which gave the actual tradition of the Bull of Minos?"

In addition to the architectural remains of the palace and the numerous art objects, many inscribed tablets were recovered in the early weeks. When he read the first enthusiastic notice of the Knossos excavations published in *The Times,* John Evans was so pleased that he immediately sent off to his son a draft for £500. In acknowledging the gift, Arthur provided his father with some up-to-the-minute information that shows that written records were still his major concern. "The great discovery is whole deposits, entire or fragmentary, of clay tablets analogous to the Babylonian but with inscriptions in the prehistoric script of Crete. I must have about seven hundred pieces by now. . . . These inscriptions engraved on the wet clay are evidently the work of practised scribes. . . . A certain number of characters are pictographic, showing what the subject of the documents was. Thus in one chamber occurred a series with chariots and horses' heads on them, others show vases [Fig. 50] . . ."

Figure 50

In his first formal report to the scholarly world Evans gives an excellent description of the tablets found in the campaign of 1900.

Of the clay records brought to light the vast majority of pieces, in number over nine hundred, present a linear form of script. The other hieroglyphic class was sparsely represented. . . . Not only were the clay slips extremely friable but the slightest touch of moisture was liable to reduce them to pulp and a few specimens on a tray which had been wetted during a nocturnal storm, owing to a leakage in the roof of the Turkish house which served as our headquarters, became a shapeless mass of clay. The marvel is that any of these clay tablets should have resisted the natural damp of the soil, and in many cases their survival was due to the extra baking they received through the conflagration of the building. In this way fire—so fatal elsewhere to historic libraries!—has acted as a preservative of these earlier records. . . . The linear tablets are for the most part elongated slips of hand-moulded clay with wedge-shaped ends from about two inches to about eight inches in length and about ⅗-inch to about three inches broad. . . . These have the inscription generally in one or two lines along their greatest length. Others, however, are broader, with the inscription in several lines across their lesser diameter. . . . The larger tablets are scored with horizontal lines for the guidance of the scribe. They are generally written only on one side but some show a short endorsement and others present a full inscription on both faces . . .

Evans then proceeds to characterize the inscriptions themselves.

About seventy characters seem to have been in common use. . . . A certain number of quasi-pictorial characters also occur which seem to have an ideographic or determinative meaning. The numerals show a certain parallelism with the Egyptian. The system is decimal [Fig. 51]. The units, consisting of upright lines, are practically the same as the

Figure 51

Egyptian. The tens are generally horizontal lines. . . . The hundreds are circles. . . . The thousands are circles with four spurs. From the frequency of ciphers on these tablets it is evident that a great number of them refer to accounts relating to the royal stores and arsenal. The general purport of the tablet, moreover, is in many cases supplied by the introduction of one or more pictorial figures. Thus on a series of tablets . . . occur designs of a typical Mycenaean chariot, . . . a horse's head and what seems to be a cuirass, sometimes replaced by the outlines of an ingot.

Some of these ideographic symbols appeared to offer the possibility of comparisons with shapes—and therefore dates—of known objects or representations.

Among other subjects thus represented were human figures, perhaps slaves, houses or barns, swine, ears of corn, various kinds of trees, saffron flowers, and vessels of clay of various shapes. . . . On one tablet two ox-heads are seen associated with a vase of the Vapheio type, both of gold, that also occur among the Keft offerings [in Egyptian tombs]. This identity of shape seems to indicate approximate contemporaneity and makes it probable that some at least of the tablets go back to the beginning of the fifteenth century B.C. . . . The words on the tablets are at times divided by upright lines, and from the average number of letters included between these it is probable that the signs have a syllabic value. The inscriptions are invariably written from left to right.

As a matter of fact, after years of intensive work and a major publication, Evans did not really get very far beyond this point in the interpretation of the tablets. Here he goes on to enunciate a policy that, if he had carried it out promptly and fully, might have resulted in a much earlier decipherment. "The full material has first to be collected by the thorough exploration of the as yet unexcavated portion of the Palace. It will then be possible to publish photographic reproductions of the whole, supplemented by careful copies of the inscriptions from the originals, together with complete tables of the letters, numerals and other signs." And as part of a footnote he adds, "No effort will be spared to publish the whole collected material at the earliest possible moment. The Oxford University Press . . . has undertaken the publication, and has already set in hand the preliminary work, including a Mycenaean Fount."

It is reminiscent of Schliemann's experience with loosely supervised workmen that some of the Knossos tablets were smuggled out of the dig and appeared on the market in Athens. Ironically enough, the offending workman's name was Aristides, whose illustrious classical ancestor was nicknamed "The Just." And to intensify the irony, the theft was proved in court by producing other tablets from the same deposit that, though un-decipherable, showed similar formulae.

Although the earlier history of the site does not concern us directly, it may be mentioned that the "Mycenaean" was not the only horizon dis-covered in the first campaign. A deep sounding in the unbuilt area that was later recognized as the great central court of the palace produced "black primitive pottery . . . some incised, and a good many celts [stone hand axes]. . . . Here we have an early site untouched in the middle of a later settlement: from religious reasons (?)." This offhand and tentative theory illustrates a tendency typical of most archaeologists—and particu-larly of Evans—to adduce religious reasons to "explain" any and every enigmatic discovery.

On June 2, 1900, the first phenomenally successful season at Knossos ended. The expedition had dug for nine weeks and had uncovered "about two acres of the Palace site." Evans explains that the very large area laid bare was "largely due to the relatively small depth below the surface at which the actual remains lay." And he continues: "The floor level varied from about 13 inches in the zone immediately above the Southern Terrace to somewhat over 10 feet in the Northern Step-way. . . . It is no exaggera-tion to say, that on no previously excavated site in the Greek lands have so many ancient relics been found within the same space at so slight a depth below the surface of the ground."

Evans is also at pains to point out the careful methods employed.

The earth was removed in layers from the surface, and owing to this method some large pieces of fallen fresco which might otherwise have been ruined by the pick were preserved intact. Wherever the earth showed traces of containing small objects it was thoroughly sifted, . . . Owing to this minute examination many small objects of great value were recovered which would otherwise have been irretrievably lost. Among these may be especially mentioned pieces of inscribed linear tablets, clay "labels" of the hieroglyphic class, and . . . clay impressions of seals, a class of object never before observed in any excavation of a Mycenaean site. That such had existed elsewhere, however, is only too probable, and the example of the native antiquary's [Minos Kalo-kairinos of Candia] dig on the Palace site itself, in which fragments of inscribed clay tablets were thrown out without attracting observation, shows how necessary is a minute examination of all the earth in which finds occur.

While Evans' criticism of the carelessness of earlier excavators is no doubt justified, it is fairly obvious from these remarks that his own attention was concentrated on recovering the objects themselves rather than on minute observation of the circumstances of their discovery *in place.*

Even in the first year Evans could utilize information already available from the Greek mainland and Egypt to place his discovery within at least tentative chronological limits. Above a neolithic level an "early" or "Kamares*" palace should date back at least to 2000; and over its ruins a "late" or "Mycenaean" palace persisted until the fourteenth or thirteenth century. (The chronological chart on p. 167–68 may help here and following.)

In spite of the complicated arrangement of some parts of the interior of the Palace, a great unity prevails throughout the main lines of its ground-plan. . . . Certain later modifications of the original plan have been noted . . . indicative of various epochs in the history of the building. . . . Many of these more massive constructions really date back to the "Kamáres" period. . . . The Magazines* [long, narrow storage rooms] in their earliest form, and with them their great stone door-jambs, go back to the latest pre-Mycenaean period. A very close parallel to these jambs and magazines has now been found by the Italian explorers in a prehistoric Palace at Phaestos and in that case the great bulk of the associated ceramic remains belongs to the Kamáres period. It is also observable in the great Eastern Court [at Knossos—later recognized as the Central Court] and certain chambers that the pavement level lies immediately over the Neolithic clay stratum and therefore probably represents also the first "Palace level," in other words that already in use at the time when the Kamáres pottery was produced. . . . To this stratum belongs the Egyptian diorite figure [of a certain User, perhaps a merchant or ambassador at the court of Knossos], the date of which has been approximately fixed at 2,000 B.C. . . ."

The period of the "second palace" and particularly the date of its "final" destruction will, of course, concern us most.

The later changes in the Palace and the arrangement and decoration of the rooms as revealed by the excavations were no doubt the work of the Mycenaean Age. . . . The later pottery was of the mature Mycenaean class, analogous to that found at Mycenae, Ialysos and Tell-el-Amarna, in which latter case the associations take us to the Age of Akhenaten (c. 1383–1365 B.C.). . . . Only a single piece of iron . . . was found. . . . Nothing was more striking . . . than the absence of all remains later than the flourishing Mycenaean period. . . . On the whole it seems difficult to bring down the period of the destruction of the Palace later than the thirteenth century B.C.

The first campaign made Evans realize that complete excavation would require years of work and a great deal of money. Public appeals for funds were not very successful, a result that seems not to have greatly disappointed the director. At any rate, in a revealing and prophetic letter to his father he writes:

> It is just as well that I should be in a more or less independent position. . . . The Palace of Knossos was my idea and my work, and it turns out to be such a find as one could not hope for in a lifetime or in many lifetimes. . . . If you like to give me the money personally that also would be quite acceptable. But we may as well keep some of Knossos in the family! I am quite resolved not to have the thing entirely "pooled" for many reasons, but largely because I must have sole control of what I am personally undertaking. With other people it may be different, but I know it is so with me; my way may not be the best but it is the only way I can work.

## THE SEASON OF 1901

Improved political conditions in Crete had opened the way for other excavations too. The Italians Halbherr and Luigi Pernier had begun to uncover another palace at Phaistos in the south. As on the mainland in the case of Mycenae and Tiryns, the Knossos palace had apparently had at least one contemporary rival or colleague. And an intrepid young American female, Harriet Boyd, had begun the explorations that were soon to lead to the discovery of a less pretentious but well-preserved hill-top town at Gournia on the north coast some thirty-five miles east of Knossos.

As one turns to Evans' report on his second campaign, it is startling to glance at Plate 1, "Ground plan of the Palace of Knossos, showing its extent as excavated in 1901." Except for unexplored areas in the northeast and southeast corners, the general impression is that almost the whole ground plan of the palace as we now know it had already been cleared in the first two seasons (Fig. 52).

One urgent problem was that of protecting the architectural remains. The Throne Room was already showing serious deterioration from the weather, and Evans decided that it had to be roofed. In effect, the method used here set the course for the whole program of architectural conservation and restoration at Knossos. "This necessity and the desire to avoid the introduction of any incongruous elements amid such surroundings," says Evans, "determined me to reproduce the form of the original Mycenaean columns. An exact model both for the shape and colouring was happily at hand in the small fresco of the temple façade [in the miniature "Grand Stand" composition] . . ." It was also becoming clear that parts

| 1 | Cupbearer Fresco | 10 | Priest-King Relief |
|---|---|---|---|
| 2 | Throne Room | 11 | Toreador Fresco |
| 3 | "Blue Boy" Fresco | 12 | Khyan Alabastron Lid |
| 4 | Grandstand Fresco | 13 | Faience Plaques (Town Mosaic) |
| 5 | Bull Relief | 14 | Palace Shrine |
| 6 | Magazines | 15 | Temple Repositories |
| 7 | Grand Staircase | 16 | Theatral Area |
| 8 | Sculptured Frieze Blocks | 17 | West Court |
| 9 | La Parisienne and Campstool Frescoes | 18 | Central Court |

Figure 52

of the palace had had at least two stories above the court level. Evans called in the architect Theodore Fyfe and after him Christian Doll. They set to work to record or calculate the exact position of the vanished wooden columns and beams and to simulate the original crude brick and timber walls with reinforced concrete.

In a later report, when excavation and restoration was further along, Evans eloquently defends his solution.

It being in any case necessary to obtain strong and durable supports for the upper structures, the *minimum* of incongruity seemed to be secured by restoring the columns themselves in their original form but in stone with a plaster facing in place of wood. . . . This work . . . involved most difficult structural problems and a large use of iron girders in place of the original architraves and cross-beams. . . . The actual size of the architraves and beams could be ascertained from some large charred sections actually preserved. The stones, moreover, of the upper flight of stairs and of their balustrades had been carefully marked and numbered so that they could be re-set in their original positions [Fig. 53]. . . . As a whole, the effect of this legitimate process of recon-stitution is such that it must appeal to the historic sense of the most unimaginative. To a height of over twenty feet there rise before us the grand staircase [in the east or domestic wing] and columnar hall of approach [in the west or public wing], practically unchanged since they were traversed, some three and a half millenniums back, by Kings and Queens of Minos' stock, on their way from the scenes of their public and sacerdotal functions in the West Wing of the Palace, to the more private quarters of the Royal household.

Although expert opinion may still be far from unanimous, generations of visitors to the site would warmly endorse Evans' decision. The excavator is always duty-bound either to protect the remains of an important build-ing or else to cover it over again with earth. Any type of permanent pro-tection is, of course, very expensive; but funds for this purpose as well as for adequate publication should be guaranteed before anyone is permitted to move on to another site. What kind of protection, then? A simple fence and roof or a genuine attempt at reconstructing the original appearance of the building? The former solution is cheaper and safer but unlikely to be as satisfying or evocative for the average visitor. Evans opted for the sec-ond and thereby incurred not only very heavy expenses but also inevitable (and partially justified) charges of going beyond the evidence.

Some of the characteristics of Minoan architecture and its essential dif-ferences from the mainland palaces were beginning to impress themselves on Evans and Mackenzie. To the east of the central court the Hall of the Double Axes was being uncovered and restored. In spite of certain similari-ties, Evans is wary about applying the term "megaron" to such halls.

It will be seen that my restored plan does not correspond with that of the type of Megaron with which we are familiar at Tiryns and Mycenae, with its quadruple group of columns clustering round the hearth. But it exactly answers to the "Minoan" halls of Crete as seen in the Palace of Phaestos. . . . The method of construction answers to a more south-ern type, in which the hearth no longer forms the fixed centre of the

Figure 53

Megaron, warmth being probably supplied when necessary by some
movable brazier like the modern Greek *thermastra*. A central roof-
opening, which could also serve as an outlet for smoke, being thus
unnecessary, it was found more convenient to have the opening, which
was still necessary for light, at the further end of the hall. This broad
well for light was probably provided above with a kind of lantern or
clear-storey as a partial shelter from rain [Fig. 54].

On the other hand, a close analogy to an architectural feature already
known on the mainland was demonstrated by a number of fragments of

Figure 54

frieze blocks in "porphyry-like limestone" found fallen in the northwest basement area. The pattern in relief consists of elongated half-rosettes separated by vertical members. "It belongs," says Evans, "to the same class as the inlaid alabaster band from the vestibule of the Palace at Tiryns, and the friezes found at Mycenae, as well as that depicted on the small Temple Fresco of Knossos itself. The present arrangement . . . finds its nearest parallel in the small glass paste relief, from the beehive tomb at Menidi [in Attica]." As we have seen, the whole scheme is reminiscent of the triglyph-metope frieze above the columns in the Doric order of classical architecture.

In the same area of the palace Evans and Mackenzie recovered a large number of fresco fragments, originally forming "zones of human figures which when perfect must have been about a fifth the natural height. The figures . . . were more carelessly executed than the Cup-bearer or those of the miniature frescoes." One piece preserved the head and upper body of a figure that was later, under the name "La Parisienne," to attract enthusiastic attention (Fig. 55). But Evans does not seem particularly struck by her at the time of discovery. "The bust of a girl characterised by a very large eye and brilliant vermeil lips as well as by the usual curling black hair displays a high-bodied [bodiced?] dress of quite a novel character. It is looped up at the shoulder into a bunch—blue with red and black

Figure 55

stripes—from which the fringed ends hang down behind . . ." Other associated fragments show still more unusual features, although Evans does
not remark on them in any detail. "The men, distinguished by their conventional red tint, seem to have been clad in short-sleeved tunics, blue
and yellow with black stripes, which descend to their ankles. . . . Two
of the fragments show goblets held in men's hands. Both of these are of
the high-stemmed type presenting in outline some resemblance to a
champagne glass, but with a handle on either side of the rim" (Fig. 56).
This so-called kylix* was one of the most distinctive and popular vase
shapes on the mainland in Mycenaean times.

Another fragmentary relief sculpture in painted plaster, as fine in its
way as the charging bull, turned up in the southern section; and again
Evans points a parallel with the mainland.

The first important piece brought to light showed the back and ear
of a male head wearing a crown, the upper part of which consisted of
a row of sloping *fleurs-de-lys*. . . . The *fleur-de-lys* ornament recurred
in the shape of a collar formed of links of this shape round the neck
of a male torso found near the relief of the crown. . . . It is executed

Figure 56

in the same low relief, and . . . shows an extraordinarily advanced style
of modelling. . . . The reliefs are all life-size, and the skin was originally
coloured a reddish brown. . . . The ornament itself is typically Mycenaean, and its derivation from the pure lily type with the stamens
attached may be traced on the gold-plaited inlaid dagger from the Fifth
Akropolis Grave [at Mycenae]. Of the natural lily as a Mycenaean hair
ornament we have an example in the coiffure of the Goddess and her
attendant handmaidens on the great signet from Mycenae. . . . But was
the personage who wears it in this case royal or divine? . . . [There is] a

real presumption that in this crowned head we see before us a Mycenaean King.

Additional fragments were later discovered, and the reconstructed composition was named the "Priest-King fresco" (Fig. 57).

A stonecutter's workshop held many objects of marble, bone, jasper, steatite and crystal in an unfinished state. Vessels in nearby basement rooms yielded carbonized remains of various seeds such as beans, and heaps of burned grain could be detected. The numerous long narrow rooms in the western basement area were lined with rows of great storage jars for wine and olive oil. It was clear that the palace had been not only a magnificent royal residence but also a more or less self-sufficient center for collecting,

Figure 57

storing and processing agricultural products and for manufacturing luxury goods.

From representations on gems, Evans had for some time been familiar with the favorite Cretan sport of bull baiting. But he is particularly intrigued to discover from fragments of a fine fresco panel that there were female as well as male acrobats (Fig. 58).

Figure 58

The most interesting feature . . . is the appearance, beside the male performers in this dangerous sport, of female *toreadors,* distinguished by their white skin, . . . the blue and red diadems round their brows, and their somewhat curlier *coiffures,* but otherwise attired in precisely the same way as the "cow-boys," with a loin-cloth and very narrow metallic girdle and striped socks and slippers. . . . We have there nothing of the mere catching of bulls, wild or otherwise, as seen on the Vaphio Cups. . . . They belong to the arena, and afford the clearest evidence that the lords of Mycenaean Knossos glutted their eyes with shows in which maidens as well as youths were trained to grapple with what was then regarded as the king of animals. The sports of the amphitheatre, which have never lost their hold on the Mediterranean world, may thus in Crete at least be traced back to prehistoric times. It may well be that, long before the days when enslaved barbarians were "butchered to make a Roman holiday," captives, perhaps of gentle blood, shared the same fate within sight of the "House of Minos," and that the legends of Athenian prisoners devoured by the Minotaur preserve a real tradition of these cruel sports.

Evans had already distinguished a class of large, handsomely decorated amphoras* (Fig. 59), to which he gave the name "Palace Style*." Since this ceramic style has played an important part in later theories of the relationship between Crete and the Greek mainland, it is interesting to

Figure 59

note his earliest observations. He speaks of it as "the magnificent style of vase-painting prevalent at Knossos in the great days of the Palace." And he goes on to say: "Nothing among the hitherto published Mycenaean ceramic types exactly corresponds with these, but Mr. J. H. Marshall, who kindly undertook the reconstruction of the Knossian fragments, has been able to identify a large vase from a recently discovered tomb of Mycenae, and fragments of another from the Vaphio tomb (left undescribed by its discoverer) as belonging to the same fabric, and with good reason regards these and some other isolated specimens found on the mainland of Greece as of Knossian importation." Who is to say whether this conclusion was originally in Marshall's or Evans' mind? In any case, the conviction was growing on Evans that, given two closely similar artefacts, the one found on the mainland and the other in Crete, the mainland example must be an import and not vice versa.

One of the neatest synchronisms between Crete and Egypt developed in the course of clearing the northwest corner of the palace. Under a floor of "Mycenaean" date, they discovered a

> well-marked archaeological stratum containing a large proportion of charcoal and representing the burnt remains of an earlier structure. In this deposit immediately under the Mycenaean wall-foundations, at a depth of about 16 inches below the later floor-level . . . was the lid of an Egyptian alabastron upon the upper face of which was finely engraved a cartouche containing the name and divine titles of the Hyksôs King Khyan. . . . The minimum date to which it is possible to refer it, can . . . hardly be lower than 1700 B.C. . . . On the other hand, the early phase of Mycenaean civilisation represented by the chamber built above the earlier stratum in which the lid lay, shows many points of contact with the Egypt of Thothmes III. Yet this later structure, which may thus be taken to go back to the fifteenth or sixteenth century B.C., was separated by over a foot of deposit from the more ancient Palace layer. . . . This result has a very important bearing on the date of the early part of the Palace fabric as a whole . . .

## THE SEASON OF 1902

Evans seems to have thought that this would probably be the last campaign at Knossos. But the residential or "domestic" area to the east of the central court proved to have extended to a much greater depth than expected, and its excavation posed difficult problems of reconstruction.

Evans was already aware that many of the objects (including inscribed tablets) found in basement rooms were in fact fallen from collapsed upper floors. But an interesting group of plaques made of faience* (colored glass paste poured into molds) proved that even ordinary houses were multi-story. The plaques had apparently been inlaid in zones and panels to decorate a wooden chest, and a large number of the better-preserved specimens depict exterior views of houses. They show two, three and even four stories, windows in the upper floors, clerestories and outlines of brick and timber wall construction. Since they were discovered under the pavement of the later phase of the palace, the necessary conclusion was that such pretentious private houses had a long history at Knossos. Other associated plaques, even more fragmentary, showed humans, animals and vegetation. "The warriors and city recall the siege scene of the silver vase [from Mycenae]. . . . The homes of civic life within the walls, the goats and oxen without, the fruit trees and running water, suggest a more literal comparison with the Homeric description of the scenes of peace and war as illustrated on Achilles' shield[42] than can be supplied from any other known source."

Inscribed tablets were continuing to appear in large numbers, and new evidence showed that writing had not been confined to formal archives. An inscription painted on a vase as part of the decorative scheme "recalls the inscribed vases of Classical Greece and is the only specimen hitherto known belonging to the 'Mycenaean Period.' " Furthermore, the interior of two plain cups revealed linear writing in ink. "The lines of the letters show occasionally a tendency to divide, which may point to the use of a reed pen. . . . These ink-written inscriptions . . . give us the first direct evidence of the existence of literary materials . . . other than the inscribed clay tablets. . . . Parchment may have been used, and the old Cretan tradition that palm leaves had once been used for writing should not be left out of account."

Almost everywhere, but especially in the western quarter of the palace, Evans saw religious connections. Like many archaeologists, he had a tendency to label as cult furniture almost any object to which an obvious utilitarian function could not be assigned. From such objects and from what he interpreted as cult scenes on rings and gems he was developing a series of ingenious hypotheses about Minoan religion. In the previous year he had published a long account of the evidence for a "Mycenaean Tree and Pillar Cult." Gradually he enlarges the catalogue of religious symbols and representations—the double ax, the bull, the horns of consecration, the Dove Goddess, the Protectress of Animals, the "divine pair." The double ax is the "labrys"; and the palace with a double ax incised on many of its wall blocks is "the place of the double axe," *i.e.,* the mysterious "labyrinth." In this campaign he discovered in the southeastern quarter a "small square chamber [that] proved to be an actual Palace Shrine with the vessels of offering, votive figures, idols, and cult objects still in position" (Fig. 60). He concludes that this installation represents "the latest period during which this part of the Palace was occupied." He points to the "crude" appearance of much of the shrine's furniture (especially the figurines) and suggests that "the contents . . . derive a special interest from the decadent period to which the bulk of them belong, since they afford a convincing proof that essentially the same religious cult . . . survived to the very latest period of occupation."

What absolute date did Evans now have in mind for the "very latest period of occupation" of the palace? He had earlier mentioned the thirteenth century; but it appears that, at least for the inscribed tablets, he is gradually coming to the conclusion that this is too late. At any rate, in describing a group of tablets that show both triangular and leaf-shaped

Figure 60

swords or daggers, he says, "The presence of the leaf-shaped form in the Palace is of great interest, as there can be little doubt that it is of Northern origin. It is not too much to say that the whole chronology of the European Bronze Age is affected by this discovery, which shows that this leaf-shaped type of sword had been developed before the approximate date of 1400 B.C." Thus, as early as 1902 Evans had decided that these particular tablets (and presumably all of the documents soon to be called Linear B) cannot date later than 1400. It is not at all clear how much later he now considered the shrine and other features belonging to the "very latest period of occupation."

It must have been about this time that Duncan Mackenzie submitted an article entitled "The Pottery of Knossos" for publication in the *Journal of Hellenic Studies*. It is a very thorough review of the evidence from the first three seasons at Knossos; and it casts its shadow far into the future. Inevitably, one wonders whether Evans' own developing theories were absorbed into it or whether they were at least in part derived from it. Mackenzie distinguishes "three distinct strata of deposit." The lowest is "prehistoric, neolithic," with a thickness "starting from the virgin soil and extending upwards to the beginnings of the painted series averaging about 20 feet." Above it comes a deposit in which "we have the first appearance of painted Cretan ware . . . and, where undisturbed, underlying the later deposit of the palace. . . . This includes what may be termed the Early and Middle Minoan classes." As for the third major division, "Last of all comes a 'late Minoan' stratum, represented all over the palace region down to the floor-levels. . . . The later phase of this class covers the fabrics elsewhere described as Mycenaean."

We cannot follow the detailed description, but some of Mackenzie's basic points require our attention. He insists on the native character of Minoan ceramics, undisturbed by outside influence, from the beginning to the end of the Bronze Age. There are no "sharp breaks" in its evolution that would signal foreign intrusion. Seemingly abrupt changes are ingeniously explained by what "may be generalised into a law for all undisturbed floor-deposits, to wit, that house-floors being regularly swept do not contain a deposit record of the whole period, during which the floored space was used but only of the close of that period when the floored area for whatever reason came to be abandoned, and that as a rule there is a record of the final period itself only if the abandonment has been an enforced and sudden one. A quiet flitting would never have left behind it the series of beautiful vessels, more or less complete, in fragments found on these Minoan floors."

Mackenzie seems already to be close to the conviction, later to be so firmly held by Evans, that *all* the major pottery types found at Knossos must have been developed there—or at least in Crete. In the case of the distinctive polychrome ware found in the "Kamares" or Middle Minoan levels it turned out that he was correct. "The scantiness and isolation of this ware in all deposits in which it has been found outside Crete are in such complete contrast to the richness of the Knossian deposits that no further proof is needed to bring us to the conclusion that Crete itself is the true source of the similar ware found elsewhere, as in Melos, Thera, Tiryns, Mycenae, Egypt."

But more sweeping assumptions creep into the discussion of the material from the upper levels. He describes the Late Minoan or "Mature Knossian period" as an "era of renewed life . . . which saw the building of the second palace at Knossos." It is characterized by such features as pottery of "a fully developed Palace style native to Knossos [that] occurs in one general context with the magnificent series of stone vases, with the frescoes of the great period, and with the written records of the Palace that now adorn the museum at Candia."

Coming to the latest pottery found in the palace, he can hardly hold that purely quantitative evidence shows that Knossos or Crete as a whole was still the nucleus.

While pottery in the grand Palace style of Knossos is comparatively rare outside of Crete, the style of pottery which is most clearly characterized by its conventional rendering of foliage and flowers is found in a much wider context, embracing the whole of the East Mediterranean basin. This decadent style at Knossos is typical of a period when the palace is only partially inhabited and probably is no longer a royal residence. The Bügelkanne [stirrup vase] which is rare in the great days of the palace is characteristic of this third period. . . . In this latest period thousands of kylix-cups, amphorae and jars exist in this pale yellow clay without any decoration. The perfectly uniform character of style in the Aegean area at this period is at once apparent on the comparison of wares from different centres. . . . If we take the proved instances of importation into particular centres in connection with the perfect uniformity of style prevalent at this period at all the centres that came into account, the hypothesis of production at one centre becomes strengthened. Furtwängler and Loeschcke [who had published in 1886 the authoritative account of Mycenaean pottery as it was known up to their time] with the evidence before them when they wrote, thought this centre must have been Mycenae. With the additional evidence before us now, taken in connection with the fact of ascertained importation into Melos and Egypt, it is more probable that this centre was Crete, to which Melos on the one hand and Egypt on the other are next-door neighbours on either side.

Here we find formulated in 1902 a number of basic ideas on which Evans later staked his reputation—the tripartite chronological scheme; the contemporaneity of the clay tablets with the spectacular Palace Style or "empire" pottery; a partial and later habitation responsible for the "decadent" pottery that was often undecorated and in shapes such as stirrup jars.

## THE SEASON OF 1903

During the fourth season the excavation of the Royal Villa, to the northeast of the palace, showed that the complex of monumental buildings extended well beyond the palace proper, and Evans continued to find the ruins of comfortable villas abutting on the palace and presumably belonging to court functionaries. But what he considers "in many respects the culminating point of interest in the whole four years' excavation" was the discovery of the Temple Repositories within the palace itself.

In most of the long narrow basement storage chambers, or magazines (Fig. 61), and in the long corridor onto which they opened, a series of rectangular cists had been cut below floor level and covered with paving blocks. All of the cists showed very careful construction and lining. Most of them had apparently been meant as receptacles to catch the oil or wine that spilled from cracked pithoi or escaped during their filling or emptying. Some may have been for the storage of liquids or grain in years of high productivity when taxes in kind exceeded expectations. But bits of gold

Figure 61

foil in a few cists indicated that they had at some time been used to contain objects of precious metals, of which the palace seemed to have been
so thoroughly looted. These considerations "made it desirable to subject
the floors of the small chambers about the Pillar Rooms [an area in the
central 'religious' section just west of the main court] to the same searching examination. . . . Might there not here too lie concealed beneath the
pavements earlier repositories belonging to the Palace Shrine?" Evans
was becoming increasingly sure that "there was a sacerdotal as well as a
royal side to the Minoan dynasts of Knossos. It would seem that there
were here, as in early Anatolia, Priest-Kings; and old tradition, that made
Minos son and 'Companion' of Zeus and a Cretan Moses, is once more
seen to have a basis in fact."

Sunk into the floor of a room just south of the Throne Room were
two small rectangular stone-lined cists, perhaps for the storage of oil, which
were apparently contemporary with the latest use of the room. Evans de-

cided to probe around and beneath them. At first the earth was red from the effects of fire; then it became dark and mixed with charred wood and fragments of gold foil. At a depth of about 44 inches was a layer of terra-cotta vases packed closely together. Another 44 inches deeper still the pottery ceased, and the earth grew "fatter and more compact." Finally in a layer about 17 inches thick, at the bottom of what turned out to be a much larger stone-built cist or repository,

> abundant fragments of faience began to come to light. . . . This faience series included figures of a Snake Goddess and votaries, their votive robes and girdles, cups and vases with painted designs, flowers, fruit, foliage, and shells in the round, small reliefs of cows and calves and wild goats with their kids, a variety of plaques for inlaying, and quantities of beads. Among the other relics were an ivory handle and inlays, bone plumes of arrows, doubtless of a votive character, the usual gold foil, a clay tablet and roundels, presenting inscriptions of a linear class different from that of the later period of the Palace, numerous clay seal impressions, many of them of a religious character, and a marble cross of orthodox Greek shape [Fig. 62].

In addition there were painted sea shells, animal horns, burned grain and steatite "Libation Tables," all of which reinforced the impression that the contents of a shrine had been buried here for safekeeping in time of danger or for some other reason.

The presence of a second even more substantially built repository was detected beside the first. The stratification was identical, but the contents were quite different. "Faience objects were here wanting, with one notable exception—a missing part namely of the figure of a Snake Goddess. . . . This circumstance pointed to a considerable disturbance of the contents of the other depository at some period, and was probably due to plunderers at the time of what seems to have been the first great catastrophe of the Later Palace." The contents of the second repository contained a very large amount of gold foil, some of it showing "traces of an elaborate design in relief apparently of circular form and recalling some of the thin gold disks found in the Akropolis tombs at Mycenae." There were gold and crystal leaves and petals, apparently for inlay in chests or other objects of some disintegrated material. Evans suggests that the heavier construction of this repository was "possibly because it contained gold treasure while the value of the objects in the other cist was more preponderantly artistic."

True to his central interest, Evans first discusses the inscribed objects. He recognizes that they represent "a distinctive form of linear writing" as compared to the hundreds of tablets discovered elsewhere in the palace. And he is able to parallel their "typical characters . . . the system of

Figure 62

numeration, the shape of the tablet itself and of the sealed disks" with a newly discovered archive found by the Italians at the "Palace or Royal Villa of Hagia Triada near Phaestos" (Fig. 63). He then proceeds to lay the foundation for a major and important distinction in Cretan writing systems.

> This early system of linear script—which may be conveniently termed Class A as opposed to Class B of the latest Palace Period at Knossos— had a wide extension in the island. An inscribed clay tablet found by the British School at Palaikastro belongs to the same class, as also the characters on a clay disk found by Miss Boyd at Gournia in 1903. There can be little doubt, moreover, that the signs on the Dictaean Libation Table [from the Psychro cave in east central Crete] fit on the same system. At Knossos itself certain graffito inscriptions on pottery and those of another isolated tablet prove to belong to the same category.

He naturally proceeds to ask, "What, then, is the relation of Class A to Class B?" After comparing the forms and the distribution and date of

Figure 63

the known examples, he concludes: "We are thus reduced to the conclusion that Class B, though of later appearance in the Palace, is fundamentally a parallel rather than a derivative system. It seems to be an alternative form of linear script, of more or less equal antiquity, which, owing to some political change, came to the fore during the latest Palace period at the expense of the other. At Hagia Triada there is no evidence of any such supersession of Class A."

The remarks that follow echo Mackenzie's earlier pronouncement; and both cast a long shadow into the future. "The change in the official style . . . is a phenomenon which seems best to explain itself on the hypothesis of a dynastic revolution. That there was no change of race appears from various indications. The two systems of script, though divergent, show a large common element. . . . It thus appears that the language was essentially the same. . . . There is no ethnic break, and the culture exhibited by the remains of the latest period of the Palace on the whole represents the natural outgrowth of the penultimate period of its history to which the contents of the Temple Repositories belong." This hypothesis (for that is all it ever was) gradually became dogma during the next half century.

We cannot follow the lengthy description of the unique and lovely faience objects. They now represent Minoan art at its best, and it seems odd to find Evans remarking that "there was nothing to prepare us for [their] extraordinary variety, the beauty and the technical perfection." Yet on reflection we realize that the palace had been thoroughly plundered of movable and precious contents. This discovery was, in a way, as startlingly new as the furnishings of Schliemann's Shaft Graves. Molds found along with the objects made from them left no doubt that they were the product of a native palace industry. They reinforce the evidence for long-term creative use by Cretans of technical processes such as sculpture in faience, which they originally learned from Egypt. The exquisite figurines provided new detail on feminine costume and opened for Evans a new dimension of Cretan religion in the Snake Cult. And he believes that the cross, originally a solar symbol depicting the sun's rays, became an actual object of worship in Minoan cult.

One more revelation of the 1903 campaign calls for mention. In following one of the characteristic narrow paved streets in the deep fill northwest of the palace, a "stepped area" was uncovered consisting of two series of stone steps or seats at right angles to one another and with a rectangular paved area delimited by their lower lines and by walls on the remaining sides (Fig. 64). It became clear that these "steps" did not lead anywhere and therefore must be very low seats accommodating between 400 and 500 spectators. A series of comparable seats in parallel straight lines had been discovered on the north edge of the west court at Phaistos.

Figure 64

A suggestion, doubtless taken from the great stairs and stepped approaches of the Minoan Palaces, has here developed into a structure which itself is no kind of approach, but the earliest existing example of a veritable theatre. . . . What performances, it may be asked, are likely to have been given in the paved area? The favourite Minoan sport is ruled out, since the enclosure was in no wise adapted for a bull ring. Shows of pugilists . . . may well have taken place here [boxers are depicted in Minoan art]. In spite of its rectangular shape . . . the area would have been also well adapted for dances, possibly of a ceremonial kind like those of the original Theatre in classical Greece.

After reviewing the evidence on gems and frescoes for a high development of the dance in Minoan Crete, Evans suggests that "it is difficult to refuse the conclusion that this first of theatres . . . supplies a material foundation for the Homeric tradition of the famous 'choros' [dancing place] 'like that which once upon a time in wide Knossos Daidalos fashioned for Ariadne of the fair tresses.' "[43] And in a particularly appealing gambit connecting ancient and modern customs, Evans goes on to say that when Dörpfeld and his party came to Knossos on their annual visit to see the newest excavation results, they were entertained in this very theater with a dance by the workmen and their wives, "a dance, may be, as ancient in its origin as the building in which it took place."

## THE SEASON OF 1904

The fifth campaign was mainly devoted to examining a large cemetery and to a more detailed study of the palace stratigraphy and chronology. In his report for that year Evans published a "Diagrammatic Section of Strata, below Pavement of West Court," which (though stratigraphic tests continued over the years) was reproduced without change as the major stratigraphic record in Volume I of *The Palace of Minos* seventeen years later (Fig. 65). Whether or not all major phases of the Bronze Age history of the site were as neatly represented as they appear in the chart, the tests established an impressive depth of over 40 feet of habitation debris.

Some 100 tombs were opened in an area called Zapher Papoura about half a mile north of the palace. They belonged mainly to the period immediately after the "final" destruction. Although there were at least three different grave types, Evans strongly resists any suggestion that intruders might have settled around Knossos. "In truth, the high interest of the Zapher Papoura cemetery lies in the fact that throughout its whole duration it attests a striking continuity of local traditions. To whatever cir-

NORTH ←   SOUTH →

ORIGINAL GROUND SURFACE

LATE MINOAN STRATUM   2.50'

PAVEMENT OF WEST COURT   5.33'

FLOOR LEVEL, MIDDLE MINOAN III  **MIDDLE MINOAN**   1.0'

FLOOR LEVEL,   MIDDLE MINOAN II   .5'

STRATUM BELONGING TO EARLY MINOAN III   .44

STRATUM BELONGING TO EARLY MINOAN II  **EARLY MINOAN**   .66

FLOOR LEVEL, EARLY MINOAN I

(SUB-NEOLITHIC)

**NEOLITHIC STRATUM**   6.43'

VIRGIN ROCK

Figure 65

cumstances was due the great overthrow of the later Palace it did not bring with it any real break in the course of the Late-Minoan culture."

About two miles still farther toward the sea a large Royal Tomb was cleared. It was built of well-cut blocks with a dromos, entrance hall with sepulchral niches on either side and a rectangular main chamber. The upper part of the walls was missing, but the roof of both entrance hall and chamber had apparently been in the form of a pointed tunnel vault— probably a Near Eastern trait. Although it had been thoroughly plundered, the chance finds scattered throughout showed clearly enough that the main burial in a cist cut in the floor of the chamber had been a very rich one. Evans dates the original construction to the end of the Middle Minoan age and quotes his architect Fyfe to the effect that "from structural evidence, we are on the whole justified in regarding the Knossos Tomb as of earlier date than any built tomb on the mainland at Mycenae or elsewhere."

Yet Evans was clearly unhappy with the dearth of tombs to rival the palace that he had found. "It can hardly be supposed indeed," he says, "that Minoan Knossos, which to the last seems to have exercised a dominant influence on the arts of mainland Greece, was unable, during the period which is marked by the great domed chambers of Mycenae, to produce at least their architectural equivalent." But he has to admit that in the Treasury of Atreus at Mycenae "the workmanship is finer, the area covered . . . is over three times as great [as in the Knossos Royal Tomb], and the domed vaulting is in accordance both with static and dynamic principles."

Several fine Palace Style amphoras and other objects show that the tomb was still in use contemporary with the later palace, and Evans speculates as to whether Homer's King Idomeneus might have been buried in it. "The site would have been specially appropriate for the tomb of the Cretan prince who led the largest [actually, not as large as those of Agamemnon and Nestor] naval contingent of any of those who took part in Agamemnon's expedition."[44] There was also plenty of evidence for its continuing use through the end of the Bronze Age and into the Iron Age. This knowledge seems to cause Evans some pain. "The later history of the Royal Tomb in fact curiously reproduces that of the Palace itself. . . . Just as the once royal and seignorial halls were parcelled out and divided up by poorer denizens, so the spacious vault, originally we may believe constructed as a last resting-place for kings of Minoan stock, became in days of ruin and decline a common burial-pit."

Only one other discovery of the 1904 season need detain us. A test pit had been sunk to try to pick up the course of the narrow paved street that led west from the Theatral Area*. The Minoan level proved to contain inscribed tablets and seal impressions, which led to the clearing of a small section just to the north of the road and to the recovery of a very important group of inscribed records (Fig. 67).

These tablets . . . lay within the opening of what seems to have been a basement Magazine, into which the wooden chests containing them had sunk when the floor above collapsed. Of these about fifty referred to chariots . . . the frames, with or without the poles and yokes, appearing on one set, and the wheels by themselves on another. The large expenditure on the last item entailed by the character of the country may be gathered from the fact that one tablet concerns a total amount of 478 wheels. . . . Still more interesting are a series of tablets showing two curved objects. . . . We have here represented the long curving horns of the Cretan Agrimi or Wild-Goat. . . . To what purpose were these pairs of horns applied? There can be little doubt that we have here the raw material for horn bows, such as that of Menelaos [Pandaros? Paris?] . . .[45]

But an even more striking coincidence was still in store.

With the above tablets was found the latter part of one referring to a large amount of arrows [Fig. 66]. The subject of this clay document

Figure 66

was made clear by the repetition of a pictographic figure of an arrow.
The tablets contained a record of two large lots of arrows, one 6010
in number, the other 2630. . . . But what adds an extraordinary interest
to the occurrence of this inscription is the discovery in its immediate
neighbourhood of the remains of two actual depôts of arrows, at a distance of about 10 feet from one another. The depôts had in each case
been contained in wooden boxes with bronze loop handles, and together
with the charred fragments of these were found the clay seals with which
their string binding had been secured. These sealings were three-sided,
the strings passing through their major axis. Both chests had been sealed
in an identical manner, and together afforded a more perfect illustration of the Minoan method of controlling and safeguarding deposits of
valuables than had as yet been supplied by similar remains from Knossos
or elsewhere. . . . Embedded in the *débris* of the chests, once so elaborately sealed and registered, were the carbonized remains of the shafts
and, partly attaching to them, the bronze heads of hundreds of arrows.
. . . The types of the bronze arrowheads are identical with those of the
arrowheads found by Tsountas in a chamber-tomb of the Lower Town

of Mycenae, where they had been laid in two bundles of ten each. . . .
It seems possible that we may be able to locate here the Royal Armoury
and Stables.

## THE SEASON OF 1905

The brief report for 1905 is the last to appear as the leading article in
the *Annual of the British School;* and that season was, in fact, Evans' last
major excavation. The very title, "The Palace of Knossos and Its Dependencies," suggests that the operation is spreading out and leveling off (Fig. 67).

1   Main Palace
2   Royal Villa
3   Armoury
4   Little Palace
5   Evans' Villa Ariadne

Figure 67

Evans had been sure that the roadway running on to the west from the
Theatral Area and past the Armory must have led to a major structure
outside of the immediate palace area. And in fact the ruins of a "large
building on the hill to the West of the Palace," later called the Little Palace,
were discovered. This building "reproduces on a reduced scale the leading
features of the Palace of Knossos as finally remodelled about the beginning of the Late Minoan Period." And Evans' description throws a good
deal of light on his developing theory of the later palace phases.

Here too, as there, were abundant traces of later occupation during the more decadent period of Minoan civilization and of the breaking up of the seignorial halls into the dwellings of humbler denizens. . . . The kings are less, the people more, and the princely building now partially explored, like the great Palace opposite and the "Royal Villa" beyond, is broken up into smaller habitations. . . . But the evidence . . . forbids us to believe that the close of the Palace period at Knossos should be connected with a successful foreign invasion. Rather it points to some internal revolution. . . . In every direction we begin to perceive decadence, but the decadence itself is simply the gradual falling away from the models of the latest Palace style. There is no real break in continuity. . . . But what is still more interesting is the evidence, now for the first time supplied by some fragmentary clay tablets . . . that the fully developed linear script of Minoan Crete continued to be at least partially in use during the later period. It thus appears that the fall of the Palace did not bring with it the absolute extinction of letters, and the true dark ages of Crete were not yet.

He is here definitely leaning again toward a date long after 1400 for some of the Linear B tablets.

We can by now begin to glimpse the reconstruction that was forming in Evans' mind as he finished the first strenuous phase of his Knossos excavations. The Minoan civilization had a strong influence on the Mycenaean mainland from the time of the Mycenae Shaft Graves at least until the destruction of the Knossos palace. But he insists with increasing vehemence that there could be no question of any mainland agency in the destruction itself or in the "decadent" Minoan phase following it.


## D E V E L O P I N G  T H E O R I E S

A radically different interpretation, however, had occurred to Mackenzie about the same time or perhaps a little earlier. In 1904 the full account of the British excavations at Phylakopi on the island of Melos was published. We will recall that Mackenzie had been a very important staff member there before the Knossos excavations began, and it is natural that he had a share in the publication. He is credited with the chapter entitled "The Successive Settlements at Phylakopi and Their Aegeo-Cretan Relations"; and some of the points he makes are strongly influenced by the finds at Knossos.

In explaining the sudden appearance of a megaron of mainland type at Phylakopi, Mackenzie puts forward the following theory:

The Cretan megaron has a special arrangement for lighting in the form of a light-well at the back, which is absent at Phylakopi as at Tiryns, and it has no hearth in the middle of the megaron such as is present both at Tiryns and at Phylakopi. The presence of the light-well and the absence of the central hearth are universal in Crete, and the light-well at the back of the megaron is as conspicuous a feature in the palaces of Phaestos and of Hagia Triada as it is at Cnossos. . . . The inevitable conclusion then, to which we are driven by all the evidence, is that in the closing era of the Third Settlement at Phylakopi, while the bulk of the population remained the same as at an earlier period, the people who built the palace were of an alien race. Whence these people came it may be possible to conjecture as a consequence of what has been said regarding the affinities of the megaron of Phylakopi. When we have pointed out that this megaron has the closest analogies with mainland types like that of Tiryns, we have virtually said that the latest rulers at Phylakopi were a mainland people, and that these formed part of a general wave of immigration into the Aegean of part of the native population of Greece, consequent on the incursion into their homes of new tribes from the north.

Just who Mackenzie thought were these new tribes from the north is never made clear. But he seems to have had in mind quite a major population movement, since he continues:

That this thrusting into the Aegean region of such sections of the late Mycenaean coast-communities as were unable or unwilling to come to terms with the new comers, or were simply ejected from their homes, was part of a general migratory movement, is proved by the fact that the same phenomenon is observable in Crete. One of the causes which contributed towards the break-up of the Minoan civilization in Crete was undoubtedly invasion from the mainland. And it was the same invasion from the mainland that submerged the earlier native civilization at Phylakopi, and that effectively arrested the course of genuine native evolution on the old lines in Minoan Crete. Thus the last "Mycenaean" people at Cnossos, those who destroyed the palace and then reoccupied parts of its ruins, like those who built the palace at Phylakopi, appear as strangers unacquainted with native institutions and forms of life . . .

Here is a revolutionary change from Evans' and Mackenzie's own repeated assertion that there is "no break" until the very end of the Bronze Age that would permit one to even imagine an occupation of any part of Crete by outsiders.

Between 1905 and 1908 Mackenzie also published four long essays, "Cretan Palaces and the Aegean Civilization." As the title implies, his starting point was architecture now, not pottery. But he is even more concerned with the broader historical and cultural implications of the whole complex of recent discoveries on Crete, particularly at Knossos. Again we sense the operation of a positive and incisive (though sometimes erratic) intellect that must have played an important part in the interpretation of the new Cretan discoveries.

The first article was written in reaction to Dörpfeld's theory that, of the two clearly marked major stages in the palaces of Knossos and Phaistos, the earlier reflects a native Cretan architectural tradition, while the later shows such strong analogies with the Greek mainland that it must be the result of an "Achaean" invasion and control of Crete. Following his position in the Phylakopi publication, Mackenzie attributes "any megara of mainland type that have ever been identified in the Aegean" to an invasion and occupation by "Mycenaeans" from the Greek mainland. It was they who destroyed the later Minoan palaces. "To the same period and type apparently belongs the late megaron at Hagia Triada which Halbherr himself regards as really Mycenaean."

Then he attempts to draw a fundamental distinction between these "Mycenaean" invaders of Crete about the time of the destruction of the Knossos palace and a still later group at the very end of the Late Bronze Age. The latter, says Mackenzie, must be Dörpfeld's "Achaeans," who were of Hellenic stock, i.e., Greek speakers.

The general cumulative tendency of the evidence afforded by excavation is to prove that the first wave of invading peoples from the mainland (who were themselves very apparently of Mycenaean race, of the same original stock as the Cretans themselves, and therefore, as we shall see in the sequel, not at all of "Achaean" origin), who were responsible for the final destruction of the later palaces at Phaestos and at Knossos, had themselves appeared too late upon the scene to play any reconstructive rôle in the development of the Minoan Civilization; they were responsible merely for the work of dissolution which, in combination with internal causes of decadence, symptomatic of the final phase, was one of the potent external influences at work in the final break-up of the Aegean Civilization as a whole. When at length the first wave of people of Achaean race and of Hellenic stock appeared upon the stage of Cretan history, the Palace of Knossos, like that of Phaestos, had already long been a venerable ruin. The evidence is fast accumulating in Crete and in the Aegean in favour of the hypothesis as to the continuity of the Mycenaeo-Minoan Civilization down to quite the end of the period after the destruction of the Palace at Knossos which we have called the Third Late Minoan Period (Late Minoan III.).

The second installment in Mackenzie's series is an extremely specula-
tive adventure in early-twentieth-century ethnography, which might perhaps be better ignored if it had not such a close connection with Evans'
later publications involving the North African connections (if not origin)
of the Minoans and many of their culture traits. Mackenzie takes the firm
position that the "Aegean Race" was essentially unchanged from the time
of the newly discovered neolithic at Knossos until the very end of the
Bronze Age. "At every later stage in inquiry we have to be on our guard
against admitting any such hypothesis of derivation from without, as
long as the conception of internal development continues to stand the
test in explanation of the phenomena." Crete itself is "so apparently the
centre of the Aegean civilization" that if there are no internally inconsistent elements observable in the development there, one can assume practical homogeneity.

But where did the people of the Knossos neolithic come from? There
is no neolithic skeletal material, but the evidence for the physical type of
the Bronze Age Cretans "turns out to be entirely in harmony . . . with
Dr. Evans's views regarding the Egypto-Libyan connections of the Aegean
race." In the light of the testimony of modern physical anthropologists to
the highly complex and mixed nature of the ancient Aegean skeletal and
cranial material, this statement is an oversimplification, to say the least.

Mackenzie then discusses the evidence of origin supposedly provided
by Minoan costume. In the scanty clothing of the males "we find the true
explanation of . . . a loin-cloth apparel there, on the hypothesis alone that
this characteristic attire of a warm climate was original to the people of
the Aegean in their original home. And it is apparent that this original
home and this warmer climate could only have been in Africa . . . What
the people of the North [apparently Dörpfeld's "Achaeans"] looked like in
costume, and what they wore next their skins when in the fulness of time
they at length appear upon the scene, is clearly shown on the Warrior
Vase . . . of Mycenae."

The elaborate female costume presents an even tougher problem, but
Mackenzie's Scottish Presbyterian Puritan instincts are fully equal to it.

When we come to consider closely the women's dress of the Aegean,
we do not find a different story as to origin and genesis, notwithstanding
all the apparent disguise of Parisian-like mode revealed to us in the
low bodices, puffed sleeves and multiple skirts worn by the fashionable
court dames of Knossos. People have been scandalized by the exces-
sively low dress of these court ladies into serious reflections as to the
decadent character of the Late Minoan culture in general, without considering that what looks so shamelessly modern, is really the survival

of very primitive custom in dress. . . . We are thus justified in surmising
that the . . . ancestresses of these women wore no bodices and no
multiple skirts. But they still wore their loin-cloth and belt like the
men. . . . This could only have been in torrid Africa!

As the pace of excavation slowed, Evans, too, had more time to devote
to the study and comprehensive publication of the Knossos finds. It is
characteristic that the materials he first turned to were the written documents. *Scripta Minoa,* Volume I, appeared in 1909. Almost all of the
documents published there are of the earliest (hieroglyphic) type. He says
in the Preface that "the remaining Volumes—II and III—of this work will
be devoted to the detailed publication of the documents of the advanced
Linear Scripts of Crete, of both Classes (A and B)"; yet at his death over
thirty years later most of these vital documents were still unavailable to
other scholars. Perhaps the reason can be guessed from another statement
in the same Preface. "In the absence of bilingual inscriptions, the material
as a whole has not reached the stage when any comprehensive attempt at
interpretation or transliteration is likely to be attended with fruitful results."
Evans naturally hoped to decipher the scripts himself, and since he had not
made much headway it was unbelievable to him that anyone else could.

Part I of the first volume of *Scripta Minoa* does contain, however, a
wide-ranging general discussion of the situation in the later Minoan context, sometimes with a rather tenuous connection to written records. Its
tone is reflected by the title, "The Pre-Phoenician Scripts of Crete. Their
Mediterranean Relations and Place in Minoan Story." In a preliminary
summation of the material to be discussed, Evans points out that

> the written documents from the Palace of Knossos and its immediate
> dependencies now amount to nearly two thousand. The overwhelming
> majority of these clay documents, including the first discovered, pre-
> sented an advanced type of linear script—referred to in the present
> work as Class B—which was in vogue throughout the whole of the
> concluding period of the Palace history. But the course of the excava-
> tions brought out the fact that the use of this highly developed form of
> writing had been in turn preceded in the "House of Minos" by two
> earlier types—one also presenting linear characters, described below as
> Class A, the other, still earlier, of conventionalized pictorial aspect,
> recalling Egyptian hieroglyphics. . . . We shall not err on the side of
> exaggeration in estimating the period covered by the successive types
> of developed script on the Palace site at Knossos at over a thousand
> years. It must at the same time be observed that the latest of the Minoan
> documents discovered on this site, those namely dating from the period
> of decline, when the Palace as a Palace had ceased to exist, are older

by several centuries than the earliest known records of Phoenician writing [*i.e.,* in the Greek alphabet]. The twelfth century before our era may be regarded as their latest limit.

Evans seems at this point in his thinking to have been willing to assign to the Linear B tablets a rather wide chronological range, since only a few pages later he says that "the great bulk of the deposits of clay tablets found in the rooms and magazines of the building [*i.e.,* the later palace] . . . represent the form of script in use at the time of its final catastrophe, about the close of the fifteenth or the early part of the fourteenth century B.C." More than that, he apparently had the curious idea that there may be considerable differences in date even for associated groups of tablets. "As to the higher limit of the use of this form of writing at Knossos we have no direct evidence, but some of the larger deposits of clay archives must have been naturally of gradual accumulation. It is possible, therefore, that it [the Linear B script] was already in existence in the earlier half of the fifteenth century before our era."

Evans is quite emphatic that "at Knossos the inscribed documents belonging to the Linear Class A only occur in this particular stratum representing the lowest limit of the Middle Minoan culture," *i.e.,* somewhat before 1600; but he adds that "finds made elsewhere in Crete [particularly at Haghia Triada but also scattered examples at Phaistos, Zakro, Palaikastro and Gournia], however, seem to point to a longer local survival of this type of script." The use of Linear A appears to have spread over all central and eastern Crete and to date from "the transitional age that covers the close of the Middle Minoan and the early part of the Late Minoan Period." On the other hand, "documents of Class B . . . have as yet only been found on the site of Knossos."

His presumption that the two scripts, with many signs in common, were used to write the same language finds a revealing expression at one point. Two different and approximately contemporary documents show the same word group made up of two signs, one of which has a slight peculiarity attributable to Linear A. This, says Evans, "clearly indicates that the language in both cases was the same." No one nowadays would contend that the same *word* occurring in two inscriptions indicates that the *language* of both is the same. In answer to the natural question of why a new script should be evolved to write the same language, he repeats his earlier suggestion that the change is connected with a "dynastic revolution," perhaps also indicated by the "widespread catastrophe that brought to a close the Middle Minoan Period of the Palace."

He has obviously studied the documents very closely and believes that "bureaucratic methods of control here visible are themselves the outcome of a long inheritance of dynastic organization." He speaks of a "Palace School of Calligraphy," and his description of the symbols and method of recordkeeping is characteristically acute yet biased.

> The characters themselves have a European aspect. They are of upright habit and of a simple and definite outline, which throws into sharp relief the cumbrous and obscure cuneiform system of Babylonia. . . . It would seem that the characters stood for syllables or even letters, though they could in most cases be also used as words. Many are obviously compounds, and certain allied groups of signs show a regular systematic variation which betrays the hand of an official grammarian. . . . The spaces and lines between the words, the espacement into distinct paragraphs, and the variation in the size of the characters on the same tablet, according to the relative importance of the text, show a striving after clearness and method such as can by no means be said to be a characteristic of classical Greek inscriptions.

Evans realizes the obvious utilitarian and economic content of the tablets; yet he does not want to deny his Minoans the creation of a real literature.

> Was there more than this? Were there still fuller records, such as chronicles and sacred writings; liturgies, and books of magic, or hymns, possibly . . . ? May we suppose that manuscript copies existed of the Laws of Minos; that Epic tradition was already partly fixed by writing in prehistoric Crete, or that early prose romance had taken literary form as in contemporary Egypt? None of these possibilities can any longer be excluded, but the perishable nature of the materials that must be presupposed for the existence of any extensive literature makes it very improbable that it should have survived the catastrophe of the Cretan Palaces.

One also gains the impression that the "great catastrophe" that took place "not later than the first half of the fourteenth century" (on Egyptian synchronisms) was not complete and final. A few sentences sound as if Evans was half convinced by Mackenzie's recent theory: "That the catastrophe at Knossos itself, and the new condition of things that characterizes the Period of Reoccupation, were partly due to the successful incursions of men representing a closely allied form of culture from the mainland of Greece is in itself quite possible. . . . The new settlers . . . represented a somewhat later stage and a humbler aspect of the same civilization." Yet, in his view, they apparently did not take over political control. "Only in the Domestic Quarter of the Palace—a part of which, perhaps, was almost continuously occupied—are there signs of attempts at restoration on a large scale which make it probable that dynasts of the old stock still maintained a diminished state on the Palace site." Furthermore, Evans is here quite explicit that some tablets belong to this later period. In the "reoccupation phase" of the building called the House of the Fetishes, west of the palace, seal impressions were found "on the later floors" and "in juxtaposition with these, remains of tablets showing inscriptions belonging to Class B, but executed in a somewhat inferior manner."

Evans is now inclined to believe that the Cretan writing system was widely exported along with other Minoan culture traits. "In spite of the negative results obtained by Schliemann at Mycenae and Tiryns, all probability seems in favour of some form of early writing having existed on the mainland side." He is also ready to concede that "during the Third Late Minoan Age [after about 1400] . . . the centre of gravity of the Minoan world tends to shift to the mainland side." Scattered mainland evidence, almost entirely on pottery, would indicate that "during the latest Minoan and Mycenaean period" there must have been in use "a system of script which fits on to a Cretan signary of distinctly earlier date."

Like Mackenzie, Evans believes in a late invasion of the mainland by "Achaean tribes, whose oldest records point to Northern Greece." He apparently thought at this point, too, that they were the people who pushed large numbers of "Mycenaeans" into the Aegean islands, including Crete. As his own contribution to the difficult question of how to distinguish archaeologically between Achaean and Mycenaean, Evans poses a simple but rather drastic theory. "How large a part of the 'Mycenaean' civilization they themselves [the Achaeans] took over from the earlier inhabitants is sufficiently proved by the living record preserved to us in the Homeric poems." The "Achaean period" was at the very end of the Bronze Age (the so-called sub-Minoan), when iron implements and weapons were beginning to appear. "This is precisely the period when the Homeric poems —the apotheosis of Achaean enterprise—take their characteristic shape, and the Idomeneus of the *Iliad* may be taken to reflect Achaean domination of Knossos itself. At the same time the Homeric poems themselves afford a convincing proof that the traditions of the earlier Minoan and Mycenaean culture lived on in that of the Viking race of Greece."

In 1912 Evans was elected to the highest office of the Hellenic Society, and his presidential address, "The Minoan and Mycenaean Element in Hellenic Life," was published in the Society's journal. Here we see clearly how far he is now prepared to go in claiming not only that the Mycenaean inhabitants of the mainland in the Late Bronze Age were completely lack-

ing in originality, but that much of the inspiration in classical Greek
civilization, particularly in the areas of art and religion, really goes back
to non-Greek, Minoan sources. The anticlassical trend of his earlier years
has now matured, and he is confident that his new Cretan evidence has
provided the ammunition he previously lacked. Nor does he hesitate to
use it bluntly and forcefully.

The flavor of the whole paper can be sensed from a few of the opening
sentences.

> In his concluding Address to this Society our late President [Professor
> Percy Gardner] remarked that he cared more for the products of the
> full maturity of the Greek spirit than for its immature struggles, and
> this preference for fruits over roots is likely to be shared by most classical
> scholars. . . . Yet I imagine that my presence in this Chair is due to
> a feeling . . . that what may be called the embryological department
> has its place among our studies. Therefore I intend to take advantage
> of my position here to-day to say something in favour of roots, and
> even of germs. These are the days of origins, and what is true of the
> higher forms of animal life and functional activities is equally true of
> many of the vital principles that inspired the mature civilization of
> Greece—they cannot be adequately studied without constant reference
> to their anterior stages of evolution. . . . I venture to believe that the
> scientific study of Greek civilization is becoming less and less possible
> without taking into constant account that of the Minoan and Mycenaean
> world that went before it."

Evans then announces his theme with obvious relish. "Let it be assumed
that the Greeks themselves were an intrusive people and that they finally
imposed their language on an old Mediterranean race. But if, as I believe,
that view is to be maintained it must yet be acknowledged that from the
ethnic point of view the older elements largely absorbed the later. . . .
Can it be doubted that the artistic genius of the later Hellenes was largely
the continuous outcome of that inherent in the earlier race in which they
had been merged?" He alludes sarcastically to those who suggest that
Minoans and Mycenaeans belonged to the "Hellenic stock" and who have
seen in the "stray specimens of the script [Linear B from Knossos] which
have as yet seen the light" evidence that their language was Greek.

Evans' major obsession for the last thirty years of his life is already
crystallizing. Mycenaean culture was "only a provincial variant," a "mainland plantation" of the Minoan. Their physical type, their religion and
their language were the same. "We must clearly recognize that down to at
least the twelfth century before our era the dominant factor both in Mainland Greece and in the Aegean world was still non-Hellenic, and must

still unquestionably be identified with one or other branch of the old Minoan race." The major cultural differences between Minoans and Mycenaeans, emphasized by Dörpfeld and even by Mackenzie, have become "slight local divergencies." The theory of Minoan political control of the mainland is much more firmly proposed and is now rather oddly stretched to allow for "a subject race of Hellenic stock during the whole, or a large part of the period of Mycenaean domination." It was against this internal threat that the Mycenaean citadels were so heavily fortified. He does not explain how he proposes to relate these earlier representatives of the Hellenic stock to the "Achaean invasion" at the very end of the Bronze Age.

After pointing to persuasive examples in art and religion where there is apparent continuity between the Minoan-Mycenaean and the classical period, Evans turns to the daring theory that caps his whole argument. It had been vaguely anticipated in *Scripta Minoa* three years before, but one can still imagine the electrifying effect it must have had on his orthodox classicist colleagues. Considerable portions of the Homeric poems, he suggests, were really translations or adaptations of the exploits of an earlier, more gifted people (the Minoans), and they were originally sung (and perhaps even written) in an alien tongue.

> How is it then that Homer, though professedly commemorating the deeds of Achaean heroes, is able to picture them among surroundings, which, in view of the absolute continuity of Minoan and Mycenaean history, we may now definitely set down as non-Hellenic? . . . I venture to believe that there is only one solution of these grave difficulties, and that this is to be found in the bilingual conditions which in the Peloponnese at least may have existed for a very considerable period. . . . Many of the difficulties with which we have to deal, are removed if we accept the view that a considerable element in the Homeric poems represents the materials of an earlier Minoan epic taken over into Greek.

Evans is as sure as Schliemann had been in the case of his Mycenaean discoveries that we can actually see in Minoan art the ultimate visual inspiration of descriptions in Homer's poetry. If there were Greek speakers on the mainland well before the end of the Bronze Age, Evans believes that they had no share in the "inner palace circle of Tiryns and Mycenae, where such works were handled and admired." It is impossible to suppose that "any Achaean bard at the time when the Homeric poems crystallized into their permanent shape [*i.e.,* in the Early Iron Age] had such lifelike compositions [art objects] before his eye or could have appreciated them in the spirit of their creation." Evans reviews a whole series of representations to prove his point. One example is a clay seal impression from

Figure 68

about 1600 found at Knossos (Fig. 68). It depicts a fearful creature with a doglike head, attacking a ship. "This sea-monster," says Evans, "is a prototype of Skylla, and though her dogs' heads were multiplied by Homer's time, we have here, in the epitomized manner of gem engraving, the essentials of Ulysses' adventure depicted half a millennium at least before the age of the Greek Epic."[46]

So Evans holds that Schliemann, although his "views on Homeric subjects were not perturbed by chronological or ethnographic discrepancies," was essentially right in seeing a direct and vivid connection between Mycenaean art objects and the Homeric poems. And Schliemann's most fulsome prose could scarcely outdo Evans' peroration, as he reiterates the glory of that bygone Creto-centric epoch. "By what means could this undimmed reflection [in Homer] of a pure great age have been perpetuated and preserved? Only in one way. . . . They were handed down intact because they were preserved in the embalming medium of an earlier Epos—the product of that older non-Hellenic race to whom alike belong the glories of Mycenae and of Minoan Crete. Thus only could the iridescent wings of that earlier phantasy have maintained their pristine form and hues through days of darkness and decline to grace the later, Achaean, world."

After World War I Evans did not return to Crete until 1922. By that time the first volume of *The Palace of Minos* had appeared. It is wholly concerned with Minoan history before 1600; but sections of the Preface mention Minoan-Mycenaean relations in the Late Bronze Age and can fairly be attributed to Evans' thinking in the prewar period. In fact, he states that "difficulties and preoccupations . . . caused by the Great War delayed the publication of this work, the materials for which were already in an advanced state in 1914." Joan Evans has an amusing paragraph describing the grief that Evans was continually causing his editors. "He had neither secretary nor typewriter, and still used a quill pen. His handwriting was growing more and more stylized, and was of a kind that produced a fertile crop of printer's errors. . . . One reference . . . turned . . . 'exotic' into 'erotic,' with astonishing results. An erratum slip that said 'for *skytotes* read *rhytons*' drew the commentary from *Punch* that they were sorry that the author thought it necessary to part with '*skytotes*': 'it is just the short word we have been wanting for aeroplanes.' "

Volume I of *The Palace of Minos* shows even in the Preface that the thesis of complete Cretan domination over Mycenaean civilization has further solidified. "I have also felt that the view here presented of the Minoan Age . . . could not be adequately drawn out without some attempt to set forth its relation to the Mycenaean culture of Mainland Greece. . . . The results will surprise many. Few probably have yet realized how absolute is the dependence which these comparisons substantiate." One also notes a characteristic forthrightness and at the same time a certain defensiveness about some of his own previous views and the contributions of colleagues. By 1914, of course, a good deal of excavation had been carried out in other parts of Crete by British, American, Italian and Greek colleagues; and syntheses of Minoan civilization were beginning to appear. "The writer has, therefore, some right to be allowed to set down his own conclusions, gradually formed, in the course of years, from a first-hand knowledge of the materials, without seeking to inquire at every turn whether similar opinions may have been already expressed in print in other quarters."

Attention is drawn to Mackenzie's twenty-one years of faithful assistance, and particularly in the preparation of this publication. "My thanks are exceptionally due to him for the continued help that he has rendered to me at every turn in the course of the present work, and for his careful revision of the proofs. His special archaeological knowledge, particularly in the ceramics field, is so widely recognized that it is with great satisfaction that I am able to record that in all main points in my scheme of classification he is in complete agreement with me."

The scheme as it had taken shape by 1921 may be formalized as follows (all dates B.C. and approximate):

| | |
|---|---|
| Neolithic | 8000–3400 |
| Early Minoan | 3400–2100 |
| Middle Minoan | 2100–1580 |
| *(Early Palaces destroyed* | |
| *at end of MM II, about 1700)* | |

| Late Minoan I | 1580–1475 |
|---|---|
| Late Minoan II | 1475–1400 |
| *(Later Palace at Knossos destroyed* | |
| *at end of LM II)* | |
| Late Minoan III | 1400–1200 |

In the preliminary pages of this introduction to the distillation of Evans' lifework, he sketches the history of Bronze Age Crete, particularly as he has reconstructed it from his own excavations. It is an appealing formulation; and he feels confident that the three major divisions of the Bronze Age (Early, Middle, Late Minoan), each in turn with three major subdivisions (I, II, III), represent an approach that "is in its very essence logical and scientific." He insists that "in every characteristic phase of culture we note in fact the period of rise, maturity, and decay." The interest in origins in general is here combined with a special sentimental concern for the history of the West. "This comparatively small island, left on one side to-day by all the main lanes of Mediterranean intercourse, was at once the starting-point and the earliest stage in the highway of European civilization."

World War I was by no means the end of Arthur Evans' scholarly career. He had, in fact, still twenty years of a green old age ahead. They were divided between the comfortable Villa Ariadne, which he had built for himself on the hillside to the west of the palace ruins, and his English estate, with its gardens and excellent private library. From these peaceful retreats came forth volume after volume of the monumental *Palace of Minos* right up to 1936. At Knossos there were occasional minor tests and small excavations; and the work of conservation went on. He entertained friends, students, admirers. He defended with vigor the views he had come to believe were irrefutable; and he attacked with fervor and sarcasm those few who were incautious enough to differ with him.

Evans' later years, especially one major controversy, will have a place in another chapter; but no argument or discovery after the war can be said to have shaken his confidence in the essential truth of his own reconstruction of historical events in the Late Aegean Bronze Age. Its broad outlines are laid down in the Introduction to the first volume of *The Palace of Minos:*

Thus the time limits with which we have to deal for the Late Minoan Age lie approximately between 1580 and 1200 B.C. The early part of this epoch . . . is the Golden Age of Crete, followed, after a level interval, by a gradual decline. The settlement already begun in M. M. III [*i.e.,* before 1600] of large tracts of mainland Greece is now continued, and the new Mycenaean culture is thus firmly planted on those shores. . . . The overthrow of the great Palace [at Knossos] took place at the close of the succeeding L. M. II Period [*i.e.,* about 1400], the result, according to the interpretation suggested below, of an internal uprising, apparently of "submerged" elements. It looks as if the Mainland enterprise had been too exhausting. The centre of gravity of Minoan culture shifted now to the Mycenaean side. Finally, some hostile intrusion from the North, which is naturally to be connected with the first Greek invasions, drove away the indigenous settlers who had partially reoccupied or rebuilt the ruined sites at Knossos and elsewhere, and put an end to the last recuperative efforts of Minoan Crete.

From this point on we hear no more from Evans about the possibility that mainlanders (even "kindred" Mycenaeans) might have been responsible for the destruction of the Knossos palace around 1400.

Looking ahead a little, we may here record that Evans' last trip to Crete in 1937 was the occasion for the dedication of a bronze bust set up in his honor at the entrance to the Knossos site. With the plaudits of Cretan friends ringing in his ears and crowned with a laurel wreath, the old man made his acceptance speech in Greek. "We know now," he said, "that the old traditions were true. We have before our eyes a wondrous spectacle— the resurgence, namely, of a civilization twice as old as that of Hellas. It is true that on the old Palace site what we see are only the ruins of ruins, but the whole is still inspired with Minos' spirit of order and organization and the free and natural art of the great architect Daedalos."

We said previously that Heinrich Schliemann was an authentic genius and a man of paradox. It is curious that Joan Evans, with all allowance for sisterly pride and love, describes her half brother in words that are almost wholly applicable to Schliemann too.

Arthur [was] a man of paradox. He was flamboyant, and oddly modest; dignified, and loveably ridiculous; imperious, and surprisingly gentle; extravagant, yet by no means self-indulgent and in some things austere. He could be subtle as an Oriental, and simple as a child. He could be fantastically kind, and fundamentally uninterested in other people; he could be fantastically generous, and extremely self-centred. . . . He was always loyal to his friends, and never gave up doing something he had set his heart on for the sake of someone he loved. He was always true to his principles, and always true, at the same time, to his own unconscious sense of the preeminent importance of the workings of his own mind.

# V

## Before Blegen: The Situation in the Early Twenties

As Tsountas' *Mycenaean Age* provided us with a synthesis of the evidence that had accumulated up to the end of the nineteenth century, so we shall depend mainly on the work of two of his successors in the next generation. Both of them attempted to sum up the impact of new discoveries and new lines of research between 1900 and World War I and to suggest revisions in older theories required by the new data.

One book was part of the ambitious French series called *L'évolution de l'humanité: synthèse collectif*. The preparation of the Greek prehistoric material had been undertaken by a promising young scholar, Adolphe Reinach. After his death in battle at the very beginning of World War I, Gustav Glotz took over the assignment. Glotz's *La civilisation égéenne* appeared in 1923 and was translated into English under the same title, *The Aegean Civilization* (1925). Our second guide will be *Die Kretisch-Mykenische Kultur* (The Creto-Mycenaean Civilization) by Diedrich Fimmen. The author was killed in action in 1916, but he had left the manuscript in the final stages of preparation. It was edited and seen through the press by Professor George Karo (1921).

Unlike Tsountas, neither Glotz nor Fimmen was an experienced field archaeologist. Perhaps this is an advantage in attempting a synthesis, although Tsountas' own excavations do not seem to have lessened his objectivity. To a striking degree, we can see in these two books characteristics that are often alleged to be typical of German and French scholarship. Fimmen's account is terse, concise, factual and methodical, although its notelike quality may in part be explained by the author's premature death. Glotz's book, in contrast, is diffuse, exuberant and imaginative. They therefore form a useful foil to one another. Both, of course, discuss major aspects of the civilization such as palaces, private homes, grave types, pottery, art and economic activities. But Fimmen is more concerned with chronology, foreign contacts and precise systematization of data; whereas

[173]

Glotz (like Tsountas) takes a wider approach, with essays on the physical type, costume, weapons and armor, religion, writing systems and political institutions. The purely topical treatment is clearly becoming a drawback since it almost precludes a successful demonstration of the *development* of a civilization within its total chronological range.

The very titles of the two books indicate the wider sweep made necessary by the recent discoveries in Crete. The emphasis has shifted away from Troy and to some extent even from mainland Greece. How overpowering a role Evans himself played in this phenomenon is made clear by a sentence in the Foreword to Glotz's book: "The present volume is devoted entirely to the civilization revealed by Evans in excavations in Crete dating from 1900 and by earlier excavations dating from 1876 on the mainland of Greece and in Asia Minor." Glotz seems almost to be unaware that Italian, American, Greek and other British archaeologists had begun work in Crete at the same time as Evans and had also achieved notable results. It is true, however, that the full text does put the situation in somewhat fairer perspective; and Fimmen's Register gives a complete summary of all the relevant exploration and excavation in Crete, the other islands and the mainland.

Two other general points strike the reader almost immediately. Crete had stolen the stage not only because the revelation of Minoan civilization was novel and exciting, but also because very little new evidence of a spectacular sort had emerged from excavations on the Greek mainland during the first decades of the twentieth century. Steady and important work on various aspects of the Mycenaean material, such as the pottery analysis so prominent in Fimmen's book, had of course been proceeding. But this rather undramatic topic does not receive much detailed attention in Glotz's account. Secondly, it is quite clear that many features of Evans' theories on Minoan civilization and on interrelationships between Crete and the mainland are already approaching the status of unchallenged dogma.

At the same time, both of our authorities have reservations about details of some of Evans' propositions. For instance, we have seen how Evans moved almost full circle in his use of the term "Mycenaean." At first it was applied to everything prehistoric in Crete; but by 1920 it was only grudgingly used to characterize decadent mainland manifestations of "Minoan" inspiration. In this connection Glotz cautiously says, "Since the authority of Evans has invested the word [Minoan] with such respectability, we shall not deny ourselves the use of it, on the understanding that we confine it to Crete and that even in Crete we apply it especially to the period of the hegemony of Knossos."

Glotz also has doubts about certain details of Evans' system of chronology in which we cannot usefully follow him. But, by and large, he is under the spell of the neat "scientific" formulation of the tripartite Minoan scheme. "Evans, it is clear, combines the data of the stratification with the universal laws of evolution and the requirements of the human mind when he assumes with such regularity a period of growth leading to a period of apogee, followed by a period of decadence and transition."

Fimmen, like Glotz, adopts Evans' Minoan terminology and tripartite scheme for the Cretan Bronze Age, but he disagrees in important respects with Evans' absolute dates. His own dates represent a careful reexamination of the Egyptian synchronisms. We must record some of his conclusions, particularly as they affect our Mycenaean focus of attention. In addition to plotting the Near Eastern synchronisms, most of them via Crete, Fimmen underlines a point of view that had been gradually forcing itself on the attention of prehistoric archaeologists. He insists that "the most important basis for the distinction of the developmental features of a culture is the pottery."

Schliemann in his later years had begun to appreciate this crucial fact; and the pioneering German studies, *Mycenaean Painted Pottery* (1879) and *Mycenaean Vases* (1886), by Furtwängler and Loeschcke, had already pointed the way. But up to the end of the nineteenth century attention was mainly concentrated on the intrinsically valuable or unusual artefacts. Archaeologists still had something in common with their predecessors, the tomb robbers, who scorned and trampled the lowly pots. They would have laughed at a prediction that, scientifically speaking, the pottery would one day be quite literally the most precious part of the contents of an undisturbed tomb. In far too many cases the pottery was neglected and never properly published.

Evans had, of course, been a pioneer in the study of Minoan pottery, but he lacked the time—and perhaps the inclination—to devote much attention to that of the mainland. A major portion of Fimmen's book consists of a careful stylistic analysis of ceramic types from the whole Aegean area. And in his studies he works on the explicit assumption, which has appealed particularly to German specialists, that "the decorative motifs [point the distinctions] in greater measure than the vase shapes, since the former have gone through the richest development."

Fimmen proposes the terms "Early Mycenaean," "Middle Mycenaean" and "Late Mycenaean" as a basis for a distinct mainland chronology. His Early Mycenaean period begins about 1700 (more than a millennium after Evans' Early Minoan) and extends down to 1550. This is the time when the distinctive gray Minyan (Fig. 69) as well as matt-painted ware* (Fig. 70) was still flourishing. Both had been represented in the Mycenae

Figure 69

Figure 70

Shaft Graves, along with the earliest actual imports of Minoan ceramics. Fimmen places the earlier phases of the mainland palaces and the Mycenae Shaft Graves before the close of his Early Mycenaean epoch. His dates for the extant remains of mainland palaces have turned out to be much too early.

His Middle Mycenaean period (1550–1400) embraces what he thought was the most flourishing period of the palaces as well as of the great tholos tombs. The Late Mycenaean (1400–1250) marks the final form of the palaces and the strengthening and extension of the fortifications at Tiryns. Troy VI (presumably its latest phases), Troy VII, the intrusive megaron of mainland type at Phylakopi and the destruction of the Minoan palaces are dated to the beginning of this period.

Glotz's chronological scheme is somewhat different in detail, and we shall avoid unnecessary confusion by ignoring it. But in both books we notice very marked progress over Tsountas' generation in relative and absolute dating. And of course a dependable system of dating forms the essential framework of any historical study, whether or not the culture involved was a literate one. It is quite impossible to form rational views of historical development and change unless one can arrange the major observable features in a fairly firm *relative** sequence, preferably with a number of *absolute* dates as anchors for the whole structure.

In beginning his ambitious "historical survey of the Aegean peoples" Glotz poses searching and valid questions. "What place did the Mycenaean civilization have in the whole Aegean world? What was its origin? Was it the end of a world or the beginning, dawn or dusk?" Anyone who attempts a similar synthesis in our own day must make clear how far present information and theory have progressed in finding answers to such basic problems. And, ironically enough, it would probably be true to say that each of the three generations of Greek prehistorians has found clear-cut solutions progressively more elusive.

Glotz frames his answers with a good deal of assurance, as is perhaps necessary if a semipopular account is to inspire confidence in a wide circle of readers. And yet one misses the optimistic view that we have repeatedly noted in the scholars of the nineteenth century, who tend to leave the impression that all of the necessary evidence is in hand—or will be very soon. For example, he points out that "in Asia Minor we are faced with only blackness" and that "excavations that should elucidate this problem [connections between the Aegean area and the Near East] are sadly lacking." Fimmen's Register shows Miletos as the only prehistoric site on the Asia Minor coast below Troy where evidence of Minoan-Mycenaean settlement or trade had been authenticated. And, in fact, though neither of our guides mentions it, most of the Greek mainland and much of Crete were still very inadequately explored.

Glotz accepts without reservation Evans' "Minoan thalassocracy* [rule of the sea]" lasting until late in the Bronze Age, the Minoan colonization and/or political domination of the Greek mainland as well as of much of the east Mediterranean area, and the overwhelming effect of Minoan culture on less developed native traditions. On the other hand, he does not hesitate to question certain aspects of Evans' historical conclusions, though the semipopular format he has adopted prevents any detailed discussion of the evidence.

For example, his view is somewhat different on the date when "Achaeans," *i.e.*, Greek speakers, occupied the mainland, and it diverges still more widely on their continuing role in Mycenaean culture:

> It was above all in the North, in the countries occupied since 2000 by the Achaians, in Hellas which was opened more and more to external influences, that from 1700 onwards Cretan civilization poured in a mighty flood. . . . Everything becomes Cretanized. The ladies dress in fashions of Knossos. In sanctuaries of Cretan type the Cretan goddess is installed, with her usual animals, attributes, and ritual objects; all the ceremonies and all the games celebrated in her honour on the island accompany her to the continent. The princes' dwellings are adorned with frescoes and filled with precious vases and jewels in which there is scarce a trace of Helladic* [mainland] inexperience.

Assuming for the sake of argument that Minoan cultural dominance was as total as this account implies, the obvious question is how such a situation developed. "Is it the effect of an armed invasion," asks Glotz, "of an immigration *en masse?*" He continues:

> No. The mass of the population has not changed. The Achaians still testify to their northern origin by their beard, by their drawers and sleeved *chiton,* by their isolated *megaron* and fixed hearth. Their chiefs . . . impress all the hands needed to carry the gigantic blocks of stone. They delight in war and raids, fine weapons and chariots. By land and sea they go, carrying off cattle and women; but above all they need gold. . . . The sudden metamorphosis of Argolis [the Mycenae-Tiryns region] appears then to be the result of sporadic and peaceful colonization. Elsewhere . . . Cretans could instal themselves as masters . . . but in Argolis they doubtless confined themselves to making the natives accept the blessings of a superior civilization. . . . This Creto-Mycenaean civilization . . . gradually reached every land in Hellas. . . . All the shores of the Peloponnese were visited by the strangers, and at many points they established factories or branches.

Perhaps it is unfair to criticize this general formulation on as tricky a point as Minoan-Mycenaean political relations. But it is difficult to see just what Glotz thinks was the situation. Were the mainland rulers Minoans or Achaeans? Apparently he is saying that only in the Mycenae area did the native kings remain in power. Yet the evidence would seem to indicate that at Mycenae in particular there might have been a Minoan dynasty.

That, at least, is what Evans believed. It is also debatable how Minoan political control could have become established everywhere else in Greece without an armed invasion.

At any rate, Evans would presumably not have been too unhappy with Glotz's account of earlier Mycenaean history. The continuation of the story, however, must have given him acute pain.

> In this continual expansion the part played by Cretan traders and colonists was for a long time predominant. But it tended to diminish as the pupils learned to do without their masters, and the power of the mainland chiefs increased. There remained to the Cretans the immense superiority which they enjoyed through their empire of the sea. But even here the Achaians were doing their apprenticeship. . . . A day came when the peoples grew tired of paying tribute to the Cretan thalassocracy. . . . One day of weakness, and the island was conquered. It was. About 1400 the glorious palace of Knossos was overthrown. It was swift and dreadful, a thunderbolt. . . . The catastrophe was universal; Gournia, Pseira, Zakro disappeared; Palaikastro went up in flame. It was no internal revolution this time. Evans would attribute all this destruction to a revolt of the plebs against the monarchy. But everything testifies to the arrival of a new population in Crete. . . . The island which had been mistress of the Mediterranean had become a distant dependency of the mainland. The jewel of the Aegean was to lose all its lustre. . . . When, at the end of a half-century, a few groups of men took possession of Knossos, they could only set up mean hovels in the ruins of the palace.

It is, if anything, more difficult for us now to picture Glotz's (presumably) foreign rulers of Knossos living in the "mean hovels" than Evans' own "miserable [Cretan] survivors." Glotz clearly experiences a letdown of inspiration as he turns to the task of following the fortunes of the rebellious mainlanders. "While the Achaians of Argolis assumed the mastery of the Aegean world the civilization which they had assimilated and transformed to their own use extended further than it had ever gone. . . . New settlements multiply. . . . The Hellas thus formed is the Hellas of the *Iliad,* and the *Catalogue of Ships,*[47] which enumerates its peoples, is a veritable chapter of political geography." Fimmen, too, notes the "thorough-going correspondence of Mycenaean settlements with the places in Homer's catalogue of the Achaeans." In this connection, a puzzling antithesis to Evans' and Glotz's bleak picture of the miserable hovels and pitiful squatters in Crete after 1400 is supplied by the description of Crete not only in this same *Catalogue* but in the general Homeric tradition of the island as "fair, fat, well-watered; and in it are many men, beyond numbering, and ninety cities."[48]

Faced with the apparent shift of material prosperity from Crete to the mainland, Glotz cannot resist a nostalgic and perhaps justifiable eulogy of the Minoan cultural achievement. "Glorious though the spectacle may be which is presented by the Mycenaean civilization if we consider only its extent, it gives the impression of a backward movement if we compare its quality with that of its predecessor. . . . There is the superiority of wealth . . . [but] art grew vulgar and degenerate. It was a characteristic sign of the intellectual decline that writing was very rarely used, and tablets were wanted nowhere outside of Crete."

One of Glotz's surest instincts about Minoan culture concerns the novelty and effect of the great architectural complexes.

> To estimate the level reached by Cretan architecture and to enjoy its charm one must first forget those intellectual qualities of order, symmetry, and balance which give Greek buildings their incomparable beauty. The Cretan architect made no effort to offer to the gods temples worthy of them. He wanted to build comfortable houses and mansions and magnificent palaces, in which the master could conveniently accommodate his whole family, an army of servants, and the offices of a complicated administrative system, and display his wealth by brilliant entertainments. The great artistic skill with which all crafts combined their resources at the call of the Cretan architect is clearly shown not so much in the majesty of the general effect or even in the splendour of the external decoration as in the perfect adaptation to climatic conditions, happy distribution of light and shade, and intelligent ventilation and drainage, in the ease of communication between the countless rooms, the arrangements made to satisfy quite modern notions of comfort [i.e., "flush toilets"] and the harmonious opulence of details, and finally in a sure sense of the spectacular and picturesque which indulges in monumental entrances, the elegant ordering of terrace upon terrace and vistas of noble landscapes on every side. These are the solid and native qualities which appear in the palaces . . . when one tries to imagine them as they were when they had taken on their final form.

When he turns to mainland architecture, Glotz is again not so lyrical.

> Then is the Cretan house of the same origin as the northern house, of which the Mycenaeans bequeathed the type to the Greece of the future? This is the opinion which archaeologists maintained at first, either deriving the Cretan type from the mainland type or *vice-versa*. But to-day it is generally admitted that between the two systems there are radical differences, due to the climates in which they had their birth. There is nothing at all Cretan about the purely "Nordic" arrangements which appear in the second half of the third millennium at Troy II and in Thessaly, reappear about 1600 at Mycenae and Tiryns [dated *far*

too early], and extend during the XIVth century to Melos and even to Crete. . . . The essential feature of the mainland palace is the *megaron,* independent and isolated. The addition of one new room after another to the original building [in Crete] is hardly possible except with a flat roofing. . . . The long straight line of the *megaron* [in the mainland] makes it possible to drain off the water by a roof with two slopes. . . . The mainland house is deep, with a single entry in the small side, so as to keep the heat in the cold season. . . . To protect their *megaron* from the weather the Mycenaeans resign themselves to having no light in it but what comes through the doors, the central louver, in which the openings are so narrow that they do not prevent the smoke from blackening the ceiling.[49] . . . Between the principles of. architecture applied in Crete and the mainland . . . the difference is profound and absolute, and lies in their very origins.

We notice that Dörpfeld's notion of a flat roof for the Tiryns megaron is here ignored. Although the "northern" pitched roof has had many adherents since Glotz's day, the evidence is now very strongly against it.

Fimmen also insists, as had his earlier German colleagues like Dörpfeld, on a "completely separate line of development in house types," and he points to the change from Cretan to mainland architectural usages both between Phylakopi II and III and even in the latest prehistoric phase at Gournia and Haghia Triada in Crete itself.

Glotz prefaces his chapter "The Social System and Government" with a useful statement of the elusive kind of evidence sometimes available to the prehistorian.

On the organization of the social group the remains of prehistoric times leave a free field to the imagination and do not, it seems, supply any information. It is not impossible, however, to form a rough idea of the lines on which the Aegean societies must have developed. . . . The poet of the *Iliad* tells us that Priam lodged in his palace all his children, his fifty sons[50] and his daughters with their husbands[51]; the poet of the *Odyssey* again shows us in the palace of Nestor six sons, six daughters-in-law, and several married daughters.[52] Here we discover the close relationship which may subsist between social organization and architecture. . . . In the earliest times collective burial was practised; the members of the family were gathered together in the life beyond the grave as they had been gathered together in this world.

There is one notable feature in which Minoan-Mycenaean society seems to show a marked contrast to the contemporary situation in the Near East. Glotz emphasizes "the large part played by women in religious ceremonies and public festivals. . . . They are not recluses. There is nothing corresponding to the harem in Cretan dwellings. . . . The Cretan artists are fond of representing high-born maidens standing up in chariots and holding the reins like Nausikaa.[53] Like Atalante they go hunting." The relatively prestigious status of women is indeed suggested by Late Bronze Age representational art, particularly that in the Minoan tradition. The Homeric poems mirror it to a lesser extent. And one has only to recall the major roles played by women in the myths embedded in Greek classical literature that had their origin in the Bronze Age social situation and that point such a striking contrast with the actual mores of classical Greek society.

Although Glotz's frame of reference in discussing political conditions is largely Minoan, it may be inferred that he saw on the mainland, at least in the region of Mycenae, later developments along similar lines. Political power passed gradually from a large number of heads of local clans to monarchs of a relatively few strategically placed power centers. Shortly after 2000 these independent kings began to build proper palaces. In the end the majority of local chieftains recognized the overlordship of Knossos.

> Only then . . . historical probability permits us to call the king of Knossos by the name of Minos. This name does not seem to have been applied to one personage only. It is less a proper name than a dynastic title. There were Minoses in Crete, as there were Pharaohs and Ptolemies in Egypt and Caesars in Rome. . . . Minos was above all the priest-king. . . . He is the representative of the Bull God, the incarnation of the Minotaur. . . . The king, like the god, had as insignia the sceptre and the double axe, the *labrys*. Two thousand years before it became the symbol of authority in Rome, the axe already held that position in the palace of the Labyrinth.

Evans' view of the Minoan priest-king has now crystallized and become a widely accepted article of faith.

Glotz also summarizes the existing evidence indicating that the later Minoan kingdoms had a very highly developed and complex bureaucratic palace administration. "One thing that gives a good idea of Minoan administration is the multitude of tablets. . . . If we could decipher the tablets we should be thoroughly acquainted with the financial administration . . ." Failing that information, it is still clear that a large number of royal services were installed in the palace.

> Along the ground floor lie the Magazines—what the Homeric epics were to call the "treasure."[54] There, lined up in rows, stand the great *pithoi* containing grain, wine, and more especially oil, and the subterranean cists . . . holding the objects of greatest value. . . . The king's "treasury" was, in the modern sense, the treasury of the State. It was fed by the State revenues and doubtless also by gifts, voluntary or other-

wise. . . . The king . . . owned workshops which had to supply him with objects of art and luxury which . . . bore brilliant witness to his glory, all the world over.

As we have noticed, Glotz follows Evans in believing that Minoan political power extended to the mainland; but he is pardonably unsure about the precise line of command.

According to Thucydides,[55] Minos sent his own sons as lieutenants to his foreign possessions. . . . In any case, on the mainland the command was in the hands of military chieftains, some of whom must have recognized the over-lordship of Minos. . . . The more favoured among them, however, were posted at the ports, such as Pylos, or watched the great roads frequented by merchants at Orchomenos, Thebes, Tiryns, Mycenae, and Vapheio; these became great and mighty dynasts. Each had his retreat on an acropolis surrounded by imposing ramparts. . . . There they lived with all their family in joy and luxury. . . . Such pomp was only possible where the many toiled and moiled for the few. Round the strongholds lived the multitude from whom forced labour could be exacted at will.

Glotz's enumeration of the food resources available to these densely settled communities recalls the Homeric picture of a highly specialized and perfected farming and herding economy. "Wheat and barley were grown throughout Crete as in the Cyclades*, in Asia Minor, and in Greece proper. . . . The olive-tree was of the greatest service to them. In the Homeric poems its oil is only used for the toilet and hygiene.[56] Thus it was believed until quite recently that oil was for a long time a rare commodity in Greece. . . . To-day doubt [about its wide use and economic importance] is no longer possible. . . . The vine was likewise cultivated . . ."

He goes on to mention archaeological proof for the cultivation of figs, dates, flax, poppy, sesame, crocus and saffron. There were flocks and herds of sheep, pigs, goats, and especially of cattle. "All the occupations proper to pastoral life were reserved for the men, and there was doubtless something noble about this privilege then as later, in the time of Homer." Beekeeping is attested by Homer and in archaeological discoveries. Hunting was a favorite pastime and must have lent variety to the food supply. "The ubiquitous sea offered endless resources in the way of fish. . . . Whereas the Homeric heroes scorn fish and leave it for the poor, in Crete it appeared on kings' tables and among the dishes of the gods."

Important evidence for widespread international trade was also accumulating; and it was generally assumed that Minoan ships carried the bulk of it, at least up to 1400. The most reliable index of the various markets is

Fimmen's careful documentation of the discovery of Minoan and Mycenaean pottery found outside of Greece and Crete. Fimmen is quite certain that by no means all the exported Mycenaean and Minoan vases contained wine or oil or some other commodity. "One must certainly not assume that all the vases were traded only for their contents. The expensive painted pottery of Crete and Mycenae with its sense of style formed in itself an important article of commerce. One can certainly dare to assume from the most beautiful vases found in Egypt and from the numerous kraters* with figured scenes in Cyprus that they were purchased for their form and decoration." He goes on to list the major imports, such as amber from the Baltic area, ivory from Africa, and various metals. He admits that it is an "open question" as to how far the Aegean area was self-sufficient in the latter. The main source of copper seems to have been in Cyprus, of tin in Spain and England, of silver in Sardinia and Spain, and of gold in Egypt and Nubia.

In discussing foreign trade, Glotz as usual strikes a more popular note.

Schliemann found at Hissarlik axes of jade and a fragment of white nephrite. Here, then, we have stones which, from stage to stage, have come from the Kuen-Lun Mountains [in central Asia] and perhaps still further to the shores of the Troad. Who can tell by what mysterious roads the amber found its way among the pre-Hellenic peoples, and to such an extent that Pylos before Nestor's day [see chapter VI for the Kakovatos site] contained quantities of it? Through what hands did the tin pass before it reached the bronze-workers of Knossos? . . . Melos, the most south-westerly island [of the Cyclades] . . . from the earliest times . . . exported . . . obsidian, of which it had the monopoly. It became the great half-way house between Crete and Argolis.

Among the most obvious Mycenaean exports were the vases already known from Egyptian tombs in Schliemann's day. "How did these Mycenaean goods make their way into Egypt?" asks Glotz. "It is probable that the Cretans made themselves the middle-men between the whole Aegean and Egypt during the XVIth century and the greater part of the XVth. . . . Before 1420, the Achaians were in direct relations with Egypt. . . . This competition was certainly not unrelated to the catastrophe which ruined Knossos to the profit of Mycenae about 1400. . . . So the trade of Mycenae, once liberated from the hegemony of Crete, poured into Egypt for two hundred years." For example, at the end of the Trojan War, "we find in the *Odyssey*[57] Menelaos and Odysseus, with the men of Crete, Laconia, and Ithaca, setting forth from Pharos [an island off Alexandria], sailing up the Aigyptos [Nile] on ventures which were half commercial and half military, and returning with coffers filled with gold." It should perhaps be injected that Glotz's account of Egyptian trade has turned out to be a particularly distorted reconstruction.

Minoan-Mycenaean traffic with Asia Minor was also coming vaguely into focus. "The Cretans from the XVIth century, and then the Mycenaeans, were constant visitors to the Syrian coast. . . . A complete colony was founded at Miletos, which bears the name of a Cretan city. . . . At the extreme point of Asia Minor, at the entrance to the straits, there was an important market, that of Troy. . . . The opulent city of Priam was for two centuries in continuous relations with the regions dominated by the city of Agamemnon."

Glotz belittles the traditional account of the rape of Helen as the cause of the Trojan War; it was a simple case of cutthroat commercial rivalry. "We already have the competition described later by Hesiod, 'between potter and potter,' but it is international; it is already, on the economic field, the Trojan War. And indeed, when the Achaians, masters of the trade and the coasts from the mouths of the Nile to the Hellespont, grow tired of seeing access to the straits barred to them, Agamemnon need only send out the call to arms and all . . . will come rushing upon the city of Priam."

Glotz also believes, with Evans, that the Minoan thalassocracy had turned its attention to the west. "They [the Minoans] could collect on the [western] coasts still more precious goods, brought from very far by cara-vans—amber, and above all, tin. Italy, Sicily, and Iberia [Spain] thus became the Far West of the Aegeans. . . . In Sicily, then, far more than in Italy, the archaeologist finds all sorts of indications which suggest the establishment of colonies rather than the extension of trade." He even follows Evans' lead in suggesting that there is archaeological evidence to support a rather tenuous later tradition that connects Minos and Daidalos with Sicily.[58] "We have no right to disdain the traditions which mention successive migrations of Cretans to Sicily. Daidalos, it is said, came the first, and then Minos, in pursuit of Daidalos. What Daidalos, who personified the industry and art of Crete, brought with him we see in the painted vases, the weapons, and the jewels laid in the [Sicilian] tombs; what Minos did, who personifies its political power, we know from the concordance of Cretan and Sicilian evidence. . . . Even Minoan writing, according to Evans, was taken up by the Iberians. If there was no colonization here, there was at least commercial contact." Glotz's confident statement of the case for Minoan colonial expansion is by no means echoed by Fimmen, who is not even sure how "colony" can be distinguished from "trading post."

In Glotz's account of Minoan-Mycenaean religion, it is again Evans' hypotheses and to a large extent Evans' discoveries that dominate his thinking. Fimmen, on the other hand, makes a careful independent study of all the grave types through the Aegean area and their dates and localities. By and large, he thinks, hints about religious practices that can be gained from art representations and the like usually prove elusive and baffling, whereas the abundant evidence of funeral ritual in the form and contents of tombs provides at least some dependable material on which to base a reconstruction of a people's religious beliefs. Fimmen comes to the conclusion that, of the three main types—the rock-cut chamber tomb, the cist grave and the tholos tomb—the first occurs in Crete, the islands and mainland Greece (except Thessaly), with the oldest examples on the islands of Melos and Euboea. The second type is especially common in the islands and in northern Greece and is very seldom found in Crete; again, the oldest examples occur on the islands. The tholos type is common on the mainland, unusual in the islands, and (except for a doubtful precedent in Early Minoan times) occurs only in late examples on Crete.

Fimmen also points out other differences between Crete and the mainland. For instance, there are no mainland examples of the common Cretan sanctuary on or near a mountaintop; only in Crete have actual examples been found of the house shrines and chapels shown in art representations; material evidence of continuing hero cults from the Late Bronze Age to classical times seems to be confined to the mainland. While Fimmen does not explicitly say so, the rather obvious conclusion from his review is that extreme caution is indicated before adopting Evans' belief that the Minoan religious tradition eventually preempted the loyalty of all Aegean peoples.

On the question of cremation versus inhumation of the dead, it now seemed safe to say that there is hardly a known case where one can speak with assurance of cremation being practiced in mainland Greece or Crete during the Late Bronze Age. The charcoal, ashes and animal bones in many mainland graves are best understood as evidence for cult offerings to the dead.

Glotz again echoes Evans' judgments in discussing Minoan-Mycenaean art. The Minoans are the creators; the mainlanders, rude and bungling imitators. Crete did, it is true, borrow much from the Near East, but everything was transformed by Minoan artistic genius. "Freedom in respect of all teachings and all traditions—that is the most characteristic feature of Cretan art. It had its conventions; none of them ever hampered personal experiment. . . . The Cretan artist has the confidence of youth and an ingenuous audacity. . . . All these artistic qualities were displayed by the Cretans, as a rule, on objects of small dimensions. They have an eye for truth and for beauty, but not for size. One might say that they reduce everything to their own stature, being small men."

In reviewing the contents of the Mycenae Shaft Graves, Glotz is, of course, puzzled by the lack of homogeneity. But in general the rule holds: Anything "good" is Cretan (or at least foreign), anything "crude" or "simple" is native. But, even granting this dangerous distinction, some peculiar subjective judgments are made.

Nowhere, not even in Troy, have such masses of jewels been found. . . . Some of them are like nothing in Crete, either in form or in decoration. Others clearly bear the stamp of Cretan influence. . . . The famous gold masks which preserve the features of buried kings speak to the imagination, but they are only clumsy impressions stamped by natives. . . . Simple-minded image-makers cut the grey-brown limestone of the country into clumsy funeral steles. . . . To fill the field the artist could think of nothing better than heavy spirals. The Cretans changed all this. . . . We come thus to certain works which do not merely indicate the influence of foreign models or masters but were actually executed by those masters and were almost all imported.

The siege scene on the silver rhyton shows

a tale of war which was told in Argos. After the *Iliad* we have the *Odyssey;* on a third fragment of the rhyton there are shipwrecked men swimming for their lives. Thus all the legend which was to be immortalized in the Achaian epic was already immortalized in Cretan art. For the authors of these works, which were buried in the Fourth Shaft Grave, were not the fellow-countrymen of the heavy-handed image-maker who carved the stele of the same tomb. They had come to Mycenae at the call of a dynast who had gold and wanted glory. . . . The art of the cups from Vapheio is more refined and more sure of itself; we pass from the Shaft Graves to the bee-hive tombs . . . One really cannot see where, except in Crete, such complete artistry could have appeared at such a time.

For Glotz, too, the gulf separating Minoan and Mycenaean ceramic products was absolute and unbridgeable for centuries, though native potters finally succeeded in uninspired imitations.

While the Cyclades and the mainland everlastingly reproduced the same types or altered them only at long intervals, without rising above an industrial technique and an uninspired geometric decoration, Crete soon learned to give superior qualities to ordinary pottery, and above all to transform a utilitarian industry into a luxurious art. . . . The education of the Cycladic and mainland potters was completed during the two centuries [1600–1400] . . . The import of Cretan vases became more and more active all over the Aegean world. Moreover, in many places vases were manufactured which we should call Cretan if certain details did not prove their local origin. These can only have been made and painted by Cretan immigrants. The native potters kept up their own types, but they became daily more imbued with a technique and a style which they considered superior.

Glotz's remarks on the distinctive Palace Style ceramics might have been written by Evans himself.

During this time [a generation or two before 1400] the Palace style became known. There is no doubt of the Cretan origin of some of these precious vases, which have been found all over Argolis, at Kakovatos, in Aigina, at Chalkis in Euboia, at Thebes, and at Orchomenos. But others, more numerous, are imitations. . . . From where do these imitations come? . . . The native potters cannot have decorated them; the most advanced of them were still incapable of it. We must, therefore, suppose that master-potters from Crete worked on the mainland in certain centres from which their work was sent far afield.

We may, perhaps, innocently inquire why Cretan "master-potters" could produce originals for export from Crete but were reduced to making obvious imitations when they emigrated to the mainland. The day of distinguishing the provenience* of clays was, of course, still far in the future.

After 1400 the fortunes of Minoan ceramic art mirrored the larger political events. "Just when the pottery of Crete was at its apogee, Mycenaean pottery borrowed its models, carried off its artists, appropriated its processes, and immensely enlarged its domain. The next thing it did was to take its place." The strikingly homogeneous later pottery, one of the leading features of the Mycenaean koinê* (common or shared culture), was exported very widely throughout the eastern Mediterranean area. Glotz has only faint commendation for its best efforts and characterizes the final manifestations as "the last phase of a once glorious art, the death agony of a civilization."

Since Evans and his followers considered the native mainland pottery almost beneath their notice, it will be worthwhile to summarize Fimmen's workmanlike description of the two most important early varieties of what he calls "the pottery of central Greece." One type is characterized by simple geometric or curvilinear decoration applied in "matt" (dull) black or brown paint on a light greenish or yellow-brown ground. This "matt-painted*" ware occurs in its most developed form in the Mycenae Shaft Graves. Another very important contemporary type has already come to our attention several times. It is a monochrome gray or yellow ware, with sharp profiles and sometimes with incised or ribbed decoration. Fimmen notes that Schliemann called this ware "Lydian" when he encountered it in Level VI at Troy and later coined a new name, "Minyan*," for essentially the same pottery at Orchomenos. Fimmen himself prefers the term

"Orchomenos ware." It was approximately contemporary with the matt-painted pottery. It will be remembered that these two very distinctive types of pottery are characteristic of Fimmen's Early Mycenaean period (1700–1550). The developed Mycenaean pottery is essentially a fusion of decorative motifs from both the Minoan and native matt-painted traditions applied in lustrous paint to the yellow Minyan fabric.

The massive impact of the highly sophisticated Minoan art forms had its strongest effect on the mainland in Fimmen's Middle Mycenaean period (1550–1400), and in this environment the so-called Mycenaean koinê began to emerge. "Crete finally developed," says Fimmen, "a completely separate rich and unique culture which soon far outstripped all the other provinces. The fusion which took place in the following period is created through the complete preponderance of Cretan culture. . . . The Cretan naturalistic style of the first Late Minoan Period comprised in a free manner a very large number of motifs which in the ornamentation of the koinê, in time completely stylized, recur again and again." Fimmen is quite prepared to explain this development by the presence of "Cretan colonists," but he does not follow Evans in believing that cultural dominance implies political control. In fact, he believes that the emergence of the koinê style is more likely to imply that the political center of gravity in the Aegean area may have been beginning to shift to the mainland.

Glotz's chapter "Writing and Language" is perhaps the best indicator of the distance we have come between 1925 and 1965 on the question of literacy in the Late Bronze Age. He begins by briefly reviewing the evidence and theories current at the end of the nineteenth century about writing in the Aegean. Evans' excavations "have brilliantly confirmed what was only an inspired divination. . . . Unfortunately these documents are still a dead letter for us and will perhaps remain undecipherable so long as no bilingual inscription is discovered to give the key. All that the penetrating sagacity of Evans has so far been able to do is to distinguish different classes of writing among the *scripta Minoa*."

The long discussion of the connections between Egyptian, Cretan and Phoenician systems of writing is an instructive example of the reckless theorizing that written documents in an unknown language and script are so likely to invite. Glotz's conclusion is that "the simplest thing is to admit, not only that the Phoenicians drew from the Cretan source as well as from the Egyptian, but that the Cretans and Egyptians both drew equally from the primitive source of the Neolithic writings." One wonders how anyone could regard such a suggestion as "simple"! But he takes a more sensible stand in connection with alleged influence from the cuneiform systems in the Near East. "As for Asiatic influence, it appears nowhere in Cretan writing. There is an outward likeness, it is true, between the clay tablets used in Crete and those of Babylonia. One might at first admit, if necessary, that the material form was borrowed, and that only, as in any case the Cretan signs have no resemblance whatever to the cuneiform characters."

Glotz is much more positive than Evans that the clay tablets represent a quite minor class of written documents in a highly literate society. "We must therefore suppose that the documents which have come down to us were not of the kinds most extensively used. The religious and literary writings have disappeared, and of the commercial and legal papers, the stamped documents, nothing remains but the seal-impressions which were attached to them." We find also a somewhat more cautious reflection of Evans' theories of the origin of Greek epic. "When Homer describes the dances which were performed in the theatre of Knossos he authorizes us to think that the bards who sang in the palace of Alkinoos[59] had their fore-runners in the palace of Minos, and that the Greek epic, with its artificial language, was inspired by poems far more ancient."

The inferences about the three writing systems of Crete have in general a familiar ring. The earliest hieroglyphic style is succeeded by Linear A "as soon as new dynasties established themselves in the Second Palaces [after about 1700] . . . The new system, perhaps enforced by the royal authority, was alone taught henceforward. . . . This system remained in general use all over Crete. But at Knossos [about 1450] . . . the chancery brought about the predominance of a script which was doubtless reserved for the royal documents, the linear script of Class B. . . . At Hagia Triada, as at Pompeii, we see *graffiti** [in Linear A] scrawled on the walls by idle passers-by. The humblest folk could read and write."

He faithfully reflects, too, the current belief about the language or languages of the tablets. "Judging by the regularity with which writing develops from the end of the Chalcolithic Period [transitional from stone to metal] to the Greek invasions [end of the Bronze Age], we have the impression that the same language is transmitted to successive generations, with inevitable changes. This speech was neither Indo-European nor Semitic. From certain groups of signs it seems to have had alterations of suffix in which we may see word-endings and inflexions; this characteristic makes it similar to the Aryan languages, but proves nothing."

In discussing the diffusion of Minoan scripts, Glotz tries to take account both of the archaeological evidence and of later traditions about the earliest Greek writing systems.

> Since the Cretans took their system of writing with them it is not surprising that they caused it to be adopted all over the Aegean. . . . Everything seems to show that in the islands it is the Cretan language which is expressed in the Cretan script. But on the mainland we do not find

things presented in such a simple fashion. While certain vase inscriptions conform to the linear Class A, others appear to mark a transitional stage between hieroglyphs and linear characters. . . . In Boeotia particularly the archaic system prevailed. The famous "Kadmeian" letters of which the Greeks spoke were indeed used on the Kadmeia [acropolis of Thebes], as at Orchomenos, and it is these no doubt which were engraved on the bronze tablets which Agesilaos found at Haliartos in the "Tomb of Alkmene," and took for Egyptian hieroglyphs.[60]

We shall be reviewing the Theban inscribed jars later; but Glotz's inferences about them are quite wrong.

There is also something prophetic (although curiously inverted) in Glotz's reconstruction of the process by which Greek speakers of the classical period in Cyprus used a syllabary derived from Bronze Age Crete for their own writing system. "This local form of the Cretan writing followed its proper destiny. When it was reduced to a syllabary Achaians from the Peloponnese [who settled in Cyprus toward the end of the Bronze Age] adapted it in a rough and ready way to their own idiom; but it always showed, by its inability to denote certain gradations, despite its 54 characters, that it had not been created to express the Greek language." He agrees with Evans that certain symbols in the later Lycian and Carian alphabets of southwest Anatolia "come direct from linear scripts A and B." And in this connection he points out that "By a curious coincidence, which has an allegorical value, the only passage in which Homer clearly mentions writing is that in which Bellerophon, leaving Argos for the shores of Asia, hands to the king of the Lycians tablets covered with signs."[61]

Glotz's final chapter, survivals of Aegean civilization, ought to be the most important for our theme of Homeric connections; but unfortunately it is far from his best effort. He characterizes the Dorian invasion that destroyed the Mycenaean strongholds as the *"Drang nach Osten* of a continental civilization, that of Hallstatt*." The conventional Dorian culture characteristics are rehearsed—use of iron, cremation burial, geometric ornament on pottery and the use of fibulae* to fasten garments. The invaders also brought with them a "very different religion," in which "a great god prevailed over the great goddess of the Cretans." Protected international trade gave place to piracy on the high seas.

Yet there were elements of the Bronze Age culture that survived the Dorian hordes. "One of the features which give the Aegeans such an original aspect is just one of those which distinguish the Greeks from the other peoples of Indo-European race, that is the liking for the gymnastic and musical contests which accompany the great festivals." He goes on to cite prehistoric associations of the later religious cults connected with important athletic contests—Corinth (the Isthmus), Olympia, Delphi, Delos. "There is as direct a connection between the boxing-matches carved on the *rhyton* from Hagia Triada and those at which Achilleus[62] and Alkinoos[63] preside as between the games described by Homer and the Olympic games."

In Glotz's summation of the relationship between Mycenaean times and the Homeric poems, one senses a firm enough commitment to the proposition that there *was* a strong thread of continuity; but one misses the late-nineteenth-century conviction that the connection was close and vital. "When the days of trial came the last of the great victories won by the Achaians, the taking of Troy, assumed legendary dimensions in the imagination of the peoples who inhabited the neighbouring region, and gradually the Aiolian* bards attached all the warlike epics to that which most flattered and best consoled the new generations. Then, when the migrations in their turn receded into the past and took on a marvelous colour, all the tales of sea-journeys were fitted into the 'Returns' from Troy, and especially into the adventures of Odysseus."

In spite of the author's learning, his notable ability to synthesize and generalize, and his stylistic flair (which comes through even in translation), Glotz's book was not a completely reliable and balanced historical reconstruction even in terms of the evidence available in the twenties. Yet it deservedly appealed to the student and general reader and was a wiser choice than most of the attempted overviews of its day. On the other hand, it is a rather alarming indication of how slowly many in the profession adjust to current developments that Glotz is still prescribed for innocent students and recommended to unsuspecting general readers. The 1952 edition (in French only) is not revised—and scarcely could have been. Professors C. Picard and P. Demargne provided *notes additionnelles;* but such an expedient cannot represent a satisfactory adjustment to the insights of a new generation.

In closing this chapter, we may refer briefly and (we hope) instructively to a publication with the interesting title *A Century of Archaeological Discoveries* by Professor A. Michaelis. The English translation of the original German text appeared in 1908, half a generation after Schliemann had died and when Evans' major excavations were already well known. Indeed, the sponsors of the English version were among those scholars whose approach to classical studies irked Evans so deeply. A few excerpts will make his reasons clear enough.

The tone is set even in the Preface written by Professor Percy Gardner, who delivers himself as follows: "Light won from most of these [Aegean] sites has been thrown on the prehistoric age in Greek lands, rather [than] on what is really Hellenic. It is a Darwinian age, when the search for origins seems to fascinate men more than the search for what is good in itself; and the fact is that our eyes are somewhat dazzled by the brilliant discoveries of Schliemann, Dörpfeld and Evans."

Michaelis, in the author's Preface, defines archaeology in rather peculiar terms, even in reference to classical art. "By the term archaeology is meant the archaeology of art; the products of civilization in so far as they express no artistic character will only be mentioned incidentally." One would be interested to know just how Professor Michaelis would have defined artefacts that have "no artistic character." In any case, he states in his single chapter on prehistory and primitive Greece that the archaeology of art "is not concerned with the questions whether the people were dolichocephalous or brachycephalous, whether there was inhumation or cremation, or whether cist graves existed, nor does it inquire into their mode of living, their dress, or their furniture . . ." Prehistory is concerned with "anthropology, ethnology, and the history of civilization"; and these subjects, says Michaelis, are "as foreign to our studies as the questions of currency, trade, and history would be to numismatics*." One can only hope that the present-day historian of classical art will have the same startled reaction to this revealing admission as would the numismatist.

Michaelis has some high praise for Schliemann's discoveries, but the reservations are ominous. "But there is a reverse to the medal. Schliemann's education and talents were quite foreign to all scientific thinking and method. He cared neither for history nor art, as his indifference to the Hermes of Praxiteles proved; primitive cultures, curiosities, and vague imaginings exhausted his interests." Michaelis admires the samples of Minoan art discovered by Evans. "Every new find deepens our sense of a great civilization and of an art which, by virtue of its frank naturalism, united to a well-trained artistic eye and a technical skill by no means contemptible, succeeded in representing men in as individual and characteristic a manner as Hellenic art only attained nearly one thousand years later . . ." He is much less enthusiastic, however, about the contents of the Mycenae Shaft Graves. While admitting "the impression of an art fresh in perception and in reproduction," he feels that "one must deny it any capacity for development. Evidently certain conservative influences have to be taken into consideration . . ." Nowadays at least, the reader is more likely to sense rather more obvious "conservative influences" elsewhere.

The ideological chasm between "prehistoric" and "Hellenic," which infuriated Evans and which we shall see A. J. B. Wace deploring as late as 1956, was already wide and deep in Michaelis' thinking. "This culture [Minoan-Mycenaean] was richer and more ancient than that called forth by the so-called Dorian Invasion, which required several centuries before it produced the beginnings of the true Hellenic art, . . . This newly discovered art in its technical perfection, its definite and at times excellent designs, anticipated actual Hellenic art. This art then had to be placed before the beginning of Greek history . . ." Evans, Wace, Michaelis and Gardner would have found the greatest difficulty in arriving at a mutually acceptable definition of "true Hellenic art" or assigning an approximate date for "the beginning of Greek history."

# VI

Blegen, Priam and Nestor:

1915-1939

*"A man who rivals in wisdom and experience,*

*though not in loquacity, the ancient hero*

*whose home he discovered."*


C ARL WILLIAM BLEGEN WAS BORN IN 1887, the second of a family of six children. His father was Professor of Greek and German at Augsburg College in Minneapolis, Minnesota, so the son came naturally by his interest in higher education and especially in classical studies. The Blegen family is well and favorably known in Minnesota, particularly among scholars, educators and the numerous residents of Norse descent; and the present generation has added to its prestige. It is probably no accident that Carl Blegen is particularly remembered by his brothers and sisters for his absorption in devising and solving puzzles as well as his ability in organizing and supervising childhood games and activities.

Blegen's introduction to classical archaeology followed the usual training in Greek and Latin languages and literature. He studied at Augsburg, at the University of Minnesota and at Yale University. After completing the course work for the Yale Ph.D. in 1910, he was awarded a traveling fellowship that allowed him to enroll at the American School of Classical Studies in Athens. His ability and promise so impressed the director of the school, Dr. Bert Hodge Hill, that he was invited to stay on as secretary. He held that post from 1913 to 1920. In those years Hill and Blegen became close personal friends as well as colleagues in administration and excavation. The friendship persisted with unfailing devotion on both sides up to Hill's death in 1958.

Blegen served his apprenticeship in excavation during the early part of World War I when neither Greece nor the United States was directly involved in hostilities. At the same time another of Blegen's close and lifelong friendships was forming with A. J. B. Wace, director of the British School of Archaeology in Athens. Already a seasoned excavator and explorer for prehistoric habitation sites—particularly those of the neolithic period in the plains and river valleys of east central Greece— Wace had learned excavation techniques from older British colleagues and in 1912 had coauthored a pioneering study called *Prehistoric Thessaly*. Blegen's first major excavation was in 1915 and 1916 at Korakou, a prehistoric mound on the gulf coast about 2 miles west of New Corinth. Wace was present for a large part of the time during both campaigns, and Blegen warmly acknowledges his assistance both in the field and in the systematic study of the pottery before publication.

Indeed, one of Blegen's most striking characteristics is a capacity for loyal friendships. In this sense he may present a fairly fundamental contrast with his predecessors, particularly in their younger days. In spite of fame and countless acquaintances, Schliemann and Evans seem to have been essentially "loners." In Schliemann's autobiography this impression is strongly conveyed in his long separation from his family and childhood sweetheart and in his lonely passion to prove his own worth to them and to the world. And in the reminiscences of Evans' sister, as well as in the anecdotes about his relationships with colleagues, there are hints of personal charm and warmth offset by a certain Olympian aloofness. Blegen, on the other hand, in spite of a reserved, almost shy manner, has a notable capacity for making devoted friends and for preserving close family ties. Yet members of his staff, like his brothers and sisters in childhood days, are always aware that he is in charge. Discipline and single-minded concentration on the job at hand are quietly but effectively enforced.

Another strongly marked contrast involves Blegen's caution and Schliemann's audacity. In this respect Evans' instinct was something of a mean between the extremes. Perhaps the difference is mainly a sign of the times in which they lived. Because of its essentially wide-open nature and lack of adequate controls, a young science encourages bold theories and radical interpretations of meager evidence. But as its outlines become firmer and a dependable basis of fact gradually emerges, the ideas of even the most imaginative participants are to some extent restrained and channeled. It is probably true that Evans made fewer gross mistakes than Schliemann, both in excavation and interpretation; and, in general, the controversies in which he was involved in his lifetime were less strident. One does not need to browse very far in the early scholarly literature to realize that sharp and even acrimonious personal exchanges in print were far more common than nowadays. The trend toward restraint is no doubt a healthy symptom of maturity. In the heat of an open and bitter argument one is much more likely to be forced into an extreme position that must later be precariously defended or ingloriously abandoned. Yet human nature being what it is, strong differences of opinion always exist; and scholarly tempers sometimes boil over even yet in unfortunate public quarrels.

Blegen's record, at any rate, is a model of caution. His is always the method of understatement. Conclusions or theories, even when radical in their implications, are expressed in a quiet and disarming style. In this respect he presents an interesting contrast to his friend Wace, who was always the impetuous crusader against complacency, easy generalities and outworn viewpoints. Perhaps Blegen's bluntest challenge to established authority was very early in his career; and it involved Walter Leaf, the great Homeric critic. Leaf had stated that the Corinth area was relatively depopulated in the Late Bronze Age. Blegen pointed out that, while there was indeed no evidence for Mycenaean habitation on the exact site of classical Corinth, the surface of several mounds in the vicinity was strewn with abundant Mycenaean pottery. In fact, the mound at Korakou may well have been Homer's "wealthy Ephyra,"[64] apparently the most important settlement in the Corinth area during the Late Bronze Age. "Wherever it [Ephyra] was," wrote Blegen, "it was no doubt the capital of the Corinthia in Achaean times and as such probably exercised sovereignty over a district which was certainly well populated and prosperous, and which from the evidence we have might appropriately be called wealthy."

This exchange between Blegen and Leaf again underlines a serious problem (which we have already mentioned) involving topographical and geographical research in classical lands. The traditional philologist often prefers to remain in his study, depending on ancient literary authorities, out-of-date secondary sources and inadequate maps. The newer breed of field explorer, on the other hand, insists on going over the ground in person and relies increasingly on the evidence of his own senses. He checks the surface pottery and is increasingly likely to ask the advice of scientists in allied fields like geography, geology, civil engineering, aerial photography, agricultural economics and biology. When philologist and field archaeologist learn to cooperate effectively and complement each other's methods, a long forward step will have been taken.

## EARLY EXCAVATIONS: 1915–1927

Blegen's success in tactfully challenging established dogmas can be partly explained by the fact that his earlier excavations were carried out at relatively unknown sites. Gonia, Korakou, Hagiorgitika, Zygouries—what do these names convey in comparison with Troy, Mycenae, Knossos, or even somewhat less famous centers like Tiryns, Pylos and Orchomenos? In fact, most of the towns and villages whose ruins Blegen investigated between 1915 and 1927 were obscure in two senses. In the first place, their ancient names are unknown; and so the toponym used by the present-day inhabitants has to serve. Sometimes excavation and research may reestablish the correct ancient name, as when Hissarlik was finally proved to the satisfaction of most scholars to be the site of ancient Troy, or Ilion. But, historically speaking, many large and important ancient sites, particularly those that flourished only in prehistoric times, are still nameless. For example, the great Minoan palace in Crete that has been in process of excavation by French archaeologists since the early 1920's and is fully comparable in importance to those of Knossos and Phaistos is still designated by the local modern name, Mallia (though *possibly* ancient Milatos).

Most of Blegen's early excavation sites are obscure in this accidental sense; but they are probably also obscure in terms of their original, relative historical importance. This, of course, has to be judged from what is often very inadequate evidence surviving in epic poetry, mythology and later tradition. If, for example, we could somehow learn the original names of the mounds now called Gonia or Zygouries, it is quite possible that they would have no historical associations for us. Yet Blegen's patient and methodical excavation of these "nameless" habitation sites has proved to be tremendously important for the reconstruction of the prehistory of the Greek mainland, and particularly for northeastern Peloponnese. Precisely because they were not major political centers in prehistoric or later times, the earlier strata of occupation are less disturbed by extensive leveling to accommodate ever more ambitious complexes of buildings.

To make a gross and obviously inexact generalization, Schliemann was most interested in identifying famous ancient places and in finding treasures of precious metals; Evans, in recovering monumental architecture and the finest ceramic, sculptural and epigraphic remains; Blegen, in observing stratification and analyzing ordinary potsherds. Perhaps this transition shows most clearly the direction in which Greek prehistory has been gradually moving. From the hundreds of thousands of broken bits extracted from carefully noted levels in these unpretentious mounds, Blegen and Wace reconstructed a sequence of ceramic fabrics, shapes and decorative motifs that recurred in roughly the same relative order at different sites. Before the end of World War I they had jointly authored an epoch-making article entitled "The Pre-Mycenaean Pottery of the Mainland."

It is difficult in such a review as ours to present these forward steps in pottery analysis in sufficient detail so that the general reader will grasp both the method and the results. Admittedly, such material lacks the glamour and popular appeal of Schliemann's treasures or Evans' mysterious writing systems. But one simply cannot understand the accomplishments of the third generation without a reasonable background in the essentials of ceramic dating.

Blegen and Wace, in fact, proposed what is still the basic stylistic and chronological framework of major pottery types in central and southern Greece during the whole Bronze Age. As the title of their paper would suggest, they paid minimum attention to the better-known and latest "period of widest diffusion of Mycenaean pottery," which they characterized as the "silver age of Mycenae and Tiryns." The system owes much to Wace's work in Thessaly and to the still earlier British work at Phylakopi and in Crete. It is their primary aim to set up a mainland analogue to Evans' Minoan framework. They examine critically the widely accepted theory that mainland culture during the Late Bronze Age was simply a pale provincial imitation of the Minoan. And they emphasize the need to study mainland developments *before* the period of strong Minoan influence. "The glory of Tiryns and Mycenae was the climax of prehistoric art on the mainland of Greece and, as shewn conclusively by Sir Arthur Evans . . . is derived from Crete. Yet though Minoan in origin, the Mycenaean civilisation is not merely transplanted from Crete, but is the fruit of the cultivated Cretan graft set on the wild stock of the mainland. . . . The underlying mainland element influenced the dominant Minoan art so as to make it Mycenaean as opposed to Cretan." So, even before the first volume of *The Palace of Minos* had appeared, these two young students of mainland prehistory were challenging Evans' basic assumption about Minoan-Mycenaean interrelations from 1600 onward.

Blegen and Wace propose for their area the substitution of the term "Helladic" (*i.e.,* applicable to mainland Greece or Hellas) for Evans' "Minoan." His three major divisions of the Bronze Age (Early, Middle and Late) are retained, though in their scheme the latest pottery classed as Early Helladic is contemporary with Middle Minoan I. Evans' further subdivisions (I, II and III) for each major unit of time are not attempted, nor are his absolute dates mentioned. Furthermore, Blegen and Wace do not claim validity for their sequence of pottery types over the whole mainland. They admit that their conclusions are based "mainly [on] the result of careful observation of the stratification of the Corinthian excavations [*i.e.,* in the vicinity of Corinth] which we have followed together"; but they do take into account published material from other rather widely scattered mainland sites. Thus, they feel, the system ought to be useful "to illustrate the development of civilisation in the Peloponnesus and East-Central Greece during this long period."

Though the implications of their new classification are more epoch-making for earlier phases of the Bronze Age, we are of course directly concerned only with the later developments. Toward the end of their Middle Helladic period, corresponding to Middle Minoan II, the earliest burials

were being made in the Mycenae Shaft Graves. About the same time, gray
Minyan pottery was being imitated in a closely similar ware called "yellow
Minyan" (Fig. 71). Fairly early in their Late Helladic period, corresponding to Late Minoan I, the last burials were made in the Shaft Graves, and
the characteristic matt-painted mainland pottery ceased. The Late Helladic
period saw a rapid development from the simpler Middle Helladic civilization into the "Golden Age of Mycenae and Tiryns," with the tholos tombs
at Mycenae, Vaphio and Kakovatos, and under continuing powerful Minoan
cultural influence.

Figure 71

In the mature phase of Late Helladic, corresponding to Late Minoan II,
the production of undecorated gray and yellow Minyan pottery ceased and
Minoan imports decreased. In this period the mainland was producing an
especially fine class of two-handled goblets on a high foot with sparing
decoration of graceful floral or marine patterns. The motifs were apparently borrowed from Crete and were painted on a polished yellow Minyan
fabric (Fig. 72). "This new kind of Mycenaean pottery was first distinguished at Korakou (which may be the Homeric Ephyra) and has for
the sake of convenience been arbitrarily christened 'Ephyraean ware*.'"
To generalize rather drastically, the combination of increasingly stylized

Figure 72

Minoan decorative motifs applied to Helladic shapes and fabric became the basis for the later Mycenaean koinê so widespread throughout the eastern Mediterranean in the succeeding phase of Late Helladic corresponding to Late Minoan III.

Evans had always insisted that the sequence of Minoan pottery styles was so gradual as to rule out major intrusions of new settlers or conquerors in Crete. There were no "breaks." Blegen and Wace, on the other hand,

see evidence—at two points especially—for real discontinuity in the mainland pottery. "The appearance of [gray] Minyan Ware in the Middle
Minoan [their Middle Helladic] period marks, as regards the mainland at
least, a break away from the earlier phase characterised by Early Helladic
Ware. The period of Minyan Ware indicates the introduction of a new
cultural strain, the origin of which is not yet clear . . ." We shall soon be
hearing a good deal more about these intrusive makers of gray Minyan
pottery. Blegen and Wace go on to describe the second major dislocation.
"Not so long after the culture marked by Minyan Ware had taken root on
the mainland, Cretan (Minoan) influence made itself felt and profoundly
modified its [the mainland's] character by the introduction of a far higher
standard of civilisation."

Although their estimate of the originality of mainland prehistoric culture differs from Evans', Blegen and Wace definitely support him in his
insistence on the cultural carry-over from prehistoric to classical times.
"All recent research tends to show that archaic and, consequently, classical
Greek art was a renaissance—after it had lain dormant during a dark
period [approximately 1100–800 B.C.] of invasion and disturbance—of the
same artistic spirit that inspired Knossos and Phaestos, Tiryns and Mycenae."

Blegen's first book, *Korakou: A Prehistoric Settlement near Corinth,*
was a development of his Ph.D. dissertation. It was published in 1921, the
same year as the first volume of Evans' *Palace of Minos.* By this time
Blegen had been promoted from secretary to assistant director of the
American School. Even in the Introduction we sense the scientific value
of the thorough examination of this relatively unknown mound. The various classes of pottery, revealed in deep pits sunk right down to bedrock
and in more extensive clearance of limited areas of the upper levels, were
in general not new. The novelty consists in the stress laid on recording the
precise layer or stratum in which they occurred, *i.e.,* on scientific stratigraphy. Blegen is quite specific. "Their exact relation to one another, however, has not hitherto been accurately ascertained. The importance of the
site at Korakou lies in the fact that, supplying the evidence which was lacking at Tiryns and Mycenae, it now definitely establishes the sequence of
these prehistoric wares."

Throughout *Korakou* Blegen uses the new terms "Early, Middle, and
Late Helladic" (EH, MH, LH) and remarks that each of these periods
may be in turn subdivided as the stratification on the particular site dictates. And he does, in fact, recognize subphases of each major division at
Korakou. Although the publication is particularly important for the earlier
Bronze Age, we must confine our attention to the Late Helladic, which is
more or less chronologically parallel to Evans' Late Minoan I, II, III. Not

only are the *relative* dates of the various types of pottery established, but a "roughly correct" chart of *absolute* chronology is worked out by means of direct or indirect synchronisms with the Cyclades, Crete and the Near East. He suggests that Late Helladic I covered the sixteenth century, 1600–1500; Late Helladic II, the fifteenth, 1500–1400; and Late Helladic III, a much longer span, from 1400 to 1100 (see chart on p. 301).

Speaking of the finest mainland pottery at the transition from Middle to Late Bronze, Blegen firmly insists on its local production. "Save, possibly, for one or two sherds from Tiryns, none of this ware can be claimed as genuine Cretan, but the ultimate Minoan source of the patterns on many of these vases cannot be questioned. Since it seems equally free from doubt that most of this ware was fabricated on the mainland, Minoan originals must have been imported for use by the mainland potters. Whether any of these actual originals, which were obviously not numerous, is ever brought to light by further excavation or not, the fact of connections with Crete is nevertheless established."

Another statement is even more explicit about the nature of the cultural interplay. "Late Helladic or 'Mycenaean' pottery . . . evolved through a gradual and regular development of Yellow Minyan ware under constantly growing Minoan influence. The early shapes are thus for the most part those taken over from the Minyan stock, chiefly the goblet on a stem, and a deep bowl with high, splaying rim; but, once the new technique has passed the experimental stage and established itself, it rapidly prevails over the older methods and, as it progresses, it undoubtedly imports from abroad along with its designs many new shapes as well" (Fig. 73).

As he surveys the ceramic evidence for the whole sweep of the Late Bronze Age, Blegen perceives a gradual waxing and waning of Minoan influence.

> Although the evidence of such [Cretan] trade relations becomes exceedingly strong in the First Late Helladic Period, it is not until the Second Late Helladic Period that the height of Cretan influence seems to be reached at Korakou. . . . In fact, in the Second Late Helladic Period the ceramic artists of Korakou apparently strive to attain as nearly as possible the standards set by their Minoan colleagues in Crete. And, finally, in the Third Late Helladic Period, when Mycenaean pottery reaches its widest distribution, the fusion of mainland and Minoan art is complete; but a return swing of the pendulum has intervened, and it is now the mainland element which is seen to be dominant over the Minoan.

One can imagine Evans' reaction to the claim that as early as 1400 the mainland exerted any kind of cultural dominance over Crete.

When he extends the survey to the results of excavation on Late Bronze

Figure 73

habitation sites in other parts of central and southern Greece, Blegen finds
no important discrepancy with his classification or with his appraisal of
Minoan-Mycenaean relations. Cretan influence may have been strongest in
western Peloponnese. At Kakovatos, which was to have a special relevance
to one of his own most important discoveries twenty years later, he feels
that the material from LHII and the end of LHI indicates that "Minoan
ascendancy appears to be practically complete, and few, if any, of the
northern elements so characteristic at Corinth can be distinguished." Yet the
Kakovatos pottery as well as that from another tholos tomb farther south
at Messenian Pylos is still "almost certainly of mainland manufacture."

In the Aegean pottery assigned to the last centuries of the Bronze Age,
there is a mainland-oriented "essential uniformity" of style that Evans
himself had partially admitted. Blegen makes no attempt to give a detailed list of the very numerous places where such ware occurs; but he
underlines the extent of Mycenaean trade and influence by mentioning
"numerous places throughout the Greek mainland, on the islands of the
Aegean, at several points on the coast of Asia Minor, in Cyprus, Syria, and
Egypt, in Southern Italy, Sicily, as well as Sardinia . . ." And he adds that
"a related type, at least, appears in the extreme west, in Spain." It is hardly

accidental that a footnote refers obliquely to Evans' insistence on the great extent of Aegean-centered trade. But Blegen does not openly challenge Evans' view that the Minoans were the pioneers of this widespread commerce and that Minoan ships were still the main carriers during the heyday of Mycenae and Tiryns.

On the vital question of what happened on the mainland during the earlier phases of Late Helladic, however, Blegen leaves no doubt of his position.

> In explanation of the evolution of the simple, sturdy culture of the Middle Helladic Period, as we first see it at Korakou, into the regal magnificence of Mycenae, there is no necessity, nor is there evidence, for assuming an armed Minoan invasion followed by actual Minoan domination. On the contrary, the development, as we have examined it, seems rather due to peaceful penetration, chiefly of Minoan commerce and Minoan standards, and perhaps of colonies of Minoan artisans, among a people ready and eager to seize upon new ideas and new inventions, and willing to modify its own. The stimulus came from the south, but it acted on a mainland race which had a vigorous spirit of progress. The importance of the evidence from Corinth lies in the new light it reflects on the evolution of Mycenaean civilization. Korakou explains Tiryns and Mycenae.

As he concludes his book, Blegen feels compelled to emphasize the importance of studying the past in the broadest possible perspective. In this sense, too, he is something of an innovator and foreshadows the day when sites and whole cultures without glamorous historical connections will be explored for their own inherent interest and importance. One infers that he is fairly sure that Korakou is the "Corinth" of the Late Bronze Age and probably the "Ephyra" of Homer. Yet, even if it remains a "nameless" site from the point of view of myth and legend, we have much to learn from its ruins.

> Agamemnon and his noble peers have long enjoyed the prominence that was their due; now light is shed also on the conditions of life of the humble commoner—the nameless *tis* ["somebody"] of the Homeric poems, who with his fellows formed the bulk of the population and rendered Agamemnon's glory possible. We have recovered his modest house, though its clay walls have long since fallen away. We can picture him conducting his household worship about the pillar in his megaron. We have seen his simple bed, raised but slightly above the earthen floor. We have found the storage jars in which he kept his oil and grain; the quern on which he ground his flour; the hearth where he prepared his food; the vessels in which he cooked, and the dishes from which he

ate his meal, and the cup from which he drank his wine. And in the disorder of his abandoned house we may recognize the haste with which he fled before that mysterious peril which, under the name of the Dorian Invasion, we believe engulfed his waning civilization.

As assistant director of the American School until 1926 and as acting director in the following year, Blegen had an opportunity to carry out a whole series of further explorations and excavations in northeast Peloponnese. At Zygouries, Phlius, Nemea, Hagiorgitika and Prosymna he uncovered settlements and cemeteries of many periods. Yet, with the exception of Nemea (the site of one of the famous Panhellenic festivals in the classical period), nearly all of them produced mainly prehistoric evidence. And there can be no doubt that, as he shifted operations from place to place, Blegen was increasingly confirmed in his interest in the history of Greece before the Iron Age.

In 1924 Blegen married Elizabeth Denny Pierce, a faculty member of Vassar College and a career archaeologist in her own right. She has continued ever since to share in his almost annual field expeditions and to contribute her part to the study and publication of the finds. In his marriage as in his relationship with his own family and close friends like Hill and Wace, Blegen unfailingly shows a quiet and steady affection. He has a remarkable capacity to inspire loyalty. His sister Anne has helped him with several books, and close academic colleagues like John L. Caskey and Marion Rawson are his constant collaborators.

The text for *Zygouries: A Prehistoric Settlement in the Valley of Cleonae* was completed before Blegen left Greece in 1927 to accept a professorship at the University of Cincinnati. This position proved to be as nearly an ideal situation as any archaeologist can hope for, even if he is independently wealthy (as Blegen is not). Schliemann and Evans had the advantages of wealth and leisure and the prestige that striking success carries with it. But in at least one important respect the impact of their work was lessened—they had no means of regular formal contact with students. It is true that the experience of actually sharing the day-to-day problems of an excavation or working in a museum with a seasoned specialist is an indispensable part of the training of the aspiring archaeologist. But so are the academic contacts in the library, classroom and seminar. For a whole generation of students of archaeology at the University of Cincinnati, Blegen alternated the indispensable role of teacher with his program of excavation. The chairman of the Department of Classics at Cincinnati for many years was Professor W. T. Semple. In negotiating the appointment, both Professor Semple and his wife had been interested in arranging that Blegen's field work should continue; and they had the private means to make this possible. Even after the death of the Semples, the Taft Memorial Fund, which they set up in the Department of Classics, continued to underwrite Blegen's excavations and publications.

The mound called Zygouries lies along the highway in a defile not far north of Mycenae. The rather odd name comes from a particular kind of wild shrub that flourishes there. The two campaigns in the early twenties showed that the town was particularly prosperous in the Early Bronze Age. In Late Helladic III, however, a modest village had existed on and around the mound. It overlooked a limited amount of good agricultural land and, as we have mentioned, lay near a main land route from Corinth to Mycenae. Little towns at that period seem to have had limited scope for either political autonomy or cultural originality. "The rise of great strongholds and the concentration of royal power on the mainland," according to Blegen, "had no doubt completely subjected all the outlying small towns and reduced them to a common Mycenaeanized cultural level. . . . The dependency of Zygouries upon Mycenae, at any rate, is complete . . ."

Blegen excavated several basement rooms of a fairly large building that may have belonged to the local "mayor." At any rate, its size and the fragments of colored fresco would suggest that it was an important building. The basement rooms contained over 1,300 painted and plain vases of about twenty different shapes. Blegen refers to it as the Potter's Shop because the pots had never been used and seem to have been meant for sale. They had almost certainly been manufactured locally, perhaps in or near the building where they were found. They thus form a very valuable "closed deposit" (*i.e.,* all were exactly contemporary) illustrating almost the full repertory of shapes, size and decorative motifs of pottery that householders in this little community found attractive and useful. By this time, Blegen could date them fairly closely within the Helladic sequence worked out at Korakou and elsewhere; but he also refers to the important new dating criteria (which we will review later) being evolved by Wace at Mycenae in those same years.

By the time *Zygouries* was published, some critical reaction to the proposed Helladic system of chronology had begun to appear. Blegen is particularly unhappy about the insistence by some critics that the mainland scheme should correspond in every detail with the Cretan formulation. In a long footnote he writes:

> The system is naturally modelled on Sir Arthur Evans' Minoan classification, which laid the foundations for all subsequent study in the field of Aegean chronology, but when applied to the mainland or to any other area outside of Crete, the subdivisions should and must correspond, not with a system worked out on the basis of internal evidence

for Crete itself, nor with any fixed mathematical formula, but with the actual facts as revealed by excavations in the region in question. If they are to have any meaning in themselves they should and must correspond with the stratification.

So, in a sense, Blegen is already reflecting uneasiness about the rigidity of Evans' system, although he does not question its general applicability to the whole of Crete.

Two of the three campaigns at the Argive Heraion just south of Mycenae were carried out when Blegen was still on the staff of the American School; the last followed very soon after his move to Cincinnati. One can observe his commitment to prehistory, so clear in the proposal of an over-all formulation for Helladic chronology, gradually intensifying as time goes on. In the preliminary publication of the 1925 season at the Argive Heraion, for example, he refers politely to the "first major enterprise of the kind undertaken by the American School" at that same site from 1892 to 1895. Actually, in spite of Schliemann's startling prehistoric discoveries at nearby Mycenae and Tiryns, the whole interest and emphasis of that first American expedition had been on the later, classical ruins of the great sanctuary of Hera. Very little attention seems to have been paid to the evidence that the site had already been an important one in prehistoric times. Blegen simply points the contrast with characteristic charity and adds: "In the years which have passed since 1895 the wonderful discoveries of Sir Arthur Evans at Cnossus and of his Greek, Italian, English, and American colleagues in Crete, of the British School at Phylakopi in Melos, of the Germans at Tiryns, the researches of Tsountas, Wace and Thompson in Thessaly, of Professor Soteriades in Phocis [the Delphi area], and recently of the British School at Mycenae, to mention only a few, have added a vast amount of material and truly opened a new vista in prehistoric archaeology."

Before the end of his first season Blegen was convinced that "the pre-Hellenic settlement on the site, covering the whole extensive hill, was a very large and flourishing one, worthy to maintain its place in the Argolid beside the strongholds of Mycenae and Tiryns and possessed of a citadel of no mean strength." He believes that the dearth of imposing ruins is "due in large measure to the fact that the site continued for centuries to be occupied by the famous shrine of Argive Hera . . ." And he feels that the two epochs must somehow have a common denominator. "It hardly seems too bold a conjecture to hold that the cult of Hera is itself an heritage from this prehistoric settlement." Such continuity between prehistoric and later phases at several famous religious centers is now (1966) so obvious that coincidence is practically excluded.

A series of Middle Helladic graves and Late Helladic chamber tombs to the north and west of the habitation site had survived much better than the inhabited area. And it is largely the contents of the tombs that Blegen published so meticulously in *Prosymna: The Helladic Settlement Preceding the Argive Heraeum.* The first word of the title is the name that still clung to the site in Pausanias' day, and it has an authentic prehistoric sound. The expensive and beautiful publication, with a whole separate volume of plates, did not appear until 1937, nine years after the last campaign. Two busy years were occupied in cleaning and photographing and studying the tremendous variety of funeral offerings recovered from fifty chamber tombs. The text and illustrations were virtually complete in 1930, and the views expressed should be interpreted as belonging to Blegen's "pre-Troy phase."

The careful description of thousands of individual objects in *Prosymna* does not stand in the way of a synoptic view, although Blegen in his usual modest way understates his accomplishment. "This detailed account of the facts, which forms the major part of the present volume, is offered to meet the obligation that rests on every excavator to set forth in plain terms the results of his work, with the hope that it will prove useful to scholars who may be more competent than the writer to interpret the evidence in its broader historical, cultural and religious significance."

Blegen notes, for instance, that the Mycenaean cemetery was strung out for the better part of a mile to the northwest of the settlement. "Its position had apparently been determined by the course of an important highway connecting 'Prosymna' with Mycenae, and the tombs were evidently constructed on either side of the route, in the fashion that was still customary in the classical Greek period a thousand years later." And indeed, it is always worthwhile to search for the main cemetery of a Mycenaean site just to the west of the inhabited area—a location perhaps conceived as the first stage of the long western journey that the spirit of the dead must take when time had separated flesh and bones.

Clear-cut groups of chamber tombs at Prosymna may represent, as Tsountas thought at Mycenae, the presence of several different clans within the community. There were a few cases of cists dug in the dromoi, and they had clearly been used to accommodate material from earlier burials for which there was no longer room on the floor of the chamber tomb. In one case only, a burial of approximately the same date as those in the tomb was made in the fill of the dromos right above the doorway. "Was this perhaps," asks Blegen, "a slave or servitor, the victim of sacrifice or of self-destruction, who was laid to rest as the faithful guardian before the door of his master's sepulchre?" We recall that Tsountas had the same idea about burials found in a similar position at Mycenae. Solid evidence to confirm or refute such theories is very hard to obtain; and in fact we still do not know but are likely to be very skeptical nowadays.

Blegen is sure that the dromoi were completely filled in after each burial. He points out that the more numerous the burials inside the tomb, the more miscellaneous sherds occurred in the earth fill of the dromos. Some of these fragments definitely represent parts of vessels originally placed as offerings in the tomb, because sherds from the dromos and from the tomb chamber sometimes join. But Blegen also believes that the fill of the dromoi testifies to a custom of drinking a last toast or pouring a libation to the dead, and then smashing the cup against the door of the tomb. The door was always blocked up with a stone wall; and in the very few cases where one or more side chambers opened off the main one, their doors were similarly blocked. A few chambers contained niches (of uncertain use), and benches along one wall sometimes provided a kind of raised bed for a burial. The careful blocking of the entrance may have been meant to prevent the ghosts of the dead from disturbing the living (Fig. 74).

In about half of the tomb chambers a shallow cist had been cut in the floor. Occasionally there were several cists. In two cases they contained primary* (original) burials; in all others the burials were secondary*, i.e., the bones had been moved after the flesh had rotted away. Often multiple remains, usually rather carelessly swept together, were found in a single cist. Broken pottery also occurred in the cists, with some pieces fitting on to others remaining on the floor of the chamber. Blegen notes that the remains from previous burials were often swept back around the walls to provide space in the center for a fresh burial. "It was clear," he writes, "that the actual physical remains of the dead were held in little respect, when the time came for a subsequent burial, at any rate." And he theorizes that the more precious offerings from previous burials were sometimes removed at the same time.

Even in the case of the final burial, the disposal of the body was often impossible to determine because of the collapse of the roof. But enough evidence was preserved to show that the orientation and posture varied. Some corpses had been extended on their backs, others laid on one side or the other; the legs were sometimes extended and sometimes flexed. Only one example occurred where the upper body had been propped up, as Tsountas believed was common at Mycenae. In one case, a wooden bier had apparently been left under the body, but the deceased was regularly laid directly on the floor. The Prosymna tombs contained only one example of the clay coffin, or larnax*, which was so popular in Crete. Blegen remarks that it is "the only larnax yet discovered in actual use in a Mycenaean chamber-tomb on the mainland of Greece. It was clearly not a

DROMOS

Figure 74

Mycenaean custom to bury in coffins of any kind." This sort of evidence should already have disturbed those who believed with Evans in a thoroughgoing "Minoization" of the mainland.

Only ten of the fifty Prosymna tombs showed evidence of fire, and two reflected rather heavy burning. In not a single case, however, could there be any question of cremation of a body on a pyre. Bones that had been exposed to the fire were burned only on the upper side. Blegen disagrees with those who interpret the burning as a regular part of funeral or commemorative ritual. If that were the explanation, he points out, all tombs ought to preserve traces of fire. His own explanation is that these fires were built for fumigation. "It must have happened occasionally that two or more members of the same family died within a comparatively short time of one another and that sepulchres sometimes had to be re-opened fairly soon after a preceding burial. Under such circumstances it is easy to imagine that need may have arisen for a drastic fumigation of the atmosphere in the chamber, and no better means toward this end could have been devised than to bring in a heap of brush or other fuel and to light a good fire in the tomb, perhaps thereby even combining a ritualistic with a practical purpose." In other tombs a layer of earth was strewn at intervals over the contents of the tomb, thus forming a series of stratified "floors." This practice, too, may have had the same effect as a fumigation by smoke.

The total number of individuals whose remains could be recognized in the fifty chamber tombs approached 500. Besides jewelry, weapons, tools, implements and terra-cotta figurines, almost 1,100 vases were reconstructed. They range in date all the way from the end of Middle Helladic to Late Helladic III. Blegen again underlines the strong element of mainland originality in Late Helladic pottery. "The rapid development of the local Middle Helladic style into the fully evolved Minoan-Mycenaean is particularly clear. This evolution under Cretan influence, although remarkably swift, appears from the evidence of the pottery to have been brought about through the deliberate initiative of the mainlanders themselves."

Presumably all or practically all of the vases had originally contained food or drink or other ingredients to minister to the comfort of the dead person. "It must be admitted," Blegen writes, "that no certain traces of food were observed in any vessel; but many of the large amphoras were found still closed with a tightly fitting lid—usually the inverted foot of a goblet or cylix—and it is not probable that such care would be taken to close an empty pot." In tombs where bones of children were observable, a characteristic spouted vessel interpreted as a "feeding bottle" was particularly common (Fig. 75B), as were terra-cotta figurines.

Even allowing fully for valuable funeral offerings being removed later by relatives, Blegen feels sure that the families who built and used the Prosymna chamber tombs were not wealthy and powerful nobles. "These tombs are those of ordinary citizens in the humbler walks of life: independent farmers, or artisans, rather than serfs or labourers. . . . We have, as it were, a cross-section of the average life of their time. And we see that the bearers of the culture known as Mycenaean were not a small band of feudal lords who had led a successful invasion from abroad and made themselves masters of the country, but the yeomen or burghers themselves, if the terms may be permitted, who must have constituted the sturdy sub-

Figure 75

structure of Mycenaean civilization." This is the typical quiet method of questioning Evans' pan-Minoan theories that Blegen is learning to use so effectively. His more outspoken friend Wace, as we shall see, had meanwhile tried the more direct challenge.

In 1928, the same year as his final campaign at Prosymna, Blegen published with Professor J. B. Haley an essay called "The Coming of the Greeks." It is an interesting attempt to combine the results of linguistic research with archaeological field exploration; and it had a strong influence on the discussion (which still continues) as to when the Greek mainland was first occupied by speakers of the branch of the Indo-European language family later known as Greek. Haley utilized evidence collected throughout the Aegean area for the occurrence of a large number of distinctive place-names that preserve suffixes such as -nthos (Corinth[os]) and -ssos (Parnassos). It had been generally agreed that they represent non-Indo-European, "pre-Greek" survivals; and Haley's data suggested that "the distribution of these names points to a pre-Greek linguistic family occupying in force Crete, the Cyclades, southern and eastern Peloponnesus and central Greece, with offshoots extending beyond to the north, northwest and west into the adjoining provinces."

Blegen's assignment was to test this evidence from the place-names against the known population distribution (as indicated by excavation or the study of surface pottery of habitation sites) of all prehistoric periods from neolithic down to Late Helladic. He found that concentrations of pre-Greek names seem to coincide most closely with the pattern of habitation in Early Helladic times. And he suggested that this congruence might have a significant connection with the archaeological evidence for a cultural "break" when many Early Helladic settlements were burned or abandoned, and the Middle Helladic gray Minyan pottery appeared about 1900. Blegen and Haley concluded that the "Minyan" newcomers most likely spoke an early form of the Greek language that was gradually adopted by most of the survivors among the conquered race. It would be natural, however, that a fair number of pre-Greek place-names and certain other common vocabulary items for plants, trees and the like would have been retained from the older language family.

Linguists like Professors P. Kretschmer and C. D. Buck had already inferred from the distribution of dialects in historical times that the Greek language must have been spoken on the mainland at least as early as 1400, and perhaps 1600. Blegen holds that after the coming of the "gray Minyan people" there is no comparable discontinuity in the development of main-land culture until after 1200, at the very end of the Bronze Age. And so Blegen and Haley strongly support the equation: makers of gray Minyan pottery = first speakers of the earliest dialect (or dialects) of Greek in the peninsula.

Here again we note the challenge to Evans' widely accepted theories. In fact, Blegen outlines the clearest counterreconstruction he has so far attempted.

In Crete the Early and Middle Minoan race and language presumably still continue to exist; but on the mainland we have almost certainly a different race, the descendants of those invaders who brought Minyan ware into Greece. They have now [*i.e.,* by LHI] come under powerful Minoan influence—so strong that many, with Evans, believe in a Minoan conquest of the mainland. . . . In Crete, perhaps as the result of invasion from abroad, perhaps from internal catastrophe, the great palaces were destroyed by fire at the end of Late Minoan II, and the succeeding stage shows only a feeble survival, probably under main-land domination. Some sites were undoubtedly abandoned for a time, at least; at any rate it looks as if henceforth two elements in the popu-lation must be taken into account: a subject class and a ruling caste, the latter not necessarily very numerous. It [the ruling class in LMIII Knossos] was presumably an offshoot from the powerful dynasties estab-lished at Mycenae and Tiryns in the Argolid; while the bulk of the population was almost surely still constituted by the survivors of the indigenous Minoan stock, who had surely not been exterminated. . . . These [pre-Greek] names [in Crete] surely go back to genuine Cretan traditions and records of an earlier age, and must have existed long before the invasion of the island by the people of the mainland in Late Helladic III.

So the lines are drawn. Evans' reconstruction postulated complete Minoan cultural domination of the mainland, beginning about 1600 with the Shaft Grave period and almost certainly including political control by a Minoan minority. At some point, probably long after 1600, Greek-speaking "Achaeans" did enter the mainland area from the north; but they did not achieve political ascendancy in Greece until after—probably long after—the destruction of the Minoan palaces. Evans reluctantly admitted in most of his publications that at some point in Late Minoan III (after 1400) the tide turned, and cultural dynamism as well as political power was centered on the mainland. But he regarded the possibility of any mainland political control in Crete before the very last phase of the Bronze Age as unproved and unlikely.

Blegen and Wace now openly advocate a clearly antithetical view. According to them, a Greek-speaking minority took over mainland political control soon after 2000. The invaders gradually fused with the Early Helladic survivors and the Greek language became dominant. After 1600 this blended mainland culture was under intensive Minoan cultural influence for a couple of centuries; but a sturdy mainland element can always be detected, and eventually it strongly reasserted itself. Minoans never had any widespread political control of the mainland. At some point fairly early in the third subdivision of Late Bronze and *possibly* as early as the time of the destruction of the great Minoan palaces about 1400, however, the Mycenaeans conquered Crete and became a ruling minority there.

# TROY

No depreciation is intended of the sites that Blegen dug in his earlier career when we say that fate seems to have reserved his best years for the sites with the most important historical ties, *i.e.,* Troy and Pylos. When the University of Cincinnati Archaeological Expedition began work at Troy in 1932, Blegen was forty-five years old. Schliemann had turned forty-eight during his first Trojan campaign; and Evans was forty-nine at the beginning of the excavation of Knossos. By normal biological standards, all three were at the height of their physical and mental vigor as they began to probe these complex sites. Yet the contrast in terms of professional experience is vast. As we have seen, both Schliemann and Evans were completely innocent of previous training in excavation technique. Blegen, on the other hand, had more than twenty years behind him, most of it as director of major excavations. He had published definitive accounts of the results; he had the benefit of the accumulation of knowledge and improved methodology from two generations of pioneer investigations; and he had for years been closely associated with men like Hill and Wace with whom to discuss problems and share theories. Furthermore, he had an established position in a large university, the support and encouragement of his colleagues and all the time and financial backing he could desire.

These are tremendous advantages and Blegen made full use of them. Yet they do not fully account for the extraordinary importance of his excavations at Troy and Pylos; and the lack of previous experience and established reputation does not dim the luster of the earliest work at Troy and Mycenae and Knossos. There seems to be a deeper affinity, not fully explicable in terms of luck or experience, between the greatest excavators and the sites where they had their rendezvous with destiny. In a sense, perhaps, a great opportunity conscientiously seized may make the reputation of a man of no more than ordinary ability. But there is something almost mystical about the remarkable success of all three of these extraordinary men.

In the case of Troy, it was usually assumed after the appearance of Dörpfeld's monumental publication *Troja und Ilion* (1902) that, as far as excavation could prove decisive, the last word had been said about its major occupation phases and their historical connections. Before coming to Blegen's work, we must briefly carry on from a previous chapter the record of Dörpfeld's discoveries, particularly of the last campaign in 1894. For it was some nagging uncertainties connected with Dörpfeld's inferences that impelled Blegen to return to that patient mound and to extract from its still-undisturbed depths important new insights, particularly in connection with the Homeric songs. It is a measure of Dörpfeld's stature that he took an unselfish interest in the renewed excavations, thereby demonstrating the sincerity of what he wrote in 1902: "Later generations, which surely will be better equipped in the technique of excavation and in the understanding of the various finds than we, can through new excavations control and eventually improve on our work."

Dörpfeld first gives a useful review of Schliemann's discoveries up until 1890 as a basis for the discussion of his own campaigns in 1893 and 1894. Everywhere his affectionate respect shines out, along with a clear realization of the limitations under which the great pioneer worked. Both of Dörpfeld's own campaigns were concentrated on Troy VI, and the publication is adorned with his meticulous architectural plans. The well-preserved lower sections of the beautifully built fortifications, gates and towers were brought to light throughout more than half of the southern perimeter, and some sixteen contemporary houses were explored in the lower terraces just inside the walls. On the date of Troy VI, Dörpfeld can only repeat in 1902 what he had said ten years before. He is sure that the phase had a "long existence" and that the imported Mycenaean pottery places it roughly in the second half of the second millennium (1500–1000). "Finally," he writes, "one need scarcely mention that this dating is in harmony with the time-setting now held for the Trojan War and the destruction of the citadel by the Greeks." But such chronological calculations are still very obviously vague.

Dörpfeld proceeds to describe the new evidence for Schliemann's Level VII. The latest excavations showed that it comprised "two pre-Greek settlements," which were labeled VII¹ and VII². It is the earlier (lower) phase, VII¹, that Blegen was to find particularly interesting. Dörpfeld points out that its inhabitants probably repaired the fortifications of Troy VI and that its house walls often rest on the destroyed foundations of houses of Troy VI. Many houses of VII¹ were actually built against the old city wall, and he admits that in his preliminary reports they were mistaken for storerooms of the very last years of Troy VI. This mistake is in itself evidence of the lack of any clear layer of burning between.

The new settlement has in general smaller houses with more rooms. Dörpfeld thinks that they had belonged to "ordinary people," whereas the sturdier and roomier houses of Troy VI would have been occupied by "leaders and their dependents." Yet he is impressed by the general similarity, especially in pottery, and comes to the conclusion that the two settlements must have had "a similar population as inhabitants." He also explains his previous view that the small rooms were used for storage by pointing to the extraordinary number of large pithoi sunk up to their rims in the floors of many of them.

As for dating Troy VII¹, Dörpfeld says that the examination of the finds shows that "in the older houses of Level VII practically only such objects were found as also occur in Level VI." And he concludes that "the beginning of Level VII surely goes back, as the vase finds show, to the time of Mycenaean influence. Therefore, it is not impossible that the founding of Settlement VII falls in the last century of the second millennium . . ."

Hubert Schmidt wrote a separate report, entitled "The Pottery of the Various Layers," in Dörpfeld's publication. Schmidt had published in the same year a catalogue, the *Schliemann Collection of Trojan Antiquities* (a gift to the Berlin Museum). In discussing the pottery of "the Sixth, the Mycenaean Level," he maintains that, quite apart from the imported pottery, the native material betrays in its shapes and decoration strong influence from Mycenaean contacts and would by itself show that the culture of the mainland and Troy VI were contemporary. He stresses the association of Mycenaean pottery with the characteristic native monochrome ware that Schliemann had called "Lydian" and that was found on the house floors of Troy VI. And he insists on the "completely similar character" of the pottery of VI and VII[1]. In his judgment, "a distinction between older and younger layers [in terms of ceramics] is completely impossible."

In the same publication, Alfred Götze provides a catalogue and brief analysis in the "Small Finds of Metal, Stone, Bone, etc.," covering all phases of the Trojan excavations. This is, above all, a convenient review of the rich contents of Schliemann's various "treasures" from the second level. But, coming to Levels VI and VII[1], Götze contrasts the rarity of the small finds with the abundance of pottery; and he consequently believes that these levels had been thoroughly pillaged. Finally, he observes that such small finds as there are, especially those from Level VII[1], often betray the influence of Mycenaean models.

It is understandable, therefore, that as Blegen saw the situation almost a generation later, certain questions occurred to him that might be settled by further excavations. Above all, the last word had scarcely been said on the transition from Troy VI to VII[1]. Exactly what was the relationship, now that Mycenaean pottery was so much better known, between the imported pottery in the two levels? Could further evidence be discovered about the way in which each had been destroyed or abandoned? Could such new evidence, if forthcoming, be used to establish a sharper and clearer connection between the archaeological history of the site and the epic story of its destruction by Agamemnon and his Greek allies? Nor was Blegen's interest exclusively confined to the history of Troy in the Late Bronze Age. He was eager to reexamine the basis for the reconstruction of Trojan prehistory at every stage, since its position marked it as a natural link between the Aegean area and the still relatively unexplored hinterland of northwest Anatolia.

So in the spring of 1932 a University of Cincinnati Expedition arrived at Hissarlik, with Professor Semple as general director, Blegen as field director and a large staff of able young archaeologists, most of whom had been trained under Blegen himself. For seven successive seasons they returned to continue excavation in areas not too much disturbed by their predecessors. The full account of the results was published between 1950 and 1958 in a series of four bulky volumes called *Troy: Excavations Conducted by the University of Cincinnati, 1932–38*.

This very detailed report is superior in most ways to those that Schlie-mann and Dörpfeld had left for the guidance of future scholars. But it is only fair to say that, between the days of Schliemann and Blegen, archaeo-logical publications have—perhaps inevitably—been written more and more for specialists. An interested layman of Schliemann's day might—and no doubt did—read the bulky publications on Troy and Mycenae from cover to cover. But even the most enthusiastic nonspecialist would be very unlikely to get very far with Dörpfeld's or Blegen's multivolume reports. So, it is fortunate—and perhaps a symptom of a renewed awareness between spe-cialists and interested laymen—that Blegen has himself written a short factual account, *Troy and the Trojans* (1963), which is meant to provide a simplified but trustworthy summary of the newest evidence on Trojan prehistory.

In his review of previous work, Blegen too pays a sincere tribute to Schliemann: "The glory of discovering Troy and making it known to the world is his, and his fame was fairly won. . . . From his own mistakes he himself learned—and he was very quick at learning. He was a pioneer, and all those who have come after him have profited from his experience. By the end of his career he had made himself an experienced, trained, observant excavator who could hold his own with anyone . . ." Of Dörp-feld, too, he speaks with warmth; and in *Troy and the Trojans* there is a photograph of the sturdy old man taken during a visit to the Cincinnati excavations.

Using all the newest techniques of stratigraphy, Blegen learned from his painstaking researches how extremely complicated is the full story of the history of human habitation at Hissarlik. He was able to retain the nine major levels distinguished by Schliemann and refined by Dörpfeld. But he showed that each of them included two to eight subphases, representing, in all, forty-nine major and minor catastrophes and reconstructions over at least some areas of the site.

We can dispose very quickly with the new discoveries regarding Levels I through V, since there was no longer any question of their connection with Homeric Troy. But those whose curiosity was aroused by our review of Schliemann's discoveries and theories concerning the earlier levels will be interested in a brief survey of the newer interpretation. Detailed pottery analysis proved that these phases represent over 1,000 years of habitation, corresponding to the Early Bronze Age in the Aegean area, *i.e.,* before about 1900. Schliemann had been right in his inference, based mainly on the pottery, that there had been no detectable cultural disruption (and presumably therefore no major incursion of new people) during all that time. The megaron plan, for instance, has a continuous vogue from Troy I right down to Troy VII; and it now appears likely that this distinctive ground plan reached the Aegean from or via Anatolia. Virtually the same type of "idol," or amulet*, persists from Troy I through V.

A settlement not far away, where the Scamander River empties into the Dardanelles, shows characteristics similar to the earliest copper-using culture of Troy I; but in still lower levels it had a purely neolithic, stone-using population. So it is a fair inference that people from this or similar communities were the first inhabitants of the site that was later to become so famous and important. The hill of Hissarlik, far lower of course at that time, was soon fortified and presumably continued from then on until the end of the Bronze Age to be *the* stronghold in northwest Asia Minor. Though admittedly insufficient, exploration of the interior of Asia Minor so far suggests that Troy's major cultural contacts were always with the west and mainly by sea, rather than with the Asiatic hinterland. Comparable sea-oriented communities have been discovered since Schliemann's and Dörpfeld's day in the northern Aegean, most notably at Thermi on the island of Lesbos and at Poliochni on Lemnos.

The great megaron in the center of the fortified area of Troy II with its flanking dependencies is curiously reminiscent of the much later Mycenaean palace. It must represent the headquarters of a dynasty that had succeeded in acquiring political control over a prosperous agricultural, industrial and trading center. In addition to income from legal trade, these early Trojan chiefs may have added to their "treasures" by piratical expeditions. The tremendous fire that brought the final (seventh) phase of Troy II to an end about 2300 was clearly so sudden that the inhabitants had no time to carry away their valuables and so complete that the survivors, if there were any, were not able to rescue them later. Hence, Schliemann's fabulous discoveries more than 4,000 years later.

The Cincinnati expedition carefully preserved and recorded all the animal bones for analysis by a zoologist, Professor M. N. Gejvall. The remarkable number of sheep bones in the debris of Troy II indicates that sheep raising was a major occupation of the population. Connecting this evidence with the tremendous number of spindle whorls found in this and succeeding levels, Blegen makes the very attractive suggestion that the production of woollen textiles was a major Trojan industry.

A hint at the extent of Trojan trade, direct or indirect, is provided by the fact that the finest of Schliemann's magnificent polished battle-axes of nephrite and other exotic material find their closest parallels in far away Bessarabia. Perhaps, too, the bronze weapons from the "treasures" are royal imports or loot to be distinguished from the run-of-the-mill copper artefacts made and used by the Trojans themselves.

Another interesting result of analysis of the animal bones is that in the time of Troy III the diet was supplemented to a spectacular extent by the consumption of venison. Blegen suggests that this might be explained by the invention of some much more effective hunting technique or by an ecological change such as a shift of climate.

Blegen fully agrees with the verdict of his predecessors that Level VI marks the advent of a new people who had little in common with the culture of earlier phases. It was, he says, "a town which in its buildings seems to have followed a wholly independent plan that took no account of walls of houses and streets that had gone before. . . . A survey of the ruins . . . and of the miscellaneous objects and pottery recovered from them reveals at once striking differences and innovations. . . . The changes seem to me so unheralded, so widespread, and so far-reaching that they can only be explained as indicating a break with the past, and the arrival and establishment on the site of a new people endowed with a heritage of its own."

He admits that in Troy V "the ruins showed no recognisable signs of a devastating fire, nothing to suggest an attack and capture by enemies with the use of force and violence." But there is always the possibility of a relatively peaceable take-over by powerful newcomers or of a new occupation after a period of abandonment. In any case, Blegen points to such novel cultural features in Troy VI as technical changes and improvements in fortifications, solid freestanding houses that are widely spaced on gradually rising concentric terraces and the general use of bronze in contrast to copper. A particularly interesting innovation is the advent of the domesticated horse, shown by the scientific study of the animal bones. This trait has important implications for the origin of the newcomers and suggests the appropriateness of Homer's epithet, "horse-taming," for the later Trojans.

The most important novelty, however, was the sudden appearance in Troy VI of a very distinctive smooth gray wheel-made pottery with new, more angular shapes. This fabric had of course been recognized since Schliemann's "Lydian" designation. Blegen shows that in the earlier phases of Troy VI it is identical with the well-known gray Minyan mainland pottery, the hallmark of the newcomers to Greece at the beginning of the Middle Helladic period. So it appears that the people who had invaded Greece and those responsible for the new culture of Troy VI were either identical or closely related. We realize at once that such a situation has intriguing implications for the identity and language of friend and foe at the time of the Trojan War.

Blegen also notes the gradual increase in Troy VI of the importation of the second distinctive type of Middle Helladic pottery, the so-called matt-painted ware. And, as time went on, the Trojan potters copied Mycenaean vase shapes in their gray Minyan fabric. He recovered a whole series of locally made and imported pottery that was fairly closely datable from mainland analogies. So he was able to set the time limits for the occupation of Troy VI much more accurately, from the early part of the Middle Bronze until well on in the Late Bronze Age. The gray Minyan of the earliest level seems to be best paralleled by mainland ware of about 1800, and the actual Mycenaean imports of the latest phase are identical with mainland pots of the beginning of Late Helladic IIIB, about 1300. So Troy VI had a long and complex existence through eight major phases for somewhat over half a millennium.

It is remarkable how little evidence has ever been recovered for the burial customs of the prehistoric Trojans. The few adult burials found within the walls were clearly exceptional, and there can be no doubt that the cemeteries were outside the fortifications. All three of the excavators have successively searched carefully but without much success. Schliemann mentions this specifically as a major purpose of one of his campaigns, and Blegen too had it prominently in mind.

Although earlier cemeteries still eluded him, Blegen did discover a badly disturbed cemetery belonging to a late phase of Troy VI. It lay about a third of a mile south of the acropolis and contained a fair number of pottery jars or urns in which had been placed burned bits of human bones along with a few gifts and offerings. The proof that cremation was the burial rite in Troy VI is a significant discovery, and its use might help to explain the lack of evidence for burials from earlier levels. But the most interesting implication concerns "Homeric" versus Mycenaean burial customs. The archaeological evidence, of course, shows that inhumation was practically universal on the Mycenaean mainland, whereas rites of cremation are invariably described in the *Iliad*. We shall have more to say on this theme at a later stage.

Blegen was also able to settle, to his own satisfaction and that of most specialists, the problem of how Troy VI was finally destroyed. The upper sections of the monumental fortification and house walls were toppled over and flung about as if by a giant hand far more powerful than any human agency. There were no convincing signs of a general conflagration, in spite of Dörpfeld's contrary though not very firmly expressed opinion. And there was evidence (which Dörpfeld had freely admitted) that the site was immediately reoccupied by the same people. To such a set of circumstances, particularly in the Aegean area, there is a fairly obvious explanation. Troy VI, the mightiest stronghold ever to crown the mound of Hissarlik, was completely destroyed about 1300 by a violent earthquake. Therefore, if any confidence can be felt in myth and tradition, the Troy of the final phase of Level VI could not be the Troy captured by the Greeks. Poseidon, the lord of the rumbling earth tremors, not Agamemnon and his host, ruined Troy VI.

But was there another candidate that could be associated with the Greek siege? After all, ancient tradition placed the capture of Troy a century or more after 1300. What about the fortress that was built so quickly over the ruins of Troy VI? Dörpfeld had been clearly embarrassed by the questions raised and left unanswered by his Level VII[1]. Blegen's new discoveries and observations about that phase, which he relabeled VIIa, suggested a plausible solution.

The last inhabitants of Troy VI were apparently warned in advance and were able to save their lives and their more valuable goods. They returned "within a few days" to the ruined site and hurriedly rebuilt the fortifications with rather heterogeneous materials. They utilized other fallen blocks and scraps to build themselves shelters, not on the plan of the heavy structures of Troy VI but consisting of a maze of small crowded rooms. Into the floors they sank large numbers of storage jars covered with slabs, which further reinforces the impression of crowding and of the expectation that they might soon have to withstand a siege.

The pottery on the house floors indicates that Troy VIIa may have existed for no more than a single generation. The forms and fabrics carry on uninterruptedly the fashions of the final phase of Troy VI. There was continuing contact with mainland centers, though the quantity of imported pottery was perhaps somewhat reduced. Blegen analyzes it as follows: "The associated Mycenaean pottery includes many fragments with painted decoration in the style of Mycenaean III A, although the greater part belongs to the early stages of III B; the Grey Minyan Ware, moreover, differs little if at all from that of Phase VIh [the last phase of Level VI]. The overthrow of Settlement VIIa must surely have been brought about by 1250 B.C., if not a decade or two earlier." Other scholars have since suggested that the latest Mycenaean pottery associated with Troy VIIa is somewhat later, in fact too late to be accommodated with other evidence for the date of the Greek siege; but Blegen holds firmly to his original opinion and has in fact slightly raised his estimate recently (1962) to "the decade around 1270 or 1260."

And how was Troy VIIa destroyed? Blegen's firm answer is that "the destruction was undoubtedly the work of human agency, and it was accompanied by violence and by fire. A great mass of stones and crude brick, along with other burned and blackened debris, was heaped up over the ruined houses as well as in the streets . . ." Amid the wreckage the Cincinnati excavators came upon several human skeletons or parts of them that gave the impression that these people had been the victims of violent death.

Blegen believes that only one conclusion fits the new data.

Here, then, in the extreme northwestern corner of Asia Minor—exactly where Greek tradition, folk memory and the epic poems place the site of Ilios—we have the physical remains of a fortified stronghold, obviously the capital of the region. As shown by persuasive archaeological evidence, it was besieged and captured by enemies and destroyed by fire, no doubt after having been thoroughly pillaged, just as Hellenic poetry and folk-tale describe the destruction of King Priam's Troy. . . . It is Settlement VIIa, then, that must be recognised as the actual Troy, the ill-fated stronghold, the siege and capture of which caught the fancy and imagination of contemporary troubadours and bards who transmitted orally to their successors their songs about the heroes who fought in the war. There were no doubt many additions as well as excisions of incident or detail from time to time in the long course of transmission until in the hands of a poetic genius the various separate lays were fused together into the epics that have come down to us.

And so another episode has been added to the record of how archaeological evidence and the Homeric tradition are linked in the famous tale of Troy. Whether Blegen has written the final chapter is not yet clear. But rumblings in some quarters would suggest that not everyone is satisfied with his reconstruction. Like Schliemann and Dörpfeld, Blegen no doubt hopes and believes that he has finally settled the problem. But all three have always sought the truth above all else, and each would be willing to abandon his position if later evidence proved that the truth was not in it.

At about the time that he was completing his excavation at Troy, Blegen coauthored with Wace an important article that appeared in a German historical journal. Entitled "Pottery as Evidence for Trade and Colonisation in the Aegean Bronze Age," the essay is a plea for greater care and precision by archaeologists and historians in drawing sweeping conclusions about trade relationships from ceramic evidence. They show that there is already a basis to distinguish the likely origin of certain vase shapes and decorative motifs. "The stirrup vase, the low alabastron* [Fig. 76], a particular form of squat jug, and the kylix, though the first at least originated in Crete, are far more popular on the Mainland side and certain patterns, the ogival canopy* for instance, are practically unknown on vases of undoubted Cretan manufacture."

They also point to the pressing need for more study to distinguish provenience (point of origin) in terms of fabric—that is, types of clay,

Figure 76

presence of impurities, techniques of manufacture. They deplore the ambiguity in the writing of some historians and archaeologists who use the terms "Mycenean" and especially "Late Minoan" to refer to the whole Aegean area in the Late Bronze Age. "Late Helladic" and "Late Minoan" should be used, they insist, for the mainland and for Crete respectively, if the origin can be ascertained; otherwise, the more neutral "Late Bronze" would be less misleading.

Blegen and Wace are also concerned about the persisting belief in Minoan control of trade with the Near East far into the Late Bronze Age.

The great spread of Mycenaean influence down the coasts of Syria and Palestine and to Egypt during and after the Amarna period, that is after the fall of Knossos, came from the mainland and not from Crete and probably via Rhodes and Cyprus and the south coast of Asia Minor. There is even evidence that the mainland was in touch with these regions before 1400 B.C. In Egypt several L.H.I and II vases have been found . . . No certain Cretan pottery of later date [than Middle Minoan] has yet been found on either the Syrian or the Palestinian coast. In Egypt Late Minoan I and II pottery is very rare. . . . Recent research shows that most of the so called L.M.I pottery from Egypt is not Cretan but Helladic. This to some degree parallels the discoveries in Syria and Palestine and shows that the plentiful L.H.III imports into Egypt were anticipated to a certain extent by L.H.I and II imports. . . . More than eight times as many mainland (Helladic) as Cretan (Minoan) vases from Egypt in the period L.B. [Late Bronze] I and II, the sixteenth and fifteenth centuries B.C., are now known.

So Blegen and Wace raise serious doubts about the widely accepted thesis of a "Minoan thalassocracy" in control of the whole eastern Mediterranean at least as late as the destruction of the Cretan palaces. They are equally skeptical about the assumption that the occurrence of pottery of "Mycenaean" type in Sicily and south Italy proves that there was regular Minoan trade with the west. "Mr. [Thomas] Dunbabin who has carefully examined these vases agrees that they are not Cretan. . . . They seem to him . . . to resemble the wares of Argolis and Rhodes and therefore more likely to come from an Aegean centre."

Also, interesting historical implications about early rivalry between mainland and Cretan traders are opened up by the pottery from both areas discovered in the Aegean islands, particularly at Phylakopi on Melos. "Already in the Middle Bronze Age," Blegen and Wace insist, "the people of the Mainland were in touch with the Islands, but the extreme scarcity of their pottery in Crete hints that direct relations between the Mainland and Crete were rare and not cordial. In the first two phases of the Late Bronze Age Mainland and Cretan pottery occur at Phylakopi side by side. In the temple repositories at Knossos, where Melian vases were found, Mainland pottery is conspicuous by its absence."

They continue to question the common assumption—based almost entirely on Evans' interpretation of the archaeological evidence—that Crete had political control of the mainland, at least in the earlier phases of the Late Bronze Age.

The theory of a Cretan conquest or colonisation of the Mainland has been taken too much for granted. There is no greater Cretan influence in the Peloponnese than there is Greek in Etruria and the Greeks never conquered or occupied Etruria. In L.H.I and II the vases of undoubted Cretan manufacture found on the Mainland are extremely few, though it is true that Cretan shapes and patterns were widely imitated on the Mainland just as Greek models were copied and adapted by the Etruscans. Further there are signs of Mainland reaction on Crete. Professor [Aeilko Sebo] Snijder has suggested that the big "Palace Style" amphorae which in Crete seem to have been made only at Knossos, but on the Mainland occur almost everywhere, Mycenae, Kakovatos, Vaphio, Argive Heraeum, Berbati, Thorikos, really have their origin on the Mainland. The Ephyraean goblets of the Mainland are imitated in Crete in L.M.II in a conventionalized manner. The differences seen by Snijder, [Martin] Nilsson, [Gerhart] Rodenwaldt, and Karo in the psychology of art, in burial customs, in architecture and in many other points between Crete and the Mainland all tell heavily against the theory of a Cretan conquest or colonisation which has been based on archaeological evidence that will not stand serious critical examination. This theory should therefore no longer be allowed to cloud the historical implications of the archaeological evidence of the Late Bronze Age in the Aegean.

By the time this article appeared Evans was a very old man, and World War II was imminent. No counterattack issued from the Minoan camp; and indeed the mounting evidence had already made Evans' position difficult to defend.

## PYLOS

Blegen's excavations at Troy ended in 1938, *Prosymna* had finally appeared the year before and the preparation of the definitive publication on Troy would require years of preparation. For the first time in almost a decade the spring and summer of 1939 were free to follow up another problem that had for years piqued his curiosity. It had, in fact, intrigued a good many scholars ever since antiquity. Where was Nestor's Pylos? Blegen and Dr. Konstantinos Kourouniotis, director of the National Museum in Athens, had for some time held an unpopular belief. They thought there was a good chance that Nestor's capital had been located somewhere close to the great bay of Navarino (see Map VII) in southwest Messenia. And they believed that careful field exploration in that area might be worthwhile.

It is a striking reminder of the youthful state of Mycenaean archaeology (or of the ravages of time—or of the lack of Homeric historicity) that very few of the capitals of the thirty-odd rulers of independent kingdoms listed in Homer's Catalogue of Ships have yet been discovered. If tradition can be trusted, each king had a citadel and palace. The general location, even the exact acropolis, is fairly safely identified in a number of cases. Yet in 1939 only three such citadels had been extensively explored. Agamemnon's Mycenae was the starting point. The kings who ruled at Tiryns and at Gla in Boeotia were not certainly known. The ruins of the palace once occupied by Oedipus' family were known to lie beneath the modern town of Thebes; but according to tradition borne out by minor excavation it had been in ruins before the Trojan War. A good deal of exploration had failed to locate convincingly even the palaces of notable leaders such as Odysseus, Menelaos and Achilles.

Old Nestor, King of Pylos, is of course a figure of comparable prestige to these protagonists in the Homeric songs; and most of the handbooks of the first half of the present century list his palace as one of the few that are definitely known. But the results of Blegen's explorations strongly challenged this confident assumption, just as he had shown the error of the identification of Troy VI with Priam's capital.

The early stages of the Pylos controversy carry us back at least as far as the classical period. Blegen states the problem in his usual precise manner.

> The Dorian Invasion, whatever its source and however it ran its course, has left a broad gash, like a fire-scar in a mountain forest, cutting through the archaeological panorama of ancient Greek history. Many towns and settlements that flourished in the preceding Heroic Age were henceforth abandoned or declined to a state of insignificance. Even some of the great and noted strongholds sank into virtual oblivion, and the places where they had stood were lost from the view of men. In late antiquity the site of Troy itself, in spite of all literary fame, was no longer remembered, and academic circles disputed as to its identification. Exactly the same fate overtook Pylos, Sandy Pylos, the seat of the Neleid King Nestor, where Telemachos was so hospitably entertained on his famous journey described in the Odyssey.[65]

In classical times it was almost universally believed that Nestor's capital had been built on the high rocky citadel of Koryphasion (now called Palaiokastro, "Old Castle") at the northwest corner of the bay of Navarino (see Map VII). Those frowning cliffs are now crowned with a ruined fortification dating back at least to Frankish, Venetian and Turkish days. In the northern face of the cliff Pausanias saw what is still called the Cave of Nestor, and somewhere nearby he was shown the House of Nestor.[66] But doubting voices had already been raised centuries before Pausanias' time. The chief objector to the Koryphasion site was the geographer Strabo. We have noticed that he played a similar role in the Hissarlik controversy, and in each case he seems to have been simply expanding on the views of certain earlier scholars. Strabo apparently enjoyed jolting popular opinion by supporting an unorthodox view. And he was, above all, a firm believer in the literal truth of the Homeric poems. Compared to Strabo, Schliemann was almost a skeptic! Strabo had absolutely no doubts that Homer was personally acquainted with every detail of geography and topography referred to in the poems.

Strabo pointed out that there were actually *three* spots on or near the west coast of the Peloponnese to which the name Pylos belonged.[67] He immediately eliminated the northern one because its location does not fit the Homeric account. But he set out with great energy and persuasiveness to prove that the middle, or "Triphylian," Pylos accords far better with Homer's allusions than does the generally accepted "Messenian" Pylos on the great southern bay. The crux of his arguments concerns specific distances and routes of communication. The southern site, he thinks, is much too far away from Ithaka and the Alpheios River to fit Homer's description of either Telemachos' voyage[68] or the driving of the captured flocks and herds to Pylos after Nestor's victory on the banks of the Alpheios.[69] Also, the southern site is unsuited to Telemachos' journey by chariot from Pylos to Sparta,[70] since the lofty Taygetos mountains bar the way; whereas a much easier route from the Triphylian site skirts the northern end of the higher mountains. And, in addition, Strabo's notion of the location of the other eight "cities" of Nestor's kingdom, listed in the Catalogue of Ships,[71] suggested to him a cluster of major towns in the vicinity of the central, Triphylian Pylos.

It is difficult to say how much impact Strabo's view had on his contemporaries; but if one takes literally some of Homer's geographical descriptions, it can be argued that singers (and audiences?) in the interval between Mycenaean times and Homer's own day may have confused or conflated the two locations. In any case, we can return to the topographical problem more profitably when new facts, utterly unknown to Strabo, have been assimilated.

The general tendency between Strabo's time and the beginning of the present century was to hold with the prevailing ancient view that Nestor had lived at the southern (Messenian) Pylos. Then a new factor swung opinion heavily to Strabo's thesis. Wilhelm Dörpfeld plays the leading role in this episode, and it is one of the many ironies of our story that Blegen was destined to revise Dörpfeld's conclusions about Pylos just as he had in the case of Troy. In 1907 Dörpfeld was informed that peasants in the village of Kakovatos had discovered a tholos tomb and were carrying off the stones from its walls. He hurried to the rescue and began a careful excavation. It turned out that three large tholoi had been constructed in a slope looking down toward the sea across a fertile coastal plain some two miles in width. As usual, the tombs had been robbed in antiquity, and the domes had later collapsed; but a number of small finds and a mass of broken pottery remained. From the fragments Dörpfeld was able to reconstruct several large amphoras of the Palace Style, closely comparable to those that Evans was finding at Knossos and that he dated in Late Minoan II. So it was a fair inference that somewhere near the Kakovatos tholoi at about the same time as the latest palace phase at Knossos, at least three generations of a mainland dynasty had lived and died. Evans and his followers saw in the pottery and other contents of the Kakovatos tholoi further evidence of Cretan domination of the mainland, in both cultural and political terms.

Dörpfeld examined the flat hilltop that faced the tholoi immediately to

the south, and on its badly eroded surface he discovered the ruins of fortifications within which were the foundations of at least one sizable building. Dörpfeld remembered Strabo's theory and realized that Kakovatos is
in the district called Triphylia in ancient as well as modern times. So he
quite understandably believed that he had discovered Nestor's capital. The
mediocre ruins on the acropolis became a "palace," and he persuasively
reargued Strabo's case, adding some ingenious points of his own. Hardly
a dissenting voice was raised. Strabo and Dörpfeld were right; the almost
unanimous ancient and modern opinion had been mistaken. The capital
of the Homeric kingdom of Pylos was at Kakovatos. The ninety ships that
Nestor led against Troy had been launched from the broad sandy beach
near Kakovatos. The local inhabitants enthusiastically renamed the site
Nestora.

But there were soon a few minor discordant notes. In 1919 Kourouniotis
excavated a tholos tomb that had been discovered near Tragana, a village
located on the rim of hills about three miles north of the bay of Navarino
(see Map VII). Excavation showed that it had been built at approximately
the same time as those at Kakovatos and that there had been a succession
of burials—or at least offerings—in it until the early Iron Age. Kourouniotis
also located but did not excavate a second tholos nearby. So the southern
Pylos had a pair of royal tombs to rival Kakovatos.

Six years later a local tomb-hunter, Charalambos Christophilopoulos,
led Kourouniotis to the site of a third tholos in the southern area. It lay in
almost flat ground, just south of the modern village of Koryphasion which is
located slightly closer to the bay than the Tragana tombs. Its dromos
could not have been horizontal, unless the whole domed chamber had
been built above ground. And, in fact, the entrance proved to have sloped
downward quite steeply to provide access to a chamber deeply hollowed
below ground level. Its original exterior appearance would have been
similar to that of the usual tholoi built into a side-hill; that is, the dome
above the level of the lintel would have protruded above ground and been
covered with a protecting mound of earth. There was another novel feature about the Koryphasion tholos, although it was not recognized at the
time. Some of the vases put together from the broken pottery on its floor
date considerably earlier than any pottery in previously discovered tholoi.
In fact, some of them seem to belong to the last years of the Middle Helladic period. This would mean, unless there was a very long cultural lag
in Messenia versus Argolis, that the Koryphasion tholos was approximately
contemporary with the Shaft Graves at Mycenae.

As time went on Kourouniotis and Blegen confirmed the existence of
several additional tholoi in the southern area; but these discoveries near

Messenian Pylos did not cause many scholars to shift their allegiance from Kakovatos. Tholos tombs were turning up fairly frequently in many parts of south and east central Greece. It was vaguely conceded that their presence should indicate that a royal citadel had existed in the vicinity; but the Triphylian connections of Nestor had by then become an article of faith that few had the courage to challenge.

Blegen and Kourouniotis, however, were becoming increasingly skeptical. It seemed to them that the Homeric evidence, taken as a whole, does not rule out the southern site; and indeed this is proved by the fact that antiquity, so slavishly devoted to the literal truth of the poems, generally opted for the Messenian Pylos. They also saw that the southern location had various natural advantages. Here was the biggest, best watered and most fertile plain along the whole west coast south of the Alpheios River. Here was the magnificent sheltered bay, an invaluable base for the naval power that sent the second-largest contingent of ships to Troy. While taking seriously the strong ancient tradition about the general location, they did not agree with it that Nestor's capital would necessarily have been built on the great rock of Koryphasion, so exposed to storms and sudden attack from the sea. They preferred to begin by searching the hills and ridges that lay inland from the plain in the general vicinity of the tholos tombs.

So, in the spring of 1939 Blegen organized a very modest exploratory campaign. Kourouniotis kept in close touch with developments and managed to snatch a few days from his duties in Athens for a visit to Messenia. Blegen and his associates ranged the country by car and on foot, not searching blindly but with certain definite aims. By that time, the Mycenaean pottery that had been used in the days of Nestor and the Trojan War was well known. One characteristic sherd could by its shape or fabric or decoration provide a clue to a habitation site. A concentration of such pieces on the surface of a plowed hilltop or a weathered slope provided sure evidence. The expedition was able to locate several new habitation sites and tholos tombs, in addition to those that had been previously located.

There were other criteria, too. Nestor's palace would probably have been located on a defensible hill commanding a clear view all around, and especially toward the bay. It would have had to be readily accessible from the sea by road. There should still be a good supply of fresh water within easy reach. Perhaps one could even hope to find some fragments of fortification or house walls still protruding above the surface or recently exposed by cultivation or an earth slide.

After a thorough search, Blegen decided that a hilltop about five miles north of the bay best suited these requirements. It is called Ano (or

Epano, *i.e.,* "upper") Englianos, and it lies right beside the main highway
—actually a miserable, bumpy, winding track in those days—which leads
inland along a ridge and approximately at right angles to the coast. The
road had been cut into the south side of the hill, exposing characteristic
Mycenaean pottery of the thirteenth century. And on the hilltop there was
a spot among the olive trees where a big solid knob protruded above the
ground. Although it looked like Roman concrete, it could be limestone
calcined by fire. At a slightly higher level a quarter of a mile farther inland
there was a fairly good spring that was fed by a whole line of copious
sources extending right up to the Aigaleon mountains paralleling the
coast.

On April 4, Blegen laid out the first trench across the hilltop of Ano
Englianos. The sequel is the dramatic stuff of which movies are made
but that seldom happens in the real context of slow, unexciting, uncomfortable and often disappointing archaeological exploration. Within a
couple of hours Blegen knew that toward the end of the Bronze Age a
very large building (or complex of buildings) had stood on the hill and
had been destroyed in a great fire. This discovery seemed likely to be the
evidence he and Kourouniotis had hoped for in the search for Nestor's
palace. But that was not all. By incredible good luck the first trench exposed the ruins of a little room that still contained broken clay tablets
inscribed in a writing system that seemed on first impression to be identical
with Evans' "Minoan" Linear B. So, here in Messenia, far distant from
the Mycenaean "heartland" of northeast Peloponnese, Blegen discovered
the earliest cache of written records then known on the continent of Europe.
Tsountas and others had apparently been wrong. The Mycenaean civilization, at least in the Pylos area, *was* a literate one.

The repercussions of this epoch-making discovery were wide enough,
but it must be remembered that the Linear B script had not been deciphered. Evans had tried for forty years and failed. Furthermore, he had
published only a fraction of the Knossos material, which meant that other
scholars anxious to work on the decipherment were seriously handicapped.
Practically everyone took it for granted, as Evans did, that all of the Cretan
tablets, both those written in Linear A and Linear B, presented the puzzle
not only of unknown scripts but also of an unknown "Minoan" language.
The Linear B tablets at Pylos did not directly challenge that assumption.

Blegen's preliminary publication of the results of the 1939 campaign
naturally reflects extreme caution on this point. "We need not hesitate to
say, with all due reserve, that the script used in our palace is almost certainly a modified or adapted form of the Knossian Linear B. Whether our
documents were written in the Minoan language or in a quite different

tongue cannot yet be stated with safety, though the former alternative seems to be almost certain." We wonder if his friend Wace would have agreed with that final clause.

In fact, the Pylos tablets could be and were taken by some to reinforce Evans' long-held theory of Minoan domination of major mainland centers. Could they not reflect the administration of a Cretan "government" of Pylos? But the date proved troublesome. Few doubted the orthodox view that the destruction of the mighty palace of Minos should be assigned to about 1400, and that only "miserable squatters" inhabited the ruins thereafter. The Linear A writing system may have been continued to a very limited degree in other parts of the island; but Evans had decided, after a good deal of vacillation, that Linear B came to an end with the "final" destruction of the Knossos palace about 1400. Yet the pottery on the floors of the burned palace at Pylos, including the archives room, seemed to date much later. "We think," says Blegen, "this destruction cannot have occurred before 1200 B.C., in round figures, and that it may indeed have come about considerably later. . . . We are thus inevitably led to the conclusion that the tablets must be dated at the earliest to the close of the thirteenth century B.C., that is, to a period when, it is almost universally agreed among archaeologists and historians, an early strain of Hellenic stock has already long been established in control of the Greek mainland."

A Knossian governor and a Minoan-speaking palace bureaucracy at Pylos were rather difficult to accept at so late a date, but Evans had lately theorized (as we shall see) about just such a move from Knossos to Mycenae. Cretan control of mainland centers might have become localized and have held on, at least at Pylos, for two centuries. This is said to have been the immediate reaction of the aged Evans. Yet evidence had been accumulating for a generation that it was the mainlanders who were masters of the eastern Mediterranean after 1400, if not earlier. Martin Nilsson, one of the greatest authorities on Greek prehistoric culture, thought that the Pylos tablets perhaps represented the spoils of a piratical strike against Crete by Pylian ships. But would they not be strange booty? And where on Crete were documents being inscribed in Linear B not long before 1200? Apparently not in Knossos, although we have seen that Evans had once thought some of his Linear B tablets were considerably later than 1400! It was all very disturbing.

Blegen's summation of the immediate impact of the discovery is indeed a masterpiece of understatement. "Whatever its full bearing when the evidence has been more thoroughly studied, the recovery of so great a collection of written records in a Mycenaean context—the first deposit of its kind to come to light on the mainland of Greece—will necessitate some revision of certain current theories regarding the state of culture in the late Mycenaean world."

During the remainder of the 1939 preliminary campaign at Pylos small groups of broken tablets were laboriously cleared with delicate tools, left in place for a few hours to dry in the sun, photographed, sketched, numbered and gingerly removed. Ominous war clouds were looming, and systematic excavation of the building complex did not seem to be an immediate possibility. The trench where the first tablets had been found, only inches below the modern surface, was gradually widened. Everywhere in an area of a few square feet they lay, broken and topsy-turvy. And even the fragments were in a truly "delicate condition," permeated with moisture and riddled with rootlets. Their outline was barely distinguishable from the surrounding soil of which they had been made and to which only by a miracle they had not quite returned. No wonder if previous excavators of major Mycenaean sites, taking it as an article of faith that no palace archives had existed on the mainland, may have allowed their workmen to dig right through similar deposits.

From the moment of their discovery the Pylos tablets were assumed to be administrative records, like their counterparts at Knossos. They were clearly a homogeneous group from the very last year of the palace's existence. Such tablets were quickly and cheaply made of local clay as the need arose. The surface was inscribed while the clay was still damp, left to dry in the sun, and provisionally stored in the archives room. When they had served the immediate purpose, significant totals were presumably transferred to more permanent records on other writing materials. Then the original clay tablets were useless and would be thrown out or reduced to pulp for the next year's records. In any case, their life would normally be short. It was only the irony of fate that had preserved this final group by partially baking them in the tremendous fire that ruined the palace and most of its contents.

As at Knossos, most of the Pylos tablets are long and narrow, the simplest shape to roll out by hand and adequate for a short entry (Fig. 77). Another type is much wider, with a correspondingly large writing surface. From Cretan parallels, it could be assumed that the writing had been in

Figure 77

one or two lines along the length of the smaller tablets, and in as many as twenty neatly ruled spaces across the shorter dimension of the larger ones. Actually, the written surface could not be seen in the excavation stage, since a hard white lime accretion completely covered the surface. The inscribed content and the similarity to the Cretan Linear B writing system had at first to be inferred for all of them from the very first fragment found. It was so near the surface that it had partially dried and therefore held together when a workman noticed its rounded upper edge and picked it up. Before he could be prevented, he had drawn his hand across the surface. That one stroke revealed the written symbols and also came perilously near to obliterating them.

After they had dried out in the sun for a few hours, however, a group of tablets could safely be removed, packed in cotton wool and taken to the excavation house in modern Pylos. Dr. Hill, Blegen's closest associate then, as twenty-five years before, had constructed wire drying racks. In a few days the tablets were rock hard and could be safely handled; but they were still illegible. It was only then that Blegen, cautious as always, allowed a few to be carefully scraped until the writing could be made out. So it could finally be safely inferred that all were inscribed, and telegrams were sent off to Athens and Cincinnati to announce the news.

In the widened trench, meanwhile, a hint of the physical context was beginning to emerge (Fig. 78). Under only one or two layers of less frag-

Figure 78

mentary tablets a narrow stuccoed bench was uncovered. It was in the form of an open rectangle facing southeast, with one arm broken off irregularly and the other ending in a neat, squared fashion. In the area enclosed by the bench broken fragments continued to appear at lower levels. Behind the bench the stone foundation of the walls of a little room was cleared. The upper walls, of sun-dried brick in timber framework, had been destroyed by fire and weather, as had happened throughout the great building. There had once been a door where the bench ended so regularly. The floor was finally reached about 10 inches below the top of the bench, and the inventory of broken tablets reached almost 700. The section of the room beyond the door had clearly suffered even more; but there was no time to investigate further in that direction.

Blegen was now able to make a preliminary reconstruction of what had happened. The tablets had been stored neatly on the bench, possibly contained in wooden boxes or wicker baskets that may have been protected against unauthorized prying by clay sealings such as those found among the tablets. When the fire struck, the roof and walls of the little room collapsed, and the tablets were hurled pell-mell to the floor. Naturally, even if the inhabitants survived to come back and comb the ruins for valuables, they would not have bothered searching for such remnants. And the attackers who were presumably responsible for the fire would not have been interested in salvaging the tablets before they set the torch.

The clearing of the archives room was not the only activity of Blegen's first campaign. A second trench was laid out at right angles to the first, and it became clear that under the surface over the whole northwestern half of the hill lay massive foundations of a complex of rooms making up a very large building indeed. Naturally, very little could be made out of the plan of rooms and corridors that were intersected in the trenches. A few tablets found in other areas showed that the concentration in the archives room did not represent all of the preserved clay records; and one or two beautiful fragments of frescoed wall paintings with figured design hinted at luxury that might rival Knossos and Mycenae. In the 1939 campaign, too, the location of at least two more tholos tombs was discovered, and the one that lay alongside the highway some distance down the ridge toward the sea was cleared by Mrs. Blegen and Mrs. Hill. It proved to contain the usual assortment of small finds and pottery overlooked by robbers; and in its floor were two cists, a large one and another barely big enough to contain the body of a child. A total of five tholoi had now been authenticated in the immediate Pylos area, a number surpassed only by "golden Mycenae."

So Blegen felt justified in ending his preliminary report of that first season's work at Ano Englianos with a confident historical reconstruction.

Through the whole body of Hellenic tradition relating to the Heroic Age a single dynasty of rulers is accredited with the overlordship of southwestern Greece, and the most famous king of the Neleid line, sage Nestor, is a peer and equal among the Achaean leaders at Troy. Though presumably represented by subordinate chieftains in his many towns, so far as the literary records tell, he clearly had no rival of like standing anywhere in the district. His royal residence might then confidently be envisaged as a palace, built on a scale commensurate with that of the abodes of the other Achaean kings, including Menelaos and even Agamemnon himself. It is just such a palace that has now been discovered at Ano Englianos, the chief citadel of Western Messenia in Mycenaean times. . . . We venture therefore without hesitation, even in these early phases of our investigation, to identify the newly found palace at Ano Englianos as the home of King Nestor, the Sandy Pylos of Homer and tradition.

That first season at Pylos was probably the climax of Blegen's long and productive career; but a paper he wrote in 1940 contains his most "philosophical" general insights on the present status and future development of the science to which he has devoted his life. The occasion was a symposium on the arts and architecture in which a number of well-known scholars participated to commemorate the bicentennial of the founding of the University of Pennsylvania. Blegen's contribution, "Preclassical Greece," was first on the program.

He notes that Schliemann had begun his own archaeological career exactly seventy years before. "With Schliemann, one may fairly maintain, a new spirit entered into archaeological research, and modern field archaeology was conceived." Blegen proceeds to pay tribute to other pioneers, especially to Dörpfeld, Tsountas and Evans. He outlines the perspective on Greek prehistoric civilization to which they and many others had contributed so much. "A long and gradual development preceded the flowering of Hellenic [classical] civilization, which cannot be regarded as a spontaneous phenomenon wholly isolated from the past. Greek genius had deep roots going far down into the early layers of culture in the land; and many of the physical and mental characteristics of the Hellenic stock were surely inherited from forgotten antecedents of a remoter antiquity."

Three main ethnic "metals" had "fused together," he suggests, during prehistoric times to form the "peculiar Hellenic alloy." The archaeological record suggests that remote neolithic ancestors could be responsible for "the superstition, coarseness, and occasional unbridled passion and cruelty exhibited in the Hellenic nature." The temperament of the Early Bronze Age people, seen in its most undiluted form throughout Minoan history, suggests the origin of "the delicacy of feeling, freedom of imagination, sobriety of judgment, and love of beauty, which endowed the Greeks with a magic touch in all forms of art." The racial stock of the Greek speakers who probably entered the peninsula in the Middle Bronze period may equally account for "that physical and mental vigor, directness of view, and that epic spirit of adventure in games, in the chase, and in war, which so deeply permeate Hellenic life."

One brief paragraph on Minoan-Mycenaean relations shows that his and Wace's reaction to Evans' preconceptions has finally attained a fully confident statement.

> With the opening of the sixteenth century Mycenae became the main-land capital, and henceforth the upper ranks of Mycenaean society, at any rate, seem deliberately to have adopted and absorbed a great many of the refinements of Minoan civilization, adapting them, when neces-sary, to their own needs and tastes. The culmination of the process may be seen in the overthrow of Cretan power and the capture of the chief Minoan centers by an expedition from the mainland early in the fourteenth century, perhaps the last and most effective in a series of warlike raids. The kings of Mycenae now preside in the Aegean world as arbiters of a civilization compounded of Minoan and mainland heri-tages. It is likely that some early form of Greek was the current lan-guage.

He seems already to be rethinking his statement of only a year before that the language behind the Pylos tablets is probably "Minoan."

Blegen also concisely reviews current assumptions about the later course of events.

> Mycenaean civilization as evolved at the outset of the fourteenth cen-tury maintained its existence some three hundred years, during which a slow progressive decline is manifest both on the material and the artistic sides. Exactly what forces were at work to bring about this internal decay we are not yet in a position to determine. When the end came, however, it was clearly the result of action from outside and not from within; for all the late Mycenaean towns seem more or less nearly synchronously to have been destroyed by fire, surely the victims of hostile attack and capture. From literary sources we know that this was the Dorian Invasion, and it is interesting to note that the archaeo-logical evidence confirms essentially the dating handed down by tra-dition.

It is true that the destruction of Mycenaean centers in the twelfth century does generally coincide with the date assigned by Greek tradition to the Dorian invasion; but we shall find that the agents of that destruction now appear to be much harder to identify than Blegen thought in 1940.

In concluding his Philadelphia address, Blegen makes two vital points about lines along which prehistoric archaeology should move in the future. After a quarter of a century spent in continuous field work, no one could have been better qualified to diagnose weak points and no one had a right to a more respectful hearing.

> The amplification of any synthesis in the present state of our knowledge has urgent need, apart from further actual digging, of a systematic comprehensive survey of the districts of Greece, province by province, with the recording and mapping of all ancient sites. Most of the large centers have long ago been noted, but scores, not to say hundreds, of smaller settlements still await discovery. Almost infallibly the numerous potsherds that lie strewn superficially over the slopes of such mounds before any digging is done, give evidence of all the periods represented by the accumulated debris below. When the whole country has thus been methodically and thoroughly explored and the results have been properly tabulated and made available, we shall know infinitely more than we now do regarding the extent of occupation and the movements and distribution of population from period to period. In each district where investigations have hitherto been inadequate, two or three promising sites might then be carefully excavated for supplementary detailed information.

This recommendation is thoroughly in the tradition of Wace's and Blegen's own early and careful survey work, which was followed by such productive excavation.

A second admonition has perhaps an even more prophetic ring in terms of what has actually begun to happen in Greece since 1940. Even before that time Blegen had followed Schliemann's precedent by collaborating with scientists, particularly physical anthropologists and palaeozoologists. "In the future I believe we shall come more and more to rely on pure science for help in solving many of the problems that face us. Anthropologists, metallurgists, chemists, and zoölogists have already been called in to collaborate, to the great advantage of many excavations; and there are tasks for physicists, botanists, and geologists as well. . . . By combined effort we shall ultimately ascertain far more than we yet know regarding the formative period in the history of the Greek people."

These two methodological prescriptions were, indeed, long overdue in the Aegean area. Efforts are being made in some quarters since World War II to repair the lag; but it is puzzling to note how often the reaction to proposed cooperation with social and natural scientists ranges from skepticism to outright opposition. Blegen's energetic leadership, however, has ensured that the Pylos area where he is now working is in the forefront.

Professor Spyridon Marinatos, who succeeded Dr. Kourouniotis as Blegen's colleague, has carried on a program of exploration as well as excavation. Dr. Nicholas Yalouris, ephor (supervisor) of the Greek Archaeological Service for western Peloponnese, has also kept a careful check on all new discoveries and has cooperated closely with Blegen and his staff.

Finally, a Messenia expedition, organized at the University of Minnesota but closely coordinated with Blegen's own postwar activities, is conducting an intensive and wide-ranging program of surface exploration, topographic mapping and land-use study. In line with Blegen's prediction, more than 150 habitation sites contemporary with the palace have been located within the area which can be reasonably assumed to have been ruled by Nestor. And more tholos tombs are now (1966) known in the same area than had been recorded in all of mainland Greece as late as 1940. The population distribution of other periods, before and after the Late Bronze Age, is also beginning to come into focus. In terms of Blegen's second prescription, the Messenia expedition includes on its staff (in addition to archaeologists and historians) specialists in civil engineering, geology, paleobotany, ceramic technology, anthropology, geography, geophysics, geochemistry and agricultural economics. Each of them, as Blegen predicted, is making a contribution to the elucidation of the archaeological picture.

Blegen himself, a generation after his greatest discovery, continues to excavate annually at Ano Englianos; and the first volume of his monumental publication of the palace of Nestor is about to appear. We shall follow the postwar results in due order; but the conclusion of this chapter seems the most appropriate place to chronicle a significant event that took place on December 29, 1965. The Archaeological Institute of America has established a prestigious annual award "for distinguished archaeological achievement." The Institute's first gold medal was presented by its president with the following citation:

> Carl W. Blegen, excavator, author and teacher, throughout his long and distinguished career has fulfilled magnificently all the manifold responsibilities of an archaeologist's profession. Excavations of major importance, beginning with Korakou and ranging from Zygouries and Prosymna through Troy to the Palace of Nestor, have steadily revealed more and more of the identity and relationships of the cultures of prehistoric Greece. . . . The stately volumes which record his excavations, clear, precise, thorough, ever illuminating their wider historical and cultural implications, stand as enduring models of scholarly publication. And beyond these achievements extends the pervasive influence of the teacher and the man . . .

We have come to know Blegen's character well enough to feel the appropriateness of his response to this greatest honor that the leading American archaeological organization can confer on one of its members.

My feelings are deeply touched and I have difficulty in finding suitable words to express them. From my heart I thank you for this recognition of my somewhat plodding and prosaic endeavors. I wish I had accomplished much more to merit this award. Field archaeology—that is, excavating—is an uncertain and fickle mistress. In addition to work, application and perseverance, many other factors too are essential for success: among the most important may be counted good luck and good comrades. Most of my failures resulted from the lack of one or both of those two elements; and most of my enterprises that somehow turned out reasonably well owed it to my able colleagues . . .

Those who know him best will testify that the modesty is as genuine as the success, and that the success is as deserved as the first AIA gold medal.

# VII

---

# Developments Between
the Wars: 1919-1939

---

FOR OUR REVIEW of the new knowledge that had accumulated between the two great wars we shall again, as in Chapter V, depend on syntheses by two recognized scholars—in this case J. D. S. Pendlebury and Martin P. Nilsson. But to understand them adequately and to continue our chronicle of the emerging evidence from the key sites of Mycenae and Knossos, we must first follow up a resounding controversy. A. J. B. Wace's work at Mycenae in the earlier 1920s (as well as later) is in the great tradition of Schliemann and Tsountas, his predecessors there. Also during the period under review Evans not only continued some limited excavation at Knossos but published his multivolume *Palace of Minos*. It would hardly be fair to deny to either Wace or Evans the opportunity to state his own views. The bulk of this chapter, therefore, will be concerned with that "Great Debate."

## WACE AT MYCENAE

Schliemann had discovered the Shaft Graves; and his own insight along with that of various later experts, particularly the German scholar George Karo, had contributed much to the understanding of their marvelous contents. Tsountas' main contribution had been the clearing of the ruined palace on the acropolis and the opening of a very large number of chamber tombs in scattered concentrations among the hills to the west of the citadel. Both Schliemann and Tsountas had shown considerable interest in the tholos tombs in the same vicinity; but despite the architectural grandeur of the tholoi, the meager contents left behind by ancient robbers had made these great monuments less attractive to full-scale study and publication. Wace's work effectively filled this gap.

There were other outstanding problems, too—particularly those concerning the chronology of various important features at Mycenae, which further excavation might help to elucidate. So Wace, as director of the British School of Archaeology, applied for permission to continue the work, and two very important campaigns between 1920 and 1923 initiated a long series of British excavations. The staff included a number of talented young scholars such as Helen Lorimer, Winifred Lamb, Ida Thallon (later Mrs. B. H. Hill), Axel Boethius, R. W. Hutchinson, W. A. Heurtley, L. B. Holland, J. P. Droop and A. W. Gomme, all of whom later became well known in their own right. Piet de Jong, a gifted British artist and draftsman, divided his time between Mycenae and Knossos. Tsountas and Blegen were generous with assistance and advice.

Such a large and able staff—American as well as British—was a relatively new phenomenon in Greek prehistoric digs. The possibility thus offered for student training and careful supervision of the work force and the division of labor for intensive field study of various classes of finds were favorable omens for the future. The labor force never exceeded fifty-five, a salutary contrast to the great gangs working under one or two supervisors in earlier days. The results of the first two seasons were fully published by Wace and his assistants in the *Annual of the British School* and in the journal *Archaeologia*.

Supplementary excavation under the Cyclopean walls at two points between the Lion Gate and the Postern Gate as well as under the threshold of the former provided useful and somewhat surprising evidence. "In every case," says Wace, "L.H.III. sherds were found. It thus seems that the circuit wall of Mycenae should be dated to this same period; in other words, it cannot be older than the beginning of the fourteenth century B.C., since the finds at Tell-el-Amarna give us a fixed point for the date of L.H.III. pottery." He points to the results of the latest German excavations under Kurt Müller and G. Rodenwaldt, who were continuing and refining Dörpfeld's work at Tiryns. Their investigations indicated a similar date for the main walls of that fortress. "The walls of both citadels have always been recognized as alike in style," says Wace, "though those of Tiryns have generally been thought the older."

Wace's allusion to the sculpture in the relieving triangle* over the Lion Gate is also worth quoting. "Sir Arthur Evans has shewn the significance of the type of this relief, the Sacred Pillar with the guardian lions, and has given illustrations of parallel types. The column is the sacred pillar of strength and protection, and is an aniconic form of a deity. . . . In this case . . . the sacred pillar possibly stands for the Great Mother Goddess. . . . The placing of such a relief over the citadel of Mycenae probably meant that it was placed under the protection of the Great Mother, and that she was the establisher of Mycenae." We might anticipate here by mentioning an attractive recent conjecture that the missing heads would have identified the beasts over the Mycenae gate as griffins rather than lions. The heraldic griffins behind the Pylos throne and the wingless griffins in the Throne Room at Knossos do suggest a very intimate connection with Mycenaean royalty.

Everywhere throughout the publication one is impressed by Wace's detailed enumeration of the pottery and its careful assignment to the newly established categories and subcategories. He and Blegen and others of their generation are pioneering in a less spectacular way, perhaps, than their predecessors; but they are establishing the basis on which the chronology—and therefore the intelligible history—of Mycenaean civilization is to be founded. For instance, Wace proves that the building just to the right inside the Lion Gate was destroyed when the citadel was finally sacked and burned. From the remnants of grain in storage jars in its basement corridors, reminiscent of the storerooms of Crete, Wace concludes that it was an official supply depot and so christens it the Granary.

In describing the pottery found in the Granary, Wace was laying the groundwork for dating levels at the very end of the Mycenaean Age, later called LHIIIC. "In the same two Corridors . . . was found the deposit that had collected on their floors during the last period when the building was in use. This consequently is particularly interesting as it shews us the kind of Late Mycenaean (L.H.III.) pottery in use at Mycenae at the time of its ruin. The pottery from these two Corridors shews the same characteristics as that from the East Basement [of the palace] and we therefore have one homogeneous class of L.H.III. ware, of such a strongly marked style that we have called it the Granary Class . . ." (Fig. 79).

The British probings in the area of the ramp leading up to the palace from the Lion Gate showed that the citadel had had a long history of occupation. The excavators discovered pottery that could be safely assigned, as a result of the stratification established by Blegen at Korakou, to an early phase of the Early Bronze Age "about the beginning of the Third Millennium B.C." And above this was found the familiar matt-painted and gray Minyan ware of the Middle Bronze Age. Because of later intensive building activity, no intelligible remains of buildings could be associated with these early classes of pottery.

Important results for the history of the site and especially for the true understanding of the Shaft Graves come from the examination of the LHIII houses, presumably belonging to courtiers and important palace officials, which occupied the lower part of the fortified area. Below the level of these houses, several shallow single cist graves could be safely assigned to Middle Helladic times. They correspond to others discovered

Figure 79

earlier within or near the Grave Circle; and Wace proved that this whole slope had contained an extensive MH cemetery long before its upper part had been enclosed within the fortified area.

More than that, Wace sees a direct development from these simple antecedents to the famous Shaft Graves. The earlier graves "are in form primitive shaft graves, and apart from the rough stone wall which lines the latter, it is of the same general type as the Second Shaft Grave [Schlie-mann's #5]. The Shaft Graves in themselves are after all only elaborate versions of the ordinary M.H. cist grave hollowed out in the rock." So, in spite of the profusion of rich burial furniture, the very form of the royal Shaft Graves would indicate a long occupation of Mycenae by the ancestors of those wealthy and ostentatious monarchs. If (as had sometimes been inferred) they had come from abroad, bringing their riches with them, they would most likely have been accustomed to a different type of tomb and would have insisted on using it.

As he begins his account of the British researches in connection with the Grave Circle itself, Wace sums up the work of the past generation as follows: "Although much has been written on this subject since the excava-tions and researches of Schliemann, Stamatakes and Tsountas, the greatest advance towards a fuller understanding of its history was made by Karo, whose able paper has unfortunately not yet been published. Thanks to his unselfish courtesy we had the opportunity of conducting our researches in the Grave Circle with the assistance of the proofs of his article."

In the first place, it is pointed out that the higher and lower levels at which Schliemann found stelae should mark two separate periods in the history of the cemetery. The stelae at the lower level represent the ground level of the original rock surface, when the graves were first dug and used, but the stelae found higher up show that a major artificial change had later been made in the contour of the slope. Wace reconstructs the earlier situation as follows: "Thus assuming that in early times there was a settlement on the summit of the citadel, where the Palace was afterwards built (and we have plenty of evidence for such an early settlement in the Early and Middle Helladic pottery found below the walls and floors of the Palace) the area of the soft rock of the Grave Circle and its neighbourhood was the nearest spot to the summit of the acropolis where it was possible to cut graves. The hard limestone rock of the upper part of the citadel was naturally most unsuitable."

The development of this cemetery of simple Middle Helladic cist graves is then carried a step further.

At the end of this period, not long before the beginning of the sixteenth century B.C., part of this cemetery became reserved for royal interments. Perhaps just about this time a new dynasty occupied the throne of Mycenae. At all events from this time onwards Mycenae, which had certainly been flourishing before, now began to be extremely prosperous. From the fact of their having been laid in these graves we may call this, the first Mycenaean dynasty that we can envisage, the Shaft Grave Dynasty. During the course of the sixteenth century B.C., six royal graves were dug here close to one another, and in them nineteen persons were buried. Further to the north of the Grave Circle under the Granary, yet another was dug, and to the south of the Grave Circle . . . there was probably once another Shaft Grave. . . . Of these graves the Sixth is now recognised, by the pottery found in it by Stamatakes, as undoubtedly the earliest, and the first interment in it should be placed at the end of the M.H. period. . . . The two latest would be the Third and First [the latter is Schliemann's #2] Graves, but even these do not come down so late as the end of the sixteenth century B.C. That is to say this series of the six royal Shaft Graves stops before the end of L.H.I. . . . It is possible that this cemetery may have no longer been used for royal interments because a new dynasty now sat on the throne of Mycenae.

In order to follow the reconstructed sequence of events, we must at this point anticipate Wace's new chronological evidence from the tholos tombs.

"From about the end of L.H.I. begins the series of Tholos Tombs which from their impressive size and noble architecture we can only regard as the tombs of kings. The Tholos Tombs, beginning towards the end of L.H.I., continue right through the next (L.H.II.) and well into the last phase (L.H.III.). The different method of burial inclines us to the belief that a change of dynasty took place at Mycenae, and we may call this, the second dynasty, the Tholos Tomb Dynasty."

Yet the altar that Schliemann found within the Grave Circle and other evidence as well suggested that the royalty buried in the Shaft Graves continued to be remembered and placated with offerings. "It seems clear," says Wace, "from the investigations of Sir Arthur Evans and others that Minoan kings were regarded as semi-divine personages. The Mycenaeans seem as far as we can tell to have adopted the Minoan religion. Thus naturally the graves of the kings buried in the Shaft Grave cemetery would have been regarded as sacred. The kings were the temporary human manifestations of divinities, and to them as such all due rites and offerings were paid." It is clear that Wace was at this point deeply under the spell of at least some of Evans' preconceptions. Within a decade Martin Nilsson and others were stressing notable differences between mainland and Minoan religion.

About the beginning of the fourteenth century, according to Wace, a particularly rapid development can be noted in the whole mainland area. By then the palace of Knossos had been destroyed and the center of political power had shifted to the mainland. In Wace's view, Mycenae itself apparently benefited most dramatically. "It would then have been under the rule of a rich and powerful prince of the Tholos Tomb Dynasty. He rebuilt the palace on the summit of the acropolis, and replanned the whole citadel and enlarged its area. We assume one king to have been responsible for all this building activity, for so far as the archaeological evidence goes, all these buildings must have been constructed within a comparatively short time."

The natural line of the new fortifications would have cut right through the revered royal Shaft Graves, and so the wall was bellied out at considerable expense to include the whole area. But even greater pains were taken to show respect.

It was resolved to enclose and preserve as a kind of temenos* the sacred area where the kings still lay in state. This was done by enclosing the sacred spot with the elaborate double ring of vertical slabs with their massive covering stones and monumental entrance leading from the Lion Gate . . . but since this was a sloping hillside special constructions had to be undertaken to level the ground. . . . When the ring wall was completed . . . the sculptured grave stelai which had stood over the graves at the original level on the sloping hillside were reerected over the graves at the new level on even ground.

This imposing fourteenth-century monument seems to have remained— honored, protected and undesecrated—through the later Bronze Age. Wace theorizes that its memory, if not the actual structure, explains the story of the graves of Agamemnon and his companions that was told to Pausanias when he visited Mycenae. Wace's reconstruction ends in a characteristically modest way.

> The intuition of Schliemann enabled him to divine the existence of royal graves within the Lion Gate, and rediscovered to the world the brilliance of the civilisation which Homer had celebrated. Schliemann, however, could not, with the scanty knowledge then at command, see his wonderful finds in their true perspective. The work of Tsountas and Evans, to mention the two most prominent investigators only, has given us an outline of the history of those times. Our knowledge is still extremely imperfect; but the little we have done towards unravelling the history of the Grave Circle, in itself an epitome of the history of Mycenae, will, we hope, make the way a little clearer for our successors.

Perhaps this rather painful awareness of the disparity between what we know and what we would like to know best characterizes not only Wace himself but also most archaeologists of the twentieth, as compared to the nineteenth century.

W. A. Heurtley made a careful study of the sculptured stelae. To explain the curious discrepancy between the perfection of the geometric decoration and the clumsiness of the naturalistic figured element he suggests that the stelae must have been sculpted by mainland artists who had as yet imperfectly assimilated the new Cretan influence. And he points a comparison with the mainland vase painters.

> The feature which distinguishes the decoration of later Middle Helladic Matt-painted pottery from that of the Cyclades on the one hand, and from the contemporary wares of Crete on the other, is the persistence of the geometric tradition. Long after the naturalistic impulse from Crete had profoundly affected the art of the Cyclades, the vase painters of the mainland were dividing the surface of their vases into vertical and horizontal compartments in the earlier manner. . . . The decorative scheme of the stelai . . . is in close relationship with this tradition. . . . It is indeed clear that during the first half of the first L.H. period, three distinct artistic currents existed side by side at Mycenae, the Helladic proper which includes the makers of Matt-painted pottery and Minyan goblets, the Creto-Mycenaean represented by the potters and metalworkers, working under Cretan teachers, and the Minoan, which is

represented by the numerous objects either made by Cretans at Mycenae or imported from Crete.

Heurtley thus places the mainland and Cretan artistic productions in the perspective of two very different traditions and rejects Evans' broad generalization that everything "good" on the mainland must be Minoan or under Minoan influence, while the locally inspired productions were beneath notice. Heurtley says:

> The stelai confirm the impression which many of the gold objects from the graves and the polychrome Matt-painted vases produce, viz. the independent character of Mycenaean art. . . . Even when Cretan art was becoming paramount at Mycenae, and almost before the last Shaft Graves were finally closed, the earlier tholos tombs were rising, and though the stelai, as such, have no successors, the architectonic genius which they foreshadow was to find, at a later period, its full expression in the Lion Gate and the great tholos tombs of the third group, and in the application of sculpture to their façades.

In his final sentence Heurtley makes a prophetic inference. "Perhaps a reflection of the same [mainland] spirit may be seen in the Palace Style [pottery] of Crete."

The British excavations in the Mycenae palace were mainly a reexamination of Tsountas' conclusions, with the advantage of more precise ceramic analysis. This rocky acropolis, however, with very little depth of earth remaining and that in a disturbed state, was a very difficult place to apply the new methods. Wace sees some evidence of a new over-all rebuilding of a much larger second palace, contemporary with the new fortification walls and the finest tholos tombs. But his proposed chronology is doubted by his colleague L. B. Holland, who thinks it more likely that the changes were gradual and piecemeal. Yet Wace's suggestions are at least appealing to the imagination.

> In L.H.I. under the Shaft Grave Dynasty a First Palace stood on the summit of the acropolis. This, with alterations, would have served in L.H.II. for the earlier kings of the Tholos Tomb Dynasty. Later, at the beginning of L.H.III., under the most powerful and wealthiest kings of the Tholos Tomb Dynasty, a Second Palace was built here and we have before us to-day the ruins of one of its sections. This Second Palace seems to have lasted till the fall of Mycenae, and it would thus have been the home of the Atreidai [descendants of Atreus, including Agamemnon], if, as we now believe, they were historical. Schliemann's imagination, which dreamt of the home of Agamemnon and Clytemnestra, was not far wrong. If there was an Agamemnon, if Homer did

not write pure fiction, it was in this Palace that the King of Men lived and hither he brought home his bride Clytemnestra from the banks of the Eurotas [a river flowing through Sparta].

We can agree with Wace on the LHIII palace; but his "First Palace" contemporary with the Shaft Graves rests on very little solid architectural evidence.

We have already reviewed Tsountas' description of the preserved ground plan. The British researches did not seriously modify the earlier work, but one new discovery must be mentioned. On an upper terrace in the northeast part of the palace, which had apparently been the royal living quarters, one room contained "a curious stepped construction covered over with red stucco" and a stone-built drain. The similarity to the tank baths or lustral area in Cretan palaces led them to christen it the Red Bath. We can imagine what Schliemann would have made of this discovery, in the light of the tradition about Agamemnon's murder in the bath on his return from Troy!

Coming to the megaron, Wace suggests that the columned porch had a flat roof, which served as a balustraded loggia or upper veranda reached from the higher level of the south corridor. He imagines that from this loggia "the royal household could watch games in the Court below, as seen in the well-known fresco found by Schliemann below the Ramp House" (Fig. 80). The porch had a doorway in the center of its east wall, as well as double doors communicating with the anteroom and, through it, with the megaron proper. The side door that connected with the Domestic Quarter was apparently covered only with a curtain (Fig. 81).

The great hall was about 43 by 40 feet and had brightly painted stucco floor and walls. In the center was the ceremonial hearth flanked by four columns, as at Tiryns. Although it had been partially destroyed when the supporting wall of the southeastern section had fallen into the gorge below, the diameter of the hearth could be calculated as about 12 feet. Where it had been broken, ten separate layers of painted stucco could be distinguished. In spite of constant redecoration, conservative taste or religious associations reproduced each time the identical "wave and star" or "notched plume" motif. This depiction of rays or flames was also used to decorate movable hearths and tables of offering at Knossos. There was, as we saw, no evidence of provision for a throne in the preserved section of the floor. Possibly, it was movable, like the rest of the furniture.

Wace speculates on the peripheral position of the Mycenae megaron as compared to that at Tiryns. He assumes (and again the fascination of pan-Minoan theories is clear) that the higher central terraces, where one would expect it to have been located, were already occupied with buildings in a

Figure 80

different tradition. "If the First Palace at Mycenae—as seems reasonable, though we know practically nothing about it—depended largely on Cretan models, and if the Megaron, as held by Dr. Duncan Mackenzie and others, is a Mycenaean and not a Minoan feature, then we can understand the late introduction of the Megaron at Mycenae and Tiryns." He also discounts the suggestion that this was the "men's megaron" and that there had been a corresponding, somewhat smaller "women's megaron" (as at Tiryns) on a higher terrace. He insists that "the old theory . . . that the men and women had separate quarters in megara in Mycenaean Palaces" must now be discarded completely. We shall see later that the newest palace plan at Pylos forces a reexamination of this problem.

The lighting and ventilating of the great hall also raise problems. Wace believes that there may have been windows in the south and east sides that "would, of course, have given a magnificent view down the precipitous Chaos ravine and over the Argive plain beyond." But the escape of smoke from the hearth is more difficult, since he rather firmly holds out for a second story over both vestibule and hall. Dörpfeld's theory of a higher section of the roof (clerestory) supported by the four columns around the hearth does not appeal to Wace.

On the other hand, L. B. Holland, in his architectural commentary, doubts that the outer megaron walls and the four interior columns would have been strong enough to support either a second story or a clerestory. He feels that a fair amount of smoke from the hearth was taken for granted,

Figure 81

as is suggested by Odysseus' advice to his son. If the suitors ask why Telemachos is removing the weapons from the megaron, he is to explain that they were getting injured by the smoke.[72] Holland proposes instead that the spacing of the four interior columns both at Tiryns and Mycenae suggests the presence of a large rectangular opening in the center of the megaron. "The arrangement is similar to that of a Roman *atrium*, which was a living room in a colder climate. There what amounts to a small court is surrounded on all four sides by porticoes of nearly uniform depth."

An amusing feature in Holland's report is that Wace keeps inserting disclaimers in footnotes. For instance, at this point he rather sensibly interjects: "Assuming the Megaron to be a living-room, a hole in its roof about 15 x 13 feet in area would be extremely inconvenient in the rainy season, when a fire on the hearth would be most needed." Yet, here again, one senses a free and healthy interplay of theories and ideas. It would be difficult to imagine a publication by Schliemann or particularly by Evans in which a subordinate openly challenged the director's point of view.

The British excavators were also able to discover new evidence for the fresco decorations on the walls of the megaron. Tsountas' material from 1886 had already been supplemented by Rodenwaldt, who in 1914 had discovered new fragments near the north wall. The British recovered still more; and it was clearly established that the megaron had been decorated with a continuous frieze or separate panels representing battle scenes. Miss Lamb published the following reconstruction: "The fresco represents a building of several stories, marked into narrow vertical divisions by walls of which the ends are seen in section, and with women standing either at the windows or outside. . . . It has some of the characteristics of the high, many-towered type of building . . . The framework is of wood, probably filled with rubble and decorated with stucco imitating stonework. Below, to the right, is part of the rock on which the castle stands . . . and faint traces of a tree. The resemblance to the silver rhyton from Mycenae . . . is particularly striking."

In a footnote she emphasizes the Homeric parallel: "Fighting before the walls of a besieged castle is in accordance with Homeric practice as described in the *Iliad*. There, the Trojan army is camped before the walls of Ilion, which we know from the excavations of Schliemann and Dörpfeld to have more nearly resembled a castle than a fortified city. . . . Here we have a frieze with the besieged castle at one end of the wall, the armies fighting before it, and the camp of the besieging army beyond. It may well be considered as illustrating a siege like the siege of Troy." Can we imagine Schliemann exercising such restraint with this tempting opportunity?

The most important feature of the earliest British excavations at Mycenae, however, was surely Wace's new classification of the nine great tholos tombs in a typological* sequence. By his day it was generally agreed that they were all later than the Shaft Graves; but there was no consensus as to the outside dates of the series or where individual tombs fitted within such a span. It will be remembered that Schliemann had briefly examined the only uncollapsed tomb, the so-called Treasury of Atreus (its later label, the Tomb of Agamemnon, is still a pure guess). Stamatakes completely cleared it in the following year. Close to the Lion Gate, Sophia Schliemann had also partially excavated the dromos and chamber of another tomb (later assigned with no more evidence to Clytemnestra). Beginning in 1886 Tsountas cleared all the previously known tholoi as far as he could safely do so; and he raised the total to nine by the discovery of three more. No addition has since been made at Mycenae, and it is usually assumed that there were no others.

Wace and his colleagues carefully reexamined all nine (Fig. 16). Evans' keen interest in mainland developments is shown by a financial contribution to this project. The Greek authorities forbade complete excavation of the so-called Aegisthus Tomb because it was feared that further digging would dangerously weaken the surviving structure. Another tomb, called by the local toponym Epano Phournos, could not be safely cleared. ("Epano Phournos" means "Upper Lime Kiln," and the resemblance of ruined tholoi to these common structures is close enough that the local peasants can hardly be blamed for confusing them.)

Wace describes his own work as an attempt to reconstruct the "history of the tholos tombs at Mycenae from the point of view of construction and material." He admits that his favorite method of dating by pottery analysis has only limited application here because sherds of far earlier and later periods got washed down or thrown into the tombs. Later cult seemed to have involved ritual offerings; and tomb robbers, modern shepherds, earlier investigators and collapsing domes had completely disturbed any stratification there might once have been.

The analysis includes one other tholos, which was located at the Argive Heraion (Prosymna) only five miles or so to the south. Wace sensibly points out that his criteria may very well be inapplicable to edifices at a greater distance. "Methods of construction are bound to vary from district to district with the variations in the local material ready to hand. It is therefore inadvisable to argue from constructional peculiarities of tholoi elsewhere in the Peloponnese, in Attica or in Thessaly, unless there is other evidence available, in support of theories as to the Mycenaean tholoi. Still more so should the architectural parallels of Crete be used with great caution, since the whole environment of the Minoan civilisation in that island was different from that prevailing at Mycenae and on the mainland."

To explain the method of building these great circular tomb chambers, we can hardly do better than quote Wace's summary of the observations made in the early nineteenth century by the architects of the French *Expédition Scientifique de Morée*. Their description, it should be added, applies particularly to those of regular ashlar* construction.

The sides of the facing blocks of the dome are not cut to fit one another so as to make a kind of horizontal arch. They merely touch at their inner angles, and the resulting interspace is packed tight with small stones driven in to make all solid. At the back the big blocks of the tholos wall are counterweighted so far as can be seen with a heavy mass of rough stones packed in behind them. The blocks in the lower courses are larger than those in the upper, and the eye or final course is capped by a large slab which has a hollow on its under surface to

continue the line of the dome to a rounded point. The top of the dome
projects above the surface of the hillside and is covered with a mound
of earth which naturally serves to hold the masonry in place. Built on
this system with well-dressed rectangular blocks of hard stone, the
dome ought not to collapse if reasonable care is taken. Each successive
ring of masonry should support itself if the joints are true, and it is well
packed and counterweighted so as to make it fit tight within the circular
excavation.

Wace's scheme divides the nine Mycenae tombs into three convenient
groups of three each, with the Heraion example falling in the second
category. The first group includes the so-called Cyclopean Tomb, that at
Epano Phournos and the Aegisthus Tomb. In the second are those called
the Kato (Lower) Phournos, the Panagia and the Lion Tomb; while the
third group comprises the Treasury of Atreus, the Tomb of Clytemnestra
and the Tomb of the Genii (sometimes called the perfect tholos). All of
the names are entirely fortuitous. There is, of course, not the slightest
evidence to assign any of the tholoi to specific individuals whom tradition
associates with the royal families of Mycenae.

Wace's major typological criteria are clear and crisp (Fig. 82). The
three tombs of Group I are built of limestone (or "poros") rubble, with
somewhat larger blocks around the doorway. Only the tomb of Aegisthus
has a stone-lined dromos; and that feature, plus a later façade of ashlar
masonry in regular horizontal courses, suggests that it is transitional to
Group II. Those in the second group have a stone-lined dromos, a door
frame of large dressed blocks of the much harder local conglomerate and
long lintel blocks that indicate the presence (proved in one case) of a
relieving triangle above the doorway. Group III displays dromoi completely lined (in two cases) with conglomerate blocks laid in ashlar technique. The doorways are built of massive and regular conglomerate blocks
cut with the saw. The sparing use of sawed blocks in the Treasury of
Atreus ought to make it the closest to a transition from Group II. The
stone lining of the circular tomb chambers is of very carefully cut conglomerate laid in regular courses. The tombs of Group III have precisely
set thresholds and frames for separate doors, whereas in all the others
except the transitional Lion Tomb the entrance had simply been sealed
with a stone wall.

Wace himself reviews the distinctions as follows: "The second group is
characterized by the discovery of the relieving triangle and by ashlar work
in poros. The third group is distinguished by the discovery of the possibility of sawing hard stone like conglomerate and by great advances in
engineering skill, which facilitated the handling of gigantic blocks." The

Figure 82

line of development, or *relative* chronology, seemed the natural one, *i.e.,* from the simpler to the more complex. But it was soon to be vigorously challenged.

On the question of *absolute* chronology, however, Wace finds much more difficulty. He begins with Group III and points out a parallel with the use of sawed conglomerate in conspicuous places in the latest phases of the palaces and fortifications (both at Tiryns and Mycenae) that are securely dated in LHIII. Since the Treasury of Atreus shows only sparing use of the saw, it ought to date at the beginning of that period, *i.e.,* about 1400. At this point he adduces some ceramic evidence gained from a small test under a section of its massive threshold, where one might expect to find no sherds later than the original construction. In the shallow bedding trench, packed with small stones and the characteristic tough yellow clay that served the Mycenaeans for mortar, a number of potsherds were found. "All are of L.H.III. date and compare well with those from the first or earliest strata by the Lion Gate, and so date from the beginning of L.H.III., or the early fourteenth century B.C." It should be noted that Wace later lowered the date to about 1330. Professor George Mylonas has recently offered evidence that would lower the date of the latest monumental phase of the fortifications (including the Lion Gate) to about mid-*thirteenth* century. And he further believes (without much more definite evidence than Wace had for his equation) that the Treasury of Atreus should be about contemporary.

Wace then goes on to assign dates to his first two groups by almost Euclidean reasoning.

> Having thus acquired a fixed point for the third group, it is easy to give approximate dates for the other two. . . . The tholos tombs are almost certainly the tombs of kings. If they are the tombs of kings, they cannot well be contemporary with the Shaft Graves, as it would be absurd to imagine two dynasties ruling simultaneously at Mycenae. The princes buried in the tholos tombs . . . must therefore have been either earlier or later than the Shaft Grave Dynasty. The tholos tombs are not Middle Helladic and so cannot be earlier, but must be later. The Shaft Graves are Late Helladic I., and the third group of tholos tombs is Late Helladic III. Thus the first and second groups should fall between the Shaft Graves [the end of the sixteenth century] and the beginning of the fourteenth century B.C. . . .

Holland adds a very brief architectural commentary in which he fully supports Wace's criteria for tracing the development of the tholos. And his concluding paragraph, although not concerned with his specialty, is particularly interesting.

There are, in all probability, few, if any, more tholos tombs to be found in the vicinity of Mycenae, though there are probably a good many more chamber tombs still undiscovered there. This is due to the fact that the latter were built entirely below ground, while in the tholos tombs, as has been shown, the lintel was regularly set at the level of the natural grade of the hillside, bringing nearly half of the structure above ground. Even with a collapsed dome the presence of such a tomb could hardly have escaped notice in all the very thorough investigations of the region. We can say safely, then, that there were at Mycenae a series of nine or at most, say, a dozen tholos tombs, built over a period of something above two hundred years; and of the nine known ones no two are contemporary. This means that on the average they were built twenty to thirty years apart, or one, and only one, to each generation. The inference is obvious: they are the tombs of a dynasty of kings who ruled, from the downfall of the Shaft Grave Dynasty, until themselves overthrown when the Palace was destroyed. For nobles, and perhaps for a short-lived king—unless laid in his predecessor's tholos—chamber tombs had to suffice; the commoners probably were content with still more humble resting-places, while tholoi were reserved for royalty alone.

We notice a difference of opinion here between Holland and Blegen. The latter had insisted that the occupants of the chamber tombs at Prosymna were not nobles but ordinary citizens. And we wonder, too, if chronological considerations on Wace's reconstruction would not require that the last kings before the final destruction were buried elsewhere or in reused ancestral tholoi.

Some additional secondary questions are raised or implied by Wace's study. One concerns access to the tholoi. The clearly artificial conical mounds were noticeable in modern times above the Heraion, Lion and Clytemnestra tombs, as is still true of the uncollapsed Treasury of Atreus. Such mounds are a reliable indication to the trained eye of a surface explorer in every corner of central and southern Greece. They must have been a sufficient clue, also, to the tomb robbers of antiquity. But how did the thieves—or even the legitimate users—enter the tomb? Was the dromos filled in after each burial and reexcavated before the next? Or was it left open so that the passerby could see its façade, adorned in the latest examples with architectural and sculptural decorations? Were the tholoi, in fact, accessible through the dromos until classical or even later times, and did the entrances only gradually fill up with wash from the hillsides?

The evidence is not easy to interpret, and Wace does not face the question directly; but he does provide important clues. In several cases, potsherds found on the floor of the dromos, some of them trodden into it, belonged to vases of which the remaining pieces lay on the floor of the tholos chamber. This could only happen when the dromos was clear, but it hardly proves whether the dromos was left open or simply reopened temporarily for another burial. Again, what is the purpose of a wall built across the outer end of the dromos in the later Mycenae tholoi? Wace says it was "probably . . . so made that it could be easily taken down when the tomb was re-opened and could be replaced later." But what would be its function if the dromos was filled between burials? On the whole, it seems likely that the dromoi *were* completely filled in after each burial; and the analogous procedure in the case of the Shaft Graves may be relevant here.

In this connection we should note the relatively rich burial that Tsountas discovered at the inner end of the dromos of the Tomb of Clytemnestra. He saw in the grave goods, particularly the bronze mirrors with carved ivory handles, clear evidence that the single occupant had been a woman; and he speculated that she was a favorite slave who was forced to accompany her royal master to the next world. At any rate, the grave goods belong to relatively late Mycenaean times, and the burial was undisturbed. At that time, the inner part at least of the dromos must have been filled and never reopened. Wace believes this was a "secondary interment*," that is, presumably, that this skeleton with its possessions was removed from the tholos chamber (or some other place) and reburied in the dromos. But if she really was a slave, would she have been buried in the tholos in the first place?

Wace also notes rather enigmatic evidence concerning late finds in the tholos chambers, though again he does not face the problem directly. Mycenaean tombs often contain pottery from geometric, classical and even Hellenistic times. Usually it was deposited before the collapse of the dome. Does it indicate reuse for later burials or a hero cult of the dead king, or both? Wace seems somewhat in favor of the cult hypothesis, which of course would not necessarily prove that the dromoi remained open. The offerings might well have been inserted through a hole just below the lintel of the doorway or through a small opening in the top of the dome. "The quantity of Geometric [Early Iron Age] ware is also very striking, and might indicate that in this tomb [that of the Lion] . . . the cult of the dead princes buried here continued long after their earthly kingdom had passed away." The parallel of the altar above the Shaft Graves and the circular wall is mentioned in a footnote. The question of a continuing hero cult, at least in the sense of an uninterrupted tradition, is still unresolved.

A further source of some uncertainty involves the cists, or pit graves, dug in the floor of the main tomb chamber in the case of at least three of the later tholoi (those of the Lion, Heraion and Genii). In each case there are three cists, varying from a size large enough for several adult burials to what could barely have accommodated a child's body. In addition, there may have been a cist just inside the door of the Aegisthus Tomb, and there was another in the side chamber in the Treasury of Atreus. They are common, too, in tholoi outside of Mycenae. In at least two of the Mycenae tombs, heavy stone slabs either covered the cists or lay nearby. What do these cist graves reveal of the royal burial ceremonies?

As Blegen was later to conclude in the case of the Prosymna chamber tombs, Wace is quite sure that they were used for reburial when a new occupant was installed on the floor of the tombs. "The number and size of these grave-pits [in the Lion Tomb] suggest that the tomb was in use for some little time, and that secondary interment was practised in these tholoi as in the private chamber tombs." But could this explanation be squared with Tsountas' description of the careful arrangement of the rich remains in the cist of the Vaphio tomb?

Wace also points out that secondary burial is very rare in Minoan tombs and suggests that "this difference in burial customs may indicate a racial distinction between the Cretans and the Mycenaeans, in spite of the fact that the latter had almost entirely adopted the religion and civilisation of the former." The last clause again emphasizes how deeply Evans' dogma had penetrated, even into independent minds like Wace's, by the early 1920s.

The theory of secondary burial is believed by Wace to be strengthened by the use of a side chamber in the Atreus tomb as well as in the Orchomenos example.

> This side chamber [in the Atreus tomb] if one can judge by the grave-pit found in the floor and by the analogy of the chamber-tombs, was probably intended to be used as a charnel chamber to receive the remains of earlier interments when the main chamber (the tholos) was being prepared for a fresh burial. It thus served as a kind of elaborate substitute for the grave-pits [cists]. . . . The procedure seems to have been that the bodies were first laid in the main chamber, and remained there till it was necessary to reopen the tomb for another interment. Then the skeleton of the first tenant with the funeral offerings which had been laid around him were removed to a pit in the side chamber, or merely piled up in a heap in one corner. Apparently it was during the process of removal that the relatives of the deceased took away any of the funeral offerings that pleased them.

A few of Wace's comments on the remaining contents of the tholoi also merit our attention. In describing an amphora in the so-called Palace Style, Wace insists firmly that these vases were local products and not imported from Crete. In his opinion one such vase "cannot be dated earlier than the end of L.H.I. and, like the Kakovatos, Vaphio and Thorikos vases, it is clearly of mainland fabric." In a footnote he adds, "The design is common on the mainland . . . but of course originated in Crete . . ." He also points to the relatively long period of popularity of this ceramic class and its value for chronology. "They are . . . characteristic of the Second Late Helladic period . . . and thus would have been in use for at least a century."

In describing the pottery from the Aegisthus Tomb, Wace (like Blegen) emphasizes the survival and vitality of the mainland ceramic tradition and its probable resurgent influence on the imported Cretan style. "These considerations seem to hint that even by the end of L.H.I. the native tradition of the mainland as exemplified in the shapes and patterns derived from the earlier Minyan and Matt-painted wares had already begun to influence the imported Minoan style, and was tending to create a distinctive Mycenaean type." In the same vein but in a larger context, he remarks that the Mycenaeans blended their own ideas with the imported Minoan culture and by the Third Late Helladic Period had evolved a specifically Mycenaean culture differing significantly from the Minoan civilization from which it had sprung.

One feature of the offerings found in the Tomb of Clytemnestra was especially involved in Evans' coming attack on Wace's chronology of the tholoi. A group of fifteen fragments of large vessels of the pithos type carved in green steatite* had been recovered, partly in Mrs. Schliemann's dig and partly during repairs carried out in 1913. They proved to belong to two very similar vases that Wace describes as "imitations in stone of one of the large medallion pithoi of Knossos, which belong to the transitional period at the end of the M.M.III. and the beginning of L.M.I." (Fig. 83).

Wace has some trouble, however, explaining this find in a mainland context that he believes is LHIII.

> No previous examples of this type of pithos in any material have been found on the mainland, so one is at a loss to date them. They would certainly be later than the Cretan originals in clay. . . . Ambitious stonework of this type corresponds well with the character of the Treasury of Atreus and the Tomb of Clytemnestra with their façades of elaborately carved stone of many colours. . . . We may therefore attribute these vases to the beginning of L.H.III. . . . In any case the vase cannot be earlier than L.H.II., as stone vases are excessively rare in the Shaft Graves; the supposition that an L.H.II. vase was placed in an L.H.III. royal tomb as a kind of heirloom would cause no difficulty.

On the origin and development of the tholos, Wace is sure of two points. He believes most emphatically that its monumental phases are to be attributed to mainland architects. And, although it was probably borrowed in

Figure 83

an undeveloped form from outside the mainland, the direct source was not Crete.

Both before and since the 1920s, scholars have suggested a connection with the so-called tholoi of the Early Minoan period in south central Crete. None of these stands to any great height; all that is usually left is a low ring of rubble masonry. There is thus no absolute proof that these tombs were roofed, or if so, how the roof was constructed. Dr. Stephanos Xanthoudides, who had excavated many of them, believed, from the enormous quantities of fallen stone found within the walls, that they were once vaulted like the tholoi of the mainland. The Cretan round tombs, however, do not appear to come down later in date than Middle Minoan I, *i.e.,* they were no longer built by the beginning of the second millennium. Yet only at the very end of LMIII, according to Wace, do true tholos tombs appear in Crete, and they seem more likely to be due to the influence of the mainland than to the reemergence of an earlier indigenous type after long disuse. "So far then as the Cretan evidence goes," Wace concludes, "it does not seem possible that the tholos tomb was brought to Mycenae from Crete, more especially since the earliest Minoan objects from Mycenae are those of the Shaft Graves."

Although he could scarcely foresee the all-out nature of Evans' reaction, Wace does try to forestall pro-Minoan arguments. "In Crete the great period of ashlar masonry . . . is the First Late Minoan Period. It might therefore be supposed by those unfamiliar with the sites of the mainland that the ashlar work of Mycenae should be assigned to a corresponding date." But he insists that imitation, especially in such monumental modes as architecture, takes considerable time to establish itself in a totally different environment; and he points to the continuing use of ashlar construction in much later Minoan building.

Wace mentions the possibility of some connection with the small Early Bronze domed tombs of the Cyclades. He also refers to the discovery of a LHIII tholos by an American expedition at Kolophon on the Asia Minor coast; and he suggests that "when the exploration of the early remains of Western Asia Minor can be undertaken, some clue to the origin of the tholos tomb may be found there. On the other hand, the late tholoi of Asia Minor, like those of Crete, may be only an importation from Mycenae."

More than forty years after Wace's pioneering study, the origin of the tholos tomb is still unresolved. A strong case has recently been reargued for a more or less continuous development from the Early Bronze "tholoi" of southern Crete to the earliest examples on the mainland; but opinion is divided on its validity. Perhaps the best statement is still Wace's final paragraph, although we would not be so sure that the earliest mainland stage appeared first at Mycenae itself.

> For the present we have no information to guide us to the home of the tholos tomb: but whatever its origin, it was certainly still in a primitive form when it was first introduced at Mycenae. It was the genius of the Mycenaean engineers and architects that, without the aid of any metal harder than bronze, transformed the mean vaults of the first group into marvellous subterranean cupolas like the Treasury of Atreus, which astonish the traveller to-day as much as they did Pausanias of old. The treasures of Atreus and his sons, which he [Pausanias] dreamt of, have long since been scattered to the four winds, but the Mycenaeans in these triumphs of structural ingenuity have bequeathed imperishable treasures to the world.

Wace makes only one or two oblique references in print to the sudden halt of the British excavations at Mycenae in 1923 and to the equally abrupt termination of his tenure as director of the British School at Athens. Few details were made public at the time, and it would serve no useful purpose to review them. Wace may have been less than tactful in private reactions against Evans' dominating personality; but it was Wace's message, not his manners, that was the real irritant. We have seen him (along with Blegen and others) groping for a synthesis that would both admit the pervasiveness of Minoan cultural influence on the mainland in LHI and II and at the same time identify a concurrent mainland individuality that strongly emerged toward the end of the Bronze Age in the full-blown Mycenaean period.

Evans' reaction, as we shall see, was to challenge in print the validity of any basis for this belief and also to make it impossible for its proponent to continue his leading part in the British School and its program of excavation. We can understand and even applaud the one action; but it is impossible to condone the second. Fortunately, saner counsel finally prevailed in British archaeological circles. Wace became a professor at Cambridge University and eventually returned to Greece as an excavator of proved and exceptional ability.

## EVANS' POSTWAR POSITION

In 1927, four years after Wace's study of the royal tombs at Mycenae, Evans published a handsome, slender monograph called *The Shaft Graves and Bee-hive Tombs of Mycenae and Their Interrelation*. His thesis had already been outlined at the general meeting of the Hellenic Society in the very year following Wace's publication. After a brief review of Wace's historical reconstruction, Evans sums up his own reading of the evidence as follows:

> In one case, then, we find magnificent mausolea without contents, in the other case mere stone-lined pits huddled together, but containing the richest group of burial deposits that has ever been brought to light. . . . But may there not be a simple explanation at hand which avoids the necessity of calling in a second dynasty at all? It had occurred to me independently long since, and the idea, indeed, had been tentatively put out in an early Ashmolean Lecture, that the two sets of monuments in fact represented the remains of one and the same dynasty, the contents of the bee-hive [tholos] tombs [including the stelae] having been transferred to the grave pits [Shaft Graves] as a measure of security in view of some external danger. The same explanation had already occurred to Professor Percy Gardner . . .

It is hardly necessary to review in detail the majority of Evans' arguments to support this reactionary view that ignores mainland evidence established as early as Tsountas' day. To Evans' credit, "the very careful enumeration and description [of the Mycenae tholoi] by Mr. A. J. B. Wace" is characterized in a footnote as "a great advance on any preceding accounts"; and some sound observations and acute comparisons are made. But a sarcastic and overbearing tone and a persistence in regarding mainland cultural features in Minoan terms clouds the whole unfortunate essay. Furthermore, although the disturbed condition of the tholos tombs made ceramic dating less dependable than usual, Evans reverted to the far more imprecise (and generally outmoded) method of trying to establish synchronisms by analysis of style in major art forms.

Evans' over-all analysis of the date and characteristics of the contents of the Shaft Graves does not claim much more for Cretan influence than had Wace's own. "In the earlier stage represented in the Shaft Graves a considerable native ingredient, as we learn from the pottery, was still perceptible. By the later phase, corresponding with L.M.Ib, however, the predominant Cretan element triumphs all along the line . . ." A couple of sentences later, however, Wace's and Blegen's whole concept of an independent mainland scheme of chronology is challenged. "Parenthetically, it may be observed," wrote Evans, "that to call this civilization 'Helladic' is both untrue to fact and misleading to students." And he continues in the same vein: "The higher aspects of the culture revealed to us at Mycenae must in any case be recognized as belonging to the Minoan world. That world doubtless included provincial areas. . . . But Minoan Crete is still its centre, and . . . the influence of Knossos itself, the 'Great City,' was still predominant."

The real bombshell, however, is still to come. Wace's criteria for his three groups of tholoi may be acceptable, but his relative dates are backwards. "Greatly as the archaeological world is indebted to Mr. Wace for his painstaking study, and logical as the above results may be regarded *per se,* the gravest objection must be taken to his chronological conclusions." Then Evans points to a very real consideration—that, after a typological series has been set up, one must still be very careful to establish the *direction* of the development. So, for instance, rubble masonry is clearly a less sophisticated technique than ashlar; but rubble may just as well represent a degeneration from, as a forerunner of ashlar. "The truth is," says Evans, "that much of the evidence can be read both ways. The 'Atreus' and 'Clytemnestra' Tombs at Mycenae, structurally the most advanced, are probably the earliest on the site in point of time . . ."

Evans insists that the round tombs in the Cretan Messara are true tholoi and that the time interval between the latest of them and the mainland tholoi is not so great as is generally assumed. Yet he cannot point to Cretan examples that, by the wildest stretch of the imagination, could be the direct ancestors of the Treasury of Atreus. So he falls back on the "argument from silence," to which there can be no empirical refutation. "It seems probable that a part of the Anatolian coast [*i.e.*, Caria in the southwest] came within the area of true Minoan culture at an early date, and this might explain how it is that the finest and earliest of the Mycenae vaults make their appearance in an already Minoized form."

Evans' first precise argument concerns the technique of stone cutting. "On the technical side the most conspicuous instance of reading the evidence backwards is Mr. Wace's contention that the use of the saw was carried to the greatest proficiency in the latest structures. . . . The use of the saw in cutting conglomerate and other materials, so far from being a late characteristic, is a typically M.M.III technique [apparently on the mainland], parallel with similar work at Knossos." He also insists that fine carving in hard stone, such as that preserved on fragments from the façade of the Treasury of Atreus, is best paralleled in MMIII work at Knossos. He continues:

> In view of the existing evidence, it is perhaps hardly necessary to dwell on Mr. Wace's attempt to bring down the date of the "Treasury of Atreus" over three centuries later than that indicated by the decorative parallels above given, mainly on the ground of a painted sherd discovered by him beneath its threshold. This sherd . . . belongs . . . to the latest Mycenaean class, equivalent in date with L.M.IIIb in Crete. To use it as a base for dating this magnificent structure . . . is peculiarly unfortunate, since the ceramic group to which it belongs shows a complete divergence from the current style of Late Minoan Crete.

Evans then discusses the fragments of steatite jars that, as mentioned above, had clearly bothered Wace himself. "The correspondence in details and contour, visible in the steatite example with those of the finest class of M.M.III jars of this type, combined with the plaitwork decoration answering to that of M.M.III stone vessels of another form, supply sufficient warrant for concluding that we have here a contemporary counterpart in stone, belonging to the earlier M.M.III phase." In a footnote that refers to Wace's attempt to explain the fragments as LHIII, he inquires rhetorically, "How then, it may well be asked, did this master lapidary of the Mycenaean decadence obtain his models? By excavation in the Palace Magazines of Knossos?" And he treats with equal disdain Wace's suggestion that the vessel may have been an heirloom.

The case against Wace is reviewed in a final summation.

The "medallion" pithoi from the "Clytemnestra" Tomb . . . like the inlaid pot and bull's head "rhyton" from the "Atreus" *dromos,* as well as the comparisons suggested by the decorative sculptures of its façade, take us back to the earlier phase, *a,* of M.M.III, to which the most ancient Minoan elements found in the Shaft Graves also belong—in other words, well back into the seventeenth century B.C. Thus the two groups, so far from representing successive chronological stages, were contemporary with one another, and the theory of a "Tholos Tomb" dynasty succeeding one represented by the Shaft Graves falls to the ground.

Thus ends the essay that, more than any other publication, shows how warped Evans' once sound judgment had become in his later years, at least in relation to questions involving the mainland versus Crete.

We have already reviewed some of Evans' developing theories about Minoan-Mycenaean interrelations as formulated in the Introduction to the first volume of his *Palace of Minos.* This work had appeared in 1921 and belongs explicitly to his pre-World War I years. Probably the same could be said for most of the contents of the three bulky volumes (in five parts) that appeared between 1928 and 1935. In this sense, it would have been neater to consider them in the context of the previous chapter. Yet it is inevitable that the later volumes reflect increasingly his reactions to post-war discoveries and theories. They also present the results of some new small-scale excavations and tests at Knossos.

By long and careful study of the Minoan pottery and of foreign synchronisms, especially with Egypt, Evans has refined his chronological scheme and assigned extremely close absolute dates to the later phases. He now feels confident that it was a severe earthquake that destroyed the early palace toward the close of MMIII. Thus, it does not represent the dividing point between Middle and Late Minoan, but is followed by a short "epoch of Restoration" before the appearance of the first features to be associated with the Late Minoan period.

After experiencing personally one of the recurrent earthquakes in 1926, Evans feels he has gained new sympathy for the religious awe with which Cretans at all periods seem to have regarded the powers of the underworld. And he suggests that earthquakes rather than the fury of human foes may explain at least some of the catastrophes in antiquity. "To archaeological science it will be certainly a new suggestion that the successive destructions at Knossos, of which we have the stratified evidence, and which can indeed be approximately dated, correspond with successive seismic overthrows."

Severe earthquakes have occurred about twice a century in historical times and are likely to have been at least as frequent in antiquity. They could, he feels, have a direct bearing on the popularity of the ubiquitous "sanctuaries" with their massive pillars in the palace basements. They might also explain the Minoan veneration of bulls, which are often connected with the worship of Poseidon the Earth-Shaker. "Nor can the possibility be ignored that these great natural convulsions had political consequences, and that they may have been productive of the uprising of depressed elements in the population, or of a change of dynasty."

Excavation in the environs had made clear that at its zenith in LMI the palace was surrounded by villas of a "prosperous burgher class," and soundings farther out suggested that beyond these were smaller homes of "poorer inhabitants," crowded into close-packed blocks. Such a centripetal scheme had already been suggested by the excavation of towns like Gournia and Palaikastro. On the basis of the known Knossos examples of each class, Evans assigns to the villas an average size of 244 square yards and to the ordinary houses, 99 square yards. The Inner Residential Quarter seems to have occupied a total area of about 145,000 square yards and the "poorer outlying Zone" perhaps three times as much. Another very rough estimate is that the villas might have had an average of eight inhabitants and the ordinary houses somewhat more. "Without endeavouring to attain any too precise results, we may yet, on the basis supplied by the existing remains and the comparative materials, conclude that the Minoan town of Knossos at its most flourishing period, including its haven [harbor town], had held a population not much, if at all, under a hundred thousand souls." Most experts would now be inclined to believe that this estimate is a serious exaggeration.

Evans draws an attractive picture of the comparative safety of the Minoan city and its freedom to expand because of the absence of cramping fortifications. "The Homeric description—eureia Knōsos[73]—'Broad Knossos,' is specially distinctive as compared with the fenced-in cities of Mainland Greece. Of the populousness of Knossos again, 'the Great City,' we have a true record in the famous passage of the *Odyssey*,[74] where the 'Ninety Cities' of Ancient Crete are mentioned."

Proceeding to archaeological comparisons, Evans sees no contemporary equal, at least in the Aegean area. "Minoan Knossos in its great days was a centre of human habitation to which no rival, certainly, could have been found on the European side. Mycenae as a great and civilized city was only just in the making at the hands of Minoan conquerors and colonists. The position of Knossos must have been in many respects unrivalled even on the East side of the Mediterranean basin. No fenced city, surely, on the Syrian coast, shut in by walls and with its fields the constant prey of the passing invader, had either its expanse or its population." This concept of a fenced city is surely a misleading one, at least for mainland Greece. Without suggesting that the population of Mycenae approached that of Knossos, no one believes that the bulk of its population lived within the fortified acropolis.

Evans is not willing to commit himself too far in regard to the internal political situation in Crete, but there are frequent hints that in the "true Golden Age of the Island" Knossos probably had more than local control. "In Crete itself some superior sway may well have been wielded by a Minoan dynasty, and the general agreement that we find in all the externals of life throughout a wide area of the Island . . . speaks in favour of some central administration and organization. . . . There is much in all this that recalls to mind the general well-being fostered by the *Pax Romana* in the best days of the Empire."

The last volume of *The Palace of Minos,* published in 1935, contains Evans' final pronouncements on mainland-Minoan relationships. As he wrote the Preface in the previous year, he looked back nostalgically over the past. "Just forty years from the beginning of my first exploration of the site of Knossos it has been given me to complete this final Volume . . ." He points to the tremendous amount of comparative material drawn together from "far beyond the Aegean and even the Libyan Sea" and notes that without the help of many colleagues the task he was now completing would "transcend the limits of individual capacity." It is indeed natural that its author should claim for this great work "some title to be regarded as an Encyclopaedia of Minoan cultural features, of its Art, and of its Religion."

The same Preface also contains a touching tribute to several associates whom death has removed from the scene. The volume is dedicated to Federico Halbherr who had been so helpful when "the urge towards exploring what lay behind the traditions of Minos and Daedalos, and of the fabled Labyrinth, together with the quest of a still earlier form of writing, had led me to Knossos." A still more poignant passage refers to Mackenzie, who had been archaeological curator at Knossos as late as 1928. If there had been friction between the two long-time associates, it was now completely erased. No warmer tribute could be written, and excerpts can scarcely give the full flavor.

It has been my grave misfortune to have been deprived through a now lengthening space of years—owing to a mental affection that had left no avenue for hope—of the invaluable services of my friend and colleague Duncan Mackenzie. . . . Nothing could replace the friendly personal contact and availability for consultation on difficult points with one of such great special knowledge. His Highland loyalty never failed, and the simple surroundings of his earlier years gave him an inner understanding of the native workmen and a fellow-feeling with them that was a real asset in the course of our spadework. . . . No wedding ceremony, no baptism, no wake was complete among the villagers without the sanction of his presence . . . [And then, a short separate paragraph]

Even as these words return from the printers' hands there reaches me from Italy the brief announcement that, a few days earlier, on August the 25th that vexed Spirit had found release at last.

But there is no softening here toward at least one living colleague. Evans repeats at great length arguments advanced six years before in connection with Wace's excavations at Mycenae. If anything, increased exasperation is betrayed with a theory that "actually refers the finest example [of the tholoi] . . . to the last age of decadence!" Such lack of taste and perception "is of a piece with the terminology—still in vogue among those who approach the Minoan world backwards, from the Mainland side— which describes the products of that unified culture, when found North of the Aegean, as 'Late Helladic.' . . . The Roman Wall itself becomes 'Late British' with equal reason!"

It is clear that Evans' final position in 1935 had hardened far beyond the prewar years. Now he not only denies any notable cultural independence on the mainland before 1400, but contradicts the position that he and Mackenzie had earlier taken about the shift of cultural as well as political leadership to the mainland in the last two centuries of the Bronze Age.

He also firmly rejects a theory that was gaining very strong support— that the "final" destruction at the end of his LMII phase at Knossos might imply the presence of newcomers from abroad.

The popular idea of the fall of the Knossian Palace [at the end of LMII] seems to be that it was due to some hostile irruption from the Mainland side, and the explanation of the new fusing process that now seems to have set in [in early LMIII] would naturally be based on this view. But the ceramic data before us . . . lend no countenance to such a conclusion. . . . Whatever local break was caused by the overthrow of the Great Palace, there was no real interruption in the local culture, and indeed the Residence of its Priest-kings may simply have been shifted to another site. It will be seen that many current ideas regarding the beginnings of the succeeding L.M.IIIa phase—to use the Cretan terminology—must be radically revised.

The only detailed information Evans ever published on the Linear B tablets from Knossos occurs in the second part of the final volume of *The Palace of Minos*. He recalls that their discovery, a generation earlier, "excited more general interest than any other." But he himself is obviously discouraged, and his prognosis for their decipherment is not bright.

> The widespread hopes of its early interpretation were not verified. No one, indeed, who understood the real conditions could expect such a speedy solution of the problem. According to every indication . . . the root affinities of the original language lay on the Anatolian side. The phonetic value of the signs themselves was itself unknown. . . . The conditions, indeed, are by no means so favourable as in the Etruscan inscriptions, where we have to deal with a known alphabet, yet in that case—after over three generations of research—how vain on the whole has been the effort at decipherment! Of the Minoan script, not only the language but the greater part of the phonetic values of its characters are both lost. . . . All that I have been able here to attempt—after copying over 1,600 documents of which the whole or some material part had survived, and as the outcome of prolonged researches into their details and as to the various applications of the signs themselves—is at most of a preliminary nature.

Actually, he provides line drawings and a few photographs for slightly over 100 examples; and he includes a series of tables of the complete syllabary, as well as a comparison with that of Linear A. There is also a careful analysis of the symbols and ideograms, their possible connection with other writing systems (especially that of Egypt), the system of numeration, the tablet shapes, the business methods and the economic and agricultural practices that they illustrate. Very little is said here about the ideas formerly expressed that some of the Linear B tablets might be considerably earlier than the destruction about 1400, and not a single word is mentioned about the possibility that others could be considerably later.

He then turns to the sparse examples of writing that had been discovered on mainland pottery, mainly stirrup jars.

> The inscriptions of the Mainland offshoot of Class B . . . in some cases give evidence of such close agreement with their Knossian palatial prototypes as equally to entail the conclusion that they were separated from the other by only a short interval of time [*i.e.,* the mainland examples must date close to 1400]. . . . It is clear that both at Knossos and the Mainland sites we have to do with the same language. This absolute correspondence, indeed, of a series of name-groups—out of the very limited number recorded—on the "stirrup vases" of the Boeotian Thebes

and Tiryns, belonging to the period immediately succeeding those on the latest clay documents of the Knossian Palace, might even suggest that in certain cases we have to do with the same individuals.

Evans' historical theories based on this new mainland evidence might almost be anticipated.

That Script B of Knossos—the system of writing that reflected the highly elaborate bureaucratic methods of its later Priest-kings—should reappear in the principal Mainland centres—at Tiryns and Mycenae, as well as Thebes and Orchomenos—in the period that succeeds the fall of the Great Palace is itself an arresting phenomenon. Its reappearance on so many urban sites would naturally imply that the language and script was current at this time not only at the Courts but among the ordinary citizens, both in the Peloponnese and throughout a large tract of Northern Greece beyond the Gulf. It follows that, to at least the middle of the Fourteenth Century B.C., there is no place either at Mycenae or at Thebes for Greek-speaking dynasts. Apart from certain innovations due to the climate and environment, including the reaction of the older indigenous element [Greek speakers?], the culture, like the language, was still Minoan to the core.

He proceeds to cast doubt on the hypothesis that Linear B continued in use on the mainland until the end of the Bronze Age and that it may have been via the mainland that Cyprus borrowed the script that continued to be used to write Greek as late as classical times. He admits that a carelessly inscribed jar rim from Asinê (firmly dated about 1200) bears three undoubted Linear B symbols, but "it seems probable that the Asinê potter—though himself illiterate—had before him some existing document of the old script, the signs of which he may have used as decorative models . . ." Evans concludes that the Knossian script is a more probable source of the Cypriote, and he suggests that "the only real hope of even approximately learning the values of the Minoan signs" rests with a careful comparison of the known phonetic equivalents of the Minoan-derived symbols in Cyprus.

In addition to the distinctive pottery types and writing system in the "last palatial phase" (LMII) at Knossos, Evans was aware of a phenomenon to which he refers as "a military and indeed militaristic aspect." Many of the tablets clearly refer to a corps of charioteers and to the issuing of weapons and armor to a garrison. Equally unmistakable is the emphasis on soldierly equipment in contemporary Knossian tombs, such as the Warrior Graves. He provides a thorough review of the available evidence for the form and development of the bow and arrow, sword, dagger, helmet, cuirass, chariot and horse's harness. It is equally characteristic that, though allowing the earlier Helladic inhabitants the use of perforated boar's tusks for necklaces, he insists that "their claim to have initiated this use for Minoan helmets must be altogether disallowed." Indeed, it is somewhat of a shock to find him conceding that "the use of the horse . . . was earlier diffused on the Mainland side, where the Argolid Plain offered more special facilities than in Crete itself."

Clearly some explanation was needed for the military emphasis during the final phases of the palace, which is in such stark contrast to the apparent peacefulness of earlier Minoan times and even to contemporary Crete, except for Knossos. Evans believes that the answer lies in the sudden accession of a new and aggressive dynasty of native priest-kings. They had not only forcibly subdued their own island but probably much of the mainland too. An ominous clue is the LMII fresco fragment that shows a red-skinned "Minoan officer" at the double with at least one black-skinned follower (Fig. 84).

Figure 84

It seems highly probable that these docile and easily drilled negro bands were actually employed in Minoan military enterprises on the Mainland side in much the same way as the swarthy troops of Ibrahim Pasha [a Turkish general during the Greek War of Independence]. Had black mercenaries, under Knossian leadership, overrun the Morea [Peloponnese] some thirty-three centuries earlier? . . . May we not here, indeed, recognize the "Second Minos" of later story—the tyrant of Athens who, according to the grim traditions, fed the Minotaur with its tribute children, but who also rose to fame as the first organizer of the "Empire of the Sea"? Had Athens, too, like contemporary Canaanite cities under Pharaoh's sway, held a negro garrison?

The militarism, the new pottery types and the intensified bureaucracy aided by the new script were not the only signs that something different was going on at Knossos in the two or three generations before 1400. Clear evidence had been found for major changes in palace architecture. The Throne Room complex now stood out as a "revolutionary intrusion, effacing all previous remains" and a "wholesale invasion of new elements." In its stylized and formal griffin mosaic, the shading of the lower contours of the body represents "the first recorded instance of a regularized attempt to render Chiaroscuro." The wonderful gypsum throne flanked by two wingless griffins faced a sunken lustral area, and a door to the right flanked by another pair of griffins gave access to the goddess' own inner shrine, though "the images of the Goddess and her votaries, the Sacral Horns, and Double Axes, such as had once been placed here, had disappeared."

Evans attains considerable suspense as he described "the Closing Scene" in the Throne Room (Fig. 47).

It would seem that preparations were on foot for some anointing ceremony in the "Lustral Basin" in which the Papa Rè [Priest-King] himself may well have been called on to play a leading part. For this it had evidently been found necessary to refill most of the alabaster oil vessels, usually placed, as the marks of their bases on the pavement show, along the wall to the left of the entrance to the Inner Shrine, where there was a convenient nook for this purpose. Five out of six of these had been removed . . . from their place of storage and set down irregularly in the area in the entrance opening of the "Room of the Throne." One of the large oil *pithoi* from the Magazines, the contents of which were conveniently low, had been carried in here and laid down on its side so that the oil could be easily ladled into the *alabastra*. But this initial task was never destined to reach its fulfilment. . . . What happened here seems exactly to have resembled what . . . took place in the "Sculptor's Workshop" . . . where the alabaster and limestone "amphoras" were left unfinished on the floor. The sudden breaking off of tasks begun—so conspicuous in the first case—surely points to an instantaneous cause.

Evans believes quite firmly now that a sudden and major earthquake explains the disaster better than an enemy attack. There was evidence of severe burning, with clear indications that a strong wind was blowing from the southwest; thus, the month was probably March. But he points out that a lamp or brazier upset by the quake could easily account for the fire after the inhabitants had fled to the open fields. And the scarcity of precious objects on the floors could be as well explained by the survivors' combing the ruins as by hostile pillagers. Furthermore, if foreign attackers had stayed, there should be evidence of cultural novelties in the following period, but "the evidence of neighbouring cemeteries . . . [shows that] the general course of civilization was not sensibly interrupted."

Why, then, was the palace not rebuilt, as it had been after several equally severe earthquakes? Evans' answer to this is startling at first, but actually not out of line with the train of reasoning that he had been gradually developing over thirty-five years.

On this occasion the catastrophe was final. Squatters, indeed, after a short interval of years, occupied the probably considerable shelter still offered by the remains of the fabric. But the Minoan augurs may have at last satisfied themselves that the Powers of the Underworld were not to be exorcized. The long experiment was given up, and there are some reasons for supposing that the residence of the Priest-kings of Knossos was, perhaps not for the first time, transferred to a Mainland site, quite probably, indeed, to Mycenae, at this time re-decorated according to the latest Knossian fashion.

It was surely the decree of some merciful Providence that this aged pioneer who had contributed so long and brilliantly to the rediscovery of Aegean civilization did not have to face the final clinching evidence that utterly destroyed his increasingly fantastic theories.

## P E N D L E B U R Y ' S   S Y N T H E S I S

Probably no human being, certainly no archaeologist, has known Crete as well as J. D. S. Pendlebury. He had worked for several seasons at Knossos and seemed to be Evans' heir apparent just as surely as Dörpfeld had succeeded Schliemann at Troy. Pendlebury's early experience in Egyptian archaeology gave him an important advantage in problems involving connection between the Aegean and the Near East. He had published, with Evans' approval and support, the useful *Handbook to the Palace of Minos* (1935). Like Schliemann, Evans and Blegen in their younger days, Pendlebury was an avid field explorer. He was a familiar and respected figure in every corner of Crete and had conducted important excavations in his own right. No one could have written with greater first-hand knowledge and recognized authority on Minoan prehistory. When *The Archaeology of Crete* appeared in 1939, it was immediately recognized as not only an up-to-date summary of Evans' bulky publication, but a more balanced synthesis of the equally important evidence that had accumulated since 1900 from many other quarters of the island. The reprinting of *The Archaeology of Crete* in 1964 shows the enduring quality of his scholarly attainments.

In addition to academic competence, Pendlebury had special qualities of personal magnetism, perseverance and courage. His heroic stature was climaxed, in the eyes of friends everywhere and particularly of all Cretans, by his death during the abortive resistance to the German parachute invasion of Crete in 1941. Cretans will never forget his valor.

In his Introduction Pendlebury makes it plain why he has decided to follow the chronological method of presentation. He fears that the topical method, as used by Glotz for instance, may obscure the understanding of over-all historical development and change. Yet within each of Evans' nine time periods Pendlebury does discuss separate topics such as architecture, sculpture, ceramics, burial customs and foreign relations. He also includes very useful site lists and maps of population distribution for each chronological subdivision. And his latest chapters follow the chronicle of ancient Cretan civilization down to Roman times.

In general Pendlebury supports the conclusions and theories drawn by Evans from the archaeological material. Nevertheless, he asked Wace to read his text in manuscript and acknowledges "many valuable criticisms and suggestions." There may be a connection here with a remark on terminology. "I have unrepentantly used the term Late Helladic I, II and III for Mycenaean I, II and III. L.H. is more convenient than Myc, it does not attempt to ram the name of a city down the throat of a country, and, as we shall see, we must have some distinction between Crete and the Mainland, so L.M. will not do." This point of view required a good deal of courage in Evans' associate, although by 1939 no other position could be defended.

On the other hand, Evans' basic chronological framework for Minoan Crete is vigorously upheld against current criticism. "In the present state of our knowledge," says Pendlebury, "it would be absurd to confuse matters by altering the arrangement. . . . Until we have got something better to put in its place the terminology which has acted so well for so long must be kept." Pendlebury states clearly, too, the basis for both absolute and relative chronology, which is so vital a framework for Aegean prehistory. "The positive dating of the Bronze Age Periods in the Aegean depends entirely on foreign contacts—mainly with Egypt. Sometimes this is simple, as for example when objects bearing the name of Amenhotep III and Ty [his queen] are found in L.H.III deposits at Mycenae and L.H.III vases are found in the city of their successor, Akhenaten, in Egypt, or when a M.M.II vase is found in a XIIth Dynasty grave and a XIIth Dynasty statue in a M.M.II deposit."

Pendlebury is somewhat less rigid than Evans in regarding the evidence from Knossos as the touchstone and measure for developments throughout Crete.

> For comparative dating in Crete itself pottery is of course our chief criterion, and the duration of the periods . . . is determined by changes of style. Naturally everything is based on Knossos, for not only was that the first and most important site to be excavated but also at Knossos alone is the series complete. But . . . we must always be prepared to accept divergencies from the Knossian series, particularly on the smaller sites. . . . Evidence from stratification and from style must go hand in hand. It is fortunate that Knossos was excavated by two men who realized this. So, also, it must be recognized that the styles and periods often slide almost imperceptibly one into the next. It was slow progress, not the town crier, that ordained the change from E.M.III to M.M.I. We must not expect watertight compartments . . .

Pendlebury is equally forthright on the vital matter of basing theories, however tentative, on the archaeological evidence at hand. "In the absence of documents which we can read and believe we are bound to progress by means of theories. Any theory is justifiable which agrees with the greatest number of facts known at the time and contradicts neither a vital fact nor human nature and reason. The most reasonable theory, which gives a connected history, should hold the field until a better one is produced or until it is flatly contradicted by some newly discovered fact." He might have added, however, that tentative theories sometimes have an unfortunate tendency to become dogma, first with the originator and then in the minds of contemporaries and successors if the originator has attained great prestige.

We are particularly interested, of course, in Pendlebury's assessment of the relationship between Crete and the mainland during the Late Bronze Age. Here he shows considerable flexibility and a willingness to accept evidence that forces him to differ from the views of Evans and Mackenzie.

He admits many of the facts already brought out in our review of Wace's and Blegen's article on trade, which appeared in the same year as *The Archaeology of Crete.* Yet he will not go nearly as far as their modest conclusions as to the implications of this evidence about mainland independence and originality long before 1400. He supports Wace in the controversy with Evans over the development of the tholos tombs, stating flatly, "Architecturally the greatest contribution of the mainland was the Tholos tomb. Nothing like this was constructed in Crete until L.M.III."

Yet, in fact, Pendlebury adopts almost completely the Evans thesis about the political situation.

So Minoanized does the rest of the Aegean become that it is impossible for the present writer at least to avoid the conclusion that it was dominated politically by Crete. Athenian tradition, always the most vocal, remembered the tyranny of Minos over the Saronic gulf. We cannot separate the legend of the youth and maidens, sent to be devoured by the Minotaur, from the bull-sports of Late Minoan Crete. . . . The peace of the seas is essential to an empire whose wealth is based on trade, and the thalassocracy of Minos is no myth. But that the empire was not obtained by a deliberate policy of fire and sword seems clear from the lack of a general catastrophe on the Mainland at the beginning of the Late Bronze Age.

The admitted dissimilarity in mainland palace architecture is explained as remodeling on essentially Minoan lines. As for the striking differences in the frescoes, a parallel is drawn with India under British colonial rule. "But equally, as in India, the native princes must have been allowed to continue ruling as vassals. Otherwise the intensely mainland character of the known frescoes could hardly have existed. Just as in the palace of an Indian Prince European artists will be employed on the condition that their subject-matter is of interest to the Indian, so with the Mainland dominions of Crete the style is Minoan, but the subjects are Mainland." Thus Pendlebury, too, reflects the lingering vestiges of modern colonial preconceptions that clouded the vision of so many nineteenth-century historians of earlier epochs.

A particular interest attaches to Pendlebury's description of the short period of a couple of generations just before 1400 that Evans called LMII. Its culture, characterized by Palace Style pottery and Linear B script, had proved to be quite exotic to the rest of Crete; and Evans had seen in it the final stage of Knossian control over the whole island with a kind of special regal exclusiveness at the capital itself. Pendlebury reveals the same Knosso-centric obsession when he remarks that "the L.M.II style appealed to the Mainland, whereas it was practically confined to Knossos

in Crete . . ." How near he was at this point, however, to considering the
fairly obvious reverse possibilities is shown by a footnote. "Snijder . . . indeed goes so far as to consider L.M.II an offshoot of the Mainland style,
and having regard to the fact that this short-lived, locally restricted style
can only have overlapped the latter part of L.H.II, it is hard to argue against
him."

We are equally concerned about Pendlebury's views on the destruction
of the center or centers of this Minoan "empire." Here again he differs considerably from Evans.

> The catastrophe which overtook the Cretan cities at the end of L.M.Ib
> (or L.M.II at Knossos) was practically universal. Knossos, Phaistos,
> Agia Triadha, Gournia, Mokhlos, Mallia, and Zakros all show traces of
> violent destruction accompanied by burning. At Palaikastro, Pseira,
> Nirou Khani, Tylissos and Platé there is a distinct break in the habita-
> tion, though no trace of burning was found. This overwhelming disaster
> must have taken place at one and the same time and it has been attrib-
> uted to a severe earthquake. Earthquakes, however, in ancient times
> are not liable to cause fires . . . Everything, indeed, points to a deliber-
> ate sacking on the part of enemies of the most powerful cities in Crete.
> We have seen the prosperity of the period and it is obvious that no
> mere Viking raid could have accomplished such destruction. It must
> have been a highly organized expedition with an avowed purpose. That
> this purpose was not to invade and colonize the island is clear from the
> way in which the Minoan culture continues, though in a very minor
> key, without any Mainland influence until the very end of L.M.III.
> The object of this thorough, relentless destruction must have been purely
> political.

Pendlebury then proceeds to outline two current theories that might
account for the above facts. He admits that "both have much to be said
for them and, curiously enough, they are diametrically opposed." Pendlebury thinks that one theory, proposed by Wace, has not previously appeared in print. According to it, Crete never had political control over the
mainland, but in LMII the mainland was strong enough to conquer Crete,
presumably without serious resistance. The widespread destruction about
1400 might then represent a Cretan nationalist revolt that threw off the
foreign yoke. Pendlebury does not agree with Wace's theory, but neither
does he attempt to refute it.

The alternate explanation, which Pendlebury accepts, could be called
the orthodox one in 1939 and for some years afterward. It held that Crete,
under Knossian leadership, had attained essential political control of the
whole Aegean area before 1400 and that the destruction of Minoan sites

about that time reflects a successful mainland revolt carried to the island itself. Pendlebury believes, in spite of the evidence for extensive mainland participation in foreign trade before 1400, that the main motivation for the invasion was mainland resentment against taxation and exclusion from foreign markets.

He carries on the historical reconstruction of the last days of Knossos in an even more dramatic fashion than Evans.

> Now there is a name which is always associated, if not with the sack of Knossos, at least with the liberation of its subjects—Theseus. . . . It has already been suggested that the seven youths and seven maidens may have been the Mainland quota for the bull-ring at Knossos. That is just the type of detail that would be remembered, the more so in that it may well have been the sentimental reason without which no purely commercial war can ever take place. No doubt the rape of Helen was a very good rallying cry when the Mycenaean Empire wished to break through to the Black Sea trade which Troy was keeping for itself. And in the last decade of the fifteenth century on a spring day, when a strong South wind was blowing which carried the flames of the burning beams almost horizontally northwards, Knossos fell. The final scene takes place in the most dramatic room ever excavated—the Throne Room. It was found in a state of complete confusion. A great oil jar lay over-turned in one corner, ritual vessels were in the act of being used when the disaster came. It looks as if the king had been hurried here to undergo too late some last ceremony in the hopes of saving the people. Theseus and Minotaur! Dare we believe that he wore the mask of a bull?

## NILSSON'S VIEW

Martin P. Nilsson is not a field archaeologist, but he follows the results of excavation closely and is an expert critic and synthesist. Now retired from his professorship at the University of Lund in Sweden, he still continues his active scholarly career. His *Homer and Mycenae* (1933)—an expansion of the Sather lectures at the University of California—presents better than any other single volume a judicious appraisal of the whole sweep of Homeric and Mycenaean studies between the wars and even before. Above all, we shall be interested in his chapter "The History of the Mycenaean Age," but throughout the book there is material that concerns our theme. Nilsson is primarily an authority on mythology and religion, but he is fully in control of the current arguments from linguistic and archaeological evidence. These three sources—mythology, linguistics and archaeology—are judiciously utilized to reconstruct Mycenaean history.

He recognizes that they offer very incomplete and often ambiguous evidence; but they are the only means available and "in dealing with the origin and development of epic poetry, which ultimately goes back to Mycenaean times, we must try to form some idea of the outlines of the history of that age." He wisely avoids the circular arguments sometimes used in which the content of the poems themselves is used to reconstruct a particular historical period. "Our best method will be to try and see what can be reasonably stated and inferred in this respect independently of Homer and to apply the results to the understanding of the genesis of the epic poetry."

To Nilsson, the main questions are: Who were the Mycenaeans? What can be inferred about the political and social contributions of the Mycenaean Age, especially about the migration of Greek speakers?

He approaches the first question with the salutary warning that there is no more perilous undertaking than the attempt to equate an archaeologically defined prehistoric group showing common traits in its material culture with a particular race and/or language. Alien languages are often adopted from or by conquerors or conquered. Race is a slippery concept even with living subjects and is especially difficult if all one has to depend on is a few skulls or stylized representations in art. Pottery, the prehistorian's most valuable evidence, is too fragile to have been used as containers by people constantly on the move. "It may be considered as pretty certain that the invading Greeks had no pottery of their own . . ."

Nilsson agrees with Blegen and others that the people of the Aegean area before 2000 definitely were not Greek speakers. "To this pre-Greek population the Minoan people belonged. . . . The Minoan language was certainly non-Greek, for if it had been Greek the efforts of the most competent and sagacious scholars to decipher the Minoan script would certainly not have failed." This last remark is surely a naïve one in view of Evans' continued delay in publishing the Knossos tablets.

At what points after 2000, asks Nilsson, does archaeology show "breaks" in civilization and the introduction of foreign elements of culture, indicating the presence of a foreign people? Like Blegen and others, he sees three such "breaks" in the record—the advent about 1900 of the "gray Minyan people," who apparently caused widespread destruction of earlier sites; the sudden appearance about 1600 of Minoan culture on the mainland; the destruction of Mycenaean strongholds between 1200 and 1100, traditionally connected with the Dorian invasion. He rules out the last because of the unanimous tradition that other Greek dialects had been spoken in the peninsula before Doric. Turning to the second, he points out that there are two explanations for the Minoization of mainland culture. We have already reviewed the theory of Minoan political supremacy championed by Evans and the explanation in terms of mainland political autonomy but cultural dependence held by Wace and Blegen. Nilsson strongly supports the latter.

In fact he goes further than Wace and Blegen in underlining mainland initiative in the early Mycenaean period. "Greek tribes, barbarous but open-minded, and very subject to the lure of a superior civilization, as Aryan peoples always have shown themselves, warlike and fond of booty, may have occupied Greece and come into contact with the Minoans. Roving and pillaging they may have raided Crete and taken booty, and they may also have carried on some trade with the Minoans. They may have acquired a taste for the rich and splendid Minoan culture, and they may have brought not only valuables but men also and among them craftsmen to their strongholds in the mainland."

He then proceeds to outline his famous "eleven points," which in sum strongly suggest that Mycenaean civilization—although heavily Minoized —had decidedly un-Minoan aspects, some of which point to a northern origin. Mackenzie and Evans had tried to refute some of these arguments, such as those about the megaron type of architecture and costume, but Nilsson is unconvinced. The use of amber, especially for beads, is another point of difference. Amber is very common in early Mycenaean graves but is practically never found in Crete. Similarly, the mainlanders were very fond of sewing rows of boar's tusks on their leather helmets, but no tusks or art representations of tusk helmets occur in Cretan contexts until Late Minoan III.

Writing, on the other hand, is very scarce on the mainland and widespread in Crete. "If the Mycenaeans had been Cretan colonists we could not imagine them allowing the art of writing to fall into disuse, but if they were barbarians who invaded Greece it is quite natural." Nilsson also feels an important "difference in spirit" between what seems to have been a Minoan emphasis on peaceful pursuits and an obvious Mycenaean liking for war, hunting and raiding. He notes an elaboration about the Mycenaean burial customs and the cult of heroes that cannot be paralleled in Crete. Again, the names of almost all those who figure in the myths going back to the Mycenaean age are Greek, not pre-Greek in etymology. And Minoan art is "essentially small art," while there is a definite tendency toward monumentality in such Mycenaean remains as the tholos tombs and the Lion Gate.

Generally speaking, Nilsson's distinctions are clear, reasonably precise and essentially sound. In sum, they lead him to a firm contradiction of Evans' view that Mycenaean civilization is essentially a watered-down colonial version of the Minoan. "So many differences exist between the Mycenaean and the Minoan civilization which cannot be explained by an organic development of the Minoan culture under different conditions, and which very definitely point northwards, that we may state confidently that they were brought in by a people with northern connections who over took [he means "took over"] the Minoan culture but mixed it up with elements of their own."

Assuming that there really was an un-Minoan and presumably Greek element in Mycenaean civilization, the question still arises as to when and how the first Greek speakers reached the peninsula. In fact, Nilsson avoids taking a stand. "The opinion embraced by many scholars, especially those of a later generation, that the first immigration of the Greeks coincides with the break between Early and Middle Helladic [about 2000] cannot be definitely disproved nor can it be proved." But, by a process of elimination, one must assume that he considered this the most likely juncture for the arrival of Greek speakers.

After discussing the successive destructions of the palace at Knossos and their apparent connection with the vicissitudes of other Minoan sites, Nilsson suggests certain connections with the mainland situation. Cretan disasters contemporary with the earlier Mycenaean period, when Minoan culture is becoming paramount on the mainland, may be explained as the raids of earlier Greek-speaking "Mycenaeans" whose dialect was Ionic. It is perhaps to this time that the Theseus myth belongs, with its implications of a strong Crete that posed a threat to the mainland, and especially to Ionic Athens. The total collapse of Minoan civilization after the destruction of Knossos about 1400 coincides with a new vigor on the mainland. "No doubt seems to be possible as to the correlation of the fall of Cnossos with the bloom of the Mycenaean centres of the mainland. It points to a vigorous and successful attack of the mainland tribes on Cnossos. This is justly the general opinion. The people to whom this war is to be ascribed are, of course, the Achaeans who certainly were the dominating population of the mainland in the late period of the Mycenaean Age."

Nilsson also tries to interpret the opinion of Near Eastern scholars as to how much, if at all, the Mycenaeans are mentioned in contemporary Hittite and Egyptian documents. He concludes that the least debatable equation from Hittite sources is that "Ahhijawā" refers to Achaea. King Mursil, who ascended the throne after 1336, wrote to his "brother, the king of Ahhijawā." This king was apparently on much the same footing with the Hittite empire as the kings of Egypt, Babylonia and Assyria. "There is, of course, no place for this great empire in Asia Minor. . . . It must be the Achaean Empire of Mycenaean Greece, members of which had taken possession of part of the southern coast of Asia Minor."

Toward the end of the Bronze Age, as the Mycenaeans intensify their trade and perhaps even colonial activities along the main route to the Near East through Rhodes and Cyprus, there are also apparent references in Egyptian documents. The Tell-el-Amarna letters of the early fourteenth century mention that the tribe of "Danuna" had settled on the coast of Palestine. Nilsson seems favorable to the suggestion that the Danuna may be equated with the "Danaoi," one of Homer's commonest names for the Greeks who attacked Troy. Toward the close of the thirteenth and in the early twelfth century a motley collection of "peoples from the sea" was attacking Egypt. The names of those who were beaten off in a great land and sea attack on the delta in 1221 include the Luka (Lycians), Turusha (Tyrsenoi = Etruscans?), Shardana (Sardinians) and "Aqaiwasha." Nilsson tends to agree with the suggestion that the last-named may again be the Achaeans.

Nilsson feels that the late Mycenaean period "was really the Heroic Age of the Greeks," and in such a context the attack on Troy is a natural event. He strongly supports the historicity of the Trojan War but is very skeptical about the economic reasons alleged by modern scholars. It is true that Schliemann's Hissarlik is in a strategic position to control trade by land and sea between Europe and Asia. But we should not read modern, highly developed economic motives into the ancient record without more justification. The Mycenaeans were ambitious, quarrelsome, avaricious plunderers without long-range economic or military strategy. We have to do with "an age of wars and of strife, of extensive wanderings and oversea expeditions, the Heroic Age of the Greeks. This is the background of the Greek myths and of the Homeric poems."

After the unsuccessful attacks on Egypt the raids of the Sea People subsided. In Greece itself Nilsson thinks that the exhaustion caused by these exertions is visible in the poverty of the sub-Mycenaean period. And Nilsson implies that the last Mycenaeans were in no condition to withstand the hardy northerners whom tradition associated with the Dorian invasion.

What is Nilsson's assessment of the main points of contact between the Mycenaean age and the Homeric poems? He notes that all Homeric scholars now believe that the poems were composed in more or less their present form at the beginning of the historical period, though exact chronological estimates range all the way from the tenth to the sixth century.

Shortly after the discovery of the Mycenaean civilization it was realized that certain descriptions in Homer correspond closely to and are explained by objects and elements appearing in the Mycenaean civilization but not in the [later] Archaic Age. . . .

But he also insists that

> On the other hand, other and not less conspicuous elements in Homer
> refer certainly to the Archaic Age. . . . It is very unwise to treat Homer
> as chiefly a product of the Mycenaean Age, and to consider the ele-
> ments from this age as survivals which may be put on one side is as
> unwise as to consider the passages referring to the Archaic Age as
> irrelevant additions. . . .

Serious problems are raised by the discovery that

> The Homeric poems contain elements from widely differing ages. . . .
> [but] we have to accept it without circumlocution and to try to com-
> prehend this state of things and to explain how it is possible and how it
> came about.

His examples are categorized as "definitely late" (*i.e.,* post-Mycenaean),
"definitely early" (*i.e.,* Mycenaean) and "controversial points." In the
late category he puts, for example, elaborate brooches like that worn by
Odysseus[75] and references to the Phoenicians, especially in the *Odyssey*.
Among the "elements deriving from the Mycenaean Age" he lists the cup
of Nestor; the boar's-tusk helmet of Meriones; the kyanos (blue glass
paste) frieze in the palace of Alkinoos; the big body-shield ("tower" and
"figure-eight" types). In addition to material objects, he states quite posi-
tively that "there are references to political and geographical conditions
which cannot possibly belong to the Archaic Age of Greece or the intermediate period but only fit in with the Mycenaean Age."

On the other hand, Nilsson regards as unprovable Evans' contention
that Minoan art is reflected in the Homeric poems. "Descriptions of works
of art are often said to refer to the Minoan art. It would not be astonishing
if they did. . . . But the question being so controversial they cannot be
adduced as reliable evidence."

Burial customs pose a particularly difficult problem for those who hold
the general belief that Homer faithfully reflects Mycenaean practices. The
bodies of Homeric heroes are always cremated in a great pyre, and of
course cremation was common in the Iron Age. On the other hand, archaeology seems to show that the universal Mycenaean rite was inhumation.
Nilsson suggests a compromise and illustrates it by referring to the recent
Swedish discovery of an almost unplundered tholos tomb at Midea, near
Mycenae.

> Professor [Axel] Persson's interpretation seems to be fully justified,
> viz. that the bones in the smaller pit are those of men and animals
> slaughtered at the funeral, and that a pyre had been erected over the

larger pit in which various precious objects were burned. To the same custom of burning offerings to the dead in the tomb, are certainly related the traces of fire, which have often been observed in Mycenaean chamber tombs and have caused so much discussion. I have no hesitation in referring the description of Patroclos' funeral to this Mycenaean custom. It is only natural that in an age in which cremation was the rule for stately funerals, the poet misunderstood the old custom and mixed it up with those prevailing at his own time, letting the corpse of Patroclos also be burned on the pyre.

In spite of such prestigious support, however, Persson's observations have not been generally accepted as typical of Mycenaean burials.

Nilsson concludes that, although certain early and late cultural elements can be isolated, the various strata have been in general inextricably blended in the poems that have reached us. "How is it credible," he asks, "that the former Mycenaean elements were preserved through the centuries and incorporated in poems whose composition may be about half a millennium later?" We cannot follow his review of epic technique among other peoples at varying times in the past; but he insists that "from the examples quoted it is easy to understand that the epics which originated in this [Mycenaean] age were preserved throughout the subsequent dark and impoverished centuries." And he believes that "with the aid of the epic technique they preserved not only their memory but certain archaizing features, in spite of an inevitable accommodation to a new environment . . ."

The migration across the Aegean Sea to Ionia at the beginning of the Iron Age "prepared the ground for a renascence of epics," and finally "a great poet appeared who infused new life and vigour into epic poetry." Neither this poet nor his audience could have had any direct knowledge of Mycenaean civilization. But echoes of it, sometimes authentic and sometimes confused, had come down in the unbroken oral tradition. Agamemnon and Nestor would no doubt have trouble in recognizing in Homer's version the songs that bards may have sung in their courts at Mycenae and Pylos. But it seems absolutely sure to Nilsson that the kernel of the action and much of the circumstantial detail did not originate in poetic imagination.

# VIII

## The Last Twenty-five Years: 1940-1965

ANOTHER BOOK, rather than the remainder of this one, would be required to do justice to the task attempted in these two final chapters. As with so many areas in modern life, so with archaeology. The pace of new discoveries and new theories seems to increase in some mysterious geometric progression. New names and new faces appear. Schliemann has been resting for more than two generations in his great marble mausoleum in the Ilissos cemetery of Athens. Evans died at the ripe old age of ninety during the early days of World War II. Blegen has retired from his university post but is still actively engaged in the great series of excavations at Pylos and in preparing the final publication of Nestor's palace. It will be even more difficult than in the past for historians to select a single pacesetter in the fourth generation of Aegean archaeologists. No attempt to do so will be made here, although the names and accomplishments of several leading contenders will naturally find a place in the narrative.

The most significant recent discoveries bearing on the Mycenaean period are perhaps somewhat easier to chronicle, but the process of selection is still painful. Unquestionably, the key development has been the decipherment of the Linear B script in 1952 and subsequent revelations about the content of the Pylos and Knossos documents. The gradual uncovering since 1952 of the extensive ruins of Nestor's palace ranks close behind. So does the excavation of a second grave circle just outside the fortified citadel of Mycenae. Burials with contents closely similar to some of those in the Mycenae Shaft Graves are now known at Peristeria, near the west coast of the Peloponnese. A large building, apparently constructed for religious purposes and containing almost life-size statues, has been discovered on the island of Keos. Linear B tablets have been recovered at Mycenae and at Thebes, and from Thebes also are seals bearing the first cuneiform inscriptions found in Greece. The ruins of a well-preserved Mycenaean palace have been detected at Iolkos, modern Volos. The list of important contributions could be spun out almost indefinitely—to the long and pro-

ductive French excavations at Argos, for example, and the renewed investigations by Germans and Greeks at Tiryns. And there is also crucial
new evidence in the closely related Minoan sphere, such as the palaces at
Zakro and Arkhanes as well as the drastic review now in progress of
Evans' chronological, typological and historical conclusions.

Intensive surface exploration on a regional basis carries on the tradition of Wace and Blegen and Pendlebury. The aim is, of course, to record
evidence of habitation at every period in the past. But in and around
Mycenaean centers increasing indications point to a real "population
explosion" during the Late Bronze Age. Organized surveys in other districts will probably reveal population concentrations comparable to those
established for Attica, Argolis, Laconia and Messenia. The mechanization
of Greek agriculture is forcing the pace on survey work before deep-plough-
ing destroys many of the surviving surface indications. Extensive drainage,
irrigation, road building and other construction projects are both obliterating evidence and uncovering material that calls for immediate salvage.

Gradually, too, the second objective to which Blegen pointed in 1940 is
being attained. Specialists in a wide variety of the natural and social sciences are joining the survey teams and excavation staffs; archaeologists are
learning to observe and record and preserve specimens so that they can
ask specialists the right questions and provide the necessary data for scientific analysis in the laboratory. So far, the most valuable of these scientific
aids to the archaeologist is the carbon 14 ($C^{14}$) technique, by which, if
conditions are right, fairly close absolute dates can be assigned to samples
of organic material. In fact, if our focus of interest were on an earlier period,
the new technique of dating by $C^{14}$ would merit a significance comparable
to the decipherment of Linear B. For the Late Bronze Age in the Aegean,
however, direct or indirect synchronisms with older literate cultures usually
provide an even closer approximation of date, and $C^{14}$ analysis finds its
place as one of a number of very useful chronological checks.

Also, Aegean prehistory seems rather suddenly to have again become, as
in its first thirty years, a subject of wide popular interest. The discovery
and decipherment of the Linear B tablets must be credited with much of
the new appeal. Several books have recently become available in which
specialists and popular writers have at last—two generations after Tsountas' *Mycenaean Age*—provided the general reader in English with more
or less reliable and readable syntheses of the present state of the evidence.
Our final chapters are in no sense intended to cover the same ground. The
aim, instead, is to try to bring the reader up to date on major new clues
that confirm or refute or modify theories and inferences and conclusions
that we have seen developing in the seventy years before 1940. Perhaps it

will be worthwhile at this point to look back very briefly before trying to assimilate the new evidence.

Schliemann's work at Troy, Mycenae, Tiryns and elsewhere established beyond doubt that a highly developed civilization had existed in the Aegean area many centuries before the classical era. In this sense, at least, his efforts authenticated Homer, and there was considerable evidence that the earlier culture had points of contact with Homeric epic as well as with later Greek developments. But Schliemann failed to convince most scholars that Homer had *firsthand* knowledge of Mycenaean Greece or Troy II; before he died, he himself had practically abandoned this belief. Dörpfeld showed that it was Troy VI that was approximately contemporary with the most prosperous phases of the citadels like Mycenae and Tiryns on the opposite side of the Aegean; but his case for a close correspondence between the material remains of that later Trojan level and the Homeric account was not much more convincing. There seemed, however, after Dörpfeld's Trojan excavations to be somewhat more reason to believe the kernel of the Homeric account, *i.e.,* that an army from Mycenae and Tiryns and other major Mycenaean centers might have attacked and conquered Troy. At the very least, Mycenaean pottery found on the house floors of the destroyed city testified to fairly close contact between the mainland and the later inhabitants of Troy VI.

Tsountas discovered evidence for habitation in Thessaly and the Cyclades long before the Mycenaean efflorescence, and he contributed materially to a more rounded picture of cultural conditions in the "Mycenaean" period, which was by then roughly defined as the last half of the second millennium. Tsountas' book showed dramatically how much had been learned in a single generation. It was reasonably clear by his time that this civilization had extended far beyond the Argolid and that the exploits of these wealthy, restless and warlike people had provided the basis for much in the tradition of Greek myth and heroic song. But Tsountas hardly came to grips with the prickly problem of the time lag between the Mycenaean age and the Homeric epics.

Then the Cretan chapter opened out, with the revelation of an even earlier and in many ways more creative and opulent society, which in its later phases had much in common with the Mycenaean. Evans saw in the Cretan palaces of the Middle Bronze Age the first highly developed European civilization, and he associated the Minoan acme around the middle of the second millennium with the persistent tradition of a "control of the sea" established by King Minos of Knossos over the whole eastern Mediterranean and even beyond. An intimate connection was obvious between art objects from the Shaft Graves and tholos tombs of the Mycenaean mainland and those of proved Minoan origin and development in Crete. No one contested the conclusion that Cretan fashions, particularly in art, had very deeply affected the mainland beginning about 1600. But Evans believed that this wave of Minoan cultural influence was sufficient proof of total domination in every significant aspect of mainland civilization, including political control of at least the major population centers. And he won the assent of most scholars to his theory.

As to the last 200 years or so of the Aegean Bronze Age—which comprise the more critical period for Homeric connections—Evans' views became increasingly Creto-centric. According to his calculations, the great age of the Minoan palaces had come to an end about 1400, and this catastrophe was interpreted by most scholars as proof of some sort of major shift in the balance of power toward the mainland. But Evans insisted that at no time until the very end of the Bronze Age was there any archaeological evidence for a cultural "break" that would be needed to mark invasion and political control of Crete by "Achaean" (*i.e.,* Greek-speaking) mainlanders. He adopted the theory that the frequent destruction and burning and rebuilding of Cretan palaces—perhaps even the "final" destruction at Knossos—was best explained as the result of recurring serious earthquakes.

Evans admitted that for two or three generations previous to the "final" destruction an aggressive and militaristic dynasty had been in control of Knossos and perhaps most of Crete, but he held that these were native rulers. In his last publication he even advanced the view that after 1400 the incumbent "priest-king" transferred the capital to the mainland, probably to Mycenae. The last two or three centuries of the Bronze Age, both in Crete and on the mainland, were in Evans' view a continuation and gradual degeneration of an essentially Minoan civilization. If Greek-speaking people were already present, they were a subject race. The heroes of Greek tradition were presumably Minoan leaders or puppets, and the first epic poems about their exploits may have been written down in the Minoan language. A long literate tradition had existed in Crete, and the Linear B script had been developed at Knossos and used on the mainland at least as early as 1400.

Practically no one else was willing to accept all of the implications of these hypotheses. In spite of Evans' awesome reputation and prestige, his own lieutenant, Pendlebury, thought the "final" destruction of Knossos to be explained by a successful mainland revolt from Cretan colonialism. Many who had long studied the mainland evidence were skeptical of Evans' repeated insistence on its total dependence on Minoan models. Nilsson published his "eleven points" of important dissimilarities in the very year that Evans' last and most extreme pronouncement appeared. But the case for a sturdy native "Helladic" cultural tradition, never totally submerged even at the height of Minoizing fashion and strongly reemerging after 1400, was put most persistently and cogently by Blegen and Wace. Their system of mainland chronology, though closely coordinated with the Minoan, was a symbol of mainland integrity.

A second crux was Wace's dating of the finest tholos tombs at Mycenae after 1400 and the insistence that the later stages in this monumental form of architecture developed in a non-Minoan environment. Even in the pottery, where they freely admitted widespread importation and imitation of Minoan ceramics over a long period, Blegen and Wace felt that mainland motifs and shapes could be traced in every period. The massive Minoan influence apparent in the fifteenth and sixteenth centuries was, they insisted, rather out of proportion because the surviving evidence tends to underline a single cultural aspect, that of minor arts, especially ceramics. They believed in an almost total loss of Minoan international power after 1400 and speculated that strong mainland competition in foreign trade had been developing considerably earlier.

In an unbiased view, no really convincing case could be made for Minoan political control of mainland power centers at any time. The dominant language of the Mycenaeans, in the opinion of most scholars, was probably an early form of Greek that had most likely been introduced to the peninsula at the beginning of the second millennium. Although they were not primarily concerned with Homeric connections, mainland archaeologists like Blegen and Wace believed in an authentic mainland Greek tradition of heroic songs originating in the Mycenaean context and with clear echoes —however they were to be explained—in Homeric epics.

This was more or less the status of the problem when the Linear B tablets were unearthed at Pylos in 1939. The news did not have any immediate and serious effect on existing theories except to contradict the common view that the mainlanders were essentially illiterate. Evans himself had declared that a few inscribed vases found earlier on the mainland (especially at Thebes) showed that at least as early as 1400 the Minoan bureaucratic palace system and the Linear B script had been transferred to the mainland; and he had implied that the failure to find tablets might be attributed to the fixed idea among mainland excavators since Tsountas' time that there were no tablets to find. To be sure, the date assigned to the Pylos records, around 1200, seemed unexpectedly late; but after all, this was close to the time of most intensive Mycenaean economic activity at home and abroad, and it was then that they would have felt the greatest need for a viable system of record keeping. There was no absolute proof to rule out the possibility that, if Minoan-speaking minorities had seized control of mainland centers around 1400 or before, they might still be in power two centuries later. In fact, Evans must have been cheered during his last months by the Pylos discovery, which seemed to lend confirmation to his views.

The preoccupations of World War II slowed almost to a standstill normal scholarly progress and cooperation in archaeology, as it did in many other scholarly areas that are judged not to "contribute to the national defense." Field work in Greece was particularly affected because of the long agony of the civil war that followed her heroic defense and foreign occupation. Even after organized fighting ended, renewed archaeological activity was long hampered by devastation, poor communications and outlaw bands. Many museums were damaged or destroyed, and their contents in some cases were not accessible for decades.

## FURUMARK'S CERAMIC ANALYSIS

The most important publication during the war years came out of a country not directly involved in the conflict, and even in this case the research had been done in peacetime. Arne Furumark's monumental feat of analyzing and classifying the evolution of ceramic shapes (typology) and decorative motifs (stylistics*) is a landmark. Almost inevitably his system is complex and some modifications have since been advocated. But *The Mycenaean Pottery,* which he published in two volumes in 1941, is still the standard against which one's own discoveries must be checked, and it has provided an organized context for comprehensive discussion. New material and further research along the general lines laid down by Furumark will gradually widen and deepen the all-important ceramic basis for relative and absolute chronology. In addition, the research of chemists, geochemists and ceramic technologists is beginning to provide very welcome approximations on such problems as the time elapsed since a vase was originally fired in the kiln or the area from which the clay comes.

As far as technical terminology is concerned, Furumark rejected both the all-inclusive Evans-Mackenzie "Late Minoan" and the distinctive Wace-Blegen "Late Helladic" to designate the Late Bronze Age on the mainland. He preferred the more general term "Mycenaean," which has been used with varying degrees of precision as to time and area ever since Schliemann's day. His major objection to "Helladic" seems to be that it implies an exclusively mainland character that does not take into account influences from various quarters, especially from Crete and other south Aegean

islands. Here Furumark has had few followers, although the general designation "Mycenaean age" is now used interchangeably with "Late Helladic
period." Late Helladic has clearly emerged as the usual technical ceramic
designation, especially when complicated subperiods (I, II, III; A. B. C.;
I, 2, 3) are involved.

Furumark's scheme of classification naturally owes a good deal to
previous formulations, but the more refined (some think too refined) subperiods were mainly the result of his own meticulous studies. The equivalent absolute dates were based on the best evidence available through
synchronisms with Crete and directly or indirectly with Egypt and the Near
East. Without following it in full detail, we reproduce the main features,
which will be an indispensable basis for much of the discussion later in
this chapter and the next. A good many authorities would now prefer a
date nearer 1200 for the transition from LHIIIB to LHIIIC.

| | |
|---|---|
| LHI | about 1550–1500 |
| LHIIA | about 1500–1450 |
| LHIIB | about 1450–1425 |
| LHIIIA | about 1425–1300 |
| LHIIIB | about 1300–1230 |
| LHIIIC | about 1230–1100 |

Furumark's book appeared in the year of Evans' death, and it completely demolished Evans' thesis that mainland pottery throughout the
Late Bronze Age was simply a "colonial" version of Minoan. A necessary
part of Furumark's task had been to analyze both mainland and Minoan
pottery of the preceding Middle Bronze period, as well as the Minoan
developments throughout the Late Bronze Age. He was therefore able to
state quite authoritatively that even during LHI, when Minoan influence
was rapidly gaining ground in the mainland, some vases were being made
in the unadulterated mainland tradition of shape and decoration and technology, while still others showed a mixture of the two traditions. Apparently the lustrous applied paint of LHI is a Cretan novelty. The mainland
potter's repertory of shapes was derived about equally from Cretan and
native sources. As one might expect, the imported shapes are generally
those of "luxury" vessels, while local shapes were retained for common
"utility" pots. Yet some finer mainland-derived shapes like the stemmed
cup (kylix) and deep bowl (krater) not only survived but eventually
became popular in Crete. There are also a few shapes, like the pilgrim·
flask* (Fig. 85), that were borrowed from Near Eastern sources. Furu-

Figure 85

mark believes that mainland potters were much less likely than their Cretan colleagues to imitate new shapes from other media, such as metal vessels.

LHIIA represents the nearest to complete Minoan domination, when contemporary Cretan fashions almost preoccupy the attention of mainland potters. On the other hand, the style of LHIIB is essentially a mainland creation. Furumark sees here the first genuine Mycenaean ceramics in which the native mainland and the Minoan traditions are successfully fused into a new style.

An increasing tendency toward typically mainland stylization and simplification is observable in LHIIIA, even though fairly strong influence from Crete resumes. The technical processes of selecting, preparing and firing the clay are being continually improved. In general, mainland and Cretan products are becoming easier to distinguish. The extremely widespread LHIIIB pottery shows a logical development of previous tendencies. It is, in general, notably homogeneous, although a recognizable eastern (Levanto-Mycenaean) style can be differentiated. Cretan influence practically ceases and mainland artistic propensities are in full control. Shape and decoration are more standardized. Design is becoming abstract and stereotyped, so that the naturalistic origin of many motifs is scarcely recognizable. These are the tendencies that earlier generations of archaeologists were inclined to characterize as "decadent."

LHIIIC is more varied and complex, reflecting the breakdown of the Mycenaean koinê and the fragmentation caused by turbulent political and cultural conditions throughout the east Mediterranean area. Two almost antithetic tendencies, implicit in LHIIIB, are separately developed. The one involves simplification, the other elaboration in decoration. They were in fact represented in the same time sequence at Mycenae and called by Wace, respectively, the Granary Class and the Close Style* (Fig. 86). LHIIIC pottery exhibits far more distinct regional features, too, and a new wave of Cretan influence is apparent. A strong element of representative art also appears in some of these vases and is apparently derived from the tradition of mainland fresco painting. The best-known single example is the Warrior Vase from Mycenae. But the style is most at home on chariot

Figure 86

Figure 87

kraters (now proved to have been made and painted in the Peloponnese) which seem to have been especially popular in Rhodes and Cyprus (Fig. 87).

The final phase of LHIIIC, often called sub-Mycenaean, reflects the last, rather fumbling attempts at elaboration and pictorial representations. At the same time, the prevailing trend is to a radical use of simple geometric designs. Here within late Mycenaean art can be found the basic elements of the so-called protogeometric* style of the earliest Iron Age.

It is difficult to breathe life and popular interest into these drastic simplifications of Furumark's conclusions. And yet it is often from such unspectacular evidence that sweeping historical generalizations can be affirmed, modified or refuted. For instance, it can no longer be seriously held that the Dorians or any other group of newcomers introduced an intrusive style of "geometric" pottery at the end of the Bronze Age. This distinctive art form represents—at least in the main—the revitalization of the native Mycenaean tradition under new conditions and doubtless with significant new elements in the population.

Furumark also showed that, although there was extremely strong Cretan influence on mainland ceramics in the sixteenth century and particularly in the earlier fifteenth century, it was never a completely overpowering phenomenon. The native tradition survived and reasserted itself. There is nothing here that could not be explained by close and fairly rapidly developed economic and cultural relations between politically independent peoples, the one possessing a much more sophisticated artistic tradition. In any case, a more closely reasoned and controlled reconstruction is emerging, indicating a period of intensive contact from about 1550 to 1450, a shorter period of stabilization and fusion from 1450 to 1425, a time of increasing mainland self-confidence and material prosperity from about 1425 to 1200 and finally a more complex, diffuse and decentralized situation from about 1200 until the end of the Bronze Age. The ceramic evidence provides an indispensable basis into which additional cultural material may be fitted and with which broader historical theories must be reconciled.

In the immediate post-World War II years there were several important developments that bore little or no relation to the resumption of excavation. Each reflects, on the contrary, the results of seasoned reflection in the study and library on the published results of earlier field work. This vital kind of archaeological activity may or may not be carried on by practicing excavators. It is usually the quiet sort of contribution that seldom is in the headlines. Yet without the synthesis that it does so much to provide, the rapidly expanding bulk of evidence from excavations would soon become chaotic and unmanageable. Indeed, there is much to be said for some kind of schedule (other than recurring wars) to impose a moratorium on new excavation at stated intervals and allow the excavators and their colleagues a respite for reappraisal.

## KANTOR'S ANALYSIS OF CONTACT WITH THE EAST

A significant shift in opinion on the question of Minoan-Mycenaean leadership in economic activities followed the publication in 1947 of an important monograph by Helene Kantor. Being in the enviable and rather unusual position of knowing at first hand the artistic traditions in both the Aegean and the Near East, she could authoritatively review the interrelations in "The Aegean and the Orient in the Second Millennium B.C." As a historian of Near Eastern art, she is particularly interested in the evidence for direct importation and imitation of Aegean decorative motifs. Her analysis shows that, contrary to Evans' belief, the critical shift in Minoan versus Mycenaean contact with Egypt and other countries of the eastern Mediterranean seems to have occurred between 1700 and 1600. In the MMII period there is a fair amount of evidence for direct or indirect trade in Cretan pottery and metalwork, probably in patterned textiles and no doubt in other raw materials and processed goods that can no longer be traced. On the other hand, the moderate amount of Aegean imports into the Near East in the earlier part of the Late Bronze Age, *i.e.*, 1600 to 1400, would seem already to derive almost exclusively from the Greek mainland. There is even some transitory impact discernible from mainland art on the conservative Egyptian tradition.

Kantor considers the evidence sufficient to prove that direct trade connections between the Mycenaeans and peoples of the Near East were solidly established during LHI and II, although she views with some skepticism Persson's attempt to show strong reverse influence from Egypt on Greece. She further maintains that the pottery and even the celebrated Egyptian tomb paintings of the Eighteenth Dynasty showing offerings of Aegean type being presented by "Keftiu" indicate that Crete by this time had a very limited share in trade with the Near East.

Blegen and Wace had stressed the Mycenaean origin of most Aegean pottery found in the Near East. Pendlebury had acknowledged the direction in which this evidence was pointing, but he had sidestepped the complementary political implications. Kantor bluntly states that it is impossible to reconcile these facts with any theory of Mycenaean payment of tribute to Cretan overlords. In fact, the whole concept of a Minoan thalassocracy in LMI and II now becomes dubious and may be a mirage. She refers obliquely to Wace's bold suggestion that LMII at Knossos might even represent a period of mainland political control and, without directly supporting it, says that the (by this time) orthodox explanation of the destruction of Knossos by mainlanders about 1400 cannot be correct, since it postulates a mainland revolt against an economic monopoly that clearly did not exist in the late fifteenth century.

The greatly expanded trade contacts between the Greek mainland and the Near East in the last centuries of the Bronze Age now appear in the perspective of a gradual buildup over the preceding century or two, rather than as a sudden burst of pent-up energy released by the conquest of Crete about 1400. During LHIII Asiatic artisans were affected by Mycenaean imports; in ivory carving Aegean motifs exercised a particularly notable influence. Kantor's summation is in its way as sweeping as any of Evans' frequent generalizations—and it directly contradicts one of his major premises. "After the close of the MMII period, and throughout the later part of the Second Millennium," she insists, "only the sailors, merchants, and craftsmen of Mycenaean Greece can justifiedly lay claim to the honor of forming the links connecting the Aegean with the Orient."

## LORIMER'S REVIEW OF HOMERIC CONNECTIONS

Another scholar, H. L. Lorimer, completed during the war years the work of a whole lifetime and in 1950 published the results in *Homer and the Monuments*. Her purpose was to bring up to date a subject much in the thoughts of earlier excavators and Homeric scholars. The available evidence had been summed up sixty-six years before in a German work, *The Homeric Epos Illustrated from the Monuments,* by Wolfgang Helbig. Unfortunately, Schliemann's work was then just getting under way, and Helbig's masterly synthesis was deprived of the results of the first organized excavations. Part of the subject was carefully handled a decade later (1894, and again in 1901) in Wolfgang Reichel's book *Homeric Weapons,* also in German. Lorimer became their distinguished successor. The whole vast problem of the relationship between material remains of varying periods as revealed by archaeology and the complex culture depicted by Homer is, of course, beyond our scope. Yet we cannot avoid some attempt to draw on Lorimer's conclusions as they affect the recurring question of how much (if any) direct or inherited knowledge of Mycenaean civilization is revealed in the Homeric poems.

Schliemann's impetuous enthusiasm had identified Troy II with the city of Priam and the occupants of the Shaft Graves at Mycenae with Agamemnon and his contemporaries. In the Homeric poems he saw (at least in the earlier years) such direct descriptions of these places and objects as could only be the result of personal experience. But few, even at that time, fully shared his conviction, and two generations of further research ruled it out completely. Closer dating showed that Troy II had been destroyed many hundreds of years before the Shaft Graves were constructed. The Shaft Graves in turn had held their hallowed dead for centuries before the days of intensive Mycenaean contact with Troy VI and VIIa in the thirteenth century. If, as was increasingly believed after Schliemann's day, the Trojan War was a real historical event, it had probably taken place between 1300 and 1200. Were there, then, in the poems authentic echoes of the culture of that period or of the immediately preceding centuries as it was revealed by archaeology? If so, it would be fair to assume a continuous tradition in oral songs originally circulating in Mycenaean courts and persisting until Homer's time (certainly centuries later), when nobody had firsthand knowledge of Mycenaean civilization.

It was to these problems that Lorimer directed much of her research, although she was equally interested in identifying the latest cultural elements of the poems, as indicated by archaeological parallels in the Early Iron Age (after 1100). The latter line of inquiry was clearly a very important means of assigning an approximate date to the poet or poets responsible for giving the *Iliad* and the *Odyssey* their more or less final form. We shall simply record here that she inferred from this evidence that Homer lived in the second half of the eighth century. Some cultural features of the *Odyssey* seem to be a little later than any in the *Iliad,* but the time lag need not exceed the span of one lifetime. This general position on one aspect of the Homeric Question had many adherents even before Lorimer's book was published, and the support of her meticulous handling of the archaeological evidence buttressed it considerably. Continuing study up to the present has lent it increasing weight.

Lorimer's major conclusion on the problems that directly concern us would have been somewhat disappointing even to Schliemann's more cautious successors like Dörpfeld and Tsountas. She finds, in short, that the poems do indeed preserve certain features of Late Bronze Age culture, but that the correspondence is not nearly as consistent as was once supposed. Perhaps the most striking examples of archaeologically known objects described in the poems occur in earlier Mycenaean contexts, especially in the Shaft Grave period. Such artefacts as the great body shield, the "cup of Nestor" and the boar's tusk helmet certainly did not physically survive the Bronze Age. The helmet, which she considers the most decisive Homeric echo, was covered with four or five rows of tusks arranged with the curve in alternating directions in each row. Thirty to forty pairs of tusks were used in making a single helmet. Lorimer says: "For four centuries at least [before the eighth century] no one could possibly have seen a boar's tusk helmet; only in the amber of traditional poetry handed down with an astonishing verbal fidelity could its image have been preserved." She also believes that the exotic niello technique of metal inlay, which is believed to have originated in Syria and is best illustrated in early Mycenaean daggers and described in connection with Achilles' shield, died out before the end of the Bronze Age. More general considerations, like the repeated references to bronze weapons centuries after that metal had been largely replaced by iron, also have validity.

The discrepancy between Mycenaean inhumation burial and Homer's rites of cremation is a stumbling block for many who want to establish a continuous tradition. But it causes no particular problem in Lorimer's perspective of a long time span involving mixed culture traits that are reflected, sometimes in rather undigested form, in the final product. She points to Blegen's discovery of a cemetery of cremation burials contemporary with Troy VI and to the probability that the Greeks attacking Troy

VIIa saw and perhaps practiced the same rite on foreign soil. During the chaotic decades toward the end of the Bronze Age, cultural novelties were disturbing many long-cherished customs, and cremation seems to have been one of them. It is probably no accident that cremation becomes popular in and near Athens, the rallying place of many Mycenaean refugees and the springboard for the Ionic migration to Asia Minor in which Homer's ancestors must have taken part.

Lorimer's chapter "The Age of Illiteracy in Greece" dramatically reflects the lack of preparation of most scholars for the shock that was to come only two years later. She seems to accept Evans' theory of foreign oligarchies in mainland centers, "where Minoan would be the court language," and she regards the Pylos archives as confirmatory evidence. Preliminary work on the tablets in her view is "wholly unfavourable to any hope entertained that the language of the inscriptions might be Greek."

A period of illiteracy in the Aegean area seems to have followed the end of the Bronze Age, except in Cyprus, where there was a continuing use of a modified version (probably derived from Crete) of linear script (probably Linear A). When writing was reintroduced to Greece, the script was a quite unrelated alphabet borrowed, directly or indirectly, from the Phoenicians. Lorimer accepts the theory most widely held at present, which would date the historical Greek alphabet no earlier than about the middle of the eighth century. It is therefore probable that the Homeric poems were composed in a milieu where renewed literacy was in its infancy, but Lorimer does not speculate on the possibility that the new system may have been used to record the poems in or soon after Homer's lifetime. The society that Homer describes is clearly illiterate, and this would point to a continuation of oral heroic poetry during the so-called dark ages between the end of the Bronze Age and the eighth century.

Up to 1950 no single example of a metal corselet or cuirass was known from the Mycenaean period; thus, in spite of the ideogram in the Knossos tablets that Evans had interpreted as representing this article of armor (though the material is, of course, unknown), Lorimer regards Homer's numerous references to metal body armor[76] as later Iron Age interpolations. The same conclusion is reached for the same reason in reference to the "bronze-greaved"[77] Greek warriors. The Mycenaean soldier was apparently equipped with a single heavy thrusting spear, and it is only in the Iron Age that pairs of lighter throwing spears appear in art representations. The spear is, of course, the favorite weapon of the Homeric fighter, and he regularly carries two of the throwing variety; so we have here still another late feature. There is practically no echo in Homer of the long slender rapier or thrusting sword, which is the only type found in Greece and

Crete until quite late in Mycenaean times (LHIIIA). Then a shorter, broader, unribbed slashing sword, obviously the weapon wielded by the Homeric hero, replaces the older type.

Chariots drawn by a pair of horses appear as early as the Shaft Graves and continue to be an important instrument of war through the later Bronze Age. Archaeology does not establish how they were used in war, and it is possible that their peacetime function for racing, for state occasions and as a means of rapid transportation was equally vital. Battle scenes on geometric vases of the Early Iron Age suggest that chariots, occasionally drawn by four horses, were a rapid means of reaching and leaving the fight, just as in Homeric descriptions. But Nestor's descriptions of the massed charge of chariots may very well constitute the record of earlier usage.[78]

Lorimer sees no echo in Homer of the very distinctive male and female clothing of Minoan Crete. Male costume of mainland type, as distinct from Minoan, consisted of a short light linen or woolen tunic (like the Homeric chiton), as shown on the Warrior Vase, and probably also a woolen cloak (like the Homeric chlaina*). The latter was fastened over the shoulder with a straight pin or sometimes (after the thirteenth century) with a fibula*, like our safety pin. There was apparently no significant change in these garments from the days of the Shaft Graves until the time of Homer.

The archaeological evidence for female costume is even more unsatisfactory. The more sophisticated Mycenaean art objects invariably show ladies (or goddesses) dressed in the elaborate, plunging neckline fashion that prevailed in Crete and may have been copied at the Mycenaean courts. But mainland representations like the terra-cotta figurines show a simpler one- or two-piece dress (perhaps akin to the Homeric peplos*), which presumably represents the native tradition. The garment was clearly cut and sewn, and the most common fastenings were probably the ubiquitous pierced conical objects that once were called loomweights but are more likely buttons. Pins and fibulae seem also to have been used. Ornate brooches apparently did not appear until the later Iron Age.

Lorimer believes that some real connection, however confused and enigmatic, must be assumed between the mainland palaces of the Late Bronze Age and the Homeric descriptions. The echoes could be explained either by a continuous oral epic tradition or by the continuation of the megaron in a less ambitious form for the kings or gods of a later time. Homeric references to the great central ceremonial hearth with the columns around it and to various details of plan and decoration seem to support the former theory. Yet it is strange, on that assumption, to find in Homer no mention of the frescoed walls and decorated floors that are such a striking feature of Mycenaean palaces.

In both the Homeric poems and Mycenaean Greece the gods seem usually to have been worshiped in open-air shrines or groves. The palace shrines of Crete may have had less obvious counterparts in the mainland, but separate buildings used as temples seem to have been a later feature. They certainly existed in Homer's time,[79] but no convincing example from Mycenaean Greece was known to Lorimer.

## VENTRIS AND LINEAR B

In the year 1952 an epoch-making discovery was announced that has every right to be ranked with Schliemann's at Troy in 1870 and at Mycenae in 1876, Evans' at Knossos in 1900 and Blegen's at Pylos in 1939. Michael Ventris was not an excavator or a "desk archaeologist" or a philologist, but an architect by profession. Already an avid linguist and amateur cryptographer, Ventris as a boy of fourteen had heard Evans lecture in 1936 on the mysterious Cretan scripts and had then made up his mind that he would someday solve the puzzle.

Unfortunately, there was not much material to work on before the war. As we have seen, Evans had published little more than 100 of the 3,000 or so Linear B tablets he had found at Knossos. And he was extremely indignant when a Finnish scholar, Johannes Sundwall, copied and published a few more without explicit permission. Photographs of a half-dozen Pylos tablets had appeared in Blegen's preliminary report in 1939, but the bulk of the tablets from both sites were unavailable, although plans were being made for their publication as rapidly as possible.

Several premature, even weird, attempts at decipherment had been made, but few experts were much impressed. The underlying language was identified as anything from Basque to a rather odd kind of primitive Greek. Several scholars were inclined to see in Linear B (and even in Linear A and Minoan hieroglyphics) some kind of Indo-European pattern at least related to Greek; but the overwhelming tendency was to follow Evans in visualizing a pre-Greek, non-Indo-European, non-Semitic "Aegean" or "Minoan" language with vague origins and perhaps survivals in southwest Asia Minor. Some saw the most attractive possibility in the Etruscan language, itself a puzzle, although the alphabet at least was familiar. In 1940 Ventris, at the tender age of eighteen, published an article in the prestigious *American Journal of Archaeology* in which he supported the Etruscan equation.

Then came the war years, when only a few scholars were able to devote their attention to the decipherment. Fortunately, there had been time for the Pylos tablets to be cleaned and photographed before they were taken off to the vaults of the Bank of Greece along with other treasures from the National Museum in Athens. The 1939 excavation photographs and notebooks as well as a full set of professional photographs of the cleaned and mended tablets had been brought back to Cincinnati. Blegen had entrusted this material to one of his graduate students, Emmett Bennett, Jr. A formidable amount of work needed to be done before the tablets could be made available to scholars, and both Blegen's and Bennett's efforts were interrupted by military service. Gradually, however, line drawings were made from painstaking tracings of each fragment, joins of one fragment to another explored, a table constructed of normative forms of each symbol of the syllabary* and a word index compiled. It is a tribute to Blegen's determination to make the full evidence quickly available to scholars and to Bennett's industry and precision that the first edition of *The Pylos Tablets: A Preliminary Transcription* appeared as early as 1951.

Immediately, the amount of available material was multiplied by five, since it had been reasonably clear from the first that, though there are minor differences, the Pylos texts and the documents in Linear B from Knossos could confidently be studied together. The impact of the new Pylos material is reflected in the rapidity of Ventris' progress toward their decipherment in the next few months. An admirably clear account of that fascinating process is provided by Ventris' closest colleague, John Chadwick, in *The Decipherment of Linear B* (1958). We shall make no attempt here to summarize this complicated story, except to record that even when the "grid*" of phonetic equivalents for the syllabary was taking encouraging shape Ventris still took it for granted that the underlying language would turn out to be an unfamiliar one.

There seems, in retrospect, to be no completely rational explanation for the fact that between 1939 and 1951 almost all scholars continued to exclude the possibility that the Linear B script was used to write Greek. Tsountas had long ago insisted that the Mycenaeans spoke Greek. Linguists such as C. D. Buck had reenforced the idea. Blegen and many colleagues believed that Greek speakers had first entered the peninsula as early as 1900. Wace's theory that several anomalous culture traits of the LMII phase at Knossos might be explained by the presence of mainlanders (presumably Greek speaking) had been recorded by Pendlebury in 1939. Professor Sterling Dow (and perhaps others) had accepted Wace's historical conclusion, although Dow's opinion was unpublished and unknown to Ventris.

Evans himself had once observed that the two-syllable word that accompanied an ideogram* (stylized picture) of a young horse on some of the Knossos Linear B tablets would, if assigned the phonetic equivalents that these symbols had in the later Cypriote syllabary, be PO-LO, which is

startlingly close to the Greek word *pōlos* (a cognate of English "foal").
A. E. Cowley in 1927 had inferred from the content of certain Knossos
tablets that two frequent word groups of two syllables and having the first
syllable in common must represent "boy" and "girl"; and he compared
the phenomenon to Greek *kouros* ("boy") and *kourē* ("girl"). Furthermore, a serious question about the usual theory that Linear A and B were
used to write the same language was raised by Bennett in 1950. He had
shown that the system used to indicate fractions was entirely different in
Linear A and Linear B.

Yet when Ventris circulated a questionnaire to a dozen or so of the
leading world authorities in 1949, not a single one who replied looked
seriously on the possibility that the language of the Linear B tablets could
be Greek. It would be difficult, indeed, to point to a more glaring example
of how one able and dynamic man's interpretation of inconclusive evidence
so thoroughly dominated the thinking of nearly all of his colleagues for
half a century.

Nor were the philologists alone in error. It is equally embarrassing to
quote a judgment such as that published in 1950 by Furumark. According
to this distinguished expert on Aegean pottery and related art, "The most
conspicuous manifestation of this Cretan period [*i.e.,* LMII], its art, has
indeed been considered so peculiar that it has been suggested that it was
due to an inspiration from abroad; this assumption has, in its turn, led to
the theory that at this time Knossos (and Crete) was under foreign rule.
But a systematic study of the material shows such views to be untenable."
The real stumbling block, by hindsight, was the acceptance of the *political*
consequences that would have to accompany the idea that Greek might
have been spoken or mainland artefacts used at the court of Knossos before
1400.

In any case, by mid-1952 Ventris was literally forced to believe that
more than chance was involved when in so many cases the substitution of
the values in his experimental grid was producing attractive Greek equivalents. Place-names like Knossos (phonetic equivalent KO-NO-SO) and its
port Amnisos (A-MI-NI-SO) were assumed to be present in the Knossos
documents and were used to provide the values for the grid. The critical
point, however, was reached when Ventris' phonetic equivalents for the
common two-syllable word known to mean "total" came out as TO-SO
(masculine) and TO-SA (feminine), which are inflected forms of the common Greek adjective meaning "so much." Other equations, though they
may appear somewhat strained at first glance, produced standard Greek
nouns like PO-ME, *poimēn* ("shepherd"), KA-KE-U, *khalkeus* ("bronze-
smith"), KU-RU-SO-WO-KO, *khrusoworgos* ("goldsmith").

It was this evidence that drove Ventris to suggest on the BBC's Third

Programme in early June, 1952, that he had found the key to the decipherment of Linear B. "During the last few weeks," he said, "I have come to the conclusion that the Knossos and Pylos tablets must, after all, be written in Greek—a difficult and archaic Greek, seeing that it is 500 years older than Homer and written in a rather abbreviated form, but Greek nevertheless."

Actually, the occasion of that broadcast was an invitation to review the long-awaited Volume II of *Scripta Minoa,* the preparation of which was a labor of love performed by Evans' old friend Sir John L. Myres. Unfortunately, the bulk of the Knossos tablets, finally published after Evans' death, appeared too late to play a major part in Ventris' decipherment. Myres' publication was, in fact, far inferior to Bennett's work, although its faults are attributable mainly to the uneven state of Evans' records and the failure to check Evans' readings against the original documents.

Ventris' modest announcement had a particularly galvanizing effect on one of his hearers, Dr. John Chadwick of Cambridge University; and within a few weeks Ventris and Chadwick had become collaborators. Chadwick had been working on Linear B for some years, and his expert linguistic knowledge of the facts already established or inferred about early Greek was exactly the right foil for Ventris' brilliance and inventiveness. Before the end of the year they submitted to the *Journal of Hellenic Studies* a historic article with the cautious title "Evidence for Greek Dialect in the Mycenaean Archives." The use of the adjective "Mycenaean" had a stronger authority because of recent news that Wace's newest excavation in a row of houses or palace annexes just outside the Mycenae citadel had produced tablets inscribed in the same Linear B script.

After stating the linguistic, historical and archaeological reasons why their thesis had a claim to a fair hearing, Ventris and Chadwick printed the grid in which phonetic equivalents were supplied for sixty-five of the more than eighty different symbols in the syllabary. They then explained their "assumed rules of Mycenaean orthography" (*i.e.,* spelling rules), which to users of an alphabet seem complicated and clumsy and inexact. For instance: (1) the same symbol serves for the syllables *pu, bu* and *phu;* (2) L and R are not distinguished; (3) consonants at the end of a word are not written; (4) S is not written at the beginning of a word if the next sound is a consonant; (5) certain combinations of consonants have the following vowel anticipated by a "dead" vowel. KO-NO-SO illustrates rules 3 and 5 and may be presumed to represent Knossos. PU-RO illustrates rules 1, 2 and 3 and must from context designate Pylos (*Pulos* in Greek), although the same two symbols would also be used to write Bylon, Phylor, Spyros (rule 4) and so on.

It is immediately apparent that the theoretical possibilities for various combinations and permutations are very numerous; and when this difficulty is compounded by many unfamiliar features of bookkeeping shorthand, archaic grammar and obsolete vocabulary, one can begin to see why jokes have developed, radically different serious translations are current and many words, phrases, clauses or even whole tablets still remain completely enigmatic.

Ventris and Chadwick gave numerous samples of words that fit the rules and context neatly, like PA-TE and MA-TE for *patēr* ("father") and *matēr* ("mother") where lists of parents and children seemed indicated. They also hazarded translations and interpretations of a few longer passages. And finally they pointed to numerous significant instances where this Mycenaean dialect is closely related to the so-called Arcado-Cypriot dialect of classical times. Arcado-Cypriot had long been assumed to represent enclaves of refugees who survived the dark days at the end of the Bronze Age in two very widely separated areas of the Mycenaean "empire," Arcadia in central Peloponnese and the island of Cyprus off the Syrian coast.

The first exposition of the decipherment convinced some scholars immediately; most experts (including Bennett) still withheld judgment, and a few were very skeptical. Almost all of those in the second category, however, were persuaded by a new and dramatic confirmation of Ventris' system. In 1952 Blegen had finally been able to begin the full-scale excavation of the palace at Ano Englianos. One of the first areas cleared was the vicinity of the little archives room uncovered in 1939. Immediately to the south and east, an area that had been disturbed by a great trench dug by later seekers for building stone yielded more than 300 additional tablets. When they were cleaned and mended the following spring (1953), Blegen experimented with the proposed system of decipherment and was so impressed with the results in one particular case that he wrote immediately to Ventris. It should be emphasized that Ventris had no knowledge of the document in question until after he had completed his original grid and announced the tentative decipherment.

This tablet (Fig. 88) is identified as Ta 641 in Bennett's rather com-

Figure 88

plicated classification system. The alphabetic letters identify it as one of a series of records inventorying containers and furniture. As is fairly often the case, this scribe added pictures of the objects being inventoried, described them carefully and recorded the number in each distinct group. The first word, followed (after three descriptive terms) by the picture of a vessel shown with three supports and the numeral "2," turned out on Ventris' system to be TI-RI-PO-DE. In the second entry (midway in the top line) only one vessel of exactly the same type is inventoried, and the corresponding word here is TI-RI-PO. Only an extremely stubborn opponent of Ventris' decipherment could refuse to agree that we have here the Greek word for a three-legged vessel, or "tripod." Its singular form is *tripos,* and the dual number (common in Homer and still occasionally found in later Greek when pairs are involved) is *tripode.* Furthermore, in the second and third lines another pair of inflections of a single word—DI-PA and DI-PA-E—occurs, along with pictures of a vessel of different shape, which narrows sharply toward the base. The word reminds us of Homer's *depas,* a bowl or goblet for libations; and the dual form DI-PA-E occurs in the only entry (midway in the second line) where two of them are inventoried.

Nor does the persuasiveness of Ta 641 end here. The DI-PA shape is pictured with four handles, three handles and no handles at all. In the entries opposite the four- and three-handled varieties respectively are the words QE-TO-RO-WE and TI-RI-O-WE; while A-NO-WE occurs with the plain vessel. These words are surely compound adjectives describing the vessels. The O-WE element is easily identified with the Greek word for "ear" that continued to be used in later Greek to denote "handle"; and QE-TO-RO, TI-RI and A(N) must be Greek *tetra* ("four"), *tri* ("three") and *a(n)* (a negative prefix).

Could any neater and more opportune confirmation of Ventris' system be imagined? It is so overwhelmingly convincing, in fact, that one persistent critic hinted at collusion; but such an allegation is unworthy of a member of the scholarly community. The established sequence of events as well as the reputations of Ventris and Blegen made the insinuation impossible and unthinkable. There are still unsolved problems about Ta 641, but we can now understand much of this inventory, and the Greek-ness of the underlying language is beyond doubt.

The 1953 article by Ventris and Chadwick did not fully explain how the grid had been built up, and some clarification and amplification was desirable. Furthermore, the new tablets from Pylos and Mycenae now had to be taken into account. The excavators allowed Ventris and Chadwick free access to the newly discovered tablets, so that in the same year they were hard at work on a much more ambitious project. Their bulky book, *Docu-*

*ments in Mycenaean Greek,* dedicated to Heinrich Schliemann, appeared in the autumn of 1956, a few weeks after Ventris' tragic death in an automobile accident. In the fraction of his short thirty-four years devoted to the decipherment Michael Ventris made the greatest contribution to Mycenaean studies of any scholar in the third generation after Schliemann. In fact, this whole chapter was at one point called "Ventris and Linear B."

Ventris and Chadwick first provide extensive chapters dealing with the development of the decipherment, the writing system, the language, the very large proportion of personal and place-names and the new data on Mycenaean civilization. But the nucleus, as the title suggests, is a translation (with commentary) of 300 selected texts from Knossos, Pylos and Mycenae. The choice of this particular group out of a total of over 4,000 was based mainly on their judgment of the most interesting documents that were then available and at least partially intelligible.

There is no doubt that our field of study has been dominated and partially restructured in the past dozen years by the results and potentialities of the decipherment. The last centuries of the Aegean Bronze Age have suddenly leaped from the prehistoric stage (although we already had the testimony of later mythology and epic poetry) to that of a "protohistoric" period for which we possess contemporary written documents that can be at least partially understood. Field archaeologists and philologists have had to collaborate and supplement each other as never before. Perhaps in another generation a more adequate adjustment will have been made to this startling change. The archaeologists will almost certainly unearth more clay tablets within closer dating brackets and will make new discoveries or better syntheses to illuminate more clearly uncertain features of the material civilization. The philologists in their turn, as they continue to work over the present texts and make use of the additional material, will gain a more adequate control of this early "Achaean" form of Greek.

It is only fair to record, however, that progress on the philological side has been somewhat disappointing since Ventris' death. The first rush of interest and enthusiasm led to excessive hopes and sometimes to rash and untenable proposals. Skeptical reactions by able philologists were to be expected and have not wholly subsided. *Documents in Mycenaean Greek* marked the zenith of the initial impetus, and nothing said or implied hereafter is meant to call into question the solid new insights it provided and the challenge it offered of extracting further dependable evidence from the tablets.

It is intriguing to speculate whether, if Ventris were living now and devoting his full time and tremendous energies to the interpretation, the present situation would have been notably different. He could certainly

have made himself a first-rate philologist. But many first-rate philologists
have been working on the tablets for more than a decade and their collective progress is slow. Doubtless Ventris' imagination and perceptiveness
and flair might have suggested solutions to some problems, but no one
could overcome the inherent difficulties of a small body of fragmentary
texts containing highly stylized and abbreviated bookkeeping shorthand
notes, in a writing system that seems to us so awkward that it was probably
adapted from one used for a completely different language ("Minoan"),
in a dialect and stage of Greek at least as difficult for scholars of classical
Greek as Chaucerian English is for users of modern English.

Yet, apart from the continuing problems of interpretation, the decipherment brusquely decided the "Great Debate." It must have been a kindly
fate that decided that Evans should die before 1952 and that Wace should
survive to write the Foreword to *Documents*. He may be pardoned for
showing in it a certain belated exasperation with the widely accepted "pan-
Minoan theories." And he has even stronger criticism for certain classical
archaeologists and philologists who continue to insist on an almost absolute
gulf between the cultures of Bronze Age and Iron Age Greece. On this quite
separate issue he and Evans had long been allies. Wace says:

> The importance of Mr. Ventris' decipherment can hardly be over-
> estimated, for it inaugurates a new phase in our study of the beginnings
> of classical Hellas. We must recognize the Mycenaean culture as Greek,
> and as one of the first stages in the advance of the Hellenes toward the
> brilliance of their later amazing achievements. We must guard against
> the facile assumptions of the past and look at everything afresh from the
> new point of view. In culture, in history and in language we must regard
> prehistoric and historic Greece as one indivisible whole. The way has
> been prepared for us by the pioneer archaeological work of Schliemann,
> Tsountas and Evans, and we must follow boldly in their footsteps under
> the guiding light now provided for us by Mr. Ventris and Mr. Chadwick.

A few years later (1962) Wace's close associate Blegen would express
the same idea with equal authority and eloquence.

> The definite recognition of the Mycenaeans as Greeks calls for some-
> thing more than mere passing mention. Let it be an early stage in the
> history of that race, perhaps before Hellenic speech had yet been fully
> evolved. Nonetheless it demonstrates the inherent strength of the Greek
> people and their astonishing power of survival: they still exist and
> flourish today, retaining their distinctive character, their language, their
> exclusiveness along with their cohesiveness, despite intense individual-
> ism. Apart possibly from the Chinese, there are few, if any, other com-
> parable peoples in their tenacity to endure. In their long history they

have at least three times blossomed out into world leadership in culture: in the Late Mycenaean Age, in the classical period, and in the heyday of the Byzantine Empire. They have withstood the impact of innumerable invasions that brought hordes of foreign intruders into their land from the north, from the east, from the south, and from the west; they have endured subjection and occupation for centuries under alien rule, and yet they have always in the end absorbed the marauders and imposed their own Greek spirit, their way of thinking and their culture on the fusion of Hellenized survivors that remained.

Wace proceeds to review very briefly some of the ground we have covered in previous chapters. He particularly emphasizes the growth of the conviction that Greek speakers had entered the peninsula as early as about 1900, the evidence that Mycenaean culture always preserved native mainland traits and the error of regarding LMII Knossos as the wide-ruling Minoan capital of the Aegean world.

Quite characteristically, he invites another controversy by assuming that the mainland Greeks never completely lost their literacy in the period between the end of the Bronze Age and the assimilation of the new alphabet some three or four centuries later. He cites the parallel of the survival of a modified form of the Minoan syllabary in classical Cyprus and insists, "It is incredible that a people as intelligent as the Greeks should have forgotten how to read and write once they had learned how to do so." Yet surely the invention and retention of a writing system is a product of need as well as of intelligence. The complex palace bureaucracies of the Late Bronze Age, which the content of the tablets has revealed and which we shall presently review, could not have operated without a system of written records; whereas all the evidence so far suggests a much simpler and less centralized economy after the destruction of these great power centers. Nothing could be more suddenly obsolete than a tax record when the power that imposed the tax has been destroyed. The onus of proof, both theoretical and actual, is clearly on those who would insist that the Greeks of the earliest Iron Age had any compelling reason to perpetuate the Mycenaean writing system.

Few, on the other hand, would deny Wace's assertion that writing was done on materials other than clay in late Mycenaean times. The flowing curves of the Linear B syllabary seem to have been developed on a more tractable material and are only possible on clay by the use of a very thin sharp stylus in a practiced hand. Bennett has identified the idiosyncracies of more than forty scribes at Pylos. This may support the thesis of a somewhat more widespread calligraphy on perishable materials like papyrus or skin (parchment). Marinatos has suggested that fine lines visible on the reverse of a clay sealing from Knossos may indicate that it was pressed against a sheet of papyrus. What such documents would have contained we can only guess. The clay tablets were apparently not used for permanent records, even of a local economic nature. They contain no year date and seldom even identify the month. There are references to "this year," "last year," "next year," but that is all. It is almost certain that other materials were used for more permanent economic records, and it is at least possible that there was written diplomatic exchange at the interkingdom level within (and possibly beyond) the Mycenaean orbit.

When we come to the theories of Wace and others about the existence of historical and literary archives, however, we are on very slippery ground. It is probably fair to see in Greek mythology, though it is so intimately bound up with the Mycenaean past, an imprecise, unhistorical, orally transmitted set of "great deeds of famous men" (Homer's *klea andrōn*). The archaeological material, such as the representations on sculpture, fresco, gems and vases, gives a similar impression of interest in the general and genre in life, rather than the specific depiction of a given historical event so noticeable in much Near Eastern art.

Wace surely carries his hypothesis to a dangerous extreme when, after outlining the orthodox modern position that Homer stands at the end of a long tradition of epic song that probably extended back in an unbroken line to Mycenaean times, he adds, "We need not therefore be surprised if excavation or some casual find in Greece gives us an early document—a letter, or a literary text, a history or a poem—from some long-forgotten forerunner of Homer." On the contrary, the recent intensive study of the technique of epic poetry suggests very strongly that the long epic tradition culminating in Homer was from the first—and almost if not quite to the last—an entirely oral one. The discovery of a fragment from a proto-Homeric epic written in Linear B would now have an even more upsetting effect on academic preconceptions than the demonstration that Greek was the language of the Knossian court before 1400.

It is difficult to estimate how far other prehistoric archaeologists of this generation would go along with Wace's severe criticism of many of their colleagues who work in the later, classical horizons. "From the beginning of Schliemann's discoveries at Mycenae," he charges, "the conservatism of classical archaeologists has obstructed progress in the study of Greek civilization as a whole. . . . It is this spirit which has impeded progress in our studies of pre-Classical Greece. . . . Greek art is one and indivisible, and has a continuous history from the first arrival of the Greeks." What Wace calls the "orthodox" classical attitude is the position (which we saw exemplified in Michaelis' book) that Mycenaean and classical culture are so completely unlike that any close organic connection is impossible. These scholars, many or few, see in the geometric culture of the early Iron Age the real origin of the "new life of pure Hellenism."

Wace believes that the wide cultural "chasm" that is supposed to exist at the end of the Bronze Age and has been traditionally explained by the Dorian invasion is a mirage comparable to Evans' pan-Minoan obsession. According to Wace, every step of the development of the form and decoration of the crisp, economical geometric artistic style so admired by Hellenists can be traced on Greek soil out of the late Mycenaean repertory. We shall review current opinion on this thorny question in our final chapter; but meanwhile Professor Wace, gadfly and controversialist extraordinary, has led us rather far from the Linear B tablets.

One gets a vivid idea of the new impact in the early years after the decipherment by comparing Wace's account in *Mycenae* (1949) about Mycenaean civilization with Chadwick's *Decipherment of Linear B* only nine years later. There are not many major features in Wace's review to which we have not made some reference in previous chapters. What Wace does is to provide a perspective on the typical inhabitant of a typical Mycenaean town, or as he himself says, "to form some idea of the average standard of life." His sketch is almost as readable as Tsountas' and much better balanced than Glotz's.

On the question of government, all Wace could say in 1949 is that indications are that each kingdom seems to have had an "orderly monarchical form of administration," with perhaps a council of elders, as in Homer's account. Although he did not fully utilize Nilsson's insight to disentangle mainland from Minoan rites and practices, he concludes that the native religion was polytheistic with a principal female divinity who may have united in her single person many local cults and the attributes of several "goddesses." A cult of the noble dead was a notable feature, and it was perhaps carried on without interruption in the hero cults of later historical times. In the intellectual realm, literacy was probably confined to a small group; but Mycenaean achievements in many fields showed that they were truly civilized and produced "skilled craftsmen, imaginative artists, capable organizers, able engineers and architects." Wace had no doubt that Mycenae was the capital of the leading kingdom, even if Homer's picture of the king of Mycenae as exercising some measure of control over the other kings is not entirely historical. As an explanation of Mycenae's celebrated wealth, he suggests that she controlled copper mines, of which he believes there are traces within her territory, especially in the neighborhood of Nemea.

Chadwick's chapter "Life in Mycenaean Greece" will form the basis for our review of highlights from the Linear B tablets. This will be supplemented by subsequent information worked out by Chadwick himself, L. R. Palmer and numerous others. Chadwick begins with the assertion that, in spite of efforts to throw doubt on the decipherment or to explain in very peculiar ways the fact that the language of the tablets is basically Greek, we are forced to believe in the testimony of the proper names themselves that Greek speakers formed at least the major segment of the population in mainland centers like Pylos and Mycenae. Greek speakers must also have controlled Knossos and much of the rest of Cretan territory for some time before 1400, and the use of Linear A at least down to the early years of the fifteenth century may provide an approximation of the length of the occupation. We shall have more to say on some of these controversial topics in the final chapter.

Chadwick admits that the contents of the tablets so far give no hint of the cause of the Mycenaean collapse. There is certainly no decisive evidence to support the belief in a massive Dorian invasion sweeping all before it. But a number of Pylos texts do appear to refer to defense measures, presumably against the enemy who actually burned the palace very soon after they were inscribed. It is hardly possible that these were routine maneuvers or precautions against chronically bothersome neighbors. There must have been some warning of a major attack. The enemy was almost surely from outside the Peloponnese, and the expected thrust was very likely from the sea. On the other hand, there is no good evidence in the Knossos tablets that a major attack was expected there.

A fair number of Pylian troops in small units, each under a designated commander, seem to have been deployed to certain key posts as "watchers to guard the coast." An important officer called E-QE-TA (compare English "count" from Latin *comes,* "companion") is assigned to each post. He may have had a chariot at his disposal and so might have been responsible for liaison with headquarters. There are also a few tablets referring to the mustering of rowers. It is a fair deduction that the Pylian fleet was concentrated to guard the heart of the kingdom while the "watchers" were more thinly spread out on either side as a precaution against a landing on the flanks. One ship with a complement of thirty rowers is said to be going to a place called Pleuron. If this is the known town in far-off Aetolia, the reason for the ship's urgent mission is intriguing.

Other records that may very well be connected with defense measures mention "masons going to build" (emergency fortifications?) and the issuance of raw material to bronzesmiths at various locations. It has been calculated that the totals listed of this very scarce and precious metal would be sufficient to manufacture over half a million arrowheads or 2,300 swords. Very precise arrangements are recorded for monthly provisioning of troops, artisans and slaves (adult and children).

One presumably important element in the Pylian war machine figures in only a minor way among the tablets. Separate chariot wheels are mentioned, which reminds us of the Homeric descriptions[80] of attaching the wheels before the vehicle is ready for a major trip. This may simply reflect a way of economizing storage space, but it could also indicate that the roads left a good deal to be desired. At Knossos the tablets inform us of the existence of a brigade of almost a hundred fully equipped chariots. Some of them were gorgeously painted and inlaid.

As for the political and social organization, such evidence as we get from the tablets presumably reflects the normal situation and is largely unaffected by the final crisis. There are repeated references both in the Knossos and Pylos records to the *wanax*. He seems to be the supreme monarch in his own kingdom. Since this title was not used in later Greek times, the Linear B documents prove that the Homeric epithet *(w)anax andrōn* ("lord of men") commonly given to Agamemnon[81] is an authentic echo of the Mycenaean title. Next in importance to the *wanax* is an officer called *lawagetas* ("leader of the warriors"), who was apparently the commander in chief of the army. Both he and the king have their own household staffs, and their parcels of land are designated by the Homeric[82] and classical word *temenos* ("cut" or "section").

Other special landholders in the very complicated and still unclear Pylian system are nobles (whose pedigree is given), officials known as *telestai* (functions debatable) and the above-mentioned counts who had a special relationship to the *lawagetas*. Among subsidiary local dignitaries the office of QA-SI-RE-U (*basileus*) is particularly interesting. The Mycenaean *basileus* may have been a very minor official, but there seems to be no possible doubt about the title. Before Homer's time this word had replaced *wanax* as the usual designation for "king." Perhaps the change is a reflection of the breakup of the big Mycenaean power centers and the consequent rise in prestige of smaller autonomous local units.

The kingdom of Pylos was divided into two major "provinces," designated as the "hither" (*i.e.,* the western one, closer to the capital) and "further" (apparently to the east, around the Gulf of Messenia). The hither province was made up of nine districts (designated by the name of the principal town) and the further province of seven. The nine towns remind us of the list of Pylian "cities" specified in the Homeric Catalogue of Ships, but there is practically no correspondence in the names. Similarly, the seven eastern districts remind us of Agamemnon's offer to Achilles of seven towns "near the sea, at the furthest border of sandy Pylos"; but again connections are tenuous and the numbers in the Homeric passages may be poetic formulas rather than authentic echoes of earlier administrative arrangements. Each Pylian district was responsible to an official called a KO-RE-TE, perhaps a sort of mayor of the major town, and he in turn had a deputy, PO-RO-KO-RE-TE (compare the prefix in Latin *procurator*).

The word KE-RO-SI-JA may refer to a *gerousia* ("council of elders") but only on a local level. It can hardly represent a parallel to the Council of Princes that Agamemnon convenes from time to time in the *Iliad*.[83] On the other hand, the Homeric assembly of warriors or free "citizens"[84] may have at least some analogy in the rights and powers of the *damos* ("the people") in Pylian law and society. The *damos* seems to have held certain village land in common and to have been able to contest tenure or ownership. If it is confirmed by future study, this is indeed a principle of crucial importance since it would show that "the people" in Greece were already different from the faceless nonentities of Near Eastern Kingdoms—and even, to some extent, of the Homeric poems. Nevertheless, their position in both Mycenaean and Homeric society suggests a sharp contrast with the classical period.

Slaves appear to have been very numerous and to have been assigned to a wide variety of specialized tasks. Most of them were no doubt connected with the large and relatively self-sufficient royal households. The complement of fifty women slaves that Homer assigns to the palaces at Ithaka[85] and Scheria[86] would have been much larger than what any household possessed after the end of the Bronze Age; yet the tablets show that over 500 slave women plus their children were attached to the palace at Pylos. Other slaves were assigned to the service of the gods and to a number of crafts connected with religious establishments.

Some of the slave women were apparently captives; and descriptive adjectives suggest that the most prized slaves were acquired from islands like Lemnos and Kythera and from towns such as Miletos and Knidos on the east Aegean shore. The picture that one glimpses here is reminiscent of the normal treatment of conquered towns described in the Homeric poems and the fears that Hector expresses for his wife's and son's future after he is dead and Troy captured.[87] The presumption is that most slaves were of foreign origin although it is possible that the Mycenaeans also enslaved native Greek speakers. The children of slaves of course inherited the same status and were expected to do their share of work (as no doubt were children of free parents). The daily rations of grain and figs for free and slave workers are reckoned on a very precise system of weights and measures borrowed from the Near East.

A good deal of controversy has been generated over the use of such a prescriptive term as "feudal" to describe the Mycenaean political and social system as it emerges faintly and uncertainly from such hints in the tablets. If the O-PA recorded in the Knossos tablets connotes the dues or services that the inferior owes his lord, then we have a striking echo in the case of Homer's Meriones, who is the *opawon* ("retainer") of Idomeneus, king of Knossos;[88] and Meriones in turn has a charioteer who is his *opawon*.[89]

T. B. L. Webster's judgment is worth quoting in this general connection, although scholars like Chadwick are even more cautious. The king was probably divine or near divine because his title, *wanax,* and the name of his special allotment of land, *temenos,* were used in later times only in connection with the gods. He lived in a palace surrounded by beautiful objects and served by a multitude of slaves. He had his counts, and there was a wider circle of nobility owning land apparently bestowed on them by the king and worked by their tenants. Some of the nobility formed the chariotry, and some were mayors of towns and villages, responsible for the craftsmen and land workers of their districts. After his death the king may have been thought of as living on in a royal tomb. All grades of society were held together by the services which they paid directly or indirectly to the palace. "With some misgiving," says Webster, "I use this word feudal as a convenient way of describing the paying of dues and services to the palace in return for privileges and possessions."

The major crafts seem to have been those connected with the various stages in the manufacture of textiles (especially woolens and linens), the making of weapons and other objects of metal, carpentry, shipbuilding, jewelry, pottery, inlaid furniture, perfumes. Motifs such as rosettes, lilies, shells, dolphins that are exquisitely carved, for example, on the little ivory plaques found by Wace at Mycenae are paralleled by decoration on pottery. Such plaques may well have been used as inlay for the elaborate furniture mentioned in the tablets. One's imagination is spurred by the description of "one ebony (?) footstool inlaid with figures of men and lions in ivory" or "one footstool inlaid with a man and horse and octopus and palm-tree (?) in ivory." We immediately think of similar elaborate and skillfully crafted possessions so lovingly described in the Homeric poems.

It is probable, in view of the size of the perfume-making industry in which various aromatic substances like rose or sage were added to an olive oil base, that a great many of the smaller closed shapes of Mycenaean vases found throughout the east Mediterranean had originally contained high-grade perfumed oil. Such ointments are known to have been a much prized commodity in areas like Egypt. Wace's discovery of the so-called

House of the Oil Merchant at Mycenae vividly illustrates the manufacturing process.

Large herds of sheep and goats and smaller numbers of pigs and cattle are inventoried. The wool-raising industry in Crete must have been very flourishing, with as many as 19,000 sheep listed on a single tablet. Apparently, most of the wool was sheared from castrated rams.

In general, the economic, political and social conditions indicated by the Linear B tablets are remarkably similar to the highly centralized kingdoms of the Near East. Something of the sort could perhaps have been guessed—but never by the remotest chance proved—from the archaeological remains. It seems clear, however, that long before Homer's time most of these Late Bronze Age features and institutions had completely faded from memory.

On the other hand, certain religious texts among the Linear B tablets held a major surprise. The cults of the Olympian deities who play so prominent a part in the Homeric poems had usually been thought to date after the end of the Bronze Age. But in the tablets most of the familiar names already appear, along with those of a large number of deities who are only shadowy memories or are completely absent in later times. We find in the tablets the names of Zeus and Hera, as well as Poseidon, Hermes, Athena, Artemis and possibly Dionysos. Several deities whose worship was later combined with that of a major Olympian are recognized very much in their own right, like the healer Paian (Apollo), the war god Enyalios (Ares), the patron of women in childbirth Eleuthia (Eileithyia). And there are still others even more remote. For instance Potnia, "the mistress" (literally "the powerful one"), may be the nearest to the old idea propounded by Evans, Wace and others of a single great mother-goddess, symbol of fertility in and control of nature. We also find references to a priestess of the winds, to the "thrice-hero," to Iphimedeia, who is once mentioned by Homer,[90] and to Zeus' and Poseidon's female counterparts called Diwia and Posidaeia. And there are tantalizing allusions to such superhuman beings as the "Dipsioi" ("thirsty ones"), perhaps the dead.

These and other divinities received precious vessels, gifts of food and additional commodities, especially oil for ritual use. Some of the deities—notably Poseidon, whose role as patron deity of Pylos is clear in Homer[91]—appear to have owned land, sanctuaries (not necessarily temples) and slaves. There are references to sanctuaries like the "Posidaion" at Pylos and the "Daidaleion" and the "Labyrinthos" at Knossos. It has been traditional to believe that life-size statues were not a usual feature of these shrines, but the Keos discovery (to be described later) warns us against blanket generalizations based on negative evidence. Religious scenes carved on rings and gems, however, reinforce Homer's witness[92] that the shrines were usually open-air precincts, perhaps surrounded by a low wall and containing an altar and sacred grove. Here, it seems, the god might appear to the worshiper in the form of a bird. The total religious context is in fact far closer to evidence in Homer and later Greek writers than it is to the hypotheses that the archaeological record had suggested. Professor W. K. C. Guthrie points out that "before the coming of the Greeks a single great goddess, personifying the earth, mother of all life, was worshipped in Crete under different aspects. It was probably the Greeks, with their more concrete imagination, who divided these aspects among different personalities, creating names out of what they had taken over as epithets . . . If this is true, the Mycenaean tablets are interesting evidence that the process of individuation was already well advanced by the thirteenth century."

The Mycenaean *wanax* seems to have had at least some divine prerogatives or associations, as is still dimly remembered in Homer. It is on this basis that his right to make legal judgments is explained.[93] Guthrie, however, shows notable caution on this question. "It has been suggested," he writes, "that, as in some of them [the Near Eastern kingdoms], the ruler (*Wanax*) was worshipped as divine. He was certainly the earthly representative of a god who himself was known as *Wanax* (Lord) in addition to any more specific name. But there is no inscriptional evidence that he was deified during his lifetime, and the palace-shrines rather suggest that he was a mortal who needed his divine protectress. Among Greece's near neighbours, the Hittites, kings were not believed divine, nor offered cult, during their lifetime, but only after death." Professor Mylonas is even more skeptical about divine honors being accorded to the Mycenaean king, in either life or death.

The solid new information already gained from the tablets is priceless, and much of it could never have been supplied by normal material remains. It will require at least a generation to interpret and assimilate the texts we now have, even if no additional documents were to be found. But, as with the material remains, the evidence is still so fragmentary and palace scribes assume in the reader so much familiarity with the system that we cannot hope to reconstruct it fully. A new term such as "protohistory" should perhaps be invented to designate a stage of knowledge about a civilization suspended somewhere between prehistory and conventionally documented history.

Chadwick was from the start more cautious than some of his colleagues in refusing to draw sweeping conclusions even from plausible hints supplied by certain tablets. And he is still more unwilling to commit himself in answer to the question "Has the decipherment so far suggested that the tradition linking the Mycenaean Age with Homer was more closely knit than used to be believed"? As we have seen, there are sound reasons for answering both yes and no to such a query; but most experts, if forced to commit themselves, would probably answer in the negative.

## The Date of the Linear B Tablets from Knossos

At approximately the same time as Chadwick published *Decipherment* Blegen was writing a very short article with the deceptively mild title "A Chronological Problem." His remarks brought into sharp focus an obvious question that begged for a straightforward answer: Are the Linear B tablets from Knossos really two centuries older than those from Pylos and Mycenae? He thus launched a storm of controversy that has not yet died down; and his doubts provided one more reason for a total reexamination of Minoan chronology that will likely result in major readjustments. Meanwhile the original question has not been answered conclusively.

Blegen took as his starting point the acknowledged fact that the Knossos tablets are in form, writing system, language and organization of content practically indistinguishable from their mainland counterparts. Yet the pottery associated with the Pylos and Mycenae texts provides an uncontested date not very far on either side of 1200; and Evans' final verdict on the Knossos Linear B tablets seems to have been that all (or practically all) belong to the year of the "final" destruction of the palace, and that this disaster occurred at the end of LMII, about 1400. How can this discrepancy of approximately two centuries be reconciled?

Those who had previously faced the problem usually spoke of scribal conservatism in a closely guarded art passed on from one generation to the next in restricted palace "schools." Parallels for an almost static writing system could perhaps be found in cuneiform texts on clay; but the Linear B is a very different kind of script that seems to have been developed and used mainly for writing on more tractable materials than clay. And later Greek alphabetic records, even on stone, show quite rapid changes in writing styles. Blegen therefore suggested that the advances in stratigraphic excavation during the half century since the Knossos tablets were discovered and the profound change in our knowledge of Minoan-Mycenaean relations in the Late Bronze Age may provide good reason for a careful review of the evidence for dating the Knossos tablets.

There is, of course, nothing incompatible now about the association of documents written in Greek with LMII levels at Knossos, since strong mainland cultural influence at Knossos is already very clear before the "final" destruction. But Blegen was inclined to believe that the closest parallels, not only for the tablets but for other features like the architectural planning and fresco decoration of the Throne Room at Knossos, are found in the securely dated context of the LHIIIB mainland palaces (*i.e.,* after 1300). Furthermore, various artefacts that were apparently found in the same context as the Knossos tablets appear to have their best parallels in mainland objects to be dated somewhat later than 1400.

Finally Blegen emphasized the serious dilemma involved in Evans' theory that fragile tablets, partially burned in a destruction around 1400, could have survived during Evans' lengthy "period of reoccupation" at Knossos. "I have long wondered," says Blegen, "if there is not a strong probability that all the Knossian texts in Linear B really came from the debris heaped up in the burning of a palace which had been reconstructed and occupied by a Mycenaean conqueror from the mainland in Late Minoan III, or—shall we say?—Late Helladic III. . . . A thorough re-examination of all evidence available for the circumstances of discovery in each specific place where tablets were found at Knossos is certainly needed to test this suggestion."

The problem of the date of the Knossos tablets has since been examined by several scholars. Certainly the most colorful of these is L. R. Palmer, Professor of Comparative Philology at Oxford University. Palmer immediately accepted Ventris' decipherment, and he has contributed a great deal to the massive task of interpreting and explaining the content of the tablets as well as to the elucidation of the early stage of the language there documented. In the latter sense, philology would seem to have a proper role in helping to solve the chronological problem, and philologists generally agree that in linguistic features as well as script the two sets of tablets show very few significant differences. Again, therefore, a gap of two centuries appears strange.

But the crucial problem of the stratigraphical context at Knossos is clearly an archaeological one. There are, roughly, two possible methods. One is to make new stratigraphical tests in unexcavated areas at Knossos in the hope of discovering new and securely datable tablets; the other is to try to review and reconstruct the circumstances of the original discoveries in Evans' and Mackenzie's early excavations. Palmer has spent a great deal of ingenuity on the second approach and has shown beyond doubt that there are serious discrepancies between the original field records, the excavators' immediate inferences and Evans' final summation of the evidence and conclusions. A rather heated exchange of views, first in the British press and later in pamphlet and book form, between Palmer and some of Evans' successors and supporters has contributed little as yet to clarifying the problem. Palmer's book *Minoans and Mycenaeans* (1961, revised 1965) sets out to show that the tablets not only belong to the last "reoccupation" phase of the palace, but that the general archaeological context and some internal evidence in the texts point to a destruction date actually *later* than 1200.

On the other hand, a reexamination of the record by such archaeologists as John Boardman, Reader in Classical Archaeology at Oxford, upholds Evans' general conclusions; and new stratigraphical tests by Sinclair Hood have been cited as further confirmation. We shall refer to the controversy again in the broader context of the final chapter, but at present most scholars are cautious about committing themselves to either extreme position. Consensus may have to wait for some further discovery, such as a new hoard of Linear B tablets securely dated around 1400 on the mainland or around 1200 in Crete. Preliminary information on the excavation at Thebes in 1963 places the few tablets so far discovered there in a context around 1300. The Greek supervisor, Dr. Nikolaos Platon, seems to consider that the date and content of the Theban documents will strengthen Evans' dating of the Knossos tablets.

Of the numerous excavations since World War II, the most striking results of only a few can be chronicled here—and even these in less detail than they deserve. Our main criterion will be that the ones we choose to review have contributed in a major way to the confirmation or modification of theories that we have seen developing in previous chapters.

## THE SECOND GRAVE CIRCLE AT MYCENAE

As late as 1951 the six Shaft Graves inside the Grave Circle and the fabulous burial offerings that Schliemann had found at Mycenae remained practically unique. It is true that fairly close parallels to the grave type had been discovered at Eleusis and Lerna; and roughly comparable circular structures enclosing cemeteries had been explored on the island of Leukas. But Schliemann's discovery continued to represent the preeminent insight on the crucial point of time, the transition from Middle to Late Helladic, when the heretofore independent and distinct mainland and Minoan traditions first met.

Although most scholars adopted Wace's view that the Shaft Grave type was simply a more monumental form of the older and simpler individual Middle Helladic cists that had been scattered over the same hillside, there were other notable innovations not easily explained as natural developments. One could point to the sculptured stelae erected over the graves, to the special reverence that seems to be indicated in the later construction of the circular parapet and also to the striking richness of the original burials. It is no wonder that Mycenae has remained *the* site for the study of early "Mycenaean" civilization. Its power and wealth seem to have surpassed that of any other area of the mainland at the same period. The new evidence that we are about to review has done little to explain this fact (if it is a fact); but it showed dramatically that the occupants of Schliemann's Shaft Graves did have earlier roots at Mycenae and that their "dynasty" did not represent quite as sudden an efflorescence of wealth and power as had been assumed.

The repair and restoration of the great tholos tomb of Clytemnestra, which Mrs. Schliemann had first excavated long before, led to the discovery. The tholos lies on ground sloping down to the west almost immediately outside of the citadel wall. Here a new Shaft Grave was discovered. This was not an entirely unexpected development; but it directed attention to the area immediately to the south, where several stone blocks formed what could be a segment of a circle. Was it possible that there had originally been another grave circle lower down on the slope? The implications were so important that the Greek Archaeological Society named a special committee, which in turn entrusted the supervision of excavation to two of its most trusted members: Dr. John Papadimitriou (deceased in 1963), then director of the Archaeological Service; and Dr. George Mylonas, a faculty member both of Washington University in St. Louis, Missouri, and of the University of Athens. Their three campaigns between 1952 and 1954 not only brought to light the second Grave Circle, but have provided vital comparative evidence on Schliemann's Grave Circle. This is next best to being able to reexcavate Schliemann's Shaft Graves using painstaking modern techniques.

Papadimitriou and Mylonas called the new circle B and used A to designate the one so long known. Such prosaic denominations are perhaps symptoms of the matter-of-fact, scientific world in which we now operate. Schliemann would no doubt have invented more colorful terms, probably with rather daring historical implications. The twenty-eight graves in Circle B were further distinguished by letters of the Greek alphabet to avoid confusion with Graves I to VI in Circle A. Circle B was surrounded by a rather roughly built wall of almost identical diameter with that of Circle A. Fourteen graves in B can be classed as true Shaft Graves. Mylonas is reasonably sure that the construction of the wall of Circle B (as well as an original, lower wall forming Circle A) preceded the digging of the graves within them. The entrance to Circle B was probably at the west, and sculptured stelae seem to have faced in that direction.

The burials in Circle B date somewhat earlier, beginning in the seventeenth century and overlapping to a considerable extent with the earlier sixteenth century graves of Circle A. The overlap is difficult to explain if (as has been usually assumed) the Shaft Graves contain the bodies of royalty only and if there was a single ruling dynasty at Mycenae. Both circles show clearly a common tradition of burial rites, and the wealth so conspicuous in A is already accumulating in the earliest graves of Circle B.

Modern excavation of the new Grave Circle has provided welcome authentication for current interpretations of Schliemann's rather scanty and confused evidence. The methods of construction and roofing, the laying of the corpse (usually at full length) on the pebble-lined floor with food and weapons and ornaments around it, the lack of any sign of cremation or embalming, the immediate filling in of the shafts, the funeral feast with fragments of food and dishes thrown over the grave, the heaping up of more earth into a low mound with a plain or rather awkwardly carved tombstone on its apex and the building of a low stone wall around its edge, the frequent reopening of the grave for later burials and when necessary pushing earlier burials and gifts aside to make room for the new occupant—all of the major features are already present.

Apparently, however, the final resting place of these earlier "kings" was not so reverently remembered as in the case of Circle A. The wall surrounding the graves in A was monumentally rebuilt at a higher level inside the later fortification walls and may have been visible as late as Pausanias' time. On the other hand, Circle B seems to have been neglected and forgotten at least as early as the time that the Clytemnestra tholos was built, because the new construction encroached on its area. The great mound of the Clytemnestra tholos deeply buried most of the earlier graves, protecting them in the same way as the later fill inside the wall had done for those in Circle A.

Some of the graves within Circle B are simple, individual Middle Helladic cists with very sparse grave furniture. So Wace's theory of a local origin of the so-called Shaft Grave dynasty seems to be reinforced. At the other end of the time spectrum represented, one of the largest Shaft Graves was reopened and enlarged, apparently in the fifteenth century; and a long, narrow tomb chamber and entrance passage with vaulted saddle-roof of cut stone blocks was constructed. This type of tomb is so far unique in Greece. The closest parallels seem to be slightly later structures at Ras Shamra on the Syrian coast. By that date we have seen that close trade contacts had already developed between mainland Greece and the Near East. Possibly the wealth of the Shaft Grave kings is to be explained mainly in this context.

As in the case of Grave Circle A, the contents of these deeply dug and rather inconspicuous tombs were practically intact. Most of the gold is again thin foil, which originally covered objects of lesser worth. Weapons are a predominant item of contents, as in Circle A. The pottery, however, seems to be almost entirely in the mainland tradition, especially the later Middle Helladic matt-painted and gray and yellow Minyan fabrics. If this distinction proves well founded, we shall have a fairly close idea of the time when Minoan pottery began to flood into Mycenae. One of the most interesting among the many important grave gifts is an amethyst bead with a tiny, beautifully carved portrait of a handsome bearded man. The single electrum death mask discovered in Circle B is another indication of direct continuity with the contents of Circle A.

Dr. Lawrence Angel, a physical anthropologist who examined the bones of these early Mycenaean rulers, concludes that they were generally big, tall men, quite different from the smaller, lithe, beardless Minoans. Perhaps their stature set them apart even from their own subjects. One skull showed a trepanation, presumably done to relieve pressure caused by a brain concussion. Two gallstones lay neatly in position with one skeleton, and several individuals had suffered from arthritis.

It was natural that, when Grave Circle B was discovered outside the fortified acropolis, its position should bring to mind Pausanias' statement that he was shown the graves of Clytemnestra and Aegisthus "outside the walls." Indeed, Wace and others inferred that part of the surrounding wall of Circle B or some of the stelae were still visible in Pausanias' time. Mylonas makes a persuasive case, however, for believing that this could not have been so. Of course, the legend might have clung to the spot long after remains of the cemetery could not be seen, but it is at least as likely that the mounds over some of the tholos tombs were the monuments pointed out to Pausanias. The tradition connecting two of the tholoi with Clytemnestra and Aegisthus may be worth mentioning here.

## NEW FINDS IN THE SOUTHWEST

An even more recent discovery (1965) provides strong support for the theory that the contents of the Mycenae Shaft Graves represent a phenomenon that was by no means confined to the Argolid. Dr. Spyridon Marinatos, Professor of Prehistoric Archaeology at the University of Athens, has discovered at Peristeria, some twenty-five miles north of Pylos, an unlooted trench that is presumably to be connected with the badly destroyed tholos tomb above it. Finds are said to include a gold plaque with a procession of young men in relief, gold dress ornaments decorated with rosettes, birds, a gold diadem and three gold cups. The best of the cups is decorated with linked spirals in relief and Professor Marinatos believes that it may have been made in the same workshop as a comparable cup from the Mycenae Shaft Graves. The associated pottery would indicate a date for graves and contents at the end of MH and in LHI, *i.e.*, contemporary with the Mycenae Circle A.

Schliemann's excavations had first dramatized the importance of northeast Peloponnese, and Evans and others continued to regard it as almost the only mainland area worth considering in the Late Bronze Age. Yet finds like Tsountas' at Vaphio and Kampos and Dörpfeld's at Kakovatos had shown quite early that rich and powerful Mycenaean centers had been located as far away as southeast and west Peloponnese. Blegen's discovery of a ruined palace at remote Messenian Pylos underlined the fact that major Mycenaean power centers were by no means confined to the Argolid. In fact, sporadic finds and organized exploration in many areas indicate an increasingly wide scattering of tholos tombs and Mycenaean pottery, which in turn strongly supported the testimony of the Catalogue of Ships in *Iliad* II that the whole of central and southern Greece had been thickly populated in later Mycenaean times. Continuous and energetic exploration of southwestern Peloponnese in the postwar years has revealed that from Early Helladic times until the end of the Mycenaean period fertile areas were intensively occupied. The Pylos region is emerging as a prosperous and highly developed equal of the Argolid, not a peripheral rural cousin. And there can be little doubt that similar intensive regional exploration will reveal a comparable situation for other Mycenaean kingdoms recorded in Homeric epic.

Dr. Kourouniotis, who had been Blegen's associate in 1939, died during the war. His successor, Professor Marinatos, has carried out a series of excavations in the Pylos area coordinated with Blegen's concentration on the palace site itself. Marinatos' attention has been mainly devoted to the numerous tholos tombs that cluster, usually in groups of two or three, about various peripheral regional centers. These sites must represent independent capitals of much smaller political units that seem to have gradually succumbed to the designs of Neleus and his son Nestor to impose their sovereignty on the whole region.

It is surely in this context that Dörpfeld's site at Kakovatos is best understood. Whether or not this general area was confused with Nestor's Pylos in post-Bronze Age times, there is absolutely no archaeological evidence that the capital of the kingdom was transferred there after the destruction of the palace at Messenian Pylos. The political system in the twelfth century and for some time thereafter would seem to exclude any large unified

Pylian kingdom. On the other hand, the floruit of the site at Kakovatos is probably too early to allow the possibility that the Neleid dynasty settled there before locating at Messenian Pylos.

The general impression from the current excavations in the Pylos region is that it was in close touch with Crete almost as early as was the Argolid and that Minoan influence and trade relations continued to be very strong.

The pottery discovered in a tholos tomb near modern Koryphasion, which was cleared by Kourouniotis in 1925, suggests that it is as early as any yet known on the mainland and that it should be contemporary with the later Shaft Graves at Mycenae. A somewhat later tholos at Peristeria, originally almost as monumental as those at Mycenae, has a façade composed of carefully cut limestone blocks, two of which bear incised Linear A signs like those in Cretan buildings. Still another at Routsi, which had somehow escaped the tomb robbers, revealed the last burial still laid out in orderly fashion on the floor in the center of the chamber. Bones and offerings from several previous sepultures had been deposited in shallow cists. Among the contents, perhaps the finest were two inlaid daggers in the same marvelous "metal painting" technique as the earlier examples from the Mycenae Shaft Graves.

One of Marinatos' interesting observations is that in at least some tholoi wheel ruts were cut in the dromos near the doorway of the tomb chamber, apparently indicating that the body and its accouterments were conveyed to the last resting place in a chariot or wagon. This theory was recently supported by the discovery of the skeletons of two horses lying on the floor of the dromos of a tholos tomb near Marathon in Attica. They must have been sacrificed after drawing their dead master to the tomb, and perhaps it was believed that these badges of luxury thus continued at his command. Also, the recently discovered practice of burying chariot and horses in later Cypriot tombs may well be a survival of Mycenaean practice.

## NESTOR'S PALACE

In the excitement of the retrieval of the Linear B tablets at Pylos in 1939 attention was somewhat distracted from the importance of the fairly well-preserved floors and lower walls that showed up in the trenches, but Blegen's painstaking clearing of the hilltop between 1952 and 1964 has fully redressed the balance. Nestor's palace now emerges as the most coherent and impressive building complex of Mycenaean times. Recently roofed over and protected, it gives the modern visitor who traverses its rooms and corridors a vivid sense of physical contact with the past. The clarity and completeness of the ground plan and the excellent preservation of the lower walls and various permanent installations is owed to the fact that no later habitation, as at so many important sites, destroyed or obscured the ruins of the latest monumental Mycenaean phase. At Pylos one gets far the best picture of how a Mycenaean king's household was arranged, but one must still go to Mycenae and Tiryns to see the massive fortifications by which such installations were in some cases protected. Perhaps Tiryns might have provided both aspects if modern techniques of excavation and preservation had been available when it was first cleared. But its palace ruins could scarcely have compared to those at Pylos, even when Schliemann and Dörpfeld first uncovered them (Fig. 91).

On the other hand, the visitor to Nestor's palace should not expect too much. The whole complex was burned to the ground in a raging conflagration fed by the great structural timbers and such especially flammable contents as big jars full of olive oil. No doubt, either the inhabitants (if they had time) or the captors carried off almost every movable object of value—vessels of precious metals, inlaid furniture, jewelry, weapons— before the fire was set. Any surviving organic materials like wood and leather and textiles have long ago disintegrated. What remains is the more or less indestructible ruins of an architectural nature and certain equipment that could not be removed or was not considered worth saving. In the latter class are the thousands of pottery vases that were smashed to pieces as the building collapsed. The majority had fallen from the wooden shelves of the "pantries" where they had been stored for local use or (just possibly) for export. Inscribed clay tablets, though concentrated in the archives area, were also in use in other parts of the building. Together with the clay sealings and particular types of pots, they sometimes help identify the original use of certain areas in the palace.

In a kind of intermediate position between the lowly objects of clay and the preserved architectural features are the innumerable fragments of fresco paintings. Blegen found masses of the decorated plaster facing fallen from the walls and not completely obliterated by the fire. But he was doubly fortunate to locate a large deposit of less damaged fragments discarded from an earlier decorative scheme and tossed over the edge of the acropolis. Many of the more important palace rooms on both the first and second stories must have presented a gay, not to say garish, appearance. Most walls and even some floors (as well, no doubt, as ceilings) were painted. Many of the wall panels, sadly fragmentary though they are, provide a good deal of information about the people themselves—their physiognomy, costumes, implements, occupations. Presumably the paintings were based mainly on contemporary local models, but we seem to detect a conservative tradition going back to Minoan originals. Other compositions show glimpses of buildings, animals (real and imagined), stylized plants or purely geometric motifs.

Finally, one sees the blackened stumps of the walls, the stuccoed floors, the drains and water pipes under the floors, the built-in clay hearths and stairs and benches and counters, and the gaps in the floors and walls that once accommodated wooden beams, columns, door frames, sentry boxes and even the king's throne.

Out of such unpromising material the archaeologist (and the visitor) must try to reconstruct the original appearance of the buildings and the life of the people who lived in them. Blegen has the advantage of a lifetime of familiarity with the remains of Mycenaean civilization, from both his own and others' excavations. Throughout the years at Nestor's palace he has worked with meticulous care and has associated with him a variety of able assistants in the task.

Piet de Jong did many of the Knossos illustrations during Evans' later years and has assisted in the study and illustration of the results of a whole generation of British and American excavations. He has been responsible for many of the architectural drawings of the Pylos palace, for the architectural reconstructions, for the illustrations of restored fresco panels, fresco fragments and some of the finer pottery. Mrs. Blegen and Miss Marion Rawson have never missed a season of excavation as section supervisors and specialists on the pottery and such material as jewelry from the nearby tombs. Professor Mabel Lang of Bryn Mawr College has become an expert in cleaning and reassembling fresco fragments, as well as in publishing and interpreting the inscribed tablets. These and others, under Blegen's direction, are in charge of the final publication entitled *The Palace of Nestor at Pylos in Western Messenia*. The first volume, describing the architectural remains and the pottery, appeared in 1966, and a good deal can also be gleaned from Blegen's annual reports in the *American Journal of Archaeology* and in the little *Guide to the Palace of Nestor*.

The history of the site is gradually coming into focus and seems to mesh remarkably well with tradition. The acropolis and its western slopes were occupied continuously from MH times. It is probable that in the LHI phase heavy fortifications guarded the hill itself. A thorough-going destruction of LHIIIA buildings about 1300 can be plausibly connected with Neleus' arrival and suggests that his new Pylian kingdom was not won without violence. It is perhaps significant that all three of the tholoi so far investigated in the immediate vicinity of the acropolis antedate this event, while the chamber tomb cemetery bridges the two periods without obvious interruption. After a drastic leveling process, Neleus' "new" palace would be represented by the older part of the surviving ruins at the western end of the hill, and it is probable that from then on no private homes were allowed to intrude on the acropolis. Well before the middle of the thirteenth century Nestor would have added the unified rectangular structure directly to the east. Perhaps some of the minor buildings are somewhat later still. Nestor was succeeded by at least two (probably short-lived) descendants. Finally, the whole complex on the acropolis as well as the lower town was put to the torch about 1200, just as the latest LHIIIB pottery styles were merging into LHIIIC. We will have a good deal to say later about the agents of that final destruction.

But let us go back a little in time and imagine ourselves in Telemachos' ship as he approaches Pylos on a fine spring day some ten years after the end of the Trojan War. Homer has given us, of course, a marvelous description of the visit,[94] and we are now on fairly safe ground in associating his frame of reference with the buildings on the hill of Ano Englianos. Telemachos has come from Ithaka in the hope of learning from Nestor some news about his father, Odysseus, who is still missing from home. Our ship identifies herself to Nestor's coast guard and runs up on the beach. We find the venerable king and hundreds of his people down on the beach engaged in sacrifices to their patron god, Poseidon, who was Nestor's reputed grandfather. Nestor greets us hospitably at the water's edge, asks us to share in the ritual meal and then insists that we go up to the palace to spend the night.

Our destination is five miles or so away—too far for distinguished guests to walk. A line of gorgeous chariots with bodies of brightly painted wood inlaid with ivory and drawn by matched pairs of gaily harnessed horses awaits us. We whirl off along the beach and join the coast road, which soon turns inland along a high ridge. As the grade steepens and the road twists its way upward, the horses slow down and we can look back through the clouds of dust from other chariots and catch glimpses of the flat coastal plan and the Pylian navy drawn up snugly on the sheltered beach. Soon we see artificial tholos mounds and chamber tombs beside the highway and we know we are approaching an important town.

Suddenly we round a slope and see ahead of us a fairly steep hill crowned with a large building (Fig. 89). Its west side faces us, presenting a flat-roofed façade of two stories with rows of windows. The heavy dun-colored walls of mud brick and timber seem almost to be a higher continuation of the hill slope. As we come closer to the acropolis we see that there is a good-sized town spreading around and below it. The chariots roll through the street below the south slope of the acropolis and turn up the easier grade at its east end. Looking inland across a little saddle we see a smaller

Figure 89

hill crowned with another of the familiar tholos mounds. Behind it, catching the evening light, a noble range of mountains apparently about five or six miles farther inland is parallel to the coast.

We clatter up onto the acropolis and notice that the nearer eastern half is free of buildings. We realize that this is where the people in the lower town would congregate in time of danger. Ahead of us looms a massive building complex with a couple of smaller separate structures intervening (Fig. 90). Grooms run out from the nearest building and catch our horses' bridles. From inside this building we hear the hum of voices and the busy sound of hammer and anvil. The grooms unhitch the horses and push the chariot through the doorway. Everywhere there is an air of system and orderliness. As we leave this building, we see a small room recessed in the wall and open in front, with an altar just outside. Here we catch up with Telemachos and Nestor, who are carrying out the initial rites by which a guest is introduced to the protection of the palace deities (Fig. 91).

Our little group then passes around to the south side of the main build-

Figure 90

ing and we realize that the main entrance faces in this direction—and no wonder, for it presents a magnificent sweep of undulating countryside covered with olive trees, vineyards and grain fields. Several distinctive mountain peaks etch the horizon. The sea is in view off to the right. We congratulate Nestor on the beauty and fertility of his country. He is obviously pleased and proud as he leads us toward the main block of the palace. One question which we cannot restrain seems to leave him a bit troubled. Why, we ask, is this rich administrative center not fortified like most of its rivals? He hesitates for a moment, and then says that the main problem is water supply. There is a long tradition that the citadel itself cannot withstand a close siege since there is no spring on the hill or its immediate slopes. The only feasible defense, he assures us, is to take advantage of the contours of the narrow ridge, with its steep slopes to north and south. The spring up the road to the east must be defended at all costs and contact maintained if possible with the harbor to the west.

Passing a strongly built guardhouse (rooms #57, etc.) on our right and continuing through the columned main entrance, we find ourselves in a handsome courtyard. Facing us is the columned porch of the megaron, which is a familiar nucleus of every royal palace; and there is also a shady columned porch to our right. We pass between the two columns of the

(*Numbers as in Blegen's plan*)

| | | | |
|---|---|---|---|
| 57 | Guard-house | 63 | Courtyard |
| 23 etc. | Oil Storage Rooms | 68 | Kitchens |
| 21 etc. | Pantries | 105 | Wine Storage Building |
| 10 | Reception Room | 7 | Archives |

Figure 91

megaron porch, are saluted by a sentry on guard and enter an anteroom with doors in the center of each of its four walls. Nestor leads the way through the door facing us. We pass another guard and find ourselves in as handsome a throne room as any Mycenaean king possesses (Fig. 92).

Almost every feature is familiar—the great circular ceremonial hearth in the center with the four columns supporting a raised section of the roof, the throne against the wall on our right, the stuccoed floor divided into squares that are decorated with various painted designs, the colorful frescoed walls and painted ceiling. The style and subject matter of the frescoes make us feel at home. We particularly notice the protecting griffins and lions behind the throne and the graceful octopus in the floor panel directly in front of it. Additional wall panels depict other animals and humans. One distinctive scene portrays a harpist (Apollo, we guess) sitting on a rock. A bird hovers near, charmed by his song (compare Fig. 36).

Nestor takes his seat on the wooden throne decorated with costly inlay and a servant brings him a cup of wine. He pledges us a welcome and passes the cup to us. When it is handed back to him, he pours the remainder

Figure 92

of the libation into a depression in the floor at his right from which it trickles along a channel to a second depression. His wife and family, servants and courtiers gather in the throne room or look down from a sort of gallery or mezzanine with its railing framed by the tall slender columns. We are formally introduced and offered light refreshments.

Nestor then assigns his beautiful daughter Polykaste the honorable task of preparing a bath for the guests. She leads us out into the anteroom, where we turn left through a door opening onto a long corridor. Straight ahead is a flight of stuccoed steps leading up to the second floor. That whole area, as well as some of the rooms ahead of us on the ground floor, are, she tells us, reserved for the royal family. We turn right, then left and into a kind of waiting room from which, one at a time, Polykaste summons us into the bathroom. She tells us to take off our dusty clothes and makes us sit down in the painted terra-cotta tub. As a mark of special honor, she herself dips warm water from a big jar set into a clay counter in the corner and pours it over our sweaty bodies. A servant then dries us off and anoints us with a fragrant oil. They bring us clean clothes of fine embroidered linen and, thoroughly refreshed, we are led back to the throne room.

Nestor courteously breaks off the business he has been attending to and dismisses the clerks. He asks us if we are too tired for a tour of the palace before dinner. We follow him as he spryly leads the way into the same corridor. He turns left along the side wall of the throne room. We pass a number of storerooms, and at the end of the corridor he shows us three big rooms (#23, etc.) lined with great jars containing olive oil. He tells us that this is one of the major agricultural products of his kingdom and that the finest oil is boiled up with aromatic herbs and sent all over the world in stirrup jars made by palace potters. From the oil stores we pass into a long corridor on the opposite side of the megaron and come to a series of small rooms (#21, etc.) in which tremendous numbers of vases, most of them unpainted, are arranged by size and shape on wooden shelves. Nestor laughingly confirms our guess that in one little pantry alone there are almost 3,000 kylixes or wine cups of various sizes. Clearly, the vine is also widely grown in Pylian territory.

Beyond the pottery stores and opposite a door leading into the megaron porch is a room (#10) equipped with a comfortable bench and a big jar of wine. The room is empty now, but Nestor says that tomorrow it will be crowded with people waiting for an audience with the king or his most trusted administrators.

We move on into a larger courtyard (#63) near the southwest edge of the hill and realize that the complex we have been inspecting forms a separate unit. Nestor seems to be particularly proud of it and tells us that early in his reign he himself supervised its construction. He says that the older section we are about to enter is the main part of the palace, which his father, Neleus, built a generation earlier when he first established control of the district. We had first sighted its outside wall as we drove up the road. The plan here seems to be less unified than that of the new section. There are two big rooms in front with interior columns. Nestor still uses these halls for state dinners and other occasions, particularly when the weather it hot. The small rooms (#68, etc.) behind continue in use as the main palace kitchens. As we go up the stairway we hear the clatter of preparation and smell the delicious odor of the meal they are preparing. Some of the rooms on the second floor are reserved for guests, and through the windows of those assigned to us we feel the evening breeze and get a lovely view of the bay and the sea far beyond to the southwest.

We descend again and stroll down an open shaded area between the old and new palaces. A turn to the right behind the oil storage rooms brings us to a long, freestanding building (#105) close to the precipitous north edge of the acropolis. Here Nestor's wine is stored in rows of big terra-cotta jars, each with a label indicating origin and age. A wine steward invites us to choose the vintages we will drink with our dinner. We continue our tour along the northeast side of the new palace and notice its particularly fine outer wall of square-cut, carefully dressed limestone blocks. Passing the building where the chariots were left, we hear workmen still busily hammering and sawing.

Nestor leads us toward the main entrance again as on first arrival, saying we have time to take a look at the real hub of the whole kingdom. We turn left opposite the guardhouse and enter a room (#7) where scribes are taking dictation from tax inspectors who all day have been receiving and storing taxes in kind brought to the palace by people from various parts of the kingdom. A huge, ribbed pithos in one corner has received the day's quota of fine olive oil, which servants are now ladling into smaller containers for transfer to the palace storerooms. An inner room (#8) is the archives proper (Fig. 93). On a low clay bench are neatly stacked newly inscribed clay tablets. Still others are stored in baskets, all labeled and in order. Here, more than anywhere on our tour, we are im-

Figure 93

pressed with the evidence for efficient and minute organization of every administrative detail.

Finally, just as darkness is falling and torches and lamps are lit, we are summoned to dinner in the great hall. Tables have been set up and are loaded with food. As eating gives way to serious sampling of the products of the Pylian vineyards, Nestor calls for a song. A distinguished figure rises from his place at table and picks up his lyre. Leaning on a column and with the torchlight fitfully illuminating his fine old face, he begins the epic tale of the Neleid conquest of the Pylos region. We all sit enchanted as the vigorous story unfolds. Telemachos finally leans over to Nestor and reminds him of the purpose of our visit. The old man obviously considers this as business for tomorrow. But he does ask the singer to give us some of the new stories of Odysseus' exploits in the Trojan War. And so we sit, far into the night, sipping our wine and enjoying the grand heroic tales.

## A TEMPLE AT KEOS

Coming back across 3,200 years, let us resume our survey of the most recent developments. The new Grave Circle at Mycenae, the uncovering of the palace of Nestor and the decipherment of the Linear B script have provided much of the major excitement since 1950. But important work has gone on elsewhere, and there have been other unexpected and significant discoveries. One of the most interesting find spots is on the island of Keos, just off the southeast tip of Attica. The excavation carried on there since 1960 is under the direction of John L. Caskey, former director of the American School of Classical Studies in Athens, a former student of Blegen's, his colleague at Troy and now his successor as chairman of the Department of Classics at the University of Cincinnati. In the sixteenth century (and perhaps even earlier), maritime towns like that on Keos seem to have been under strong Cretan cultural influence, but contact with the mainland even before the end of the MH period is also certified. Minoan pottery found on Keos—and even more recently on the island of Kythera —suggests that Cretan cultural and commerical (if not political) influence was still strong in the fifteenth century. The apparent use of the Linear A script confirms this impression.

But the results of Caskey's excavations should warn us not to expect in the islands simply local adoption or adaptation of features already certified in Greece or Crete. Among the buildings in the main town of Keos one large structure appears to have been a temple from the time of its foundation. It was in continuous use from the beginning of the sixteenth century until the end of the Bronze Age—and on into the Iron Age even as late as the Hellenistic period. Furthermore, in the earlier strata lay the broken remains of at least nineteen terra-cotta female statues, some of them almost life-size. So at one blow two long-held generalizations about the Aegean Late Bronze Age are shown to be untenable.

The so-called "argument from silence" is always an uneasy one, and yet it was impossible to ignore the fact that three generations of active excavation had not produced a single certain example of a monumental freestanding building devoted solely to religious purposes or of a really monumental statue in the round. In spite of some equivocal cases (particularly at the very end of the Bronze Age), it was natural to infer that these features were unknown in Mycenaean times. Indeed, this statement was regularly made by leading authorities, including Lorimer, but they were wrong. Numerous indications of cult installations and religious paraphernalia in addition to the statues—particularly in one room at the inner end of the Keos building that Caskey identifies as the most holy shrine or "adyton*"—and the clear evidence of continuing religious use extending down past the classical period leave little doubt about its major purpose from the time it was built. Several of the statues can be repaired from the fragments; and the stance, the full skirt, the open-fronted jacket exposing ample breasts are quite clearly in the authentic Aegean plastic tradition. The oval face and jutting chin may hark back to Cycladic marble sculpture of the Early Bronze Age, and other features such as the "archaic" smile may anticipate Greek sculpture of the Iron Age (Fig. 94). The presence of numerous female representations in a single shrine has Bronze Age parallels, especially in Crete. In such cases we might perhaps recognize all of them as representations of "the goddess" or (more likely) of her priestesses or devotees.

The Keos excavations prove that small shrines in private homes or palaces were not the only places of worship and that miniature representations of deity were not the absolute rule. There were, in fact, scattered (and generally late) indications from earlier excavation that a few freestanding structures might have been wholly dedicated to religious use, and the occasional monumental relief sculptures and rare fragments of large-scale sculpture in the round should have prepared us to some extent for the new evidence. At any rate, another archaeological "proof" of the supposed lateness of certain features in the Homeric poems now loses much of its cogency. When Homer tells, for example, of temples at Troy and of the offering of a new and magnificent garment to be draped on an obviously life-size statue of Athena,[95] we can still say that this fits better into the known archaeological milieu of the late eighth century; but we can no longer assert that it directly clashes with the archaeological evidence (or lack of it) for the Late Bronze Age.

Figure 94

## Bronze Armor at Dendra

Similar revision in another area has been forced on us by recent archaeological discoveries. In a rich and almost unrobbed chamber tomb at Dendra
just east of Mycenae, the latest of a long and productive series of Swedish
excavations uncovered in 1960 the burial of a Mycenaean warrior with
his full battle dress placed beside him in the tomb. Buried about 1400,
he had worn a helmet, onto which were neatly sewn rows of boar's tusks.

The upper part of his body had been protected by a bronze cuirass (Fig. 95) consisting of a separate front and back section laced together at the sides. His neck had been shielded by a separate bronze collar, his groin by overlapping flexible bands of bronze and his legs by bronze greaves. Also, a pair of bronze greaves was found recently in a late Mycenaean tomb in northwest Peloponnese. And among the spectacular 1962 discoveries at Thebes, which we shall review later, there are recognizable parts of a second bronze cuirass. The general design of this body armor ties in neatly with an ideogram in a series of Linear B tablets from Knossos, which record the issue to individuals of horses, chariots and what has long been recognized as some kind of corselet with loops over the shoulders (Fig. 50).

Yet, as we saw in our review of Lorimer's conclusions, the absence of metal body armor in Mycenaean graves was taken as late as 1950 to

Figure 95

prove that the lovingly detailed Homeric descriptions of the "bronze clad Achaeans" could not be derived from the authentic context of the Late Bronze Age and must reflect the equipment of a later period. It was said that Mycenaean defensive body armor must have been made of some perishable material like leather; and no doubt most of it was. Again, however, one can see in retrospect that it was dangerous to rule out metal armor completely. Nearly all of the richer Mycenaean tombs, where such precious objects might have been deposited, have been robbed. And, in fact, metal was so costly and the skill to fashion such formidable and difficult equipment so rare that it would have required extraordinary restraint and respect for the dead if relatives had abandoned such precious objects in a grave or failed to retrieve them when the grave was reopened.

The new evidence shows that the Homeric descriptions correspond in a wholly convincing manner with the complicated fabrication of Mycenaean body armor. Coincidence or personal knowledge of later fashions seems to be ruled out, although Webster suggests that such "antique" fashions as the great body shield and boar's-tusk helmets survived longer in art representations of gods and heroes. In any case, the poems prove once more to embody an authentic Mycenaean tradition. The fact that details were so little distorted by generations of bards who must have been increasingly out of touch with the actual objects is a powerful confirmation of the conservatism and veracity of oral transmission in the epic.

## MYCENAEAN ATHENS

Among the many interesting post-World War II discoveries, we cannot fail to mention new evidence at three other important power centers— Athens, Thebes and Iolkos. Fairly intensive surface exploration has shown that Attica was heavily populated in Mycenaean times. Numerous widely scattered royal tholos tombs may indicate the truth of the tradition that it was only toward the end of the Bronze Age under Theseus that Athens asserted herself as the political capital of the whole region. Due to constant and intensive later occupation very little early evidence except broken pottery has survived on and around the Athenian acropolis. But there can be no doubt that a Mycenaean palace occupied the north central section of the "well-built fortress of great-hearted Erechtheus,"[96] not far from where the classical temple called the Erechtheion still stands.

We are also sure that a great Cyclopean fortification more or less on the lines of the later classical walls protected the acropolis in the late Mycenaean era, and indeed sections of it were incorporated in the later construction. Professor Oscar Broneer discovered traces of an ingenious "water stair," very reminiscent of the well-preserved arrangement at Mycenae and rather similarly placed alongside the north wall. Like its counterpart, it was built to ensure access to a water supply in time of siege. Most of the construction was of wood, a symptom of urgency and fear. Private houses clustered below the fortress, and ruined chamber tombs in the Areopagos hill to the west and in the Agora just north of it give us a glimpse of where and how the wealthy inhabitants were buried. The forty-five Mycenaean graves discovered to date provide at least a suggestion of Athens' important status during our period.

## THE PALACE OF KADMOS AT THEBES

The existence and vicissitudes of Gla, which we reviewed earlier, are almost surely tied in to some extent with the history of Thebes as well as with Orchomenos. The Theban acropolis rises in the heart of the flat and fertile south Boeotian plain, and it has had a much longer record of occupation than Gla, both before and after Mycenaean times. Most of what we know of Theban prehistory, however, depends so far on legend and myth. Systematic excavation has been impossible because a modern town completely covers the ruins left from continuous earlier habitation.

Very limited and tentative excavation in the first three decades of the present century showed that an extensive Mycenaean palace had once stood on the acropolis; and it seemed plausible to see in it the home of the mythical Kadmos, who is said to have come to Greece from Phoenicia in search of his sister Europa. According to legend, Kadmos settled at Thebes in obedience to an oracle from Apollo of Delphi and introduced "Phoenician letters" to his adopted countrymen. The so-called Theban cycle of Greek mythology recounts the tragic fate of Kadmos' descendants, especially the ill-starred Oedipus. The destruction of Thebes in a fratricidal struggle between Oedipus' sons two or three generations before the Trojan War seems to account plausibly for the striking absence of Thebes and Thebans in the *Iliad*.

The earliest excavator thought, on rather unsatisfactory evidence, that the destruction date was early in the fourteenth century, but at least this did not contradict the literary tradition that Thebes had been destroyed considerably earlier than Mycenae and Tiryns. The few basement rooms and corridors that could be explored suggested that this had been a storage and industrial area of the palace. In one room, fragments of an early Mycenaean fresco panel (perhaps fallen from an upper story) showed a procession of women in costumes and poses very reminiscent of Evans' discoveries at Knossos.

Perhaps the most significant discovery, however, was a series of about eighty large stirrup jars, of which some thirty had short inscriptions painted on their shoulders (Fig. 96). The script was recognized as comparable to Evans' Linear B, and Sir Arthur made full use of this discovery to support his thesis of Knossian political control of important mainland power centers. Some very interesting recent evidence about the origin of these vases will be reported at the end of this chapter.

Figure 96

Again, just before World War II, a second minor excavation confirmed previous indications that the ruins of a great Mycenaean building underlay additional areas of the center of modern Thebes. But it was not until a deep foundation for a new building was being sunk in 1963 that archaeologists had a rather better opportunity to probe a limited new area. The results of this work, so far only briefly reported by Dr. Platon and Mrs. Eva Stassinopoulou-Touloupa of the Greek Archaeological Service, are particularly tantalizing.

It is no longer surprising when a few Linear B tablets are discovered at another Mycenaean capital. The Pylos archives, Wace's discovery in palace annexes just outside the acropolis at Mycenae and an even more recent British discovery of a few fragments inside the Mycenae citadel have conditioned us to expect tablets and inscribed objects in any new excavation of an important administrative center. The new Theban examples were found in what seems to have been a separate annex, perhaps an arsenal, some distance to the east of the earlier excavations and apparently separated from the palace by a wide roadway. But their date is very important, if it is authenticated. Platon assigns the destruction of the "arsenal" to about 1300. The new tablets from Thebes would therefore be the earliest yet found on the mainland and would fall midway between Evans' date for the Knossos tablets and Blegen's and Wace's for those from Pylos and Mycenae. The Theban tablets show no significant difference from the Pylos archives in script and in what they reflect of the particular stage of the language, so that, if the date is right, the Linear B system will indeed have been shown to be a very conservative one. In that case, as far as internal evidence goes, an even longer gap between the Knossos and Pylos tablets is not ruled out.

In addition to the tablets, the newest excavations at Thebes produced gold jewelry, carved ivory plaques, onyx beads, numerous bronze implements, vessels and weapons and the defensive armor mentioned earlier. Fragments of horse harness represent another "first." In the main area of new excavation, a mass of closely datable pottery lying on floors in two distinguishable layers of ash indicate that the main Mycenaean building was destroyed by fire at least twice. Reports on the destruction dates are somewhat contradictory, but Platon apparently tends to assign the first to the later fourteenth century and the second almost at its end. The complex in which the inscribed stirrup vases were found in earlier excavations has a similar orientation to the older structure. Platon refers to the latter as the "Kadmeian" palace, though Kadmos is supposed to have arrived in Greece as early as the sixteenth century. Tradition tells us that its destruction was caused by lightning. The rebuilt palace which was destroyed about 1300 had a different orientation. It would presumably be the one over which Oedipus' sons fought and died.

But Platon's major discovery, which guarantees that the fabled Theban palace ranked with those of Priam, Agamemnon, Minos and Nestor, was a "hoard" fallen from a higher floor into a basement room connected with the later building. The cache includes typical Mycenaean and "Aegean" seals, as well as jewelry of gold and glass paste and ivory; but the really startling element in its contents is a group of almost thirty oriental cylinder seals of lapis lazuli and agate. They bear characteristic carved representations of gods, demons, humans and animals; fourteen have cuneiform inscriptions. A preliminary classification by E. Porada indicates that all can be dated before 1300 and that they are a mixed lot—mostly Baby-

Ionian, Kassite and Mitannian. A few are pre-Babylonian and one is Syro-Hittite. One published inscription identifies a certain Kidin-Marduk, an official of King Burraburrias II, twentieth king of the Kassite dynasty, who reigned 1367 to 1346.

As with previous "bombshells" like Schliemann's Shaft Graves and the Pylos archives, it will require some time for the archaeological community to assimilate the new evidence. Naturally, one thinks of the legendary Kadmos and his mysterious "Phoenician" system of writing, which has usually been vaguely associated with the much later borrowing of the Greek alphabet directly or indirectly from Phoenician sources. But, again, the discovery of Near Eastern seals in a Mycenaean context should not cause undue surprise. It has long been known that there were close trade relations between Mycenaean centers and markets at the east end of the Mediterranean. Objects manufactured in one milieu occasionally occur in the other, and art forms and techniques were mutually borrowed. It would not be at all difficult for a wealthy Theban king to have his agents collect and send to him this fine selection of inscribed oriental seals.

Problems arise mainly when we try to assess his motives. Did he intend to keep them merely as curios? Did they serve as valuable convertible currency? Were they objects of religious veneration such as amulets? Had they been imported as models for his own gemcutters? Perhaps the last is at present the most likely explanation. Certainly, there is plenty of evidence on contemporary Mycenaean seals for direct or indirect imitation of oriental models. Some of the imported seals seem to have been reworked, and rumors of a "half-finished" example raise still further questions.

## THE PALACE OF JASON AND PELIAS

More tentative and much less sensational results were obtained still farther north between 1956 and 1960 at the town of Volos, a busy modern seaport at the head of a deep protected gulf on the east central coast. The great acropolis, formed almost entirely from the debris of millennia of continuous human occupation, has usually been identified since Tsountas' day with the famous Mycenaean capital of Iolkos, from which Jason and the Argonauts set out to recover the Golden Fleece. Iolkos was also the original home of Nestor's father Neleus, brother of Pelias. The overlying modern buildings have presented the same problem to excavators as in the case of Thebes. The Greek archaeologist Demetrios Theocharis decided to try to cut into the northwest edge of the acropolis below the overhanging medieval fortifications.

Theocharis was able to substantiate that a thick layer of debris from the Late Bronze Age contains well-preserved foundations of a monumental building with typical Mycenaean remains, including fragments of fresco painting. Again, two major phases were indicated by layers of ash and destruction. The later building apparently survived longer than most of the power centers farther south. A heavy stone foundation over 90 feet long was uncovered, and partitions dividing the building into three large rooms extend under the fill. No more than the edge of the structure can be explored without the removal of the modern buildings above. Even then a monumental operation of examining and removing later walls and deep overlying deposits of debris will be necessary before reaching the prehistoric levels. But Theocharis believes that a very large and relatively well-preserved palace awaits further excavation. He even suggests that a vase fragment discovered in a test excavation at the nearby harbor site and showing a ship propelled by a large number of rowers may reflect the story of the Argonauts.

## A BRONZE AGE SHIPWRECK

Speaking of ships, a fascinating area of archaeological discovery is being opened by new developments in scientific underwater exploration and salvage. The most valuable evidence bearing on our period has been produced by a University of Pennsylvania expedition under the direction of Dr. George Bass and with the assistance of Peter Throckmorton. Local sponge divers led them to the wreck of a small ship, which (it turned out) had sunk about the end of the thirteenth century off the rocky coast of Cape Gelidonya in southwest Turkey. Little could be learned about the ship itself, but its cargo and the light shed on its business operations are of great interest and importance.

The general nature of the contents and, particularly, the standard employed for the hematite weights suggest that its home was some east Mediterranean port and that it was proceeding westward, stopping off at coastal points to bargain and barter. It was apparently a kind of floating blacksmith's shop, carrying its own supplies of copper (probably loaded in Cyprus) in the familiar form of stamped ingots occasionally found in Aegean sites and portrayed on the Linear B tablets. Tin oxide was used to temper the copper, and bronze scrap in such form as broken implements seems to have been acquired along the way. New tools such as hoes, plowshares, axes, adzes, chisels, spades and meat grills were available on board for the customer's inspection. If a desired object was not obtainable ready-made, it could have been quickly forged to order on board. Probably such eastern ships competed with Achaean bronzesmiths in Greek ports. Bigger craft no doubt transported most of the raw copper direct to mainland markets, where they picked up a return cargo of perfumed oil and other mainland specialties.

## SCIENCE AND ARCHAEOLOGY

No more appropriate conclusion could be chosen for this chapter than a glimpse at the tentative results of just one of the many areas where new scientific techniques are being applied to archaeological materials. As early as 1939 Blegen and Wace, among others, had foreseen the possibility and importance of this particular line of research applied to ceramics. Dr. H. W. Catling and two of his associates in the Research Laboratory for Archaeology and the History of Art at Oxford University reported in 1961 and 1963 on the spectrographic analysis of a group of over 500 Mycenaean and Minoan potsherds dated after 1400 and collected from some thirty known sites. The purpose was to determine whether there are detectable differences in chemical content of the clays that might identify place (or at least area) of manufacture.

The preliminary results are most encouraging, although the Oxford researchers stress that only a beginning has yet been made. They distinguished thirteen distinct kinds of composition, which were labeled Type A through Type M. Two major points were established: 108 out of 110 samples from sites in the Peloponnese fell in their Type A; and nearly all the samples from Knossos and central Crete could be assigned to Type B.

Pottery of Type A (Peloponnesian) was identified in relative abundance in Rhodes, Melos and in the sites represented in Egypt and Syria. Conversely, pottery of Type B (central Cretan) did not occur at all in the east Aegean and Near Eastern sites. This neatly confirms other evidence we have reviewed for the supersession of Minoan by Mycenaean traders in the east Mediterranean, particularly during the fourteenth and thirteenth centuries. A somewhat unexpected corollary seems also to be indicated, that is, that Mycenaean "colonies" in the Aegean were importing large numbers of pots (or their contents) from the mainland and that the fine Mycenaean pottery reaching the east end of the Mediterranean was largely manufactured on the Greek mainland rather than in the much closer island settlements. For example, the distinctive kraters with chariot scenes, found much more frequently in Cypriote graves than on mainland sites, were apparently manufactured in the Peloponnese.

The preliminary analysis also seems to confirm a widespread belief in minimum contact between Crete and the mainland after 1400. Pottery of Type A was extremely rare in Crete; and that of Type B was very uncommon on the mainland, except at Thebes. Catling was inclined to explain the latter anomaly as an accidental similarity of the local clays rather than as evidence for some exclusive trade connection between Knossos and Thebes.

The results of the tests in the Oxford laboratory suggested a good many other interesting possibilities about the minor centers of trade and manufacture. Catling pointed out that future refinements will no doubt be possible and much wider samplings analyzed. An immediate problem is to find means of distinguishing pottery manufactured in different parts of the Peloponnese. It will be vital to know, for example, how much of the Type A pottery found in the Near East came from the vicinity of Mycenae. Similarly, the problem of distinguishing between sherds from Thebes in Boeotia and central Crete clearly needed further investigation.

The last-mentioned puzzle has now (1966) been solved. Catling (with A. Millett) describes the reanalysis of the Theban sherds and the addition of a further group of twenty from the new excavations at Thebes. Nineteen of the latter proved to belong to Type B. The breakthrough came in isolating a previously uncounted component in the spectrum: germanium. This element was found to be present in very small quantity but consistently in all of the Type B sherds from Thebes, whereas it is completely absent in all of the Type B sherds from central Crete. Furthermore, the scattered Type B sherds from elsewhere on the mainland are of the Theban variety now distinguished as Type "B*."

An equally absorbing result of the research most recently reported by Catling and Millett concerns the inscribed stirrup jars found at Thebes in 1921. The date originally assigned (early fourteenth century) has been both supported and attacked on the basis of both shapes (typology) and inscriptions (epigraphy). But neither criterion is yet precise enough for close dating, and the original context of their discovery (like that of some possible parallels elsewhere) is poorly documented. Estimates all the way from 1400 to 1200 are current. Spectrographic analysis cannot pin down date; but, as we have seen, it is most useful to indicate origin (or provenience) and there can be no doubt that the inscriptions were painted on the jars at the time and place of their manufacture.

Evans, of course, believed firmly that the Linear B inscriptions were in the "Minoan" language and that these jars found at Thebes (as well as scattered examples at Mycenae, Tiryns, Eleusis and Orchomenos) proved that the mainland sites were under Minoan political control. The fact that no inscribed jars were known from any Cretan site and that Linear B tablets had been found only at Knossos convinced him that the Minoan rulers came from Knossos.

After the decipherment, Evans' view had of course to be abandoned, but the supposed connection with Crete persisted. Typically the inscriptions consist of three words—a personal name (official?), a place-name (origin of jar and contents?) and an adjective indicating "belonging to the *wanax* (king)." Palmer had already pointed out that several of the personal and place-names recur in the Knossos Linear B tablets, and that the presumption should be that the jars and their contents were shipped to Thebes and other mainland sites from Crete.

The Oxford scientists were allowed to take drillings from twenty-five of the Theban jars. Spectrographic analyses revealed three distinct groups of twelve, six and five examples, with the remaining two jars perhaps forming another group. There are additional significant variations within each group; but, over-all, Group I is closest to Type F of the 1963 analyses and Group II to Type O. Both of these types, therefore, indicate a provenience in extreme eastern Crete, Type O in the neighborhood of Palaikastro and Type F in or near Zakro. In Group III, three jars appear to have been manufactured in Thebes itself and two are closely comparable to Type A (Peloponnese). Not a single jar seems to have come from Knossos or central Crete.

The repercussions of this analysis go far beyond the obvious commercial implications. It appears, for instance, that the Linear B writing system was used in eastern Crete as well as at Knossos. If the date of the jars is eventually shown to be around 1400, this would have very interesting implications about the political situation contemporary with Evans' dating of the "final" destruction of the Knossos palace. If, on the other hand, the date is a century or more later, we shall have to revise the traditional view of Cretan literacy as well as overseas trade in the closing part of the Late Bronze Age.

# IX

## Some Current Theories and Problems

T HE FOLLOWING PARAGRAPHS are not intended as an attempt to summarize and synthesize the information on Mycenaean civilization that is now (1966) in our control. Fortunately, up-to-date and dependable handbooks are at last available to fill this need. Our purposes are quite different. We want particularly to take a final and necessarily oversimplified look at the most pressing historical problems that have arisen over the past century and to review them in the context of the most recent evidence and of relevant theories based on it. Most of the inferences and arguments to be cited can be found in scattered publications by prominent authorities over the last decade.

This final chapter also has two secondary and perhaps somewhat presumptuous aims. The first is to sound a tactful warning on several vital issues where (as so often in the past) unproved conclusions threaten to assume the status of dogma. The second is to indicate from time to time specific directions that future research might usefully take in an effort to pinpoint some of the more troublesome outstanding questions.

We have already seen that the situation in Greek prehistoric archaeology is never static; as in any lively science, it changes and shifts in a kaleidoscopic series of developments with every passing year. We now have much solid new knowledge denied to Schliemann and Evans and even to Blegen in his earlier years. This advantage allows us to recognize certain wrong inferences and conclusions reached by them and their contemporaries. But it would be grossly misleading to give the impression (as J. Irving Manatt did as early as 1897) that we are now or very soon will be in possession of "the facts" about Mycenaean civilization. Indeed, an honest assessment of the developing situation requires us to admit that the more we learn, the more unanswered (and perhaps unanswerable) questions we encounter.

It is unlikely, for example, that any relevant publication of Schliemann's or Evans' generation contains in the same number of pages as many qualifications (ifs, mights, possibles) as does this concluding chapter. Yet reasonable caution and the awareness of what is not known dictates most if not all of them. Such continual understatement may annoy some readers, but it is inherent in the scholar's as opposed to the popularizer's and generalist's method. The archaeologist and historian has to recognize the unsolved problems, and he views them as a challenge to his curiosity and ingenuity. If the questions are stated clearly and the background has been filled in with a minimum of technical jargon, there is no reason why non-specialists cannot also enjoy the puzzles and follow new developments that contribute to their solution or deepen their mystery. That is the hope in which these final pages have been written.

Specialist readers, too, may be somewhat unhappy about the presentation. It is quite possible that certain issues have been oversimplified, that a lack of balance or special pleading has crept in at times, that important discoveries, problems and hypotheses are ignored and that the evidence on some that are included is not fully developed. Every scholar who dares to write for his own colleagues must to some extent run these risks; and when he attempts a more popular overview he is doubly vulnerable. Yet the interested public needs and deserves direct communication on its nonspecialized level with the expert; and when the specialist attempts to fill this need he has a right to expect that his colleagues will take into account the extenuating circumstances before passing judgment on his efforts.

Probably Schliemann and Tsountas would be somewhat surprised yet on the whole pleased with what has been built on their foundations. In fact, as Professor Palmer has remarked, Homer would also be astonished. It is quite misleading to suggest, as Joseph Alsop has recently (1964), that "Homer has now been justified by the archaeologists, and every bit as fully as old Schliemann could have wished." Professor G. S. Kirk's verdict (1964) on the prevailing scholarly attitude is very different. After warning of "the almost infinite complexity of the process of oral transmission and elaboration," he continues as follows: "And yet they [the poems] *do* provide a wonderful picture, erratic and confused admittedly, but full of colour and vitality, of a Greek Heroic Age—an age that we should otherwise have barely guessed at; an age seen, as most such ages are, through the flattering vision of a diminished posterity, but one which did have existence of some kind, and which the historian, however imprecise his evidence, must try to understand and assess."

Dörpfeld might be disappointed to find that his identifications of Priam's Troy and Nestor's Pylos have been upset; but he would be recompensed with the assurance that the integrity of his work at those and many other sites has not been seriously questioned. Evans and Mackenzie, on the other hand, would be almost incredulous to learn that mainlanders had gradually encroached on Minoan trade and finally occupied the Knossos palace, at least as early as the mid-fifteenth century. But they might be mollified to realize that no one takes lightly the fundamental influence that the brilliant Minoan culture had on so many aspects of mainland life. Wace lived to see most of his major theories vindicated and the present situation would hold no real surprises for him. Blegen is still actively extending the frontiers of present knowledge, and it is hoped that he will find no serious fault with the generalizations here outlined.

In the preceding chapters we have reviewed, selectively but as fairly as we could, the major discoveries over the past century. Now, looking at the Mycenaean age more specifically as a historical phenomenon, what are the firm facts and where are the major areas of uncertainty and controversy?

# ORIGINS

The population of central and southern Greece and the neighboring islands during the Late Bronze Age was already a very mixed one. Probably there was still a considerable admixture of blood from ancestors who inhabited the area as far back as neolithic times (about 6000–3000). Almost certainly descendants of the gifted and progressive people of the Early Bronze Age (about 3000–2000) formed an important element. According to the "orthodox" view, it was these people who would have spoken an "Aegean" language (or family of languages), which was widely used also in Crete, in the islands and in western Anatolia. Many vocabulary items by which this "pre-Greek" language designated islands, mountains, towns, trees, plants, animals and mythological persons persisted as a distinctive substratum in later Greek.

Palmer (1961), Huxley (1961) and others now propose to connect at least some of these words and suffixes with the newly discovered Luwian language of western Anatolia. Since the existence of Luwian cannot be traced in Asia Minor before about 2000, Palmer associates its introduction into Greece with the later *Middle* Helladic invaders. But leaving questions of language aside for the moment, it is probable that most of the Early Helladic population was absorbed into the developing mainstream of the population. Enclaves of earlier people, however, may have survived until well into the Iron Age in isolated communities where a non-Greek language or languages continued to be spoken. The classical Greeks vaguely referred to such groups and their language(s) as Pelasgian.

A new people with quite distinctive culture traits appeared on the Greek mainland probably as early as 2100. The century 2000–1900 is still the usual date assigned to their arrival, but John L. Caskey (1964) has made a strong case for putting their capture and occupation of several sites some two centuries earlier. Their first settlements seem to have been in east central Greece and to have spread gradually through the peninsula, taking over and in many cases destroying the Early Helladic settlements. The lack of traces so far discovered north of Thessaly might suggest that they arrived by sea. Yet they apparently did not penetrate far into the Aegean islands and certainly not to Crete, where Minoan civilization seems to have been affected by quite different external influences and where a non-Greek language (or languages) seems to have predominated until the end of the Bronze Age.

These Middle Helladic folk (as we shall probably continue to call them, even if their earlier arrival is fully established) are traced mainly through their very distinctive wheel-made gray Minyan pottery. We recall that this is the ware that Schliemann first identified and named at Orchomenos. He had found even earlier a very closely related ware associated with the sixth level of Troy, and there he called it "Lydian." Dörpfeld and Blegen confirmed the sudden appearance of gray Minyan pottery in the earliest levels of Troy VI; and it continued in use throughout that long phase, dated by Blegen about 1900 until 1300. The shapes of gray Minyan pots, with their characteristic sharp angular profiles and ribbed surface, seem in many cases to have been copied from metal prototypes, and it is possible that the distinctive color and fabric were meant to simulate silver. A special surface sheen was produced by firing the clay under reduction conditions by which smoke penetrates the fabric. The makers apparently brought with them to Greece both the potter's wheel and the knowledge of this special technique of firing their pottery. Earlier and rather desperate theories that the pottery itself or the "molds" or even the clay was imported should be completely discarded.

It would appear, then, that these newcomers may have reached Greece from the general direction of Troy. Essentially similar pottery has been found south of the Black Sea, which may somewhat further point the direction from which they approached the Aegean area. The long-standing fixation that "the Greeks" must have come from the north is now under review. According to Guthrie (1964) we have to reckon with "the possibility that the first Greeks . . . came into Greece rather from the east than from the north . . ."

Another distinctive material feature of their culture is the building of houses with neat thin stone foundations, often on the megaron plan with an apsidal end opposite the porch. A third feature is the burial of the dead, sometimes inside their towns, in shallow single cist graves that are often lined with stone slabs or rubble.

In Troy VI bones of the domesticated horse are a novel feature. There is as yet, however, very little (if any) dependable evidence for the presence of horses in mainland towns of the Middle Helladic period. Frequent and categorical statements that these "earliest Greeks" were "horsemen" are attractive and may turn out to be true; but at this point the assumption is hazardous, as are assertions that the Middle Helladic invaders possessed "improved bronze weapons." Even the statement that some of their towns were fortified rests on rather tenuous evidence.

The "gray Minyan people" must have been fairly numerous and aggressive to be able to take over control of so many prosperous Early Helladic towns. Burned levels on numerous sites indicate that the transition was not accomplished without violence. Their advent caused a severe cultural setback, and for several centuries mainland Greece fell far behind such areas as Crete. Middle Helladic towns and cemeteries show very little evidence of prosperity or extensive foreign trade. Metal in the form of weapons, implements, utensils or even jewelry is scarce. It seems likely that the conquerors gradually blended with the survivors of earlier peoples, but it required a lengthy interval for Greece to recover from the shock of the invasion. Perhaps the so-called matt-painted pottery, which occurs somewhat later along with gray Minyan and which in some way recalls a type of Early Helladic ware, is an indication of the resurgence of the Early Helladic cultural tradition. Others see in the matt-painted pottery the result of increasingly close contact with the islands of the central Aegean (but not Crete). This Cycladic culture is still very inadequately known, but it was no doubt a factor in mainland development throughout the first half of the second millennium.

It is very widely believed that the gray Minyan people were the first "Greek speakers" in the peninsula. A somewhat more cautious statement would be Chadwick's formulation (1963) that this period of cultural change marks the arrival of "an Indo-European idiom which, after influence by the surviving indigenous peoples, emerged as Greek." Blegen, who, as we saw, had a prominent part in launching the theory a generation ago, more recently (1962) writes that "some held and still hold" this theory. Another eminent authority, Professor Sterling Dow, insists (1960) that "Greeks came to Greece by the start of MH I: that may be regarded now as certain." Professor Denys Page takes a less dogmatic position when he says (1959), "This is now as certain as such things can be."

It should be clearly realized, however, that these propositions rest on inference and not on direct evidence, archaeological or otherwise. The relevant points usually cited are: (1) that about 1400 (if Evans' date for the Linear B tablets from Knossos is correct) or at least by about 1300 (Thebes) an early form of what is unmistakably Greek was in use; and (2) that before that time no major cultural "break" has been detected in the archaeological picture until one backs up to the advent of the "gray Minyan people." Actually, the second point can be challenged by those who infer considerable cultural disturbance at the time of the appearance of the Shaft Grave dynasty at Mycenae in the late seventeenth century.

In any case, those who believe that the equation "makers of gray Minyan pottery = speakers of an Indo-European language" is certain or nearly so must support it by the assumption that a change of *language* is likely (or even certain?) to be indicated by radical changes in the *material* culture. Or, to put it another way, they assume that in a prehistoric setting, when no actual written documents can be expected, one may use archaeological evidence for the intrusion of distinctive new traits in material culture as a basis for an otherwise inferred change in language. This was the argument Evans and Mackenzie used for *denying* Achaean (Greek) control of Crete. As we have seen, they kept insisting that in the Minoan cultural record there is no archaeological "break," which they believed would have to accompany such a change. In that case it turned out that one can indeed detect an archaeological "break" at Knossos in LMII, which now fits in with the evidence of the Linear B tablets. But, as pointed out very forcefully by scholars like Fritz Schachermeyr, Palmer and Friedrich Matz, who are not themselves excavators, the assumption still remains in general a very insecure basis for asserting or denying changes of either "race" or language.

Joseph Alsop has most directly challenged the validity of such an inference. He insists that, given a conquering minority at a cultural level inferior to the subjugated inhabitants (as was almost surely the case with the "gray Minyan" invaders), recorded history shows hardly a single example where the language of the newcomers has prevailed. But our modern preconceptions about "superior" and "inferior" cultures and our view of language as a key factor in "national" integrity may be quite misleading when applied to prehistoric situations. There has probably been at all times and places a powerful individual advantage in learning the language of one's rulers, who are superior enough (at least in a military sense) to seize and hold power. At any rate, Stuart Piggott (1965) has recently summed up very persuasively the evidence for connecting a whole series of incursions into Asia Minor, the Aegean area and far into east central and western Europe about the end of the third millennium with the spread of Indo-European dialects to these areas. And there is documentary evidence that

Luwian and Hittite speakers of Indo-European languages must have reached Anatolia about this time. The languages or dialects spoken by these widely diffused newcomers seem to have prevailed or at least survived, and it is most difficult to believe that they were in all cases culturally "superior" to the earlier inhabitants.

Yet Alsop's point is at the very least a salutary warning against a second assumption that is implicit in some current statements. There is no compelling reason to believe that a new language (whether introduced by military, political, economic or religious means) quickly spreads to all areas and social levels. An Indo-European dialect could not have been imposed by fiat on the older population in Greece nor have we any reason to assume it was so "naturally superior" or carried such prestige that it quickly crowded out competitors. It is possible that, even in later times when the language of the Linear B tablets was Achaean Greek, speakers of one or more non-Greek languages formed a considerable proportion of the total population.

## THE EARLY MYCENAEANS (ABOUT 1600–1400)

There appears to have been a quite sudden burst of energy, prosperity and foreign contacts in at least some Middle Helladic communities a generation or two before and after 1600. This phenomenon is still most startlingly exemplified in the fabulous contents of Schliemann's Shaft Graves. It is no wonder that the fortunate finder concluded that these kings must belong to the era of "golden Mycenae" and "wide-ruling Agamemnon." Nor should we be surprised that Schliemann's friends as well as critics reached such incompatible conclusions in trying to analyze and explain the contents of the Shaft Graves.

The slightly earlier Grave Circle B does not solve, even for Mycenae, the enigma of the rapid transition from Middle Helladic stagnation to Early Mycenaean dynamism. In fact, the new discovery adds a further problem as to why there were *two* circles partially overlapping in date. But the newer evidence does make less likely the theories of scholars like Nilsson, V. Gordon Childe, Schachermeyr and (most recently) Frank H. Stubbings (1965), who have seen in the kings buried in Schliemann's Shaft Graves an intrusive dynasty whose founder had seized control and brought his own burial customs and wealth with him from abroad. The situation at Mycenae seems rather to have been one of sharply rising prosperity, as measured by kingly ostentation, over several generations. And the thesis championed long ago by Wace in regard to the local evolution of the royal Shaft Graves from the ordinary Middle Helladic cists has gained added weight with the discovery of the slightly older Grave Circle.

How are we, then, to explain what still appears to have been the rather sudden and unprecedented wealth of (presumably) native kings at Mycenae? Was Mycenae a kind of "sport" or anomaly in relation to contemporary mainland political units? Marinatos' recent discovery at Peristeria, reported in the previous chapter, suggests that it was not. But so far the contents of the Mycenae Shaft Graves constitute the major evidence for a sharply altered economic (and political?) situation in this first stage of "Mycenaean" culture.

Evans was right in pointing to the strong Cretan influence, if not actual Cretan origin of many objects in the later Grave Circle. But it would appear that the same cannot be said for the earlier one. From Mylonas' preliminary publications one infers that he regards most of the contents as native. At least, few parallels are cited in Crete or elsewhere in the Aegean orbit. Yet much in the more elaborate graves of Circle B is new in terms of normal Middle Helladic or Minoan culture traits—the deeper bigger graves with multiple burials, the method of roofing, the profusion of weapons, the face mask, the sculptured stelae and (to some extent) the circle itself. The pottery alone seems to have authentic, demonstrable, direct Middle Helladic parallels and antecedents. Clearly, new ideas were astir and new external contacts were developing. Could the novelties have originated with native rulers?

In this connection, we might profitably remind ourselves of Blegen's warning against fixing our attention on royalty alone. By implication he suggests that in the Prosymna chamber tombs there is a more reliable record of unbroken cultural development from MH to mature LH times. He does not detect in this record any abrupt change in culture patterns at the beginning of the Shaft Grave phase; and he regards this as a strong indication of essential continuity in the ruling power at nearby Mycenae.

Perhaps the emphasis on weapons is a clue that the new wealth was not so much gained in legitimate trade as extorted directly or indirectly by threat, piracy, raids or outright war from weaker neighbors in Greece and far beyond its borders. As we have mentioned, some scholars believe that the change is too sudden and sweeping to be explained on any basis but the seizure of power by foreign usurpers, perhaps the first speakers of an Indo-European language in the Aegean orbit. But if so, their point of origin is not easy to identify. As Piggott shows, the external contacts betrayed by the contents of the Shaft Graves are amazingly diverse. The gold and silver ornaments can be linked stylistically with the Caucasus and Iran, the amber with the far north, the horse-drawn chariot, some of the swords and various small luxury articles with the Near East, the form of the graves themselves and the burial posture with western Anatolia and south Russia.

Whatever the story of their rise to wealth and power, the sixteenth-century kings of Mycenae (and probably their counterparts elsewhere in Greece) can no longer be regarded as an isolated phenomenon. From western Asia to eastern and central Europe through the second millennium a warlike and aristocratic stratified society was developing. Everywhere, the kings or chieftains and their families were buried with utmost ostentation and luxury. Because of their proximity to the sophisticated cultures of Crete and the Near East, the Mycenaean kingdoms had a head start in technology, trade and opportunities for plunder. In time they adopted such civilized culture traits as literacy and bureaucratic palace administrations. But the archaeological record supports the testimony of the Homeric poems that they remained essentially part of a specifically European heroic tradition.

The richer graves in Schliemann's circle point unmistakably to a rapidly increasing involvement overseas. Yet it is extremely difficult to reconstruct what form it took. It has been suggested that much or all of this heterogeneous material is reflected in the fabled wealth of the legendary Danaos* and may have resulted from mainland raids on a weakened Egypt or payment for the services of Greek mercenaries who assisted in the expulsion of the Hyksos* usurpers. Stubbings suggests that Danaos may actually represent a kind of collective folk memory of a limited number of Hyksos adventurers who seized control of backward Middle Helladic centers like Mycenae when they were forced to leave Egypt. He is also prepared to believe that the story of Kadmos' coming to Boeotian Thebes from Phoenicia (Syria) represents a similar and perhaps closely contemporaneous historical event.

But (apart from other serious objections) such theories scarcely explain the curious variety of the contents of the Shaft Graves. Certainly Egyptian contact, direct or indirect, is proved by such objects as the ostrich eggs, the alabaster vase, the dagger with the inlaid scene of "Nilotic" type and perhaps by the face masks; but the influence or trade route may have been via Crete or Syria or the Cyclades. Increasing contact with island centers is proved not only by the contents of the Shaft Graves, but by Middle Helladic pottery found at Phylakopi and Keos. Perhaps island merchants were the chief intermediaries at this time, bringing to the mainland luxury goods and exotic ideas and raw materials from Troy, Syria, Egypt, Crete and even greater distances.

But, if the main source was legitimate trade, we are faced with the question of what the Mycenaeans used to pay for these imports and how they acquired such "purchasing power." The same consideration seems to make it very unlikely that these precious objects represent a collection of gifts to the kings of Mycenae from their counterparts around the known world. It is quite possible that the system of gift exchange so prominent in the Homeric epic was already well established among Greek monarchs. Certainly the once fabulous contents of the tholos tombs may have consisted very largely of gifts. But it is doubtful that the kings of the sixteenth century could have commanded the respect of distant monarchs or carried on diplomatic negotiations with foreign powers or possessed the necessary countergifts to account for the contents of the Shaft Graves.

Wace's suggestion that Mycenae controlled copper mines in the Nemea district is intriguing but unproved. Another theory originated a generation ago with O. Davies, who was familiar with metallurgy and claimed to have discovered near Delphi evidence for tin mining and smelting in context with Mycenaean pottery. He noted that in the Homeric catalogue the area immediately south of the Gulf of Corinth belonged to Mycenae, and he suggested that she might have controlled the production of this vital commodity on the opposite side of the gulf. Although Davies' claims have since been denied, they ought to be thoroughly checked by a specialist working with archaeologists. An organized survey by a competent metallurgist might also produce other important evidence for ancient mining in various parts of the Aegean world. But it would seem that the Delphi district is too far distant to have been controlled by the kings of Mycenae as early as the sixteenth century.

Another theory—that the salt-pan method of evaporating precious salt from seawater was a Minoan-Mycenaean patent (and if so of course an important source of wealth)—also needs expert study. A more likely source of Mycenae's wealth, however, is her strategic position. She could control traffic and exact taxes on goods moving by land between the Isthmus of Corinth and the Gulf of Argolis. This was surely an important factor in her later prosperity, but it is unproved that such traffic had reached major proportions by the time of the Shaft Graves. In fact, no satisfactory explanation has yet been suggested to account for the Shaft Graves treasure as the result of legitimate trade.

The single most striking impression of the contents of Circle A is still the sudden and powerful influence of Minoan craftsmanship. Evans was wrong in taking this to prove complete cultural domination, which in turn implied to him Minoan political control. But the appearance of many objects made either in Crete or at least by Cretans continues to beg for an explanation. Mainland artisans simply could not have learned so fast and so well, and no known earlier evidence at Mycenae or elsewhere on the mainland suggests a believable transition. If they were manufactured in Crete, their presence is presumably to be explained either by trade (direct or indirect) or by war and/or piracy. The latter possibility may receive some support from the analogy of what happened in the fifteenth century, from the emphasis on war and weapons in the graves and from the lack of evidence on Crete for reverse trade goods from the mainland.

One could even suggest that *all* of the exotic contents of the Shaft Graves were seized in Crete and had been amassed there from various sources by legitimate Minoan trade. Cretan provenience makes far better sense than Egyptian for the bulk of the precious objects. And the objection that no parallels for many articles in the Shaft Graves have been found in Crete might be met by pointing out that the survival and discovery of the Mycenae treasures is an almost unique accident and that comparable hoards of portable wealth are almost certain to have been stored in the strong rooms and deposited in the graves of more than one Minoan Minos.

The new generation of Greek, Italian, French and British excavators in Crete is carefully reviewing both the stratigraphical and typological basis of Evans' chronological system. They now envision (again in Evans' terms) a period of the early palaces ending somewhere between 1700 and 1600 and of the later palaces, beginning about 1600. And some are raising the possibility, unorthodox even now and unthinkable in Evans' day, that raiders from the mainland rather than earthquakes or other natural disasters or internal disorders destroyed the early palaces. One may be tempted to adduce in this connection the silver siege rhyton from the Shaft Graves that Evans was so sure is a Cretan product; but, while the attackers may be wearing a Mycenaean type of helmet, the citadel itself is heavily fortified and presumably not Minoan. At any rate, the rhyton (if Cretan) would suggest that siege and piracy were taken for granted there.

Successful raids by pirates or extortion of "tribute" by mainland free-booters at such an early date, however, run counter to the persistent ancient tradition of a strong Minoan fleet that protected the island's "empire" and imposed a Minoan "thalassocracy" around the east Mediterranean. We shall have more to say on this tradition later. Its reliability has now been seriously challenged, and it is becoming almost unbelievable for the succeeding fifteenth century. If there was such an entity as a Knossian or Minoan navy, it apparently could not or at least did not prevent mainland encroachment on its "colonies" and trade routes, and it finally failed to protect Knossos itself from Greek occupation.

In fact, the traditional belief in Minoan invincibility at sea is incompatible with the general impression that the material remains indicate about Minoan interests and temperament. It may be that Minoan prosperity and autonomy were relatively unchallenged up to some undetermined point in time, not so much because of the might of her fleet but because no one else had the courage and resources and nautical experience to invade a heavily populated island so far off in an inhospitable and relatively open part of the Mediterranean Sea. It is at least credible that, if this eventuality threatened from a dynamic Greek challenger such as Mycenae (perhaps with allies), the Minoans preferred to buy them off and to share and diversify and extend their trade contacts rather than risk a direct military confrontation.

On the other hand, one cannot yet exclude the possibility that the "Minoan" objects in the Shaft Graves were made in Mycenae or at least on the mainland. In that case the craftsmen must have been Cretans who came to Greece either willingly or as captives. To judge from later Mycenaean practices of raids and enslavement, the latter would be quite in character. But from what little is known of the contemporary situation, voluntary cooperation for mutual benefit is perhaps more likely. In either case, there is much to be said for the theory of Minoan artisans working for mainland masters or employers. Their presence in considerable numbers would explain better than would continued raids or even intensive (one-way?) trade the intensity of the Minoan influence by the later sixteenth century. It would account for the perfection of certain objects made in the current Minoan tradition as well as the more tentative experimenting with new materials and techniques and motifs that mainland taste and resources seem to have dictated. Undoubtedly, such émigré artisans might be expected to train a guild of mainland pupils, and it would have been the grandsons and great-grandsons of these masters and pupils who gradually attained a blending of the Minoan and mainland traditions to produce the finest examples of indigenous Mycenaean art. This result was, of course, achieved in the context of continuing intimate contact with the developing art of Crete itself.

The Shaft Graves and their baffling implications for Mycenae shed even less light on the contemporary situation elsewhere in Greece. The type of burial itself can so far be paralleled at only two or three widely scattered sites. If it developed naturally from the normal Middle Helladic cist grave, there is as yet little evidence that the fashion spread very far. Instead, the sudden thrust toward monumentality and regal ostentation seems to have been concentrated very soon on the tholos tomb. Wace was right in insisting, against Evans, on the priority in time of the Shaft Graves over the tholos tombs at Mycenae. But there is little evidence that the same sequence was the norm elsewhere. This in itself is perhaps an indication that the developments at Mycenae were abnormal. According to one report in connection with Marinatos' newest discovery at Peristeria near the west coast of the Peloponnese, a tholos tomb was built above one or more Shaft Graves. On the other hand, we have seen that a tholos tomb somewhat further south along the west coast seems to be practically contemporary with the Mycenae Shaft Graves. And one or two other widely scattered tholoi also contained pottery from the end of the Middle Helladic period.

The origin of the essential features of the tholos is even more controversial than that of the Shaft Grave. The earliest examples now known on the mainland surely had a long tradition behind them and may have evolved outside of Greece. In spite of a fairly formidable gap in time and other difficulties, some authorities have continued to believe that the round tombs associated with the Early Bronze and the earlier Middle Bronze Age in southern Crete and in some of the Aegean islands may represent previous stages in the same tradition. These forms could perhaps have persisted there or elsewhere through Middle Bronze and sprung to new and monumental vigor, with important modifications, in the mainland during the sixteenth and fifteenth centuries.

Unfortunately, the tholoi were such "sitting ducks" for robbers that we cannot often draw on their undisturbed contents to supplement the evidence supplied by the architectural shell. Yet what is known of their distribution and formal development permits some useful statements about conditions in Greece outside of Mycenae. If there were more and better preserved remains of palaces and fortifications and houses contemporary with the early tholoi, the reconstruction could be much fuller and surer.

The earlier kings, who diverted so much of the resources of their kingdoms to constructing and equipping a suitable receptacle for their mortal remains and thus memorializing their reigns to men of later generations, were apparently willing to live in relatively modest homes and to guard the treasure they were amassing with much less monumental fortifications than in later Mycenaean times. We can be reasonably confident that most houses, from the humblest to the most ostentatious, carried on the MH traditions. They were set on a stone base and had walls of sun-dried brick or rubble in a timber framework. Such structures seem always to have been considered safest in countries like Greece, where earthquakes are frequent. The distinctive roof tiles so popular in classical times and later are almost never found. Roofs seem to have been flat or nearly so with wooden rafters covered by branches, clay and thatch. One can at least infer the predominance of the megaron house with forecourt—a quite different effect than the Minoan agglutination of rooms clustered around a central court.

The remains of the early tholoi prove that Mycenae was by no means the only mainland center that experienced a rather sudden rise in its standard of living, at least at the royal level. It may be that rulers of no other kingdom in the early Mycenaean age could have provided as rich a complement of possessions to molder with their bodies as Schliemann found in the Shaft Graves; but kings in many another center were incomparably better off in material possessions and in the means to amass them than the most powerful ruler of Middle Helladic times seems to have been.

In the case of the "provincial" kingdoms we have even fewer clues to explain the increase in wealth and centralized power. The distribution of the early tholoi would suggest that the territory that most of these kings controlled was much larger than that of the average (probably independent) Middle Helladic village. And the early Mycenaean kingdoms were, in turn, much smaller than those carved out after 1400. We do not yet find much evidence for great power centers. In Messenia, for instance, the late Mycenaean kingdom won by Nestor and his father, Neleus, and centered at Ano Englianos must have absorbed a score or more of once independent smaller kingdoms, each of which had its own headquarters and cluster of tholos tombs.

Nevertheless, the aggrandizement of a strong king's territory at the expense of weaker neighbors must have begun long before 1400. It is fairly clear that most of the offensive weapons buried with the kings in the Mycenae Shaft Graves had not been used in their owner's lifetime solely for ostentation. The scanty evidence in the early tholoi tells the same story. It is altogether likely that such weapons were turned against mainland neighbors at least as often as they were used overseas. Perhaps in terms of freedom from outside aggression and threats, Mrs. Emily Vermeule (1964) is justified in saying that "the Early Mycenaean Age was the most peaceable of any Greek age of innovation"; but Lord William Taylour (1964) is surely nearer the mark when he observes: "It would almost seem as if they loved strife for its own sake. This element in their nature is conspicuous from the very first . . ." It is indeed doubtful if even the concept or possibility of peace would have occurred to any king or noble in the Mycenaean orbit. The obsession with building bigger and bigger political units by force of arms seems already to have been well started in Greece and may perhaps be echoed in tales of the exploits of the older generations of heroes like Perseus and Herakles, who lived long before the Trojan War.

To organize and maintain the military power necessary to control far larger territories, the kings of the early Mycenaean period were probably able to exploit natural resources more effectively than their Middle Helladic predecessors. This age is likely to have witnessed notable improvements in methods of agriculture and stock breeding, whether the skill was developed locally or acquired as a result of foreign contacts.

This could well have been the period, too, when the Copaic basin was first drained (see Chapter III), although recent excavation at Gla by J. Threp-

siadis confirms the previous impression that it was not extensively occupied or fortified until LHIIIB. In the late Mycenaean period Orchomenos
seems to have found it necessary to take drastic measures to protect the
hydraulic installations at the northeastern end of the basin. It is obvious
that if an enemy had got control of this area he could have interrupted the
emissaries and ruined Orchomenos' agricultural production. Gla must have
formed the key defensive anchor, but there are remains of several other
fortified strongholds and watch towers surrounding this vital sector. It is
in the context of a critically situated military installation, not the administrative capital of an independent kingdom, that what we know of Gla
makes the best sense.

The unique and relatively well-preserved evidence from the Copaic
basin deserves far more thorough and expert attention than it has so far
received. A third big channel in the center of the western basin, with retaining walls of earth only, could belong to the late Mycenaean period.
Irrigation as well as drainage facilities are by no means ruled out. On the
other hand, a series of vertical shafts sunk in the solid rock and the beginning of a rock-cut tunnel to replace the natural emissaries at the northeast
end of the basin seem to date from Hellenistic times.

Our information on land use and on the technical competence of engineers is still meager. In the early Mycenaean period spectacular improvement in monumental tomb architecture and in the ability to produce or
procure articles of ostentation and luxury suggests that the bigger political
units were made possible by corresponding improvements in the economic
basis of the society. Whether or not piratical raids are the most likely
explanation of the wealth in the Shaft Graves, piracy could never have
formed the stable basis of Mycenaean prosperity. And trading, especially
in the days of barter, requires that one have a surplus of desirable commodities to exchange.

The Mycenaean economy, even in its most advanced stage, surely continued to depend mainly on agriculture and stock raising. Goods manufactured from these products probably paid for most of the standard
imports—raw materials like copper, tin, ivory and amber, as well as luxury
goods manufactured abroad. We may take it for granted that the carefully
supervised agriculture and huge flocks reflected in the Linear B tablets and
the descriptions of lovingly tended gardens and orchards and vineyards
in the Homeric poems already had their modest counterparts in the small
but ambitious early Mycenaean kingdoms. The search for solid evidence
along these lines, utilizing all the analytical and comparative resources of
modern science, is one of the most important directions that future archaeological research should follow.

Improved farming and stock breeding would have formed the basis for manufacturing and processing enterprises based on surpluses of such products as oil, wine, wool, flax and hides. Supervisors appointed by the kings may already have largely controlled these activities, although free enterprise on a small scale is perhaps more likely in the early than in the late Mycenaean period. No doubt there was a certain amount of exchange of agricultural and manufactured products between independent Mycenaean kingdoms, but the increasing homogeneity of the material remains shows that foreign trade was a necessity. Basic raw materials that were unobtainable in Greece as well as many luxury goods had to be imported from abroad; and most of them had to be paid for in goods or services, even if piracy and war booty continued to account for some of the royal treasures. There is, in fact, mounting evidence of extensive foreign trade in the sixteenth and fifteenth centuries. Mycenaean products, reflected mainly in the indestructible potsherd, were penetrating to more and more distant points in every direction, and exotic objects appear increasingly in Mycenaean contexts.

In the west, evidence has been slower in accumulating; but there are indications that Mycenaean traders turned in that direction at least as early as they did to the more civilized east. It may have been easier to find markets and sources of needed raw materials in the relatively unexploited west than to break in on long established trading patterns of older economies. For instance, Middle Helladic vases of the matt-painted style were already reaching southeastern Sicily and one or two of the Aeolian islands off the north coast of Sicily in the seventeenth century; and an exact duplicate of a scepter from Grave Circle B at Mycenae was found in the grave of a British chieftain in Wessex. Contact with central Europe and southern England is proved by the influence of Mycenaean vessels and armor on the flourishing native metal-working tradition as early as the sixteenth century.

On a deeply stratified acropolis on the island of Lipari in the Aeolian group so much Mycenaean pottery of the sixteenth and fifteenth century (along with a very modest amount of contemporary Minoan ware) has been found that an important trading station must have been located there. The nearby island of Filicudi has also produced a moderate amount. The Aeolian islands lie at the center of the Mediterranean basin and appear to have been a strategic focus for early long-distance sea traffic. Small islands do, of course, provide an ideal situation for trading entrepôts.

Marinatos (1962) envisages Lipari as the intersection of a great inverted T. To the east across two almost equal stretches of water lie Kephallenia/Pylos and Rhodes/Cyprus. To the west at approximately equal distances are Sardinia and the Balearic islands off Spain. Looking north, the islands of Ischia and Vivara off the Bay of Naples are somewhat closer to Lipari, and there are indications of Mycenaean contacts there at least as early as the fifteenth century. Marinatos might well have added still another hypothetical stage toward the north, from Ischia to the Etruscan coast, with its abundant copper.

Pottery is our main evidence for trade with coastal points, and the vases themselves must have been attractive as well as useful to native peoples. Dr. Stubbings suggests that the demand for Mycenaean pottery may be partly due to the fact that it was fired at higher temperatures than most contemporary pottery. Marinatos contends that the ceramic types found on Lipari indicate that the Pylos district was the chief source. He assumes that pottery and other trade goods were carried in Mycenaean ships and suggests that long familiarity with such voyages would explain Homer's emphasis on Nestor's daring in sailing straight across the open Aegean on the return from Troy.[97]

Yet we need not conclude that the ceramic containers or even their contents such as oil and wine constituted the only, or even the major Mycenaean export. Since pottery is confined almost entirely to coastal sites, it used to be taken for granted that Mycenaean trade goods did not penetrate far inland. Professor Marinatos has pointed out quite logically, however, that overland caravans, unlike ships, cannot afford to transport cheap articles. Since pottery would (he thinks) by and large fall into this category and is also extremely fragile, its scarcity does not necessarily prove that valuable and durable goods—particularly metal weapons and implements and jewelry—did not move inland. One might also observe that a fair proportion of the goods received in exchange at a foreign port must have come from the interior, and caravans would not willingly return empty-handed.

What product (or products) was sought by the merchants—presumably Mycenaeans—who established the Lipari base? The obsidian (liparite*) so abundant there is one possibility. Preliminary geochemical investigation suggests, however, that it was not in serious competition with the much more accessible obsidian of Melos as a raw material for the manufacture of knives, razors and arrowheads. As mentioned above, the copper of Etruria or Spain or central Europe is another candidate. It has been commonly assumed that the Mycenaeans procured their copper from the east, particularly from Cyprus, but Piggott suggests that they may have had considerable initial difficulty in tapping eastern sources. Here again (discouraging reports to the contrary) new methods of geochemical analysis can probably establish the source(s) of supply.

British or Spanish tin is a third possibility, although again an eastern source has usually been taken for granted. The often repeated report of Aegean pottery in Spain has been categorically refuted by Lord William Taylour (1958), who finds no dependable ceramic evidence for Mycenaean contacts farther west than Malta and Sardinia. Yet in view of the Early Cycladic copper-working "colonies" now known to have been established in southern Spain and Portugal in the mid-*third* millennium, it would be unwise to deny that Mycenaean or Cycladic or Cretan ships could have transported Spanish metals if the demand made it worthwhile.

In fact, Piggott and others have shown that there is good reason to believe that by the middle of the second millennium ships from the Aegean area were ranging all the way to the western end of the Mediterranean in a more or less routine fashion. An easily recognizable class of segmented blue faience beads (Fig. 97), manufactured in the Aegean or the Near East, has been found sparsely in southern France in the neighborhood of Narbonne and very frequently in the British Isles, with a concentration in southern England. They represent a type of trade goods that is much more easily transportable over land than pottery. It can scarcely be doubted that we have proof here of a major trade route from the Mediterranean to Britain, probably across southwestern France by the Narbonne-Carcassonne-Loire route to the Atlantic and on to southern England. British gold and copper as well as the precious tin could have moved to the east Mediterranean along this route. In addition to trinkets, the raw materials may have been paid for in part by sharing knowledge of advanced technology and metallurgy. The sophisticated architectural knowledge behind the final monument at Stonehenge should probably be seen in the same context, whether or not the dagger carved on it represents a Mycenaean shape. At any rate, it would appear that contacts with England began as early as the sixteenth century.

A second concentration of trade goods has emerged far inland in eastern and central Europe, generally north of the Danube and stretching from Hungary to Czechoslovakia. In addition to the distinctive faience beads, decorated bonework bearing characteristic incised Mycenaean patterns has been identified (Fig. 97). Similar scattered finds, as well as a few Mycenaean metal objects found at or near the north end of both the Adriatic and the Aegean suggest that as much as possible of these trade routes was over water. Here again abundant copper, tin and gold must have been the major attraction for Mycenaean merchants, who seem to have been tapping this great area by the fifteenth century.

Marinatos believes, however, that the importance of the early trading station on Lipari is owed mainly to the amber trade. This substance, which held such fascination for many ancient peoples, occurs in various parts of northern, central and southern Europe. It seems likely that refined methods of chemical analysis will soon be able to at least roughly identify the origin of archaeological specimens. Although definite conclusions must await formal scientific proof, we should probably proceed on the long-standing assumption that the amber found in the southeast Mediterranean reached there from the far-distant southern shores of the Baltic Sea, especially Denmark. Various land routes are believed to have converged at the head of the Adriatic Sea. Ships based in western Peloponnese or the Ionian islands seem to have been particularly active in the amber trade. The early tholoi in that area, robbed as they are, still yield disproportionately large quantities of amber beads.

A most striking recent indication of long-distance commerce in amber concerns a distinctive type of small flat plate or spacer bead with complicated perforations (Fig. 97). Examples in Mycenaean contexts were found in both circles of the Mycenae Shaft Graves and in the tholos tombs of Kakovatos. Very similar objects also occur in south Germany and in southern England. R. Hachmann (1957) claims that the Greek and British plates belonged to necklaces and collars, whereas the German examples came from a longer kind of pectoral. He believes, therefore, that the Greek and British plates must have been manufactured at the same center. If they originated in Britain (and not at some intermediary point), Marinatos' inference could be right that amber moved along an east-west trade route via Lipari as well as by the better documented north-south routes.

The identity of the merchants who were operating in the western

Figure 97

Mediterranean during the sixteenth and fifteenth centuries is scarcely debatable now, in spite of such attempts as Huxley's to reopen the question. Evans, of course, believed that the Minoans controlled the western seas at this time, and he referred rather vaguely to Minoan pottery occurring as far west as Spain. We have already mentioned the increasing skepticism about the extent and duration of the fabled Cretan thalassocracy, and in a moment we must discuss that vexed question in some detail. Meanwhile, it should be emphasized that almost all of the sixteenth- and fifteenth-century Aegean vases and other artefacts found on western sites seem to be Mycenaean, not Minoan. If absolute proof along these lines is needed, we now have geochemical means to certify provenience.

It would be difficult, of course, to prove that Minoan ships did not have a monopoly or a share in transporting these goods; but this would be exceedingly odd in view of present indications that the eastern terminus for both exports and imports was almost exclusively the mainland. The evidence for the amber trade is particularly relevant here, since it appears that amber was practically unknown in Crete. One might therefore infer that, instead of controlling the seas, Cretan ships were excluded from, or uninterested in western trade even as early as the sixteenth century. It is far more in line with present evidence to see the carriers as ships from the Greek mainland (particularly western Peloponnese) and possibly also from the Cyclades. If there is a historical basis to the legendary Cretan expedition to southeast Sicily to bring back Daidalos, the context—as Huxley admits—is in all probability a period when a Greek Minos occupied the throne of Knossos.

We need not spend much time in reviewing the better-known evidence (already discussed at various earlier stages) for the nature of Aegean contacts with the Near East in the sixteenth and fifteenth centuries. Although he finds the results "certainly surprising," Dr. Stubbings in his thorough study (1951) of the Aegean pottery found in the East essentially confirms the thesis of Wace, Blegen, Kantor and others. Minoan trade, at least as far as pottery is an index, seems to have yielded to Mycenaean competitors almost from the beginning of the Late Bronze Age. Nor can Stubbings' explanation of the phenomenon, i.e. that Mycenaean trade was carried on by independent "colonies" on islands like Rhodes and Kos, any longer be accepted uncritically. Catling's analyses, as we have seen, indicate that the later Mycenaean pottery in the east originated largely in the mainland, not in the islands of the southeast Aegean, and it would be extremely unlikely that this situation was reversed in the earlier centuries.

One feels a certain sympathy for the scholars who were so long under Evans' spell as they grope for evidence to support his rapidly crumbling pan-Minoan theories. "If, as is generally assumed, Crete was at this time the dominant Aegean power, and Greece not more than a tributary ally, how," asks Stubbings, "could Greece trade more freely with Egypt than Crete, which lies geographically between the two?" The real question, of course, is whether the evidence will any longer allow us to see Crete as the dominant power, even in the more circumscribed Aegean area, in the sixteenth and fifteenth centuries.

Huxley is a most vigorous proponent of the position that it was. He points once again to a strong tradition in later Greek history about a Minoan thalassocracy and to a number of specific tales about successful Minoan expeditions against islands like Keos and mainland strongholds like Athens, and to various places "colonized" by the Minoans (some apparently preserving the memory by their name, Minoa). "In the Aegean," he says, "trade was followed by colonisation in Middle Minoan III. In that era, about 1600 B.C., the palaces of Crete achieved their greatest prosperity, and to it we may assign the creation of the Cretan thalassocracy by the kings of Knossos. . . . The Minoan navy rid the sea of pirates and made them safe for commerce."

Without intending to preclude the judicious use of tradition, whether embedded in Homer or in later Greek literature, one must still insist that it be supported by some other kind of evidence before being accepted as essentially historical. In the first place, there is the problem of whether this tradition is based on the exploits of a Minos who is a Mycenaean Greek or a Minoan. Huxley himself ascribes to the former the tradition of the "Minoan" expedition to Sicily. Also, one could construct from equally believable tradition a fairly strong case from the exploits of the older heroes like Bellerophon, Jason and Herakles for a Mycenaean Greek thalassocracy. They, too, travel widely from the Black Sea to Troy to Lycia and to the Pillars of Herakles (Strait of Gibraltar) in the far west. And, if the legends of their "colonies" are fewer than those of Minos, the archaeological evidence for the spread of Mycenaean culture in the Aegean area more than evens the balance.

Before we come to the archaeological record, however, it may be worthwhile to think for a moment about the whole concept of "rule of the sea." May we not be reading much later ideas of navies and fleets and armadas and maritime policemen into Thucydides' remarks, which themselves were made in the very different context of the Athenian empire a thousand years after the time with which we are concerned? Professor Chester Starr (1955), for instance, completely rules out the possibility that such a thalassocracy could have been a historical fact. In his words, "neither logically, archaeologically, nor historically can the existence of a Cretan mastery of the seas be proved. . . . The presuppositions which underlie the concept—dynamic commercial expansion, trade preserves, a strategy designed to ward off the enemy at sea, developed warcraft—have virtually no justification when placed in the actual structure of economic and political life in the second millennium B.C."

What, then, is the archaeological evidence that scholars like Stubbings and Huxley adduce? To bolster his claim that "of the historical fact of Cretan maritime power there is proof in the archaeological record" Huxley cites first the occurrence of Middle Minoan pottery at many sites around the Aegean, including Lerna, the Cyclades, Miletos, Rhodes, Samos, Kythera, Melos, Cyprus, Thera, Byblos and Egypt, as well as possible contact at Delos, Megara and Krisa. No one doubts that this constitutes good evidence for wide-ranging Minoan trade before 1600 and that there was practically no competition from the Greek mainland. But when he looks for evidence of expansion or even continuation in the period between 1600 and 1400 the record is quite different.

Minoan influence continues to be strong but actual imported LMI pots are very scarce. Apart from Mycenae, Huxley mentions Aegina and Attica (one vase). The list could now be supplemented somewhat, particularly from Keos and his own recent excavations on Kythera. Yet Huxley's inventory of LHI and II (*i.e.*, Early Mycenaean) pottery found east of the Greek mainland is much longer. One is therefore at a loss to understand the implication in the statement "The amount of known Mycenaean pottery exported before 1400 B.C is not great . . ." By the same standard, he would have to admit that the amount of LMI pottery exported is almost infinitesimal. Much is made of Minoan pottery in Egypt, although (as we have seen) the record suggests that it was overbalanced 8 to 1 by Mycenaean imports. The Egyptian tomb paintings representing men of "Keftiu" offering gifts or "tribute" of Minoan-looking vessels and other objects have been much more thoroughly reviewed by Furumark (1950), who questions the common assumption that they "prove" direct and contemporary Minoan-Egyptian trade.

Furumark actually makes a much stronger case than Huxley for aggressive Minoan trade and colonization during the first century or so of the Late Bronze Age; but at the same time he admits that "the Cretan expansion was counteracted by a Mainland one, which began much earlier than has generally been supposed." In addition to older Minoan "colonies" such as that on Kythera, he posits similar settlements on Rhodes (Ialysos-Trianda) and Karpathos, as well as total cultural and probably political control of central Aegean islands like Melos (Phylakopi). To this must now be added the evidence from Keos. On the other hand, he points to increasing proof of mainland contact with Troy and the Near East, as well as to the early Mycenaean "colony" at Miletos and the likelihood that "Miletos was probably not the only Mycenaean colony in the Eastern Aegean dating back to the Late Aegean I–II period."

The total weight of the archaeological evidence, then, is not very impressive support for the grandiose concept of a LMI "thalassocracy." Even if Minoan pottery proved to be far more widespread and in larger quantities, it would simply indicate trade relations and cultural contacts, not "dominion" or "control" or "suppression of piracy." And evidence of trade can be deceptive unless one knows that it was direct and that the goods were carried in Cretan ships and that Cretan ships were controlled by Cretan kings.

If the reverse argument has been somewhat overstated, a balanced view might be that in the sixteenth and fifteenth centuries Crete was rather rapidly losing her former predominance in Aegean and east Mediterranean commerce. Whether she resisted this trend in a military sense, we have no sure way of knowing as yet. It would appear to have been a gradual process rather than a sudden shift. In this connection, the events revealed by excavation at Trianda on Rhodes are instructive. A group of Minoan settlers seems to have arrived about 1600, followed by Mycenaeans perhaps a century later. For several generations the two groups apparently lived side by side quite peacefully, but about 1400 the Minoan settlement was hurriedly abandoned and the inference is that the agents were their Mycenaean neighbors.

This may be as good a point as any to review current theories about the political situation in Crete itself during the sixteenth and fifteenth centuries. We have noted the recent tendency to speak simply of an early and late palace period, separated by a longer or shorter cultural "trough" somewhere between 1700 and 1600. If a possible explanation for the contents of the Mycenae Shaft Graves (and also for the destruction of the early Minoan palaces) is a series of mainland raids, the increasingly strong Minoan cultural influence on the mainland in the following century might fall into place as support for Alsop's principle that less cultured military conquerors (the mainlanders) will inevitably adopt the customs of their more highly civilized subjects (the Minoans). The same evidence, then, *can* be interpreted in exactly the opposite sense to Evans' assumptions, which were so natural a result of the nineteenth-century A.D. colonial situation. The scarcity of proof of reverse influence (*i.e.,* mainland influence on Crete) for several generations would in a sense be a natural corollary and scarcely rules out actual political control by mainlanders of rebuilt Minoan centers.

But it would be rash to push such a theory very hard at present. There are surely more credible possibilities intermediate between the extremes. Successful mainland raids may have been followed by a shorter or longer period in which the Minoan way of life continued to develop wholly or largely independent of mainland political control. The first forcible contacts may have included the abduction of Minoan artists and artisans, or the products of their skill brought back by the raiders to the mainland may have created such a demand in Mycenaean courts that Minoan artisans and/or their products continued to be attracted to the mainland.

Recurring theories of devastating earthquakes on Crete itself suggest possibilities for new local political alignments as well as a tempting target for outsiders to take advantage of the temporary vacuum caused by shock and paralysis. Marinatos has been the leading follower of Evans in seeking to explain destruction layers by such natural phenomena. Most recently he is reported to be seeking to link his theories with a closer geological dating of tremendous volcanic disturbances on the island of Thera (Santorin). He suggests (according to the press) that the greatest eruption, which may have taken place about mid-fifteenth century or a little earlier, caused heavy destruction and loss of life on Crete and temporarily ruined the Minoan economy. If so, this would have made Crete an easy target for large-scale raiding from the mainland, and it might have been the time when the Greeks first took over political control. The Minoan activity in the Aegean during the sixteenth and earlier fifteenth century could have been with the permission of our hypothetical Mycenaean pirates; or (more likely) it could indicate that Mycenaean sea power, though sufficient for a quick strike, did not yet have the resources to seriously interfere.

As we have seen, Minoan commerce seems to have been giving way to mainland dynamism throughout the early Mycenaean period. The gradualness (if it is a fact) does not prove that the transition was relatively peaceful. Rather, this impression (not subscribed to by all scholars) is produced by a general observation that the Minoans were essentially an unwarlike, and the Mycenaeans a warlike people. In that case, mutual self-interest may have dictated restraint and accommodation, with the self-interest of the stronger party increasingly asserted as it adopted and adapted the more sophisticated culture traits of its teacher. Some such transitional situation is at least not inconsistent with the archaeological evidence so far available.

But again the tradition of a Minoan thalassocracy must be reckoned with. One can suggest two general theories that might account for a historical basis that modern consensus still seeks in these stories. Either a true Minoan power was really centered at Knossos (as Evans thought he had proved) or some non-Minoan dynasty that occupied Knossos succeeded in attributing its ambitious acts to a legitimate Minoan power.

Some scholars still believe that the former is more likely. For example, Dr. Stubbings takes it for granted that the Theseus legend proves that Athens was at one time under a genuine Minoan political yoke. He and those who support his position must now conclude, however, that the Minoan thalassocracy antedated the Achaean control of Knossos that is proved by the Linear B tablets; that is, it has to date before the mid-fifteenth century (unless they accept Palmer's extremely low dating of the Knossos tablets). If they are right, we would probably have to abandon any theory of serious mainland challenge to Minoan power in the sixteenth century, and the proposed explanation of the contents of the Shaft Graves as booty from raids on Crete by mainlanders would be quite unlikely.

If, on the other hand, we explore the alternative explanation, the likeliest line of argumentation will be that a group of Achaean-speaking mainlanders, with a veneer of Minoan culture already acquired through sporadic contact, took over actual control at Knossos some time in the later sixteenth or earlier fifteenth century. It is too soon to speculate as to whether a new discovery at Arkhanes, very close to Knossos, might have any bearing on the political situation. A sixteenth-century building, possibly a palace, is reported to have been "larger and finer" than the contemporary palace at Knossos.

Several authorities are now insisting that there need be no striking archaeological "break" to mark this occupation. The intrusive mainland culture traits that Wace first pointed out at Knossos in Evans' LMII period (beginning perhaps before the mid-fifteenth century) still represent in the "orthodox" view the earliest time for such a take-over. But it is possible that they are simply signs of a later intensification of mainland control.

Whenever the mainlanders first seized power, the process outlined by Alsop whereby a conquering minority on a lower cultural plane adjusts to controlling a more sophisticated people would have gone into effect. The previous Minoan dynasty at Knossos may already have been exacting taxes from much of that fertile and prosperous island, and the new Achaean Minos may have taken over the whole area intact or regained it with a minimum of violence. So far, he and his fellow adventurers would have been acting as we have reason to believe similar bands of Achaeans were (or soon would be) in other areas, particularly among the southeast Aegean islands.

No immediate jealousy or friction with other Achaean powers need have developed. But this particular group succeeded to no ordinary situation. They inherited a well-developed, highly organized administrative system, and it would have been very much in their own interest to preserve and even extend it. Indeed, it is as certain as any conclusion can be in Mycenaean-Minoan relations that, at whatever time Achaeans took over control at Knossos, they did so with minimum violence and destruction and that they appropriated and perpetuated the local system. The Linear B tablets make it perfectly clear that they eventually levied taxes on most of Crete, though it is at present impossible to be sure how far back this situation goes.

Alsop contends that the new Achaean-speaking rulers would be likely to adopt the current language ("Minoan") and script (Linear A) as well as most other features of the sophisticated Minoan culture. He is surely right in believing that there is no compelling reason to assume (as nearly everyone has) that Greek-speaking conquerors would immediately decree that hundreds of Minoan clerks must learn Greek, construct a new syllabary to write it and henceforth conduct the delicate and complicated administrative machinery in a new language. Even if it were possible, such a sudden and major change would have thrown the whole system out of gear for years and caused economic chaos and serious financial loss. It would have been infinitely simpler for the rulers to learn the Minoan language (if they did not already know it) or to supervise the bureaucracy they inherited through trusted interpreters.

At whatever time it turns out that Achaeans took over at Knossos, Alsop's reasoning is valid. The archaeological record is clear enough that Crete prospered remarkably for two centuries or so after 1600. Although Evans' insistence that there is no evidence of foreign cultural intrusions during this period must now be modified, it is still true that mainland culture seems to have had very little effect on Crete until about the mid-fifteenth century.

If the first occupation happened considerably earlier, the material evidence of mainland influence in the later fifteenth century might logically be interpreted as evidence for an intensification of mainland control, possibly by a new Achaean dynasty (as Starr suggests) that replaced more or less Minoized predecessors. They would have brought with them the new and larger garrison that is reflected in some of the Linear B tablets, by the so-called Warrior Graves and other archaeological evidence. If the review of Minoan chronology that is now under way confirms the view that the widespread destruction of Cretan palaces at the end of Evans' LMIb preceded the "final" LMII phase at Knossos, this situation might be connected with the militaristic tone of LMII Knossos. The importation of fairly numerous mainland troops might represent either a reaction to a serious Cretan revolt that had broken out against previously established

Achaean rulers or else the military strength supporting the first formal occupation.

If the latter proves to be correct, it would be possible to connect it (as Marinatos, Platon and Alsop have suggested) with the previously mentioned volcanic convulsion on Thera (Santorin) about the mid-fifteenth century. Earthquakes and tidal waves may have destroyed or seriously damaged *all* of the Cretan palaces and many of the smaller settlements, as well as the Minoan "navy." Mycenaean adventurers may then have moved in on the defenseless and demoralized survivors, repaired the palace at Knossos and used it as their base to control (or perpetuate Knossian control of) the rest of the island. In that case, it might have been necessary to bring along their own scribes (assuming they already used Linear B) and to rebuild the ruined administrative system. Under such circumstances, they could quite reasonably have decided to use from the start the language and script familiar to them.

In any case, we have to reckon with the fact that Achaean Greek is the basic language of the Knossos Linear B tablets and that Greek was therefore the official language in which the administrative machinery was conducted by the time of the "final" destruction of the palace. The question is when and how and why this significant change took place. The answer depends in part on our reconstruction of the growth of the Near Eastern type of bureaucratic administrative system in Crete and mainland Greece. The earlier Linear A tablets found at several Cretan sites indicate that Minoan power centers adopted the bureaucratic system before there is any chance of mainland intrusion. Did mainland centers in turn adopt the system from Crete or directly from the Near East?

Since literacy is an integral and necessary part of such a complicated organization, the likelihood is overwhelming that the source imitated on the mainland was Crete—simply because Linear B is clearly an adaptation of Minoan Linear A for writing Greek. This invention in turn required close contact between at least one mainland and one Minoan power center. The most natural opportunity (though there are other possibilities) seems to be that outlined above of an Achaean dynasty occupying Knossos but operating through a system where "Minoan" continued to be spoken and written in Linear A. Then, a mainland king (perhaps the former sovereign of the group of Achaeans who first seized Knossos) would have sooner or later realized the immense economic advantages of organizing his own kingdom under such a system. Again, as Alsop insists, the mainland kingdom is likely to have adopted the complicated Minoan bureaucratic machinery (so far as feasible) as a whole and within a very short time, rather than gradually and piecemeal. For the mainland kingdom there would, of course, be no question of taking over the Minoan language. A system of writing Greek would have to be devised, and one or more Minoan clerks—presumably already bilingual—would have been imported for the task.

It is, indeed, quite likely that Linear B was invented at some mainland center and was used there—and later at other mainland capitals—before it migrated to Knossos at some time before the "final" destruction of the palace. The occasion might well have been the more intensive Achaean control that may have occurred around the middle of the fifteenth century. The easiest explanation of the shift in language (and script) is that a whole corps of scribes trained on the mainland was imported at one time. Even then the problems of coping with Minoan scribes and taxpayers must have been formidable.

It is of course possible that for some reason (obscure to us but sufficiently compelling at the time) the switch was made to Linear B at Knossos only a few years before the surviving tablets were inscribed. This possibility, coupled with the revised date (to be discussed later) for the "final" destruction, would allow us to lower by as much as a century the absolute dates in the timetable suggested above. And it is indeed rather unsettling (but by no means impossible) to envisage records being kept in Linear B at mainland centers before 1450.

Incidentally, literacy probably remained very largely a monopoly of palace scribes. It is at least as likely that the kings themselves could not read and write as that this rather abstruse accomplishment was a "status symbol" of the upper class. Written texts were probably in the main economic, although we have a fair number of what are almost certainly religious dedications in Linear A. Near Eastern models of writing used for much wider purposes must have been known, however, and a broader application of literacy cannot be excluded.

To return to the Greek mainland, the evidence for the early Mycenaean age already hints at most of the interests and potentialities and ambitions that were increasingly fulfilled in the "empire" period of the fourteenth and thirteenth centuries. Local monarchs seem to have had almost unlimited autocratic (and probably theocratic) power over a docile, industrious and skillful proletariat. Perhaps individual clans already occupied small villages, and several of the separate villages in turn clustered close to the king's citadel. Such complex groupings may be reflected in the feminine plural case ending *ai* (which we often replace with our plural in -s) in names of prominent power centers like Mycen*ae,* Thebe*s* and Athen*s*.

The burial practices, some of them carried over from MH times into the Shaft Grave period and beyond, strongly suggest that mainland religion remained essentially distinct from Minoan. No doubt Cretan beliefs did have some impact, particularly among the rulers. For example, the later Greek idea of Elysium or the Isles of the Blessed, where Rhadamanthys, brother of Minos, reigns, was in all likelihood borrowed from Crete in prehistoric times. But there is very little proof that a given cult object imported from Crete had anything beyond artistic and intrinsic value for its mainland possessor. Nilsson's broad distinctions in this field still seem valid.

The kings must have shared with a small and privileged warrior class a ruthless, restless and ambitious temperament. They got their greatest satisfaction in pitting their strength and skill against leaders of other kingdoms (and probably foreigners to an increasing extent) or against powerful beasts such as wild boar and lions. At least a few of the latter may still have existed in the wild state in central and southern Greece, as they still did (we are told) in northern Greece in the following millennium. Perhaps others were imported for the dangerous sport. At any rate, it need not be taken for granted that the favorite art representations of lions and lion hunts were simply stock motifs borrowed from Syria or some such exotic environment.

Like their counterparts in the Near East, the kings of early Mycenaean times were very proud of their horses and chariots. They may perhaps have regarded them more as symbols of wealth and power than as effective means of warfare; but there are hints that, although the ground is generally less favorable than in the Near East, battles of massed chariotry may have preceded the stage remembered in the Homeric poems. There, of course, the chariot is a vehicle for travel and for transportation to and from the battle. It is as yet unclear whether highways for wide-ranging travel by chariot had been built before the fourteenth century.

Like their successors of the "empire" period, these kings were violently acquisitive of precious possessions and interested in them as objects of beauty and fine craftsmanship as well as for their intrinsic and prestige value. They mustered large labor forces and skilled architects to build monumental tombs that would one day house their families and their possessions. They enjoyed good food and no doubt liked best of all to hear the court bard sing of their own adventures and military exploits as well as those of their peers, living and dead.

In fact, the Age of Heroes in Greece can properly be said to extend back as far as 1600. It seems initially to have had more in common with Piggott's "High Barbarian Europe" than with the sophisticated societies of Crete and the Near East to which Greece turned increasingly in the succeeding "empire" period. The extent and nature of the Minoan role as intermediary and civilizer is under intensive reconsideration, and something akin to Evans' position still has supporters. Yet the tide of opinion seems to be turning. Although Evans would have regarded it as the ultimate heresy and although—like most generalizations—it represents a drastic oversimplification of Minoan-Mycenaean relations, there is probably a strong element of truth in Furumark's assertion that "the insular civilization of Crete was only a picturesque episode, and its lasting contribution to European history is that it wakened Greece from its prehistoric slumber and brought it into contact with the civilizations of the Ancient East."

## THE LATER MYCENAEANS
## (ABOUT 1400–1200)

A date around 1400, which Evans and Mackenzie fixed for the "final" destruction of the Knossos palace, still serves as a kind of marker between the early and mature Mycenaean phases. In spite of Evans' vehement denials, most scholars in the past generation identified that destruction with a successful mainland revolt from Cretan political control. And they rather naturally inferred that a sudden upsurge in mainland fortunes, comparable to that of the Shaft Grave period, would have occurred almost immediately after 1400. In spite of recent developments, there are still authorities who seem to have scarcely revised that view. Yet, if we accept Evans' chronology, the Knossos Linear B tablets show that Achaean-speaking mainlanders were masters of most of Crete well before this so-called turning point. In fact, Greek speakers may have controlled Knossos when the men of "Keftiu" are shown presenting gifts or tribute in fifteenth-century tombs like those of Senmut and Rekmire in Egyptian Thebes.

On the mainland itself, there do not seem to have been any very obvious revolutionary developments that would associate the end of the fifteenth century with significant political, economic or social changes like those of the Shaft Grave era. The earlier pottery styles merge gradually into the so-called Late Helladic III, with increasing mainland independence from Cretan models. Before the end of the fourteenth century (and very probably several generations before), records in Linear B began to be kept at the mainland palaces. This proves that the political, economic and social system was moving toward the centralization long known in the Near East and presumably also in Crete. The population was growing rapidly. Foreign trade was becoming more intensive. There is increasing evidence for monumental tholos tombs, and the smaller kingdoms of early Mycenaean days were being absorbed into larger units.

We might remind ourselves at this point, however, of the pitfalls of the "break" fallacy. Political and linguistic and even racial changes of major proportions need leave no clear imprint on the archaeological record, particularly if the intruders constitute a minority at a lower cultural level than the established population. Archaeological evidence can hardly be expected to confirm or refute recurring hypotheses about new rulers in mainland centers in the fourteenth century. Professor John L. Myres long ago called attention to an intriguing fact about the "short pedigrees" of most Homeric heroes. Their beloved genealogies are usually traced back through three human generations before the family claims divine ancestry. Myres' explanation is that these families were newcomers to Greece who had seized political control only a century or so before the Trojan War.

According to such eminent authorities as Blegen and Arnold Gomme, we cannot at present dismiss the possibility that something of the sort happened. The new ruling aristocracy might have been composed of native families who seized control from older local dynasties, though it would be rather odd if the same phenomenon was repeated in so many power centers. It is somewhat more believable that a single group of determined and ambitious militarists, either originating abroad, as Nilsson thought, or from one mainland center such as Mycenae, took over control of other Mycenaean kingdoms. New and vigorous ruling dynasties *might* be relevant —but are surely not required—to explain various phenomena such as the rather sudden appearance (as far as we can now see) of splendid Mycenaean palaces and massive fortifications and bureaucratic government with its elaborate record-keeping. But their beginning—like major political changes of the type recorded about Neleus' migration to Pylos—is perhaps closer to the end than to the beginning of the fourteenth century.

In the Homeric account, the king of Mycenae has a certain primacy in relation to other Achaean kings. If this situation represents an authentic memory, it might still be explained in terms of the necessities of a specific military campaign, rather than the normal political system. Yet the archaeological record, ever since Schliemann's day, has continued to suggest that no other power center in the Greek orbit equaled Mycenae. Possibly at some point a measure of political consolidation under the strongest king was considered necessary to meet the threat of external pressure; or Mycenae may have had the power to impose her will on others. Professor Palmer has suggested that Mycenae disposed of both Knossos and Thebes (presumably in separate campaigns) in a kind of "Greek War of the Roses." Agamemnon's insistence on his special divinely appointed status may echo a kind of theocratic pyramid that placed the king of Mycenae above the rulers of lesser kingdoms. Such an interkingdom chain of command might have had analogies with the complicated intrakingdom system implicit in the Pylos tablets. For instance, it has been suggested that Agamemnon and Menelaos are represented in the *Iliad* in a relationship somewhat akin to *wanax* versus *lawagetas*.

V. R. d'A. Desborough, to whose authority we shall be appealing in other connections, maintains that only in terms of an over-all unified political structure can one explain the remarkable phenomenon of the Mycenaean cultural koinê; and he believes that Mycenae was the center from which the pottery styles of the fourteenth and thirteenth centuries were diffused to the rest of the Mycenaean world. Blegen, on the other hand, thinks it unlikely that any unified political structure existed as early as the fourteenth century.

There are other Homeric hints of a unified power that seem to make better sense for late Mycenaean times than for the early Iron Age. For example, Agamemnon offers Achilles seven "cities" located on the Gulf of Messenia, which is far removed from the area assigned to the kingdom of Mycenae.[98] Relatively easy and rapid communications between the kingdoms, so essential for any unified control, are taken for granted. Of course, sea routes connected most capitals, which were usually on or near the coast. But, especially when navigation was closed by winter storms, supplementary land routes would have been necessary. And there is increasing archaeological evidence of an ambitious system of carefully built highways for wheeled traffic within (and probably between) major Mycenaean political units. It is interesting to reflect that land communications in Greece were probably better in the thirteenth century B.C. than at any time before or afterward until the late nineteenth century A.D.

With our present knowledge, we can only note the remarkable cultural uniformity and admit that some measure of over-all political control may have existed. The massive fortifications in the thirteenth century, the warlike Mycenaean temperament and the tradition of interkingdom struggles suggest that any structure of superpower would have been uneasy and precarious; but such considerations also reinforce the likelihood that a single powerful king would have aspired to over-all control. Furthermore, there is no way to estimate the effectiveness of religious sanctions. Near Eastern analogies may apply here as closely as in the economic sphere. The lack of any convincing evidence for a united defense in the final "time of troubles" is not a very strong negative argument. An overarching political control might very well have broken down in or before that emergency.

There is one additional argument often made in support of a unified Mycenaean power, but it is an extremely slippery one. Hittite records of the fourteenth and thirteenth century mention a kingdom called Ahhijawā (or occasionally Ahhiyā). The kings of Hatti and Ahhijawā exchange gifts; the king of Ahhijawā is listed (but later erased) in the same context as the kings of Egypt, Babylon and Assyria; the god of Ahhijawā is summoned to cure a Hittite king; a Hittite exile is sent to Ahhijawā; the two royal families were intimate enough that Ahhijawans were sent to Hatti to learn chariot driving. In particular, the two kingdoms carry on negotiations, which gradually become less friendly, concerning a town (or country) called Millawanda (or Milawatas). Millawanda seems to be more or less under the political control of Ahhijawā and to have been located on the Anatolian coast. Most authorities now believe that the name represents Miletos, which in this period was a fortified settlement in which the pottery indicates that a good many Mycenaeans were living and that it might have been a Mycenaean "colony."

There is much less certainty, however, on a second proposed equation, which would identify Ahhijawā with Achaea. Ahhijawā (unlike Hatti) was clearly a sea power, and it remains to be seen whether there is room for such a powerful independent kingdom somewhere in southwest Anatolia. Apart from its location, there are serious but perhaps not insurmountable philological difficulties in equating the two names. Hittite specialists like Professors Hans Güterbock and R. O. Gurney at present regard the problem as unsolved, while Greek prehistorians are more inclined to accept the equation.

If for the sake of argument, however, we assume that the Hittite documents do refer to a Greek kingdom of Achaea, where was it located? One thinks first of the Greek mainland and the most likely capital at Mycenae. But hints in the documents are thought by some to fit better with an island (or islands) nearer Anatolia in the southeast Aegean. Professor Denys Page has made a persuasive case for Rhodes. Cyprus seems to be excluded because it was called Alasiya by the Hittites. Professor Gurney suggests that a Greek Minos installed at Knossos in Crete is another possibility, although this would require us to accept the thesis of Palmer (backed by Homeric tradition) that a powerful Greek dynasty occupied Knossos long after 1400. It is clearly too soon to base any theory of a unified Mycenaean kingdom of Achaea on the fascinating but elusive Hittite evidence.

Speaking generally now of developments in the "empire" period, expanding trade and better utilization of the land must have broadened the distribution of wealth to a limited number of royal clients. But Professor Vermeule is probably stretching the evidence in suggesting that "new merchant and professional classes" were emerging as a kind of bourgeoisie between "the gold-guarding aristocracy and the anonymous peasantry." Substantial houses within and outside the citadels, numerous chamber tombs and the complicated officialdom revealed by the tablets can be cited to support this point of view. Yet, other hints indicate that caution is in order. Mycenaean kings seem never to have developed any notable tendency to share the wealth, except in the special status-seeking sense of gift giving among themselves. In fact, Professor Dow theorizes that the rise of the great fortified citadels is probably to be interpreted as proof of increasing interkingdom competition and desire to safeguard royal possessions. The evidence for bigger kingdoms and more elaborate royal tombs points in the same direction. It was surely for good reason that the tholos tombs were called treasuries at least as early as Pausanias' day.

Taken over-all, the tightly bureaucratic palace organization of the Linear B records suggests an overwhelming concentration of wealth in a few hands. It was a "superplanned" economy, and the surplus must have accrued overwhelmingly to the *wanax*. The tablets, of course, show that each kingdom had a large number of important officials who made up the pyramid of command with the *wanax* at its apex. It is granted, too, that as the Mycenaean kingdoms increased in size, many formerly independent dynasties seem to have been allowed to continue use of the local tholos tombs and perhaps to perpetuate some measure of local power. Yet the total effect may have been to concentrate rather than distribute the rapidly increasing wealth. A king of fourteenth- or thirteenth-century Mycenae must have been richer than any monarch of the Shaft Grave period. Agamemnon's enumeration of the gifts he offers to salve Achilles' wounded pride and Achilles' disdainful reply that he has plenty of the same at home[99] may reflect the substantial resources at the disposal of a ruler of the first rank. The financial stakes must have crept higher and higher as raiding and trading ventures grew in scope. The increasing monumentality of tombs, fortifications, palaces and highways suggests a continually tightening centralized control of labor and financial resources.

There is no compelling reason, on the other hand, to believe that Mycenaean "merchants" were anything but servants or slaves. The profits from their ventures probably accrued for the most part to the royal treasury, as was the case with foreign trade in the Near Eastern kingdoms. The so-called House of the Oil Merchant and large nearby buildings excavated by Wace and Verdelis just west of Grave Circle B at Mycenae are now regarded by most authorities as annexes for palace-controlled industries.

This is not to deny that a modicum of the increasing affluence filtered down to high officials and perhaps to merchant entrepreneurs and even to the free peasantry. There was certainly a good deal of wealth among the royal relatives and other "courtiers." The Homeric picture suggests that an important distinction could be drawn between a small group wealthy enough to afford horses, chariots and all the expensive paraphernalia of offensive and defensive bronze armament versus the nameless camp followers who rowed the ships, cooked the meals and tended to the warriors' wants. The same impression is gained from the relatively pretentious homes crowded close around the palaces at Mycenae and Knossos. It would be interesting to know whether the "counts" of the Pylos tablets owned their own horses and chariots or were supplied from royal stables. The second alternative is perhaps suggested by the Knossos chariot tablets.

It is, however, the chamber tombs in the environs of many Mycenaean settlements that constitute the major argument for a certain leveling of economic distinctions in the later Mycenaean period. But how sure are we that commoners or even middle-class merchants were buried in them? Elaborate chamber tombs may indeed have taken the place of royal tholoi, as is suggested by the apparent cessation of tholoi at some sites considerably before the final destruction. Like the tholoi, the chamber tombs contained multiple burials, probably of a single family over one or more generations. Their number is probably not excessive for the use of a relatively small class of nobles with considerable wealth. Certainly, there are not enough known, even at Mycenae or Prosymna, to accommodate a fraction of the free peasant population which must have lived in the vicinity. In spite of the assumption by Blegen and others that the chamber tombs belonged to ordinary citizens, we do not really know whether a peasant family or group of families could have afforded or would have been allowed such ostentation in the era of strict social stratification before 1200.

It is difficult to assess the social status of the soldiers who were buried in the later Knossos cemeteries or depicted on the Warrior Vase. They scarcely give the impression of army privates. Perhaps in later years, as danger became more imminent, the professional warrior class was considerably extended and its prestige increased. Some of the tablets from Knossos and Pylos seem to support such an assumption. They would have at least as good a claim as merchants to some sort of intermediate social status.

The fourteenth and thirteenth centuries mark the high point of Mycenaean prosperity. Increasing population as well as commercial ventures abroad apparently encouraged a good deal of emigration. We recall the settlements at Trianda (Rhodes) and Miletos. Mycenaean "colonies" or trading stations were established in other islands of the southeast Aegean, particularly Kos and Cyprus. Some were perhaps carved out and held by force. Others must have been "free ports" maintained in foreign territory by the sufferance and at the convenience of the local ruling powers. At Tell Atchana (Alalakh), Ras Shamra (Ugarit) and Byblos in Syria and at Gezer and Lachish in Palestine, Mycenaean merchants seem to have formed part of a varied foreign population. Egyptian Thebes appears in the *Odyssey*[100] as the source from which Greek visitors might return loaded down with riches; but this situation, as Dorothea Gray points out, was possible only before the early fourteenth century. Every year reveals new deposits of Mycenaean pottery in areas as disparate as Halikarnassos, Jerusalem and Cyrene in north Africa.

Unless further analyses along the lines of Catling's alter the picture radically, it seems likely that at least a few of the colonies, especially on Rhodes and Cyprus, developed independent manufacturing. Their ceramic styles can probably be recognized as far off as Tarentum in southeast Italy. Kylixes and deep bowls are rare in the eastern centers; kraters with painted scenes (especially chariots), pilgrim flasks and shallow bowls are favorites.

In the northern Aegean, in addition to Troy, Mycenaean goods were reaching coastal spots in Macedonia and Thrace. The earlier trade in the west seems to have changed somewhat in pattern. Decreasing Mycenaean pottery on Lipari coincides with a decrease of amber in mainland tombs. One could view this as support for the theory that the Aeolian islands had been a major depot for the amber traffic in earlier centuries. It is also possible that copper from Cyprus had largely replaced imports from western sources. Large-scale geochemical analyses of bronze samples of known provenience and date should shed new light on this and related problems.

Mycenaean concentration now appears to shift to the Syracuse area of southeast Sicily and to the heel of Italy. It is becoming clear, too, that trade was developing between these Italian trading stations and the so-called Terramara* civilization in north-central Italy. Continued contact even farther west as late as the thirteenth century is proved by the discovery of several typical Mycenaean double axes of bronze in the British Isles. In terms of percentage of total trade, however, indications are that intensive late Mycenaean trade operations were increasingly concentrated in the east. Perhaps some of the "Sea People" (to be discussed later) were already a serious menace to shipping in the Adriatic and waters farther to the west.

The major products moving in trade over this relatively large area had probably not changed radically. Some of the important Mycenaean exports were perfumed olive oil, textiles, weapons, metal work, ceramics, wines. The slow-pouring stirrup jar was a favorite container for transporting liquids, and its fragments are prime evidence for Mycenaean trade penetration. Return products probably consisted chiefly of raw metal—copper, tin, gold, silver (the last apparently in small amounts since local supplies existed in the Aegean islands; the tholoi at Thorikos in east Attica hardly in themselves constitute evidence that the Laurion mines had already been tapped). But the Mycenaeans also imported dyes, spices, ebony, ivory, lapis lazuli and exotic manufactured products like textiles, fine wines, faience objects, ceramics, cylinder seals, bronze statuettes and carved ivory. Even the Greek words for some of these commodities were borrowed from the Near East.

Vermeule and others have suggested that food staples, particularly grain, may have formed a major import, just as sections of mainland Greece and the islands in later times depended heavily on the Black Sea region, Egypt and Cyrenaica. This may be a somewhat premature conjecture until we learn far more about population density, agricultural methods and land use (*i.e.*, local consumption and production). Yet it might help to explain Mycenaean interest in east Sicily and southeast Italy, the Magna Graecia of classical times.

It can probably be taken for granted that most of these goods were carried in Mycenaean ships. Native Cretan traders were certainly no longer serious rivals. The documents suggest that the territory under Hittite control (except Ugarit) could not muster a fleet. Egyptian ships seem not to have ventured too far north and west. The range and intensity of Phoenician commerce portrayed in the *Odyssey* was mainly a post-Bronze Age development. Yet the swarms of ships manned by "Sea People" that attacked wealthy coastal centers of the Near East in the later thirteenth century warn us that it is quite unsafe to assume that the east Mediterranean was largely or wholly under Mycenaean control. It is surely going to the opposite extreme, however, to deny that the Mycenaeans engaged in fairly aggressive commercial expansion and that confrontations must have occurred on the sea as well as on land. Starr's idea that the nearest the Mycenaeans had to warships were little craft propelled by ten oars is derived from a literal interpretation of the scrappy representations in art. The Pylos tablets suggest that they had considerably larger ships that could be used for military missions.

Direct trade contact with the Near East as well as indirect influence via Crete is indicated by a good many of the favorite motifs in Mycenaean art. Hybrid animals were particularly popular and would have been seen on imported textiles, seals and worked ivory and metal ware. The griffin, a combination of lion and eagle—that is, uniting the qualities of the king of birds and the king of beasts—guarded the thrones at Pylos and Knossos and appears on royal seals. His lofty crest is a Syrian motif. The sphinx, a combination of lioness and human, begins her long popularity in Greek art. The unique bronze ax from the Vaphio tholos, which Tsountas compared to those that Odysseus set up for the archery contest, is an import from Syria. Antithetic or heraldic composition, as in the Lion Gate, is originally from Near Eastern sources. Reverse influences, as in the "flying gallop" animal motif, seem to be considerably rarer, but Mycenaean carved ivories were imported and copied in Syria.

We have already referred to the Mycenaean koinê (common or shared culture), which is increasingly noticeable as the fourteenth yields to the thirteenth century. Manufacturing processes and artistic styles were becoming stereotyped, and popular items tended to be mass produced to supply widening markets. It is almost impossible by applying the usual stylistic criteria to distinguish between contemporary material remains from widely separated kingdoms, although the new geochemical analyses offer promise here. Not only were the products of artists and armorers and jewelers and potters and architects and scribes closely similar, but there is reason to believe that the koinê extended to practically every nonmaterial cultural characteristic. Undoubtedly, dialectal differences existed in Achaean Greek, and there may have been enclaves or even social levels where Greek was not the first language. But, as far as the written record has been recovered and can be understood, the language as well as the script of the courts shows remarkable similarity. If the early dating for the Knossos tablets is sustained, we shall have evidence for notable conservatism too.

Political, social, religious and economic institutions were apparently very much alike. Travel by sea and land between independent kingdoms was relatively easy and frequent. Interdynastic marriages and alliances (as well as feuds) were routine. Alsop's assumption that "there must of course have been wide variations among the late Bronze Age Greek kingdoms" has so far extremely little basis in fact. Individual kingdoms may well have had industrial or agricultural specialties, as is suggested by the great quantities of pottery at Pylos and the huge flocks of sheep recorded in the Knossos tablets, but we cannot yet distinguish with much assurance.

It is at least as difficult to establish valid regional distinctions in the categories of major art as it is to see qualitative differences in contemporary ceramic products of the various kingdoms. While potters were presumably local, it is perfectly possible that architects and painters and sculptors (the latter were mainly miniaturists working in ivory and cutting gems) may have moved freely from one kingdom to another. The questions are compounded when we try to envisage the situation in peripheral areas, such as Crete under mainland control. The problem of how its long-established tradition in the major arts adjusted to the new political realities needs close study. Although the material in most categories is less in bulk than one could wish, there is a promising field for the kind of synthesis that Furumark achieved in ceramics and that V. Kenna is approaching in glyptic* art.

In spite of a shared culture at home and opportunities abroad, the Mycenaean kingdoms seem to have intensified efforts to expand their own territory or sphere of influence on the mainland, even if this involved challenging a major adversary. There must have been almost continuous internal and external wars and alarms. One can only wonder how anyone could characterize the late Mycenaean period "until well into the thirteenth century" as "a period . . . of peace." In fact, the record of massive fortifications (at least in the thirteenth century) and the obvious emphasis on warfare, as well as the traditions of dynastic intrigues, royal exiles, domestic and interkingdom wars and rumors of wars amply prove that differing political and social philosophies are not needed to produce instability.

One must reckon with tensions fanned by royal ambition and a tradition of violence even in the midst of prosperity and common values. It is in this milieu that we can place Neleus' long voyage from Thessaly to Pylos to establish a new power center there, or the legendary attacks on Kalydon and Thebes, or the grisly rivalry between Atreus and Thyestes at Mycenae. The same restless and aggressive attitude, perhaps linked to some extent with economic motives, would explain both the Achaean occupation of Knossos and the Achaean attack on Troy. The former was surely a more significant event in Mycenaean history, yet the irony of time and selective human memory decreed that it should be forgotten while the Tale of Troy became the earliest great political and military event to permeate the history of the West.

## THE DATE OF THE KNOSSOS TABLETS

We have discussed earlier the uncertainties that cloud the capture of Knossos by Achaeans from the mainland. That problem, however, is not nearly as controversial as another concerning Knossos: What is the destruction date for the phase of the palace to which the surviving Linear B tablets belong? We have already seen how Blegen questioned the basis for Evans' date of about 1400 and we have been warned of the furor that followed. Now we can no longer avoid making an attempt to explain the very complicated issues involved. As Professor Henri van Effenterre has recently written in his impeccable Gallic way: "*Pauvre* Evans! Firmly but courteously attacked by the Italian School for his observations on the 'Early Minoan,' he is being taken to task by some of his compatriots, and in a more severe tone, for his presentation of the 'Late Minoan.' "

At the risk of oversimplifying, one might say that there are now three proposed dating brackets for the Knossos tablets. Evans' own final position is still perhaps the most widely supported—that is, the tablets belong to the "last palace," which was burned about 1400, although at least part of the site was later reoccupied by "miserable squatters" who were presumably illiterate. At the other extreme, Professor Palmer insists that the tablets belong to the reoccupation era, that the site was then occupied by the palace of a Mycenaean king (Idomeneus) and his descendants and th this palace was destroyed at least as late as its counterparts on the mainland, probably around 1150. A compromise position remains much closer to Evans, but its supporters in turn seem to be divided on the reality of the reoccupation period.

M. R. Popham (1966) concedes that some of the pottery associated with Evans' "last palace" should be dated as much as twenty-five years after 1400. Sinclair Hood, on the other hand, believes (1965) that the reoccupation period is a "mirage" and that the date of the destruction of the "last palace" and of the tablets must be reconciled with that of the latest pottery now usually assigned to the reoccupation period. He suggests that the pithoi and Palace Style vases were already heirlooms at the time of the destruction and that the painted stirrup vases and undecorated household pottery should date in the Amarna period, around the middle of the fourteenth century or a little later.

It is probably safe to say that the majority opinion (however arrived at) is gradually tending to date the "final" destruction and the tablets between 1370 and 1350. Assuming its correctness for the sake of the argument, how are we then to reconstruct events leading up to this catastrophe? The tablets prove that Achaeans were already in control of Knossos and that most of Crete was administered from there. The archaeological evidence, too, shows considerable penetration of mainland culture traits in the Knossos area before the destruction. The large garrison was equipped with weapons and armor of mainland type. Many personal names in the tablets are Greek. The "civil servants" certainly spoke and wrote Greek, and it is not impossible that many or most originated on the mainland. There is not a single hint in the Knossos tablets that danger threatened at home or abroad. The attack must have been sudden and was presumably unexpected since Achaeans were familiar with fortifications and certainly had the necessary labor at their command. Accidental destruction would seem to be excluded if Hood is right that there was no "reoccupation."

How can we best explain such an enigmatic set of circumstances? Professor Dow theorized that Minoan resistance to Achaean control in those days proved as desperate as the modern Cretan reaction to Turkish and (most recently) to German occupation. He suggested that in utter exasperation the Achaean forces themselves put the torch to Knossos and other Minoan centers and left the rebellious islanders to their own devices. But this is surely as desperate an explanation as the supposed plight of the occupation forces. Would those in control, no matter how harassed, voluntarily give up the ample income that the tablets prove was being collected in the very year of the destruction? And, as mentioned above, the picture we have rightly or wrongly formed of the Bronze Age Cretans suggests that last-ditch resistance was hardly their forte. If it was, Professor A. Severyns' theory (1960) of a massive native rebellion and capture of the capital held by the hated interlopers would be a more likely explanation. But in either case, why is there no hint in the tablets and why was there not an almost immediate rebuilding of Knossos under a restored Minoan king?

It seems somewhat more likely that the fate of Knossos is to be attributed to the same general cause as is reflected in the legends about Troy and Thebes and Kalydon. If there is anything we know of the Mycenaeans from myth and archaeology, it is that they were restless, aggressive, thin-skinned, acquisitive. There can be no doubt that at least one group had occupied Knossos earlier. The tablets tell the story of how rich a prize they seized. It is altogether believable that another group or a coalition (as in the case of Troy) should have decided to pillage this rich center, even though it was controlled by their own kinsmen. As at Troy and apparently at Thebes, they may have planned simply to destroy and not to supplant. Whether they had a deeper economic motive than pillage is not clear. Possibly the Knossian Achaeans posed a threat or impediment to the conquerors' trade routes or to a planned manufacturing monopoly or source of raw materials, but it is at least as likely that the motive was high-level piracy perhaps coupled with some personal or dynastic feud.

The known facts might even be manipulated to conform to the Minoan thalassocracy and the Theseus legend, although the following reconstruction seems more consistent with the situation in the fifteenth than the fourteenth century. Might the Achaean dynasts at Knossos have seized control of one or more vulnerable areas outside of Crete? Unfortunately for our theory, very few, if any, non-Cretan place-names have been authenticated in the Knossos tablets. But after all, there is the tradition of the expedition against Sicily that Professor Huxley believes was led by an Achaean Minos. Could an Achaean Minos have for a short time exacted tribute from Athens? If so, might Athens have taken the lead in organizing an expedition from the mainland to rid the Aegean once and for all of the oppressors?

Whatever the provocation, if the "final" destruction at Knossos took place in the first half of the fourteenth century, the attackers are likely to have been Achaean kinsmen of those who already controlled most of Crete. Yet there are serious considerations that require us to think very carefully before we dismiss Professor Palmer's basic point. The "orthodox" view of the island's history during the remainder of the Bronze Age is curiously ambiguous and obscure. According to its proponents, Crete never became a fully fledged part of the later Mycenaean koinê. Desborough simply reflects standard opinion when he describes the Cretan situation in the last two centuries of the Bronze Age as a "period of stagnation." It is said that a good many important centers were destroyed and abandoned or seriously depopulated at about the same time as Knossos. Yet their places were taken by other towns that were perhaps smaller but apparently more numerous. The total population seems actually to have increased and to have spilled over into previously unoccupied territory, particularly in the very broken and mountainous western area.

The obvious prosperity of LMIII towns could have depended more on internal resources than on foreign trade, yet there are disquieting problems. What are we to make of tripods in the Pylos tablets that are said to be of Cretan workmanship? Or does the word simply mean of Cretan *type*? We recall Furumark's insistence on a renewal of Cretan influence on mainland ceramics toward the end of the Bronze Age. Again, Catling's analyses prove that some of the stirrup jars found in the palace at Thebes were made and identified with Linear B writing in eastern Crete; and there seems to be at least an even chance that their date is later than mid-fourteenth century. Also, if the muster roll in *Iliad* II can be trusted (and informed opinion increasingly supports its authenticity), Crete was one of the most prosperous areas of the Mycenaean orbit at or not too far from the time of the Trojan War. It is portrayed as having some kind of unified political organization under King Idomeneus of Knossos. Numerous passages in the Homeric poems offer additional testimony of Cretan wealth and importance. These passages would seem on their face to have as good a chance of representing authentic Mycenaean echoes as references to the mainland kingdoms.

Yet, if we have lost Evans' bugbear, the Knossos palace of the "reconstruction" period, where are we to look for Idomeneus' headquarters? The newly discovered palace at Arkhanes, about six miles inland from Knossos, holds interesting possibilities. Dr. Ioannis Sakellarakis claims that it will prove to have been fully comparable in size and elegance to those previously known. He dates it to the neopalatial period soon after 1600, but at least two nearby tholos tombs of mainland type may well be *after* 1400. This reinforces the growing suspicion that centralized power did not necessarily collapse at the end of the fifteenth century.

Evans' whole elaborate chronological edifice is now under review, and the judgments of Greek and Italian and French experts working at other important sites will have to be taken into stricter account. The neat equations of given ceramic styles with distinct chronological periods must be rechecked. Knossos itself may still hold some surprises, unless undisturbed evidence is gone beyond recall. Blegen continues to regard the Knossos and Pylos tablets as fairly closely contemporaneous. If it should turn out that there was a major reconstruction period or that the destruction date of the "last" palace can be put as late as 1300, Palmer's thesis that the agents were essentially the same as at Pylos and Mycenae might have to be considered seriously. There is no better reason for insisting on a historical kernel in the Theseus-Minotaur legend than in that of Herakles killing the Cretan bull. And we have Nestor's testimony that the descendants of Herakles were already probing Pylian defenses at least two generations before the Trojan War. If the attack on Pylos was a hit-and-run affair from the sea, could not the same marauders have attacked Knossos even earlier?

In any case, no reasonable scholar could quarrel with the judgment of Professor van Effenterre that "when a new synthesis of the history of the Minoan world is written, one can at least be sure that it will be quite different from those of Evans and Glotz." At present, in spite of Professor Palmer's announced mission to save the archaeologists from themselves, few seem willing to view seriously his thesis that "it was the Palace of Idomeneus and his descendants that Evans excavated in 1900."

The immediate task is to reach some consensus on the archaeological "facts" relating to Minoan Crete. This may require considerable time, but only then will it be safe to attempt a synthesis of what happened on Crete with our somewhat firmer grasp of what happened on the mainland.

## THE TROJAN WAR

Little need be added to the review in a previous chapter of the newest archaeological evidence on the historicity of the Trojan War. Very few authorities nowadays doubt that Schliemann correctly identified the site. There are, however, scattered skeptics who see no compelling reason to believe that the Greeks ever attacked and destroyed the fortress at Hissarlik. More are dissatisfied either with the date assigned by Blegen to Level VIIa or with its identification in preference to Level VI as the object of the siege. Gray, for instance, stresses the "curious accuracy" of the description of Troy in the *Iliad* and suggests that it is based on Mycenaean memory of the power and wealth of Troy VI conflated with its poorer successor.

On the whole, however, the Trojan episode is emerging as a remarkably satisfactory correlation of tradition and archaeological evidence. Such a venture, as we have seen, is completely in character with what is known of Mycenaean psychology and exploits around and beyond the Aegean. Nature's destruction of Troy VI and the obviously more vulnerable condition of Troy VIIa may have encouraged the Achaean attack. Troy seems to have had reasonably close and constant trade connections with the Achaeans during the final centuries of the Bronze Age.

It used to be taken for granted that Trojan prosperity was due to its strategic position controlling the water route between the Aegean and the Black Sea as well as the easiest land route between Asia and Europe. It was further believed that the Greeks finally acted to remove this impediment to their expanding trade. Professor Rhys Carpenter has argued, however, that the most direct north-south land route crossed the strait farther east and that heavily loaded merchant ships of the type used in the Late Bronze Age could not negotiate under sail the swift currents in the narrows of the Hellespont (Dardanelles) and particularly of the Bosporos. Light, fast craft with a strong crew of rowers might have managed it, he thinks, and perhaps the story of Jason and the Golden Fleece is an authentic echo of such a daring and dangerous enterprise.

Actually, if east-bound seaborne goods had to be transshipped near Troy, the old theory of exacting tolls on commerce would make more sense. But Carpenter's theory has been categorically denied and the lack of evidence so far that Mycenaean goods penetrated to the Black Sea area throws increasing doubt on the whole problem of long-range economic motives. One could, of course, fall back on the argument that the supposed Trojan impediment to Mycenaean trade was removed too late for the Greeks to exploit the new opportunities because of danger threatening their home bases. There is, however, more inclination now to attribute Trojan prosperity mainly to shrewd management of resources such as raising horses and sheep within her own immediate territory.

Quite apart from Blegen's more precise dating of the destruction levels of Troy VIh and VIIa, we would have to conclude now that if the Mycenaeans did launch a massive attack against Troy (or any other distant target) the time must have been before 1200. Thereafter they were clearly too preoccupied with the menace and actuality of enemy attacks on their own power centers.

T. B. L. Webster (1958) makes several interesting suggestions about the relation of Troy to the Mycenaeans. He thinks that the amount of Mycenaean pottery indicates that there might have been a Greek trading station at Troy, as there was apparently at Ugarit. He even considers it possible that "Troy VII A was a Greek-speaking kingdom and a member of the circle of Mycenaean kingdoms like Knossos and Pylos." It is indeed an intriguing fact that, among the names so far identified in the Linear B tablets, about one quarter are names that Homer assigns to Trojans. In Webster's opinion, too, it is quite possible that the well-documented "story of the siege of a town by the sea was elaborated for centuries in the Mycenaean circle, and then given a new setting in the East when Troy VII A was attacked."

Professor Page (1959) has produced an ambitious synthesis of the evidence on the Trojan War from contemporary Near Eastern documents, the Homeric poems and the archaeological data. He speaks for an increasing number of scholars who believe the Catalogue of Ships in Book II of the *Iliad* is an authentic muster roll of Mycenaean forces mobilized against some overseas target, and he is impressed by the survival of many authentic Mycenaean echoes elsewhere in the poems. Page accepts almost all of Blegen's conclusions about Troy VI and VIIa. He has also studied documents belonging to the final phases of the Hittite empire in the fourteenth and thirteenth centuries in which a power called Ahhijawā is mentioned. Its identification with Achaea is, as we have already mentioned, far from universally admitted. Page's equation of Ahhijawā with Rhodes remains only an attractive theory.

In the latest Hittite records Page also finds evidence in Anatolian politics for a strong rivalry (or at least antipathy) between Ahhijawā and a power coalition called Arzawa, which seized control of western Asia Minor as Hittite power crumbled. He explains the dearth of Mycenaean pottery in the coastal area between Troy and Miletos (although since he wrote Mycenaean pottery has been found at several sites, including Ephesos) as the result of a long-standing Arzawan embargo on Mycenaean trade. He suggests that, willingly or unwillingly, Troy finally joined the hostile coalition and thus became one of the targets of Achaean attack. This is at least a credible historical reconstruction and has come a long way from a war to avenge Paris' ravishing of the fair Helen. Page concludes that "our two sources—the Hittite records written at the time, and the Iliad four hundred years later—fit easily enough together. The Iliad is concentrated on one incident, the siege of Troy . . ."

There are other possible connections, too, between Troy and the Hittite documents. Gurney discusses several proposed equations. Ta-ru-(u)-i-sa (perhaps Trōisa), which seems to have been the most northerly of a number of towns in the district of Assuwa on the west Anatolian coast, reminds us of Greek "Troia." A kingdom called U-i-lu-sa (Wilusa) is not an impossible equivalent to Greek "Ilion," which was originally pronounced "Wilion." And Wilusa was ruled about 1300 by a king called Alaksandus, which is suspiciously close to Alexandros, the more common Homeric name for Paris. Moreover, Homer often calls the Trojans "Dardanians"; and an Egyptian text shows that the *Drdny* were Hittite allies at the battle of Kadesh in 1285. So we have some reason to hope that, even if the mound of Hissarlik yields no more evidence, Troy's presently obscure relationships with the Hittites and other powers in Asia Minor may be gradually illuminated by continuing discoveries in that area.

## THE COLLAPSE OF MYCENAEAN POWER

The fall of a great civilization is a particularly fascinating subject for both professional historians and reflective laymen. Elements of mystery solving are combined with vague hopes that previous mistakes (especially moral ones, in the minds of the Christian West) can be recognized and avoided. The fate of the Mycenaean power centers certainly holds its share of mystery, which we shall review but (unfortunately) not succeed in solving. Any moral lesson to be learned from the following account is left to the individual reader's perception.

The associated events that we can trace took place during a hundred years or more, roughly in the twelfth century (1200–1100). Contemporary Near Eastern documentary sources may be relevant to the story, and Greek legend and early epic poetry certainly are. But, as usual, this kind of evidence is extraordinarily difficult to interpret with any degree of assurance. Fragmentary and unsatisfactory though it is, the archaeological material places us on somewhat firmer ground and we shall have to use it as our major guide. A careful and systematic review of the present evidence for the Greek mainland has been carried out by Per Ålin (1962).

In the late thirteenth century energetic repairs and reinforcement and extension of fortifications are proved for such key centers as Mycenae, Tiryns and Athens. Large depots for the storage of provisions were apparently constructed and almost desperate arrangements were made to ensure that a safe water supply was accessible from inside the walls. A line of fortifications was at least partially carried across the Isthmus of Corinth at about the same time. Mylonas (1966) insists that the evidence is inconclusive and that it can equally well be interpreted as proof that the acme of Mycenaean power (including the attack on Troy) may date from that period. The reaction to his point of view cannot yet be gauged, but it is hardly likely that it will reverse the belief that these are reasonably clear indications that a number of Mycenaean power centers were anticipating some kind of serious attack. The fundamental problem is to identify the threatening foe.

As we have seen, the Linear B tablets have so far provided very little specific information in this larger frame of reference. Apart from vague (and disputed) allusions in the Pylos records to an expected local attack by an unnamed enemy, the texts seem to be preoccupied with "business as usual." Indeed, although in their palace economies and in various other characteristics the Mycenaean kingdoms closely resemble their Near Eastern neighbors, they were apparently very different in a curious lack of historical sense. Not only in their written documents but in their representative art in fresco, sculpture and other media, one misses the Near Eastern passion for chronicling historical events, however misleadingly. What seems like a stock representation of a citadel under siege in Mycenaean frescoes and other art media may of course have had specific and local historical overtones. It is also possible that poetry performed a somewhat comparable function for the Mycenaeans. There are hints in the epic tradition that the old songs and stories had a spicing of international travel and adventure.

A firm tradition in later Greek literature, certified by Thucydides' authority,[101] holds that the "heroic" or "Homeric" capitals were attacked and destroyed by the Dorians some two generations or eighty years after the fall of Troy. The most common traditional date for the latter event was Eratosthenes' calculation, which can be equated with 1184. Thus the "Dorian invasion" was placed about the end of the twelfth century. Until recently it had always been taken for granted that, although the ancient calculation is rather too late, the invaders were indeed the Dorians of legend who arrived by land from the general direction of northwest and central Greece. They were said to have bypassed or failed to capture Athens and then proceeded to conquer practically all of the Peloponnese before going on to occupy Crete, most of the southern Aegean islands and the coast of Asia Minor opposite them. Especially in the Peloponnese, we are told, they immediately carved out new kingdoms. Since these are the areas that gradually evolved into the Dorian state of historical times, it was quite naturally assumed that the invaders spoke a primitive Doric dialect of Greek.

Although scholars from classical times until World War II believed implicitly that this "Dorian invasion" was responsible for the ruin of Mycenaean power, the Homeric poems ignore it. No mention of a Dorian conquest of the mainland ever penetrated the hallowed lines so dear to the later Greeks whose dialect was the Attic-Ionic branch. Homer does, however, refer to attacks on the mature Mycenaean kingdoms by enemies who are called the Herakleidai* (descendants of Herakles). Their advent is described as a *kathodos,* which has usually been interpreted as a "return" but which can also mean a "coming down" (presumably from the north).

Dr. Stubbings confidently assumes that the Herakleidai "of course represent the Argolid."

According to Greek tradition, the mighty hero Herakles, king of Tiryns, had been subjugated by Eurystheus, king of Mycenae, and had been forced to perform the famous labors. Eurystheus is said to have died later while fighting against Herakles' sons north of the Isthmus of Corinth. His maternal uncle, Atreus, then succeeded to the throne of Mycenae and replaced the dynasty descended from Perseus with that of Pelops. About the same time, apparently, all eleven brothers of Nestor were killed while defending Pylos against this same mysterious "Heraklid might."[102] Legend also preserves the account of a pact by which the Herakleidai agreed to suspend their attacks for a hundred years. It is at least worth remarking that the span of time between Nestor's youth (about 1300 or a little later) and the final destruction of the Pylos palace would indeed cover approximately a century.

Could the Herakleidai have been the same Greek-speaking invaders as the Dorians, or could the two have joined forces to attack the Peloponnese? Thucydides tells us rather cryptically that eighty years after the Trojan War "the Dorians led by the Herakleidai" conquered the Peloponnese.[103] And we remember that the kings of Sparta, the Dorian state par excellence, claimed descent from Herakles. Did the attack come by land from the north? The wall across the Isthmus of Corinth might indicate that this was the expected route. On the other hand, the attack (or attacks) on Pylos in Nestor's boyhood sounds more like a series of raids by sea, since Pylos was one of the most remote Mycenaean capitals from the supposed base of both Dorians and Herakleidai in central and northwest Greece. The final attack on Pylos, too, may well have been seaborne.

As we have said, the Dorian invasion was unanimously accepted by the historians of antiquity as the cause of the destruction of the celebrated "heroic" civilization. Until very recently modern historians and archaeologists fully agreed, although they might differ about its base of operation, route and timing. Less than a generation ago neat and impressive archaeological evidence for the Dorian arrival in the late thirteenth or twelfth century was confidently enumerated, much as that for the invasion of the "gray Minyan people" almost a millennium earlier.

The most striking new culture traits (it was said) were the use of iron, cremation burial and geometric pottery. These "geometric" features seemed to mark as persuasive a cultural "break" as one could wish for, but the alleged break (in the positive sense of new culture traits) is now undergoing drastic reevaluation. Evidence is accumulating that these supposed hallmarks of the Early Iron Age were apparently coming gradually into use among the Mycenaeans themselves in the last phases of the Bronze Age. They are almost surely natural developments or cultural "loans" rather than innovations brought in by alien invaders.

The mysterious magnetic properties of pure metallic iron were vaguely known in Greece well before the turn of the second to first millennium, when we say (roughly) that the Aegean Iron Age begins. In Hittite Asia Minor as early as the fifteenth century notable progress was being made in solving the complicated technological problem of extracting, smelting and forging iron ore. Because of iron's relative abundance, its potentialities in the production of cheaper weapons and armor and implements were of course revolutionary in the military, economic and social spheres. The point is not so much that ancient iron weapons are inherently "superior" to those made of bronze (as is so often stated) but that a heavily armed aristocratic minority could no longer completely dominate a defenseless proletariat. The commoner could eventually afford to arm himself; and this possibility doomed the absolute political monopoly of the wealthy few.

The new metallurgy apparently radiated southward long before it was known in Greece. Iron objects are found at Egyptian sites and are mentioned in written documents as early as the fourteenth century. It is odd, therefore, that useful iron, as distinct from precious iron, cannot be documented in the Aegean area until at least two centuries later, when sporadic objects such as knives began to appear in late Mycenaean graves. The main point, however, is that forged iron artefacts were known at the very end of the Mycenaean period and that iron technology seems to have reached Greece from the east. Nevertheless, it is probably still a sound generalization that any Homeric passage referring to iron is likely to be of post-Mycenaean date, since the Greeks do not seem to have firmly assimilated the new technology until the so-called protogeometric period.

Again, in some late Mycenaean cemeteries cremation burials begin to occur side by side with the usual inhumations. There is no hint that the families that chose the new rite were notably differentiated in origin or traditions. It is, of course, possible that inhumation was more compatible with older beliefs that the *psyche* of the deceased continued to live in the tomb at least as long as flesh clung to bones, whereas cremation allowed the immediate transition to the world of Hades, which the dead in Homer crave. No doubt contacts with such alien cultures as that of Troy, through war and trade, had long familiarized some of the Mycenaeans with cremation. A situation where warriors died in foreign lands or where refugees were living apart from their ancestral homes may have linked up with new religious beliefs to encourage its use. Yet the dominant burial custom, even in late Mycenaean times, was still inhumation; and there is, again,

no very compelling reason to believe that the Homeric descriptions of
cremation rites are derived from Mycenaean practice.

Also, in the pottery from the latest Mycenaean cemeteries and settlements a gradual transition in most vase shapes as well as the beginning
of the new "tectonic" decorative tradition characteristic of geometric times
can already be detected (Fig. 98). Webster has described the art of the
early Iron Age as "an art stripped down to essentials just as life was
stripped down to essentials with the collapse of the Mycenaean palaces."
These were times when the drive for mere survival must have forced im-

Figure 98

poverished Mycenaean refugees to adopt a much simpler way of life. Many features of their past had to be discarded or transformed, but the potential for creative adaptation to a new environment seems to have been primarily a Mycenaean phenomenon and not the result of intrusive culture traits.

In fact, practically the only indisputable archaeological evidence that *may* now be connected with the traditional Dorian invasion is the destruction and burning of Mycenaean centers—and even that is attributed by Mylonas to sporadic and localized civil disturbances. It should be mentioned, however, that some scholars also point to the appearance of certain secondary cultural novelties toward the end of this turbulent period.

Let us first review briefly the evidence for widespread destruction. Important buildings outside the citadel at Mycenae were heavily burned about the middle of the thirteenth century and not rebuilt. Accident is an unlikely explanation because of the known intensification of defense measures. Civil war is not ruled out, of course, nor is an attack by a coalition of Mycenaean powers, like that which is assumed to explain the destruction of Thebes earlier in the same century. But in view of the total destruction of other major power centers that begins toward the end of the century, it is tempting to see the Mycenae incident as possibly one of the first of a long series of hit-and-run attacks by foreign enemies.

Flimsy houses outside the fortifications on the north slope of the Athenian acropolis were suddenly abandoned not long after their construction in the late thirteenth century. There was heavy destruction within the citadel of Mycenae, but some of the inhabitants either held out or reoccupied the citadel almost immediately. Pylos was captured about the end of the century. The era of Tiryns' prosperity seems to come to an end about the same time, although N. Verdelis (1962) discovered later Mycenaean pottery in the two tunnels that led to a secret water supply outside the walls at the northwest. Strong points like Gla seem to have been destroyed or abandoned. Even smaller settlements such as Zygouries, Prosymna and Berbati were burned or deserted, although there are known exceptions like Korakou. Wherever intensive exploration has been carried out in the areas of the Mycenaean kingdoms there is impressive evidence of drastic depopulation in the decades following 1200, when the LHIIIB pottery phase was evolving into LHIIIC.

In the Argolid there was an attempt under Mycenae's lead to perpetuate the old way of life; but this was cut short by a complete destruction some two generations later when LHIIIC pottery was in full vogue. According to legend, another thrust seems to have been made against Athens in this same general period and the defense was led by King Kodros, a descendant of Nestor. The excavator believes that the final destruction of the citadel of Iolkos took place at about the same time. If so, it may have originally held out or been partially reoccupied. (Or did the newer Mycenaean kingdoms of Thessaly join, or at least not oppose, the invaders?) A connection has been suggested between these latest mainland events and the approximately contemporary burning of Miletos, across the Aegean.

We cannot even estimate the proportion of the inhabitants who survived the tribulations of the twelfth century. Custom would suggest that the victors killed adult male captives and enslaved the women and children, but a sizable number either anticipated the attacks or were allowed to escape. Indeed, it has been suggested that the references to ships and rowers in the Pylos tablets have to do with a planned escape by sea in case of attack. Mycenaeans who were already settled in marginal and inaccessible areas such as central (Arkadia) and northwest (Achaea) Peloponnese seem to have been undisturbed by the enemy. Their numbers were greatly increased by refugees from the formerly more prosperous areas. In these remote enclaves a simplified version of the Mycenaean way of life continued for several generations. It may have been then that northwestern Peloponnese acquired the name Achaea, which it bore in classical times. A very strong tradition records that many refugees, especially from Pylos, reached Athens. We have not as yet very firm archaeological confirmation of the last-mentioned population shift, but the Athenian acropolis does appear to have survived intact, and there were some fairly populous late Mycenaean settlements like Perati along the east coat of Attica.

Both tradition and archaeological evidence informs us that many refugees from major centers escaped by ship. The island of Kephallenia sheltered a fair number who came from the nearby coast of west Peloponnese, and there are indications in the following generations that some trade developed between Kephallenia and central and eastern Europe. No doubt some of the Aegean islands, since they were apparently unaffected by the disaster and presumably friendly, received other refugees.

There seems to be archaeological confirmation for two waves of new Mycenaean settlers on Cyprus, and an interesting linguistic phenomenon fits neatly with this situation. Scholars have long distinguished a so-called Arkado-Cypriot branch of classical Greek that preserved very old features of the language. The survival of two closely related enclaves of archaic Greek in areas as widely separated as mountainous Arkadia in central Peloponnese and faraway Cyprus almost at the eastern end of the Mediterranean now finds a plausible explanation in the fact that these were major havens for Mycenaean survivors, especially from the Argolid. And the language of the Linear B tablets shows elements of close connection with the later Arkado-Cypriot dialect. We should also note that as late as the third century B.C. a syllabary derived from the linear scripts of the Bronze Age was still employed on Cyprus to write Greek, although the current tendency is to derive the Cypriot syllabary from the Minoan Linear A.

A major puzzle, however, involves what happened to the rich agricultural areas formerly occupied by the great Mycenaean powers. Very few of the burned or abandoned Mycenaean sites seem to have been immediately reoccupied, and new settlements dating from the twelfth and eleventh centuries are very scarce. Were these once fruitful lands lying untended? As we have seen, the cultural features once linked with the supposed Dorian invaders have proved undependable. It is now urged by those who still believe in an immediate Dorian occupation that the conquerors were just another group of Greeks with an essentially similar though much less sophisticated culture. Also, the early Iron Age villages are supposed to have been small and scattered, with buildings constructed flimsily of perishable materials and whose inhabitants had little in the way of portable wealth or durable artefacts.

Yet a nagging suspicion is spreading that the Dorian-speaking Greeks arrived considerably later (but still, of course, before historical times) and that there must be some other explanation for the widespread destruction of Mycenaean strongholds and for the very drastic depopulation and impoverishment that clearly followed. At present many questions are being raised and various theories proposed, but confirmation and consensus is notably lacking. We shall first list some of the likelier suggestions and arguments made to support them; then a critical review of the problem will be attempted.

Might the destruction be attributed to hit-and-run attacks by some other outsider or outsiders? Some scholars suggest that pressure from farther north may have forced the fierce barbarians of Illyria (northwest of Greece) into a destructive invasion. Others suspect the "Sea People," who were harrying the rich and settled populations farther east and south at about the same time. Egyptian records tell how that country was barely able to beat back a desperate attack by the Sea People in about 1225 and a second in the early years of the twelfth century. A great (possibly coordinated) land invasion administered the *coup de grâce* to the weakened Hittite empire around 1200. Towns in Syria were destroyed at about the same time. One unit of the Sea People, called Peleset, settled in Palestine and appear as the biblical Philistines. The known time of their settlement and their clear imitation of late Mycenaean pottery provides an important "fix" to date the transition from the LHIIIB to the LHIIIC style in the years close to 1200.

The names of some of the allies who made up the motley hordes of Sea People are preserved in Egyptian documents; and a few equations such as Lycians, Sardinians, Tyrrhenians and Sicilians have been proposed, although most Near Eastern specialists are very uncertain of their validity. Some scholars have suggested that the Achaeans are represented by a group called Akawasha, but it is as yet utterly problematical whether Achaeans joined the Sea People in their attacks on the Near East or were themselves among the objects of these attacks. Possibly they were willing or unwilling allies at first, only to become eventual victims of their undisciplined and rapacious comrades in arms. If the mainland Achaeans refused to cooperate and the islanders were forced to join the Sea People, this could explain the survival of the latter unscathed.

The facts that several mainland centers show the same concern at the same time and that great marauding "armadas" are known to have been prowling the east Mediterranean may point to a foreign, not an Achaean or even a Dorian threat. The wealthy Mycenaean citadels, most of them situated near the sea, would have been tempting targets in a lawless era of large-scale piracy. And there may be some truth in the statements so often made that the Trojan War (and no doubt other similar expeditions) had lessened Mycenaean resilience against attack. It is believable, too, that other kings, as well as Agamemnon and Odysseus, returned home from long absences to face severe local challenges that would have weakened their defensive potential.

If it was not a matter of direct attack by the Sea People, may their activities have disrupted Mycenaean trade and brought on a disastrous economic crisis? Vermeule suggests that the Achaeans may have had to face the "double threat of conquest and starvation." Their territory as a whole was not rich in natural resources compared (say) to many parts of the Near East. And there was too great uniformity in Achaean industries to promote prosperous and independent interkingdom commerce. The economy would certainly have been hard hit by any interruption and harassment of foreign trade. But this hardly explains the wholesale destruction.

Quite different theories for the Mycenaean demise are also under discussion. Could the destroyers have been Achaean kinsmen, perhaps a combination of the numerous and prosperous "colonies" in the southern Aegean? They were in a sense beneficiaries of the mainland disaster and Catling's analyses suggest that they may have been barred from eastern markets by mainland powers. Or might the destruction be attributed to a general civil war touched off by dynastic troubles such as are hinted at in Homer's allusions to the "Return of the Herakleidai?" Might a great revolt have been led by the middle-class merchants (if there was such a "class") or by the free peasants (perhaps of different racial stock and even language) or by the masses of slaves? Possibly they all made common cause against the autocratic Achaean kings and nobles. There must have been some independent souls who chafed under the severe regimentation indicated by the Linear B tablets. Potential dissidents like Homer's Thersites may have started the fatal train of events. May the majority of the elusive Dorians have actually formed a submerged section of the local population who joined forces with ousted kinsmen (hence the "return" of tradition) to overthrow their Achaean-Ionic rulers?

Still other proposed explanations partially or wholly eliminate human agents. Could the deforestation that may have followed the construction boom and spreading agriculture of LHIIIB have caused such serious erosion of the soil that (coupled with a cessation of foreign trade) famine and/or revolution resulted? Might there have been a tremendous plague or series of epidemics that hastened the fall of Mycenaean power and could perhaps be tied in with the novel practice of cremation burial? Was there a change to a cooler and wetter climate beginning about 1100? Or, conversely, were late Mycenaean times affected by a serious drought? No one seems yet to have proposed that the destruction was due to one or a series of tremendous earthquakes, although mainland Greece appears to be as vulnerable as Crete to this manifestation of nature's power.

None of the hypothetical natural or economic disasters can be proved at present. Those involving climatic change can perhaps be checked by proper scientific study. But, even if future research should confirm one or more of them, we can be reasonably sure that it was the violence of man that the Mycenaeans feared. The feverish construction of fortifications, the provision of access to water supply from within the walls, the dispatch of watchers along the Pylian coasts, the apparently urgent distribution of metals for the manufacture of weapons seem to prove this point conclusively. Then who were the human enemies that threatened?

The Pylos tablets and the relatively few documents recovered from Mycenae indicate that right up to the year of the attacks there was no hint of an internal breakdown of the elaborate system of production and distribution. The arrears in taxes owed to the *wanax* of Pylos were probably normal and scarcely suggest disastrous drought or incipient revolution. On the other hand, the fact that the bronzesmiths seem to have been seriously short of raw materials might very well indicate an interruption of foreign trade.

Rather cryptic entries in some of the Pylos tablets are usually interpreted to indicate that the attack was expected and that the defenders looked for an external enemy who would approach by sea. We get no hint in the tablets as to whether Achaeans or non-Achaeans were threatening. Nestor's boyhood reminiscences of attacks on Pylos by the "might of Herakles," in which all of his eleven elder brothers were killed, and of later battles by the weakened Pylians against the Epeians,[104] who lived beyond Pylos' northern borders, might suggest a continuation of inter-Greek feuds. The legends and myths show clearly that this kind of civil war was endemic and vicious. A parallel could be drawn with Neleus' earlier occupation of the Pylos area, which surely was not accomplished without considerable fighting.

Yet it is difficult to believe that a single Achaean political unit or even a temporary alliance of several could have so thoroughly overwhelmed the rest, including Mycenae; and it is still more unlikely that any class or combination of classes from within the Mycenaean social system could have successfully made common cause against the well-financed and well-armed ruling minority. It is true that the removal of a very few at the top would have literally decapitated these kingdoms and that the disruption of the intricate administrative system would have precipitated a sudden and complete economic and social breakdown, but the bulk of the population could have managed to carry on along simpler lines of survival economy.

The meager evidence as yet available, as well as historical plausibility, points rather firmly to an external enemy or enemies. The attacks were scattered over a considerable period of time, and in this sense at least the term "Dorian invasion," with its implications of a single massive successful thrust, is surely wrong. But since there was apparently plenty of warning, it seems odd that some concerted Mycenaean defense effort was not made. One would think that an imminent threat or a successful attack by outsiders on one mainland power center would cause the other kingdoms to mobilize at least as powerful a defense force as they supposedly used to attack Troy. Actually, for all we can tell, they may have done so. The wall across the Isthmus could have been a defense measure undertaken by the unified political structure that some scholars believe must have existed. But it would be difficult to anticipate where the enemy would strike, particularly if he came by sea, and the tendency would likely be for each center to concentrate all its resources on its own defense.

Furthermore, our instinct that the reasonable course of action is for potential victims to unite against the common enemy seems to be contrary to Mycenaean psychology. Temporary submission of local autonomy to a centralized authority might be possible when the stakes were as attractive as the plunder of a fabulously wealthy (and perhaps troublesome) non-Greek target. Even then Homer preserves echoes of lack of cooperation in the organization of the expedition, and Achilles' mutiny suggests the fragility of pan-Achaean enterprises. On the other hand, it would probably have seemed quite a different matter to come to the aid of an independent and perhaps rival Achaean kingdom in its hour of need. History is full of parallels where small sovereign states, often related by ties of race, religion, language and culture, failed to unite against an external threat.

If we have somewhat narrowed down the problem, we still have to ask: Who were the external enemies who burned and plundered the major Mycenaean capitals one after another and spread devastation over the countryside as well? Casual raids, even in overwhelming force, could not have so thoroughly depopulated these thriving areas. Since the conquerors apparently did not remain to rule the survivors, the threat of their return at any time with fire and sword must have frightened their victims into taking refuge in less vulnerable places. The facts are admittedly few and ambiguous. The orthodox view, represented by Blegen's recent (1962) restatement, remains committed to a rather more flexible interpretation of the traditional Dorian invasion; but an increasing number of historians seem to feel that what we now know of the events may fit a foreign enemy or coalition better than Dorian Greeks. If we could be sure that the damage was done by strikes from the sea or by a series of land raids from the north, the conclusion might be easier. As of now, we have to admit the possibility of either—or both.

Although seventeen years of active excavation and research have passed since John Franklin Daniel recorded his last remarks about the Mycenaean disaster, it would be difficult to improve on his brilliant summation. "The Dorian invasion," said Daniel, "was neither a single military campaign nor a purely Greek phenomenon. Rather it was the peninsular Greek phase of the overwhelming movement of peoples who swept out of the north and engulfed the ancient world at the end of the Bronze Age. Their eruption into the civilized lands around the eastern Mediterranean brought to a cataclysmic end an age of brilliant cultural development and prepared the way for the emergence, many years later, of a new and vastly different world."

## THE FINAL PHASES

It is, if anything, even more hazardous to thread the maze of current opinion about what happened in the generations immediately following the great disruption of the twelfth century. We shall take as our main guide V. R. d'A. Desborough, who has published (1964) a careful account of the evidence for the transition from the Bronze to the Iron Age.

Desborough believes quite firmly that there was a late Mycenaean "empire" under which the other kingdoms owed at least some vague sort of allegiance to the *wanax* of Mycenae. He further holds that the empire suffered its final destruction at the hands of northern enemies who attacked by land, very much (apparently) as in the traditional account of the Dorian invasion. He identifies no specific culture traits that can be plausibly connected with the attackers, although he agrees with Schachermeyr and others that several novel features of likely northern origin appear in Mycenaean contexts about the end of LHIIIB. He concludes, however, that the intruders, after they had burned, pillaged, killed and enslaved to the limit, withdrew and left the most productive areas of central and southern Greece to the few native survivors. This view calls into question the reliability of the tradition cherished in later Dorian communities that their ancestors had conquered and immediately occupied large parts of the ancient Mycenaean kingdoms, especially in the Peloponnese.

On the origins of early Iron Age culture in Greece, then, Desborough appears to steer a middle path between those who (like Wace) are inclined to see the Mycenaeans as the direct originators of an almost uninterrupted development and those who (like Gardner) assume a radical new departure—presumably as a result of the Dorian migration—at the beginning of the first millennium. As mentioned above, Desborough sees no evidence of new settlers at the end of LHIIIB. He assumes that such rare novelties as the slashing sword, the flame-shaped spearheads and the violin-bow fibula, if they are of northern origin, were casual imports coming in by different routes, or cultural "loans," or possibly possessions of northern mercenary soldiers hired by the Mycenaeans in their time of trouble.

The use of the fibula to fasten shawls or other heavy outer garments is apparently not a native Mycenaean trait. The Mycenaeans seem to have begun very tentatively to replace the characteristic conical buttons (once called spindle whorls) toward the end of LHIIIB. Of the two main types, the so-called violin-bow preceded the arched shape (Fig. 99). Both types are common in Italy and the Balkans, and their appropriateness in a colder climate is said to indicate (though it by no means proves) that their use began earlier in the north. It has even been suggested that their appearance in Greece coincided with the beginning of a period of colder and wetter weather supposed to have lasted from about 1100 to 800. Expert opinion on whether there is any reliable physical evidence for such a change should be sought. Meanwhile, the disruption of the highly developed Mycenaean textile industry might provide a more natural reason.

Certain types of weapons and armor have also been receiving a good deal of study recently, and they may eventually provide somewhat clearer

Figure 99

evidence for contacts with the north. The distinctive slashing sword (Fig. 100), which had been popular in east central Europe since the fourteenth century, appears suddenly in the Aegean in the latter half of the thirteenth century, a little earlier than the fibulae. Piggott believes that their presence in Greece shows that "here we must have central and west European adventurers and mercenaries forming part of the raiding bands along with the Luka and the rest [*i.e.,* the Sea People]." This interpretation is certainly possible, but such mercenaries could equally well have been supporting the Mycenaeans, as Desborough suggests. And if Piggott is right that "some [swords were] copied" in Greece, his own explanation would seem less likely.

On the other hand, Desborough views very differently a series of innovations appearing sporadically in areas of late Mycenaean occupation between 1125 and 1025. About the same time various persistent features of the old Mycenaean culture, such as multiple burials in family chamber tombs and the distinctive terra-cotta figurines, seem to disappear. The scanty trade goods from Syria and Egypt still found in the cemeteries of at least a few LHIIIC settlements cease altogether. The siting of some settlements shifts slightly, and the later cemetery may actually lie above the old habitation site. The long pin joins the fibula as a common accouterment of dress. The most "fundamental" change of all, however, is the common mode of burial (mostly inhumations) in individual or double cist graves and occasionally in pithoi.

Desborough concludes that these features (in sum) strongly suggest the arrival of newcomers from outside the Mycenaean sphere. There may,

Figure 100

he thinks, have been several groups of intruders, and they apparently originated in the northwest and arrived by land. Some confirmation seems to be provided by the verdict of two physical anthropologists that skeletal remains from Athens and Argos include characteristics of a new strain of northern origin in the population.

The newcomers could have met little opposition from the weak Mycenaean survivors, who may have gradually fused with them to produce the so-called protogeometric culture. Desborough sees no firm evidence for externally derived ceramic innovations at this time. The characteristic pottery of the Greek mainland during the eleventh century is fundamentally and almost entirely Mycenaean in origin. Yet he believes that protogeometric pottery, which clearly stands at the beginning of a continuous development traceable down to classical times and beyond, may owe something to the newcomers as well as to this latest (so-called sub-Mycenaean*) style of the original inhabitants. He implies that one or more groups of these newcomers may have spoken a primitive Doric dialect of Greek; other scholars, too, have seen in this later folk movement the real Dorian invasion.

One of the most pressing problems in Greek archaeology is the discovery of the location and careful excavation of several habitation sites where these newcomers settled—if possible at spots where Mycenaean survivors had still held on. Building in stone may have largely died out, but newer field methods should recover a fair amount of information about these scattered and marginal settlers. The well-preserved LHIIIC and proto-geometric phases at Lefkandi in western Euboea, where members of the British School of Archaeology are now excavating, hold much promise in this connection.

## HOMERIC AND LATER CONNECTIONS

The earliest stages of the Greek "dark ages" following the collapse of Mycenaean civilization lead us naturally to a brief discussion of another difficult question that has an important bearing on the interpretation of the Homeric evidence. With the obvious exception of the poems themselves, what direct connections (if any) can be established between the culture of the later second millennium, which we have been reviewing, and that of the archaic and classical age of Greece in the middle centuries of the first millennium B.C.?

We have seen that many classical scholars strongly resisted and resented Schliemann's efforts to prove that there had been a brilliant preclassical period of Greek history from which the Homeric epics directly derived. As time went on it became impossible to ignore the reality of Mycenaean civilization, but we have had to modify drastically Schliemann's confident early claims that Homer's account is so closely congruent with the archaeological facts that it must reflect firsthand knowledge. Indeed, some of the newer developments, particularly our very tentative understanding of the content of the Linear B tablets, have emphasized how tenuous and confused and anachronistic are many elements of Homer's account when compared with the emerging reality. For example, very distinctive traits of Mycenaean times like tholos tombs, fresco painting and literate palace bureaucracies seem to be completely unknown to Homer. Such blurring is exactly what one would expect in the centuries-long oral transmission of the shorter stories that were finally embedded in the poems as we have inherited them.

Yet the fact is established beyond any reasonable argument that there *was* a continuous tradition (probably poetic from the start) linking the Mycenaean with the early Iron Age and on down through Homer to archaic and classical times. Professor Page eloquently sums up the modern verdict: "It adds something to the appeal of Homeric poetry, to know not only that its subject is historical, but also that its leading people are, for the most part, real people, remembered and idealized figures of men and women who played no small part on the stage of history, living brilliantly and richly on the verge of the darkest night which was ever to fall over ancient Greece."

We have, then, strong consensus that the poems contain episodes, descriptions of artefacts, names, as well as at least a few linguistic and stylistic traits that can only be explained on the theory that they were handed down from Late Bronze Age to Homer's time in a continuous oral tradition. The occurrence in the poems of many culture traits obsolete long before the mid-eighth century—chariot fighting, the bronze helmet, the single thrusting spear, the long cut-and-thrust sword, the body shield, the boar's tusk helmet, the silver-studded sword, highly developed archery, metal sculpture in the niello technique, intricately inlaid furniture, the complex palace plans, luxurious bathing customs—allow no doubt on this point.

But there is a difficult related problem. As T. B. L. Webster phrases it, "The general principle must be that elements of Mycenaean civilization in Homer . . . can only be accepted as evidence of Mycenaean poetry when we have reason to suppose that these elements did not survive the Mycenaean age." In other words, we have to know that they died (*i.e.,* went out of use) before the end of the Mycenaean age in order to assert that they could only have continued to live in "a poetic tradition" (Webster) or perhaps in "a loose prose tradition *later* incorporated in poetry" (Kirk).

Sometimes the "dead" trait appears to have been embalmed quite successfully, as in the case of the "sword silver-studded,"[105] which may preserve an actual phrase from Mycenaean Greek describing a metal-working technique that probably went out of use about the end of the fifteenth century. On the other hand, Professor Kirk points to an instance where the embalming process may have been only partial or else delayed too long. He is surely right that the kind of "equine taxi service" usually taken for granted in the poems cannot conform to strict reality at any period. The poetic tradition (except in a few passages) has lost touch with the way Mycenaean chariots were actually used in battle. Professor Kirk is, in general, less confident than most authorities that there was a developed tradition of epic poetry in Mycenaean times. He thinks that the heroic tales might have been passed on to the earliest Iron Age in less formal ways.

Were there, on the other hand, important elements of a living, vital Mycenaean cultural tradition (quite apart from the embalming process of epic poetry) that survived the early Iron Age and emerged to renewed brilliance in the archaic and classical periods? If so, how many and how strong and how direct were the connections? It is in this context that Wace, as recently as 1956, felt impelled to criticize pointedly the attitude of many modern classicists. He takes the position that the prehistoric and the later phases of Greek history are one and indivisible. In his eyes, no one can properly claim scholarly status in the one and ignore the other.

We have also reviewed Evans' and Nilsson's arguments emphasizing important elements of continuity that may have been obscured but were never lost. Evans' claims provoked almost as violent opposition as Schliemann's, but his massive influence, bold hypotheses and brilliant analyses forced most open-minded classicists to admit that the classical Greeks may indeed have owed (and quite naturally) a good deal to their own quite distant past. Nilsson's more cautious and carefully documented claims, particularly in the field of religion, carried still more conviction. Most recently, Webster's review of Minoan-Mycenaean representational art not only supports Nilsson but tends to revert to Evans' hypothesis that at least some of the germs of epic may be Minoan.

Yet resistance is still deeply rooted in some quarters. It has to be admitted (again quite naturally) that many features of archaic and classical Greek culture show little or no evidence of continuity. In political and social organizations, for instance, the highly formalized system of the relatively large Mycenaean kingdoms is comparable to Near Eastern institutions, which are regularly cited as the antithesis of those in the small independent classical city-state. The serious gap in the evidence for the early centuries of the Iron Age can be cited as a basis for the belief in the almost total abandonment of "civilized" living. And this situation tends to reinforce a very long and strongly held assumption that the wonder and perfection of classical Greek culture had no authentic forebears, that it was a kind of miracle or sport relatively independent of time and space and normal historical process.

Scholars who implicitly or explicitly hold such a view are not much interested in looking even in Greece itself for antecedents of classical modes and institutions and beliefs; they are still more reluctant to admit that the preclassical stages in Greece cannot properly be evaluated without reference to Crete, Anatolia and the Near East generally. Well-excavated habitation sites spanning this critical period are still far too scarce, particularly in the Aegean islands and on the Asia Minor coast.

Yet the skeptics must even now face up to certain concrete questions. Wace formulated them somewhat impetuously; Nilsson stated them firmly and soberly. How, for example, are we to explain the typical plan of the classical temple—with the two columns of the porch in line with the end walls and with the main shrine, or naos, and its central statue base—except as a carry-over of the plan of the Mycenaean megaron? We remember, too, that the megaron was itself a home for a personage who must have had at least attributes of divinity. And, as Guthrie emphasizes, there can be no doubt that later temples were purposely built on the same spot, presumably as a home for the same divinity who had dwelled with or in the Mycenaean king. On the other hand, it must be admitted that we usually cannot be absolutely sure whether their location was due to an uninterrupted cult or to a lucky reidentification in the early archaic period, when the popularity of the Homeric poems and a general idealization of the heroic past gave a great impetus to hero cults. The new Keos temple may provide the first undoubted example of an uninterrupted cult, but several of the most important religious centers in the classical period—like Delphi, Delos, Eleusis and Athens—appear to have had a Bronze Age predecessor.

If one moves to the architectural orders of the classical period, there is, first of all, the general column and lintel arrangement. And the so-called Doric column and capital (an order popular among the later Dorian Greek states that were previously mentioned) bear an unmistakable similarity to earlier examples like the column in the relieving triangle over the Lion Gate at Mycenae, as well as to some of those depicted in fresco fragments from Knossos and Pylos. Even the stone-carved and fresco examples of Minoan-Mycenaean friezes (Fig. 101) of split rosettes alternating with groups of vertical fasciae are strikingly close to the triglyph and metope pattern of the later Doric order of architecture.

Figure 101

O          in          6

In athletic contests (where there are religious overtones in both prehistoric and later times) and in many details of cult and ritual the resemblances are equally notable. Webster and others have shown that in Minoan-Mycenaean representational art there are many convincing parallels with singing, dancing and instrumental performances connected with later religious observances. Continuity in religion—particularly in divine names—is strongly reinforced by the Linear B tablets. The evidence (or at least general probability) hardly invalidates the hypothesis that worship at the graves of some of the Bronze Age heroes continued uninterrupted through the early Iron Age and on into classical, Hellenistic and Roman days. Mylonas is the most persistent challenger (even in the case of the Mycenae Shaft Graves) of the hypothesis of continuing cult that was accepted by Tsountas and Nilsson. Recent skepticism, however, is supported by many authorities, including Guthrie. Yet Guthrie admits that "it is doubtful . . . whether the archaeological evidence has finally solved the problem of the Mycenaean attitude to the dead."

The myths and legends show us that the classical Greeks were quite aware of many nonmaterial facets of their heritage. And in more ways than they realized they were heirs of the Mycenaean past—just as modern Western man is in turn the inheritor of classical Greek culture. In aspects as varied as the methods by which they cultivated their fields and the stories of heroic and tragic deeds that formed the basis of their literature, one detects the kinship. Nestor's son, Peisistratos, had a vital tie in culture as well as in blood with his illustrious Athenian descendant of the sixth century B.C.

Yet the more one becomes aware of the evidence for tradition and continuity from other sources, the more he realizes that the absolutely unique and incomparable tie between Mycenaean and classical times is the Homeric poems themselves. A secondary theme throughout our story has been a review of the evidence accumulating over the past century on the nature and dependability of those ties. We have seen how much caution is needed and how misleading the views at either extreme can be. There is much to be said for Alsop's generalization that the poems represent selective recollection, remembering the glamorous and forgetting the dull. It is granted that the imagination in every age is likely to be more stirred by the anger of Achilles or the guile of Odysseus than by tax records and LHIIIB pottery.

We must continually remind ourselves that to each generation during the earlier oral and later written transmission these songs were an inspiration and a delight. The mind and instinct of classical Greece cannot be understood apart from Homer. However much time has altered the original courtly forms and content, the Homeric poems provide a far truer insight into the most important aspects of the heroic age of Greece than can be expected from archaeology. Archaeologists whose interests lie primarily in the Late Bronze Age must be deeply grateful that this magnificent guide and touchstone has survived to bring alive and make relevant so many of their discoveries.

But, conversely, every classicist should realize that his discipline is founded on Homer and that archaeological discoveries are important and relevant to him. The least he and every true lover of Homeric epic must concede to archaeology is that the material objects—be they inlaid swords, broken walls or common pots—supplement and control and support Homer's marvelous stories in a useful and occasionally in a spectacular way.

# Chapter Bibliographies and

# Sources of Quotations

MAJOR SOURCES, both books and articles, on which the particular phase of the chronicle is based are first listed in sequence for each chapter. The direct quotations are then keyed in by a triple reference system: (1) page number(s) in our text; (2) identification of the source by its number in the chapter bibliography; (3) page number(s) in the source.

> AJA   American Journal of Archaeology
> BSA   Annual of the British School in Athens
> JHS   Journal of Hellenic Studies

## CHAPTER II

1. Heinrich Schliemann, *Troy and its Remains* (London: 1875)
2. ———— *Ilios: The City and Country of the Trojans* . . . (London: 1880)
3. ———— *Troja: Results of the Latest Researches* . . . (London: 1884)
4. ———— *Mycenae: A Narrative of Researches* . . . (London: 1878)
5. ———— *Tiryns: The Prehistoric Palace of the Kings of Tiryns* (London: 1886)
6. Carl Schuchhardt, *Schliemann's Excavations: An Archaeological and Historical Study* (London: 1891)

| | | | | | | |
|---|---|---|---|---|---|---|
| 9 | . | 2 | . xvi | 17, 18 | . I . | 194 |
| 11 | . | I | . 76 | 18 | . I . | 219 |
| 12 | . | 2 | . 213 | 18 | . I . | 80 |
| 13 | . | I | . 62 | 20 | . I . | 304, 305 |
| 15 | . | 3 | . 237 | 21, 22 | . I . | 323, 324 |
| 16 | . | I | . 68–70 | 23 | . I . | 335 |
| 17 | . | I | . 58 | 23, 24 | . I . | 332, 333 |
| 17 | . | I | . 41 | 24 | . I . | 347, 348 |

| | | |
|---|---|---|
| 25 . | I . | 343, 344 |
| 25, 26 . | I . | 349, 350 |
| 27 . | 2 . | ix |
| 27 . | 2 . | xiv |
| 27 . | 2 . | 51 |
| 28 . | 2 . | 675, 676 |
| 28 . | 2 . | 682 |
| 29 . | 2 . | 229 |
| 29 . | 2 . | 232 |
| 29 . | 2 . | 252 |
| 30 . | 2 . | 279 |
| 30, 31 . | 6 . | 69 |
| 31 . | 2 . | 324 |
| 31 . | 2 . | 454 |
| 32 . | 2 . | 485 |
| 32 . | 2 . | 487, 488 |
| 33 | 2 . | 463 |
| 33 . | 2 . | 467 |
| 34 . | 2 . | 379 |
| 34, 35 . | 2 . | 510, 511 |
| 35, 36 . | 2 . | 517 |
| 36 . | 2 . | 518 |
| 36 . | 2 . | 518 |
| 36 . | 2 . | 588 |
| 36, 37 . | 2 . | 587 |
| 37 . | 2 . | 587 |
| 38 . | 2 . | 607 |
| 38 . | 3 . | Dedication |
| 38 . | 3 . | 6 |
| 39 . | 3 . | 52 |
| 40 . | 3 . | 76 |
| 40 . | 3 . | 84 |
| 40 . | 3 . | 86 |
| 40, 41 . | 3 . | 169 |
| 42 . | 3 . | 279 |
| 45 . | 6 . | 51 |
| 45 . | 6 . | 91 |
| 46 . | 6 . | 72 |
| 46 . | 6 . | 92 |
| 48 . | 4 . | 60, 61 |
| 50 . | 4 . | 28, 29 |
| 50, 51 . | 4 . | 61, 62 |
| 51 . | 4 . | 63 |
| 52 . | 4 . | 80 |
| 52 . | 4 . | 85 |
| 53 . | 4 . | 84 |
| 53 . | 4 . | 88 |
| 53 . | 4 . | 100, 93 |
| 53 . | 4 . | 101, 102 |
| 53, 54 . | 4 . | 132, 134 |
| 55 . | 4 . | 135, 136 |
| 56 . | 4 . | 151 |
| 56 . | 4 . | 155 |
| 56, 57 . | 4 . | 161–165 |
| 59 . | 4 . | 214 |
| 59, 60 . | 4 . | 214 |
| 60 . | 4 . | 290 |
| 61 . | 4 . | 214, 215 |
| 62 . | 4 . | 226 |
| 62, 63 . | 4 . | 227 |
| 63 . | 4 . | 236, 238 |
| 65 . | 4 . | 296, 298 |
| 65 . | 4 . | 334, 335 |
| 66 . | 4 . | 337, 340 |
| 66 . | 4 . | 343, 344 |
| 66, 67 . | 4 . | 102 |
| 67 . | 4 . | 345 |
| 72 . | 5 . | 191, 192 |
| 75 . | 5 . | 223 |
| 75 . | 5 . | 232, 230 |
| 78 . | 6 . | 231 |
| 79 . | 6 . | xxi |

## C H A P T E R   I I I

1. Christos Tsountas and J. Irving Manatt, *The Mycenaean Age: a Study of the Monuments and Culture of pre-Homeric Greece* (Boston: 1897)

2. Wilhelm Dörpfeld, *Troja 1893: Bericht über die im Jahre 1893 veranstalteten Ausgrabungen* (Leipzig: 1894)

## CHAPTER IV

1. Joan Evans, *Time and Chance: the Story of Arthur Evans and his Forebears* (London: 1943)
2. Arthur Evans, "Knossos: the Palace," *BSA* 6 (1899–1900) 3–70
3. ———— "The Palace of Knossos," *BSA* 7 (1900–1901) 1–120
4. ———— "The Palace of Knossos," *BSA* 8 (1901–1902) 1–124
5. Duncan Mackenzie, "The Pottery of Knossos," *JHS* 23 (1903) 157–205
6. Arthur Evans, "The Palace of Knossos," *BSA* 9 (1902–1903) 1–153
7. ———— "The Palace of Knossos," *BSA* 10 (1903–1904) 1–62
8. ———— "The Palace of Knossos and its Dependencies," *BSA* 11 (1904–1905) 1–26
9. ———— "The Prehistoric Tombs of Knossos," *Archaeologia* 59 (1905) 391–562
10. Duncan Mackenzie, *et al., Excavations at Phylakopi in Melos* (London: 1904)
11. Duncan Mackenzie, "Cretan Palaces and the Aegean Civilization," *BSA* 11 (1904–1905) 181–223
12. ———— "Cretan Palaces and the Aegean Civilization," *BSA* 12 (1905–1906) 216–258
13. Arthur Evans, *Scripta Minoa: the Written Documents of Minoan Crete,* Vol. I (Oxford: 1909)
14. ———— "The Minoan and Mycenaean Element in Hellenic Life," *JHS* 32 (1912) 277–297

15. ——— *The Palace of Minos: a Comparative Account of the Successive Stages of Early Cretan Civilization as Illustrated by the Discoveries at Knossos,* Vol. I (London: 1921)

162 . 13 . 52, 53
162, 163 . 13 . 55
163 . 13 . 58
163 . 13 . 60, 61
164 . 14 . 277
164 . 14 . 278, 279
164, 165 . 14 . 283
165 . 14 . 287, 288
166 . 14 . 291
166 . 14 . 293

166, 167 . 15 . xi
167 . 1 . 363
167 . 15 . x
167 . 15 . xi
168 . 15 . 25
168 . 15 . 24
168, 169 . 15 . 27, 28
169 . 1 . 392
169 . 1 . 350, 351

## CHAPTER V

1. Gustav Glotz, *The Aegean Civilization* (New York: 1925), tr. by M. R. Dobie and E. M. Riley; 2nd ed. 1926; 3rd ed. 1952, in French only, with additional notes by C. Picard and P. Demargne
2. Diedrich Fimmen, *Die Kretisch-Mykenische Kultur* (Leipzig: 1921)
3. A. Michaelis, *A Century of Archaeological Discoveries* (New York: 1908), tr. by B. Kahnweiler

174 . 1 . v
174 . 1 . 21
175 . 1 . 21
175 . 2 . 125
175 . 2 . 211
177 . 1 . 13
178 . 1 . 44–46
179 . 1 . 47–49
179 . 1 . 50, 51
179 . 2 . 38
180 . 1 . 52
180 . 1 . 119
180, 181 . 1 . 125–130
181 . 1 . 131–134
181, 182 . 1 . 143
182 . 1 . 148, 149
182 . 1 . 150, 152
182, 183 . 1 . 152, 154
183 . 1 . 158
183 . 1 . 162, 163
183 . 1 . 165
183 . 1 . 170
184 . 2 . 118, 119
184 . 1 . 197, 198

184 . 1 . 211, 212
184 . 1 . 226
185 . 1 . 215–218
185 . 1 . 219
185 . 1 . 220, 223
185 . 1 . 223, 224
186 . 1 . 306, 308
187 . 1 . 325, 334
187 . 1 . 336–338
187, 188 . 1 . 347, 348, 364, 365
188 . 1 . 366
188 . 1 . 367, 369
189 . 2 . 75–79
189 . 1 . 371
189 . 1 . 373, 374
190 . 1 . 374
190 . 1 . 388
190 . 1 . 376–380
190 . 1 . 385
190, 191 . 1 . 380
191 . 1 . 383
191 . 1 . 389

## CHAPTER VI

1. Carl Blegen, "Corinth in Prehistoric Times," *AJA* 27 (1923) 151–163
2. ——— and Alan Wace, "The Pre-Mycenaean Pottery of the Mainland," *BSA* 22 (1916–17; 1917–18) 175–189
3. Carl Blegen, *Korakou: a Prehistoric Settlement near Corinth* (New York: 1921)
4. ——— *Zygouries: a Prehistoric Settlement in the Valley of Cleonae* (Harvard: 1928)
5. ——— "Excavations at the Argive Heraeum," *AJA* 29 (1925) 413–418
6. ——— *Prosymna: the Helladic Settlement Preceding the Argive Heraeum,* 2 vols. (Harvard: 1937)
7. ——— and J. B. Haley, "The Coming of the Greeks," *AJA* 32 (1928) 141–154
8. Wilhelm Dörpfeld, *Troja und Ilion,* 2 vols. (Athens: 1902)
9. Carl Blegen, *Troy and the Trojans* (London: 1963)
10. ——— and Alan Wace, "Pottery as Evidence for Trade and Colonisation in the Aegean Bronze Age," *Klio: Beiträge zur alten Geschichte* 32 (1939) 131–147
11. Carl Blegen, "Excavations at Pylos, 1939," *AJA* 43 (1939) 557–576
12. ——— "Preclassical Greece," *Studies in the Arts and Architecture* (Philadelphia: 1941) 1–14

212, 213 . 6 . 249
214 . 6 . 251
214 . 6 . 257
214 . 6 . 259
214 . 6 . 260
215 . 7 . 148
216, 217 . 7 . 151, 152
218 . 8 . 24
219 . 8 . 182
219 . 8 . 199, 200
220 . 8 . 281–287
221 . 9 . 27
223 . 9 . 110, 111
223 . 9 . 110
225 . 9 . 160
225 . 9 . 161
226 . 9 . 162, 164
226 . 10 . 135
227 . 10 . 137, 141, 147

228 . 10 . 136
228 . 10 . 141
228, 229 . 10 . 138, 139
230 . 11 . 557
234, 235 . 11 . 569
235 . 11 . 569, 570
235, 236 . 11 . 570
239 . 11 . 576
239 . 12 . 1
239 . 12 . 6
239, 240 . 12 . 11
240 . 12 . 9
240 . 12 . 10
241 . 12 . 12, 13
241 . 12 . 13, 14
242 . Citation with A.I.A. medal
243 . Blegen's reply to citation

## CHAPTER VII

1. Alan Wace, *et al.,* "Excavations at Mycenae 1921–23," *BSA* 25 (1921–22; 1922–23) 1–402
2. Arthur Evans, *The Shaft Graves and Bee-hive Tombs of Mycenae and their Interrelation* (London: 1927)
3. ——— *The Palace of Minos . . .,* Vol. II (London: 1928)
4. ——— *The Palace of Minos . . .,* Vol. IV (London: 1935)
5. John Pendlebury, *The Archaeology of Crete* (London: 1939)
6. Martin Nilsson, *Homer and Mycenae* (Berkeley: 1933)

248 . 1 . 12
248 . 1 . 13
248 . 1 . 16
249 . 1 . 40
250 . 1 . 78
250, 251 . 1 . 103
251 . 1 . 118
251 . 1 . 119, 120
252 . 1 . 120
252 . 1 . 121
252 . 1 . 122
252, 253 . 1 . 122, 123
253 . 1 . 126
253, 254 . 1 . 140, 145

254 . 1 . 146
254, 255 . 1 . 269, 270
255 . 1 . 234, 235
256 . 1 . 247, 248
256 . 1 . 265
256, 257 . 1 . 256
257 . 1 . 278
258 . 1 . 249, 250
258 . 1 . 253, 254
259 . 1 . 284, 285
259, 260 . 1 . 350
260 . 1 . 390
262 . 1 . 349
262 . 1 . 391

263 . 1 . 397
264 . 1 . 358
264 . 1 . 329
265 . 1 . 328
265 . 1 . 328
265 . 1 . 351, 352
265, 266 . 1 . 296
266 . 1 . 308
266 . 1 . 368
267, 268 . 1 . 395
268 . 1 . 392
268 . 1 . 395
268 . 1 . 395, 396
269 . 2 . 1, 2
270 . 2 . 49
270 . 2 . 67
271 . 2 . 69
271 . 2 . 70, 71
271 . 2 . 76, 77
271 . 2 . 88
272 . 2 . 89, 90
272 . 3 . viii, 321
273 . 3 . 564
273 . 3 . 566
273, 274 . 3 . 564
274 . 3 . 571
274 . 4 . vii
274 . 4 . ix
274, 275 . 4 . vii, viii
275 . 4 . xiv
275 . 4 . 371, 373
276 . 4 . xix
276, 277 . 4 . 750, 752
277 . 4 . 754, 755
277 . 4 . 758
278 . 4 . 870
278 . 4 . 831

279 . 4 . 887, 888
279 . 4 . 902, 912, 920
279, 280 . 4 . 942
280 . 4 . 944
280 . 4 . xxiii
281 . 5 . xxiv
281, 282 . 5 . xxiii, xxiv
282 . 5 . xxvi
282 . 5 . xxvii
282 . 5 . xxviii
283 . 5 . 225
283 . 5 . 225, 287
283 . 5 . 226
283, 284 . 5 . 227
284 . 5 . 228, 229
285 . 5 . 230, 231
286 . 6 . 56
286 . 6 . 60, 61
286 . 6 . 63
286 . 6 . 65
287 . 6 . 71
287 . 6 . 78, 79
287, 288 . 6 . 82
288 . 6 . 85
288 . 6 . 95
288 . 6 . 104
289 . 6 . 118
289 . 6 . 119
290 . 6 . 158, 159
290 . 6 . 122
290 . 6 . 156
290 . 6 . 151
290, 291 . 6 . 156
291 . 6 . 159
291 . 6 . 206, 208
291 . 6 . 208
291 . 6 . 209

CHAPTER VIII

1. Arne Furumark, *The Mycenaean Pottery,* 2 vols. (Stockholm: 1941)
2. Helene Kantor, *The Aegean and the Orient in the Second Millennium B.C.* Monograph #1, Archaeological Institute of America (Bloomington: 1947)

3. Helen Lorimer, *Homer and the Monuments* (London: 1950)
4. Arne Furumark, "The Settlement at Ialysos and Aegean Prehistory c. 1550–1400 B.C.," *Opuscula Archaeologica* 6 (1950) 150–271
5. John Chadwick, *The Decipherment of Linear B* (Cambridge: 1958)
6. Michael Ventris and John Chadwick, "Evidence for Greek Dialect in the Mycenaean Archives," *JHS* 73 (1953) 84–103
7. ——— *Documents in Mycenaean Greek* (Cambridge: 1956)
8. Carl Blegen, *The Mycenaean Age, The Trojan War, The Dorian Invasion, and Other Problems* (Cincinnati: 1962)
9. Alan Wace, *Mycenae: An Archaeological History and Guide* (Princeton: 1949)
10. T. B. L. Webster, *From Homer to Mycenae* (London: 1958)
11. W. K. C. Guthrie, "The Religion and Mythology of the Greeks," *The Cambridge Ancient History,*[2] Vol. II, Chap. XL (Cambridge: 1964)
12. Carl Blegen, "A Chronological Problem," *Minoica: Festschrift zum 80. Geburtstag von J. Sundwall* (Berlin: 1958) 61–66
13. George Mylonas, "Grave Circle B of Mycenae," *Studies in Mediterranean Archaeology* VII (Lund: 1964)
14. Spyridon Marinatos, "The Minoan and Mycenaean Civilization and Its Influence on the Mediterranean and on Europe," *Atti del VI Congresso Internazionale delle Scienze Preistoriche e Protostoriche* (Rome: 1962)
15. Carl Blegen and Marion Rawson, *A Guide to the Palace of Nestor* (Cincinnati: 1962)
16. John Caskey, "Excavations at Ceos," *Archaeology* 16 (1963) 284, 285; 17 (1964) 277–279
17. N. Platon and E. Stassinopoulou-Touloupa, "Oriental Seals from the Palace of Cadmus . . ." *Illustrated London News,* Nov. 28, 1964, 859–861; "Ivories and Linear B from Thebes," *ILN,* Dec. 5, 1964, 896, 897
18. D. Theocharis, "Iolkos: Whence Sailed the Argonauts," *Archaeology* 11 (1958) 13–18
19. George Bass, "The Cape Gelidonya Wreck," *AJA* 65 (1961) 267–276
20. H. W. Catling, *et al.,* "Correlations between Composition and Provenance of Mycenaean and Minoan Pottery," *BSA* 58 (1963) 94–115
21. H. W. Catling and A. Millett, "A Study of the Inscribed Stirrup-Jars from Thebes," *Archaeometry* 8 (1965) 3–95

| | | | | | | |
|---|---|---|---|---|---|---|
| 306 | . | 2 | . 103 | 314 . | 5 | . 68 |
| 308 | . | 3 | . 453 | 318 . | 7 | . xxxi |
| 309 | . | 3 | . 123 | 318, 319 . | 8 | . 11, 12 |
| 313 | . | 4 | . 256 | 319 . | 7 | . xxviii |

320 . 7 . xxix
320 . 7 . xxvii, xxviii
325 . 10 . 15

327 . 11 . 28, 29
329 . 12 . 64, 66

## CHAPTER IX

1. Joseph Alsop, *From the Silent Earth* (New York: 1964)
2. G. S. Kirk, "The Homeric Poems as History," *The Cambridge Ancient History,*[2] Vol. II, Chap. XXXIX (b) (Cambridge: 1964)
3. W. K. C. Guthrie, "The Religion and Mythology of the Greeks," *The Cambridge Ancient History,*[2] Vol. II, Chap. XL (Cambridge: 1964)
4. L. R. Palmer, *Minoans and Mycenaeans* (London: 1961, 1965)
5. George Huxley, *Crete and the Luwians* (Oxford: 1961)
6. John Caskey, "Greece, Crete and the Aegean Islands in the Early Bronze Age," *The Cambridge Ancient History,*[2] Vol. I, Chap. XXVI (a) (Cambridge: 1964)
7. John Chadwick, "The Prehistory of the Greek Language," *The Cambridge Ancient History,*[2] Vol. II, Chap. XXXIX (Cambridge: 1963)
8. Carl Blegen, *The Mycenaean Age* . . . (Cincinnati: 1962)
9. Sterling Dow, "The Greeks in the Bronze Age," *XIe Congrès International des Sciences Historiques* (Stockholm: 1960)
10. Denys Page, *History and the Homeric Iliad* (Berkeley: 1959; Cambridge: 1963)
11. Dorothea Gray, "Homer and the Archaeologists," *Fifty Years of Classical Scholarship,* ed. M. Platnauer (Oxford: 1954) 24–31
12. Fritz Schachermeyr, *Hethiter und Achäer* (Leipzig: 1935)
13. Friedrich Matz, "The Minoan Civilization: Maturity and Zenith," *The Cambridge Ancient History,*[2] Vol. II, Chaps. IV, XII (Cambridge: 1962)
14. Stuart Piggott, *Ancient Europe* (Chicago: 1965)
15. Frank Stubbings, "The Rise of Mycenaean Civilization," *The Cambridge Ancient History,*[2] Vol. II, Chap. XIV (Cambridge: 1965)
16. Emily Vermeule, *Greece in the Bronze Age* (Chicago: 1964)
17. Lord William Taylour, *The Mycenaeans* (London: 1964)
18. Spyridon Marinatos, "The Minoan and Mycenaean Civilization and its Influence on the Mediterranean and on Europe," *Atti del Congresso Internazionale delle Scienze Preistoriche e Protostoriche* (Rome: 1962)
19. Lord William Taylour, *Mycenaean Pottery in Italy and Adjacent Areas* (Cambridge: 1958)
20. R. Hachmann, "Bronzezeitliche Bernsteinschieber," *Kommission für Bayrische Landgeschichte, Bayer. Akad. d. Wissenschaft* XXII (1957) 1–36

21. Frank Stubbings, *Mycenaean Pottery from the Levant* (Cambridge: 1951)

22. Chester Starr, "The Myth of the Minoan Thalassocracy," *Historia* 3 (1955) 282–291

23. Arne Furumark, "The Settlement at Ialysos and Aegean History c. 1550–1400 B.C.," *Opuscula Archaeologica* 6 (1950) 150–271

24. John L. Myres, *Who Were the Greeks?* (Berkeley: 1930)

25. O. R. Gurney, *The Hittites* (Baltimore: 1961)

26. Henri Van Effenterre, "L'Archéologie renouvelle l'histoire de la Crète," Supplement #144 *Preuves* (Paris: 1963) 15–23

27. M. R. Popham, "The Destruction of the Palace of Knossos and its Pottery," *Antiquity* 40 (1966) 24–28

28. M. S. F. Hood, " 'Last Palace' and 'Reoccupation' at Knossos," *Kadmos* 4 (1965) 16–44

29. A. Severyns, *Grèce et Proche-Orient avant Homère* (Brussels: 1960)

30. V. R. d'A. Desborough, *The Last Mycenaeans and their Successors* (Oxford: 1964)

31. T. B. L. Webster, *From Mycenae to Homer* (London: 1958)

32. Per Ålin, "Das Ende der Mykenischen Fundstätten auf dem griechischen Festland," *Studies in Mediterranean Archaeology* Vol. I (Lund: 1962)

33. George Mylonas, *Mycenae and the Mycenaean Age* (Princeton: 1966)

34. J. F. Daniel, "The Dorian Invasion: the Setting," *AJA* 52 (1948) 107–110

362 . 1 . 81
362 . 2 . 32
364 . 3 . 33
364 . 7 . 15
364 . 8 . 11
364 . 9 . 4
364 . 10 . 88
374 . 16 . 126
374 . 17 . 139
381 . 21 . 102
381 . 5 . 3
381, 382 . 22 . 283, 291
382 . 5 . 6
382 . 23 . 201
383 . 23 . 202
390 . 23 . 271

393 . 16 . 156, 157
398 . 1 . 105
399 . 26 . 17
402 . 30 . 229
403 . 26 . 16
404 . 31 . 116
405 . 10 . 111
408 . 21 . 23
414 . 16 . 257
417 . 34 . 107
419 . 14 . 159, 160
422 . 10 . 258
422 . 31 . 91
422 . 2 . 18
425 . 3 . 30

# Homeric References

*(including a few later ancient sources)*

1. *Il* 22. 147–152
2. *Il* 3. 145–242
3. *Il* 1. 584
4. *Il* 24. 228
5. Herodotus I. 94
6. *Il* 6. 316
7. *Od* 6. 303–309
8. Pausanias I. 16. 5–7
9. *Od* 3. 263
10. *Il* 18. 497–505
11. *Il* 1. 450
12. *Il* 10. 257–259
13. *Od* 4. 524–527; cf. Aeschylus' *Agamemnon* 1–39
14. *Il* 7. 219
15. *Il* 11. 632–635
16. Herodotus VII. 102
17. Pausanias II. 25. 8
18. *Il* 2. 559–564.
19. *Od* 7. 87
20. *Od* 7. 81–106
21. Pausanias IX. 38. 2
22. *Od* 11. 284
23. *Il* 5. 446; 6. 88
24. *Il* 6. 248
25. *Il* 19. 38, 39
26. *Il* 23. 186, 187
27. *Il* 7. 85; 16. 456
28. *Il* 19. 212
29. *Od* 11. 23–36
30. *Il* 23. 28–34
31. *Il* 23. 175–177
32. *Od* 24. 227–231
33. *Od* 8. 337, 342
34. *Il* 7. 219–223
35. *Il* 3. 332
36. *Il* 1. 17
37. *Il* 10. 261–265
38. *Od* 21. 120–123, 420–423
39. Hesiod, *Shield* 139–317; cf. *Il* 18. 509–540
40. *Il* 6. 450–465
41. *Od* 19. 172–174
42. *Il* 18. 490–605
43. *Il* 18. 590–592
44. *Il* 2. 645–652
45. *Il* 4. 105–111
46. *Od* 12. 235, 236
47. *Il* 2. 494–759
48. *Od* 19. 172–174
49. *Od* 19. 18
50. *Il* 6. 243–246
51. *Il* 6. 247–250
52. *Od* 3. 387, 412–415
53. *Od* 6. 81, 82
54. *Od* 21. 1–14
55. Thucydides I. 4, 8
56. *Il* 10. 577
57. *Od* 3. 299–301; 4. 355
58. Diodorus IV. 76–79
59. *Od* 8. 256–268
60. Plutarch, *Moralia* 579A
61. *Il* 6. 168, 169
62. *Il* 23. 257–897
63. *Od* 8. 104–194

64. *Od* 2. 328
65. *Od* 3. 1 ff
66. Pausanias IV. 36. 2, 3
67. Strabo VIII. 3. 7
68. *Od* 15. 292–300
69. *Il* 11. 670–762
70. *Od* 3. 475–497
71. *Il* 2. 591–602
72. *Od* 19. 4–9
73. *Il* 18. 591
74. *Od* 19. 173, 174
75. *Od* 19. 226–231
76. *Il* 1. 371
77. *Il* 7. 41
78. *Il* 4. 297–309; 11. 735–758
79. *Il* 6. 297
80. *Il* 5. 722, 723
81. *Il* 1. 7
82. *Il* 18. 550
83. *Il* 2. 53
84. *Il* 2. 94–100

85. *Od* 22. 421–423
86. *Od* 7. 103–107
87. *Il* 6. 450–465
88. *Il* 7. 165, 166
89. *Il* 17. 610, 611
90. *Od* 11. 305–310
91. *Od* 3. 1–61
92. *Od* 6. 291, 292
93. *Il* 2. 100–108; *Od.* 3. 403–412
94. *Od* 3. 1–486
95. *Il* 6. 86–95
96. *Il* 2. 546, 547
97. *Od* 3. 165–179
98. *Il* 9. 149–153
99. *Il* 9. 260–400
100. *Od* 4. 125–132
101. Thucydides I. 12
102. *Il* 11. 690–693
103. Thucydides I. 12
104. *Il* 11. 670–761
105. *Il* 14. 405

# Suggested Reading

READERS who first wish to consult a reliable, general, up-to-date synthesis on Mycenaean civilization might find the items marked with an asterisk particularly useful. A new edition of the *Cambridge Ancient History* is now in preparation and individual chapters on various aspects of Mycenaean civilization are available in pamphlet form.

Some newspapers occasionally feature archaeological discoveries. Among popular magazines, the *Illustrated London News* has been outstanding in this respect. *Life* and *The New Yorker* have good features occasionally. Of the archaeological journals, the American publication *Archaeology* is meant for the interested amateur and the British *Antiquity* aims skillfully at a middle ground between amateur and specialist.

Alsop, J., *From the Silent Earth* (New York: 1964)
Bernabo Brea, L., *Sicily before the Greeks* (London: 1957)
Blegen, C. W., *Troy and the Trojans* (London: 1963)
———, *The Mycenaean Age* . . . (Cincinnati: 1962) 37 pp.
——— and M. Rawson, *A Guide to the Palace of Nestor* (Cincinnati: 1962) 32 pp.
Bowra, M., *Homer and his Forerunners* (Edinburgh: 1955)
———, *Heroic Poetry* (London: 1952)
Brothwell, D., and E. Higgs, *Science in Archaeology* (London: 1963)
Chadwick, J., *The Decipherment of Linear B* (Cambridge: 1959; Random House paperback 1966)
Clarke, J. G. D., *Prehistoric Europe: the Economic Basis* (London: 1952)
Daniel, G. E., *The Idea of Prehistory* (London: 1962)
Desborough, V. R. d'A., *The Last Mycenaeans and their Successors* (Oxford: 1964)
Evans, Joan, *Time and Chance: the Story of Arthur Evans and his Forebears* (London: 1943)
Finley, M. I., *The World of Odysseus* (London: 1956)
Glotz, G., *The Aegean Civilization* (New York: 1925)
Graham, J. W., *The Palaces of Crete* (Princeton: 1962)
Gray, D., "Homer and the Archaeologists," *Fifty Years of Classical Scholarship,* ed. M. Platnauer (Oxford: 1954)

Gurney, O. R., *The Hittites* (1952; rev. ed. 1961)

Hutchinson, R. W., *Prehistoric Crete* (1962)

Kirk, G., *The Songs of Homer* (Cambridge: 1962)

Lord, A., *The Singer of Tales* (Harvard: 1960)

Lorimer, H. L., *Homer and the Monuments* (London: 1950)

Marinatos, S. and M. Hirmer, *Crete and Mycenae* (London: 1960)

Matz, F., *The Art of Crete and Early Greece* (London: 1962)

*Mylonas, G. E., *Mycenae and the Mycenaean Age* (Princeton: 1966)

Nilsson, M. P., *Homer and Mycenae* (London: 1933)

———, *The Minoan-Mycenaean Religion,* 2nd ed. (Lund: 1950)

———, *The Mycenaean Origin of Greek Mythology* (Berkeley: 1932)

Page, D., *History and the Homeric Iliad* (Berkeley: 1959; Cambridge: 1963)

Palmer, L. R., *Mycenaeans and Minoans* (London: 1961; 2nd ed., 1965)

———, *The Interpretation of Mycenaean Texts* (Oxford: 1963)

Pendlebury, J. D. S., *The Archaeology of Crete* (London: 1939; Norton paperback 1965)

Persson, A., *The Religion of Greece in Prehistoric Times* (Los Angeles: 1942)

Piggott, S., *Ancient Europe* (Chicago: 1965)

———, *Approach to Archaeology* (Cambridge: 1959)

Samuel, A. E., *The Mycenaeans in History* (New York: 1966)

Schliemann, H., *Troy and its Remains* (London: 1875)

———, *Ilios: The City and Country of the Trojans* (London: 1880)

———, *Troja: Results of the Latest Researches . . .* (London: 1884)

———, *Mycenae: A Narrative of Researches . . .* (London: 1878)

———, *Tiryns: The Prehistoric Palace of the Kings of Tiryns* (London: 1886)

Schuchhardt, C., *Schliemann's Excavations: An Archaeological and Historical Study* (London: 1891)

*Taylour, W., *The Mycenaeans* (London: 1964)

Tsountas, C. and J. I. Manatt, *The Mycenaean Age: a Study of the Monuments and Culture of pre-Homeric Greece* (Boston: 1897)

Ventris, M. and J. Chadwick, *Documents in Mycenaean Greek* (Cambridge: 1956)

*Vermeule, E., *Greece in the Bronze Age* (Chicago: 1964)

Wace, A. J. B., *Mycenae: an Archaeological History and Guide* (Princeton: 1949)

——— and F. H. Stubbings, *A Companion to Homer* (London: 1962)

Wace, H. and C. Williams, *Mycenae Guide* (Meriden, Conn., U.S.A.; 2nd ed., 1962) 49 pp.

Webster, T. B. L., *From Mycenae to Homer* (London: 1958)

# *Portraits*

IN THE FOLLOWING PAGES we reproduce pictures of seven men whose discoveries and theories play a very prominent part in the story just concluded. It seems fitting that their physical appearance as well as their own words should be a matter of record in an account that is as largely biographical as this has been. The reader may judge for himself whether he sees any correspondence between these men's physiognomy and their unusual drive and devotion to the quest for new knowledge. At the very least, the pictures will satisfy a normal human curiosity to associate in one's memory a man's appearance with his deeds.

In telling the story of Greek prehistoric archaeology, we chose Schliemann, Evans and Blegen to personify, as it were, the attitudes and methods and preoccupations of their respective generations. Perhaps the equal prominence given here to the portraits of Tsountas, Dörpfeld, Wace and Ventris is an appropriate reflection of their strong claim to no less credit.

When the sequel is written a generation or two from now, there will of course be new faces and new finds but the contributions of these seven men will not thereby be diminished.

Heinrich Schliemann (1822-1890)

Arthur J. Evans (1851-1941)

DEPARTMENT OF ANTIQUITIES, ASHMOLEAN MUSEUM, OXFORD

Carl W. Blegen (1887-    )

Michael Ventris (1922-1956)

Alan J. B. Wace (1879-1957)

Wilhelm Dörpfeld (1853-1940)

Christos Tsountas (1857-1934)

# Glossary

---

*absolute chronology*   the determination that one object or grave or stratum can be assigned a specific date, at least within a quarter century

*Achaean* (Achaian)   one of Homer's names for the Greeks at Troy; now often used to denominate speakers of Greek (especially on the mainland) in the Late Bronze Age; also applied to the language of the Linear B tablets

*adyton*   isolated room in a temple, often used for the safekeeping of treasure and/or for particularly secret rites

*Aegisthus*   seducer of Clytemnestra in Agamemnon's absence at Troy who planned with her Agamemnon's murder on his return

*Aeolic* (Aeolian)   a major dialect of Greek (along with Ionic and Doric); spoken in historic times in east central Greece and on the islands and coast of northern Anatolia; had some effect on the language of Homeric epic

*Agamemnon*   king of Mycenae and leader of the Greek expedition against Troy

*Ahhijawā*   a political unit (*possibly* Achaea) with which Hittite kings were in diplomatic contact

*alabastron*   a low, closed vase, usually with three small handles, and probably used as a container for fine oil (Fig. 76)

*amphora*   a high, closed vase, probably used as a container for wine and water; the name literally means that it has two handles, but three are usually spaced around the shoulder (Fig. 75A)

*amulet*   an ornament or gem worn as a charm against ill luck

*Anatolia*   Asia Minor or modern Turkey; literally "the land where the sun rises" (*i.e.,* east to the Greeks)

*arch*   (see *corbelled arch*)

*archaic*   in Greek archaeology and history designates specifically the period from about mid-eighth until end sixth century B.C.

*ashlar*   wall construction in regular parallel horizontal courses; vertical joints are usually at approximate right angles (Fig. 82C)

*Athena*    one of the major deities in Olympian pantheon; protecting goddess of Troy and Athens

*bas-relief*    geometric or figured decoration sculpted in low relief on a flat surface

*brachycephalic*    round-headed, *i.e.*, width of skull relatively great in proportion to length

*Bügelkanne*    (see *stirrup jar*)

*cartouche*    a stamped or incised identification on objects manufactured in Egypt specifying date and other information

*Cassandra*    Trojan priestess and daughter of Priam; seized as Agamemnon's concubine after the capture of Troy and brought back with him to Mycenae where she (with her twin boys) was murdered by Clytemnestra and Aegisthus

*celt*    stone hand ax, one of the earliest general-purpose tools made by Stone Age people

*chamber tomb*    a communal or family tomb cut into the soft rock of a hillside and approached by an open corridor or dromos; *may* have been used by commoners as well as nobles (Figs. 39, 74)

*chiton*    a shirt worn next to the upper body by men; made of wool or linen

*chlaina*    a woolen mantle or cloak

*cist grave*    dug in rock or earth very much as modern graves; sometimes lined with stone and covered; normally rectangular and meant for single burial

*classical*    in Greek archaeology and (technically) in Greek history designates the period from the Persian invasions (490 B.C.) until the death of Alexander the Great (323 B.C.)

*clerestory*    a higher central section of the flat roof of a large building; small windows in its sides would admit light and air and allow smoke to escape (Fig. 90)

*close style*    a fussy but effective over-all decorative scheme, geometric and sometimes figured, on some LHIIIC vases (Fig. 86)

*Clytemnestra*    unfaithful wife of Agamemnon

*corbelled arch*    unlike the true arch (not used by the Mycenaeans), it is constructed by slightly overlapping each course of blocks in two parallel walls until the vault can be completed by wedging it securely with the final course (Fig. 37)

*crater*    (see *krater*)

*cross-dating*    (see *synchronism*)

*cuirass*   armor covering the neck and upper body (Fig. 95)

*Cyclades* (Cycladic)   a group of islands in the central Aegean, so named because they were thought to form a circle (cycle) around Delos; Bronze Age civilization in the islands is labeled Early, Middle, Late Cycladic

*Cyclopean*   fortifications, walls of buildings, etc., in which very large unworked boulders are used, with smaller stones and clay mortar in the interstices; thought by the ancient Greeks to have been constructed by giants (Cyclopes)

*cylix*   (see *kylix*)

*Danaos*   cheated by his brother of his rightful share in Egyptian government, he migrated to the Argolid with his fifty daughters

*depas amphikypellon*   Homer's description of a two-handled drinking cup

*dolichocephalic*   long headed, *i.e.,* length of skull relatively great in proportion to width

*Dorian invasion*   the cause of the destruction of heroic (Mycenaean) civilization, according to later Greek tradition; supposedly a single overwhelming thrust from the north overland by speakers of the historic Doric dialect of Greek

*Doric*   a major dialect of Greek used in historic times in much of the Peloponnese as well as areas colonized from there; also applied to one of the three orders of classical Greek architecture with a somewhat similar distribution

*dromos*   the "street" or approach to a tholos or chamber tomb; a long corridor, usually cut into a hill slope, open at the top and with its increasingly high walls ending at the doorway of the tomb proper (Figs. 39, 82)

*Eileithyia*   goddess who assists women in childbirth

*Electra*   daughter of Agamemnon and Clytemnestra

*electrum*   a natural alloy of gold and silver

*Ephyraean ware*   a class of pottery first identified by Blegen at Korakou (perhaps Homeric Ephyra = Corinth) (Fig. 72)

*epigraphy*   the scientific study of written records inscribed on stone, clay, metal, etc.

*faience*   colored glass paste, poured into molds; used for miniature sculpture, appliqué, beads, etc. (Fig. 62)

*fibula* (plural: *fibulae*)   ancestor of the safety pin, used in place of buttons to secure clothing (Fig. 99)

*fillet*   a decorative band to hold the hair in place

*fresco*   a technique of monumental painting by which the design is applied to wet plaster (*al fresco*)

*geometric*   decorative design, strictly speaking nonrepresentational, tending to neat repetitive patterns and motifs; used especially to designate the crisp and careful work of the Early Iron Age

*glyptic*   cutting, carving, sculpting miniature designs, particularly in hard stone, as for seals and gems (Fig. 68)

*graffito* (plural: *graffiti*)   writing (usually casual) on such surfaces as walls

*granary class pottery*   vase shapes typical of LHIIIC, with rather sparse, stylized and often careless decoration (Fig. 79)

*grave circle*   any circular construction in which burials are made; particularly the monumental structure (A) at Mycenae within which Schliemann discovered the Shaft Graves; and also the earlier structure (B) at Mycenae (Fig. 19)

*gray Minyan pottery*   distinctive, smooth, silvery fabric (with soapy feel) produced by reduction firing in the kiln; angular profiles with sharp transitions (perhaps copying metal shapes) and liking for ribbed stems (Fig. 69)

*greaves*   armor to protect shins

*grid*   a series of contiguous rectangles in which one arranges vertically and horizontally syllabic combinations of vowels and diphthongs used in a given language

*griffin*   hybrid animal combining the body of a lion with the head (and usually wings) of an eagle (Figs. 47, 92)

*Halstatt*   generic name for a distinctive iron-using culture extending over much of central and western Europe in the seventh and sixth centuries B.C.

*Hector*   son of Priam and the greatest warrior of Troy

*Helladic*   chronological term to designate mainland Greece (Hellas) in the Bronze Age

*Hellenistic*   chronological term to designate Greek culture in its widest penetration from the death of Alexander the Great (323) until the destruction of Corinth by the Romans (146 B.C.)

*Herakleidai*   the sons (or descendants) of Herakles; they were responsible, according to Greek tradition, for depredations on the Mycenaean kingdoms

*Herodotus*   a writer of the fifth century B.C. who incorporated in his *History* much legendary material about earlier events and customs (which he did not necessarily believe in full)

*Hesiod*  a poet who lived slightly after Homer's time and who continued to use the epic form for new themes such as genealogies of gods and a handbook on agriculture

*hieroglyphics*  a highly developed and standardized form of picture writing; literally "priestly incising"

*Hittites*  a people speaking a basically Indo-European language who invaded Anatolia at the beginning of the second millennium and controlled most of it until about 1200 B.C.

*Homeric Question*  Who was "Homer"? When and where did he live? Did he compose one or both of the epic poems attributed to him? Were the stories invented by him or are the poems the culmination of a long oral tradition?

*Hyksos*  an intrusive minority who controlled Egypt in the earlier second millennium and were expelled by Ahmose, founder of the eighteenth dynasty

*ideogram*  a stylized picture used in early writing systems (Fig. 88)

*Idomeneus*  king of Knossos in Crete and leader of the Cretan contingent of Greek forces in the Trojan War

*Ilion* (Ilios)  alternate name for Troy

*inhumation*  placing a corpse in a grave or tomb (as opposed to reducing it to ashes, *i.e.,* cremation)

*Ionic*  a major dialect of Greek used in historical times in Attica and neighboring areas as well as in regions colonized by these states; possibly a descendant of the earliest major Indo-European dialect to be spoken in Greece

*Jason*  leader of the Argonauts from Iolkos who sailed to Cholcis in the Black Sea to carry off the Golden Fleece

*Kadmos*  a native of Phoenicia who, according to tradition, occupied Thebes and introduced "Phoenician letters" to Greece

*Kamares*  a cave sanctuary in central Crete from which the first samples of a distinctive type of Minoan pottery were first recovered; by extension sometimes used to designate the period of the early palaces when this pottery was in use

*Keftiu*  a name used by the Egyptians to designate the homeland of people who appear in eighteenth dynasty tomb paintings and bear gifts, some of which are Aegean in appearance; usually assumed to be Crete

*koinê*  the common or shared culture so noticeable throughout the whole Aegean area in the later Mycenaean Age; also applied to a form of Greek language widely used in Hellenistic and Roman times

*krater*  a large open bowl for mixing wine with water (Fig. 75C) *kylix*   a stemmed two-handled goblet resembling a champagne glass (Figs. 56, 72 )

*larnax*   clay coffin or sarcophagos, usually with painted decoration; used in Crete but not in mainland Greece

*light-well*   rectangular shaft that provided light and circulation of air for interior living units in large Minoan buildings (Fig. 54B)

*Linear A*   syllabic writing system developed by the Minoans out of the earlier hieroglyphics; used throughout Crete in the early palaces and probably continuing everywhere except at Knossos until at least the fifteenth century (Fig. 63)

*Linear B*   modified version of Linear A adapted to writing Greek; so far certified in Crete only at Knossos but apparently widespread at mainland capitals (Fig. 88)

*Lion Gate*   the main gate in the Mycenae fortifications; so named for the heraldic lionesses sculpted on the relieving triangle above the lintel (Fig. 15)

*liparite*   shiny volcanic stone from the Lipari islands; flakes easily and was used for making sharp blades, etc.

*loomweight*   artefact of clay or stone, usually conical and pierced vertically, used to exert desired tension on vertical threads suspended from the loom; apparently some previously so categorized are really buttons

*lustral area*   a small "room" (possibly for bathing) sunk below level of surrounding floors and approached by stairs in Minoan palaces

*Luwian*   an early Indo-European language used in western Anatolia in the second millennium; believed by some scholars to have been spoken also in Crete

*Lydian ware*   Schliemann's designation of a very distinctive class of pottery in the sixth level at Troy; later equated with gray Minyan (Fig. 10)

*magazines*   long, narrow basement storage rooms typical of Minoan palaces (Fig. 61)

*matt-painted pottery*   basically MH vase shapes in light-colored clay on which rather simple geometric decoration is applied in a dark, dull (*i.e.,* matt) paint (Fig. 70)

*megaron* (plural: *megara*)   Homeric term for king's palace, or specifically the throne room; in general a relatively long and narrow architectural unit consisting of (columned) porch and main living room with hearth; often a third room lies in front of or (less commonly) behind living room (Fig. 54A, C)

*Menelaos*   king of Sparta and brother of Agamemnon

*Minos*   generic (probably) name for the king of Knossos in Crete

*Minotaur* hybrid monster (literally "Minos-bull") said to have inhabited the labyrinth at Knossos and to have been killed by Theseus

*Minoan* coined by Evans to designate the culture of Bronze Age Crete and used as the basic terminology for his chronological system

*Minyan* (see *gray, yellow*) coined by Schliemann to designate a kind of pottery he first recognized at Orchomenos, the home of the legendary king Minyas

*Mycenaean* (Mykenaian) adjective derived from Mycenae (Mykenai) and originally designating culture traits first recognized there; now regularly denominates the Late Bronze Age culture of south and central Greece as well as its wide extension in the Aegean area

*naos* Greek term for "temple"; more specifically the main room in which the statue of the deity was located

*Near East* in general the countries bordering the east end of the Mediterranean from Anatolia on the north through Syria to Egypt; more vaguely may include Mesopotamia

*Neleus* Nestor's father, who came from Iolkos in Thessaly and founded a kingdom in Messenia with capital at Pylos

*neolithic* the "new stone age" distinguished by food production and domestication of animals; about 6000–3000 B.C. in Greece

*Nestor* son of Neleus and his successor as king of Pylos; leader of the Pylian contingent in the Trojan War

*niello* a complicated technique of "metal painting" whereby geometric and figured designs in various metals are inset on a metal (usually bronze) background (Fig. 30)

*numismatics* the scientific study of coins (nomismata)

*obsidian* a fine-grained volcanic stone used for small, sharp blades; the most common color is a shiny black; the Aegean supply seems to have come mainly from Phylakopi on the island of Melos

*Odysseus* king of the island of Ithaka and hero of Homer's *Odyssey*

*ogival canopy* a distinctive decorative motif, so named by Evans (Fig. 76)

*palace style pottery* rather "monumental" style both in size of vases and in decorative schemes; found in the "final" palace at Knossos and common in mainland tholoi (Fig. 59)

*Palladium* the primitive statue of Athena that was particularly sacred to the Trojans

*Patrokles* (Patroclus) Achilles' close friend who was killed by Hector

*Pausanias* a learned "tourist" of the second century A.D. who wrote a lengthy account of his travels in Greece, noting buildings, monuments and the legends connected with them

*Pelopid dynasty*   a line of kings at Mycenae beginning with Atreus, father of Agamemnon; Atreus was descended from the legendary Pelops

*Peloponnese*   literally "island of Pelops"; the whole of southern Greece below the Isthmus of Corinth

*peplos*   a sewn garment or dress of linen or fine wool worn by women on the mainland

*peristyle*   columned porches on all four sides of an open court

*Perseid dynasty*   a line of kings at Mycenae beginning with the legendary Perseus and ending with Eurystheus, who was succeeded by Atreus (see *Pelopid dynasty*)

*pilgrim flask*   a "drum-shaped" water container fairly common in the eastern Aegean and borrowed from the Near East (Fig. 85)

*pithos* (plural: *pithoi*)   large terra-cotta storage jars for both liquids and solids (Fig. 7)

*Poseidon*   brother of Zeus and reputed grandfather of Nestor; patron deity of Pylos; god of the sea and lord of earthquakes

*prehistory*   all stages in the development of a culture before the availability of written documents that can be deciphered

*Priam*   aged king of Troy at the time of the Greek attack

*primary burial*   the original burial of a body in a prepared grave

*pronaos*   technical name for the porch in front of the main room of a temple (see *naos*)

*propylon* (plural: *propylaea*)   a columned gateway into a fortified area; the plural is used for a particularly monumental plan with columns both inside and outside the entrance

*protogeometric*   the earliest culture stage in the Iron Age; roughly the tenth century B.C.

*provenience* (provenance)   original geographical source from which an object or custom derives

*relative chronology*   determining that one object or burial or stratum is younger or older than another

*relieving triangle*   the triangular space above the lintel of monumental entrances; designed to lighten weight on center of lintel; often filled with a slab bearing bas-reliefs (Fig. 15)

*repoussé*   a technique of relief sculpture in metal whereby the designs or figures are hammered out from the inside; details may be added on the outside by engraving (Fig. 40) *rhyton*   a term used for two types of vessel, the one conical (Fig. 43), the other in the shape of an animal head (Fig. 24)

*sauceboat*   a vessel with a handle at one side and a spout (often quite long) at the other; distinctive shape of the Early Helladic period (Fig. 5)

*Scaean Gate*   the major entrance in the walls of Troy, according to Homer

*scarab*   Egyptian sealstone carved in the shape of a beetle

*Sea People*   a motley horde of warriors from the middle Mediterranean and probably beyond to the north and west; they attacked the settled civilizations of the Near East (and possibly Greece) in the thirteenth and twelfth centuries B.C.

*seal*   a small signet (usually of stone) and decorated with a distinctive pattern; when pressed on clay or other soft substance, the impression signified ownership or endorsement

*sealing*   the impression of a seal (Fig. 68)

*secondary burial*   the removal of the bones (and sometimes the funeral offerings) of a previously buried body to another place

*sequence dating* (seriation)   the arrangement of a series of artefacts of the same basic type in the order of their progressive development

*shaft grave*   essentially a large, deep, cist grave in which several burials were made at different times; typically lined with stone walls and roofed over before the earth is filled in; perhaps marked by a low mound, a gravestone and a low circular wall (Fig. 29)

*spindle whorl*   an artefact of terra-cotta or stone, pierced vertically; used to form tight threads from individual fibers; often difficult to distinguish from loomweight or button

*steatite*   a soft stone, usually black but occasionally green, which is shaped easily and often decorated with bas-relief

*stela* (*stele;* plural: *stelae, stelai*)   a stone grave marker or tombstone, usually with fairly flat front and back surfaces and sometimes decorated with bas-relief (Fig. 18)

*stemmed goblet* (see *kylix*)

*stirrup jar*   a closed terra-cotta container for shipping fine oil; at the top two small handles join a false spout or neck, while the real spout is on the shoulder (Fig. 45)

*Strabo*   a writer on geography who lived about the time of Christ; his book describes most of the Roman Empire

*stratigraphy*   the various techniques by which successive strata (singular: stratum) are identified; in archaeology the reference is to the layers of a habitation site or other deposits of man-made debris *stylistics*　(see *sequence dating*)

*sub-Mycenaean*　the final impoverished phase of Mycenaean culture, covering roughly the eleventh century

*syllabary*　a series of symbols or stylized ideograms used to write syllabically, *i.e.*, one symbol for each syllable of a word

*synchronism*　a situation where it is possible to associate an artefact or stratum or closed tomb group (possibly dated absolutely) at one site or in one culture with an artefact or stratum or closed tomb group in another (possibly undated previously)

*Telemachos*　son of Odysseus; he traveled from Ithaka to mainland Greece, according to Homer, in search of his father

*Temple Repository*　a cache of objects, many of faience and most, if not all, with religious connection, found by Evans at Knossos; some of the sculpture represents Minoan art at its acme (Fig. 62)

*temenos*　a plot (literally "cut") of land set aside for the use of a king, god, etc

*Terramara* (plural: *Terramare*)　Early Bronze culture of eastern Po valley; named for habitations resembling "lake dwellings on land"; perhaps introducers of bronze-working to Italy from central Europe

*thalassocracy*　"rule of the sea"; according to a Greek tradition as recorded by Thucydides and others, King Minos of Knossos had once controlled the whole eastern Mediterranean with his fleet

*Theatral Area*　a series of seats (L-shaped at Knossos) closely connected with Minoan palaces (Fig. 64)

*Theseus*　son of Erechtheus; prince and later king of Athens; according to tradition, he insisted on joining the Athenian "tribute" of chosen young men and women sent to Knossos; with the help of the Cretan princess Ariadne, he killed the Minotaur in the labyrinth and freed Athens from her subjugation

*Thetis*　a sea nymph; wife of Peleus and mother of Achilles

*tholos* (plural: *tholoi*)　the term is used by Homer to designate a round building; it is applied in modern times to the great round royal tombs scattered throughout Mycenaean Greece in the LH period; usually the dromos is cut into a side hill and the circular tomb chamber is lined with stone in the shape of a dome that protrudes above ground; the dome was covered with a mound, or tumulus, on the apex of which there may have been a stela or marker (Fig. 38)

*Thucydides*　the most "scientific" of Greek historians; he lived at Athens in the fifth century B.C. and introduced his *History of the Peloponnesian War* with a reconstruction (often called the "archaeology") of conditions in Greece in earlier times *treasury*   the term applied by Pausanias (and often since) to the tholos tombs; no doubt originated from the discovery of one from which robbers had not carried off the precious grave goods

*triglyph-metope frieze*   the characteristic band of decoration above the columns and architrave of a classical temple of the Doric order; its origin is probably to be seen as a decorative design used in monumental buildings of the Mycenaean period (Fig. 32)

*tumulus*   an artificial mound heaped up over a tomb or other revered monument

*typology*   (see *sequence dating*)

*Ulysses*   (see *Odysseus*)

*Warrior Vase*   a LHIIIC krater preserving perhaps the most important example of Mycenaean painting; most of the fragments were found by Schliemann in a house near the Grave Circle, although additional pieces have since been recovered (Fig. 20)

*Warrior Graves*   found by Evans at Knossos and closely connected with the LMII period just before the "final" destruction

*whorl*   (see *spindle whorl*)

*xoanon*   primitive wooden statue (ordinarily of a deity)

*yellow Minyan pottery*   undecorated MH vessels imitating the shapes of gray Minyan pottery; the fabric is often extremely fine and the surface is covered with an excellent slip of dilute clay; Mycenaean pottery consists essentially of Minoan and native decorative motifs applied in a lustrous paint to this fabric (Fig. 71)

# AEGEAN AREA REFERENCE KEY

*Spelling variants:*
  Dimini (Dimeni)
*Equivalent names:*
  Hissarlik = Troy =
  Ilion
*Ancient vs. modern names:*
  Thera: Santorin
*Closely contiguous places:*
  Ialysos-Trianda

## WESTERN MEDITERRANEAN

| | |
|---|---|
| 1 Aeolian Islands | 10 Gulf of Naples (detail) |
| 2 Balearic Islands | 11 Narbonne |
| 3 Carcassone | 12 Sardinia |
| 4 Etruria | 13 Sicily |
| 5 Filicudi (detail) | 14 Syracuse |
| 6 Ischia (detail) | 15 Tarentum |
| 7 Lipari (detail) | 16 Vivara (detail) |
| 8 Loire Valley | 17 Wessex |
| 9 Malta | |

## EASTERN MEDITERRANEAN

| | | | |
|---|---|---|---|
| 1 | Tell-el-Amarna | 8 | Gezer |
| 2 | Tell Atchana (Alalach) | 9 | Jerusalem |
| 3 | Bosporos | 10 | Kahun |
| 4 | Byblos | 11 | Lachish |
| 5 | Cyprus | 12 | Pharos |
| 6 | Cyrene | 13 | Ras Shamra (Ugarit) |
| 7 | Cape Gelidonya | | |

IMBROS

GALLIPOLI

ÆGEAN SEA

DARDANELLES
*(HELLESPONT)*

supposed area of
Greek camp

HISSARLIK-ILION-TROY

*SCAMANDER PLAIN*

TENEDOS

*SPRINGS*

BURNARBASHI

BALLI DAGH

0    miles    4

## TROY DISTRICT

**MYCENAE DISTRICT**

KNOSSOS DISTRICT

CHORA

SPRING ×
THOLOS ○
ANO ENGLIANOS ◉ (NESTOR'S PALACE)
THOLOS ○ BOUTSI THOLOS ○
THOLOI ○
○
TRAGANA

OSMANAGA
LAGOON

MODERN KORYPHASION

OX BELLY BAY
CAVE OF NESTOR
THOLOS
KORYPHASION

BAY OF
NAVARINO

MODERN PYLOS

0    miles    4

**PYLOS DISTRICT**

# INDEX

For over-all information on Mycenaean civilization, the following major headings (and the sub-headings listed under each of them in the body of the Index) should be of particular use:

*archaeological methodology*
*armor*
*arts*
*burial customs*
*chronology*
*communications*
*costume*
*crafts*
*cultural influences*
*economic basis*
*engineering*
*environment*
*epic poetry*
*food*
*jewelry*

*language*
*materials*
*military*
*movements of people*
*palace*
*physical type*
*political institutions*
*pottery*
*recreation*
*religion*
*sciences*
*shapes of containers*
*social structure*
*weapons*
*writing*

# A *selected list of* MIDLAND BOOKS

*(continued on next page)*

# MIDLAND BOOKS